MILITARY ADVISER TO THE
SECRETARY-GENERAL

INDAR JIT RIKHYE

Military Adviser
to the
Secretary-General

*U.N. Peacekeeping and
the Congo Crisis*

HURST & COMPANY, LONDON
ST. MARTIN'S PRESS, NEW YORK

in association with the International Peace Academy

First published in the United Kingdom by
C. Hurst & Co. (Publishers) Ltd.,
38 King Street, London WC2E 8JT,
and in the United States of America by
St. Martin's Press, Inc.,
175 Fifth Avenue, New York, NY 10010,
in association with the
International Peace Academy,
777 United Nations Plaza, New York, NY 10017.
© 1993 by Indar Jit Rikhye
Printed in India

ISBNs
1-85065-085-3 (Hurst)
0-312-06737-2 (St. Martin's)

Library of Congress Cataloging-in-Publication Data

Rikhye, Indar Jit, 1920 -

    Military adviser to the secretary-general: UN peacekeeping and
the Congo Crisis / Indar Jit Rikhye.

       p. cm.
    Includes index.
    ISBN 0-312-06737-2
    1. United Nations—Armed Forces—Zaire. 2. Zaire—History—Civil
War. 1960-1965. 3. Rikhye, Indar Jit, 1920- . I. Title.
JX1981.P7R527 1992
341.5'84—dc20
                                         92–13978
                                           CIP

To the memory of my father
and of my brother Satinder

CONTENTS

MAPS

PHOTOGRAPHS

PREFACE AND ACKNOWLEDGEMENTS

I was appointed Military Adviser for the Congo Operations to the United Nations Secretary-General, Dag Hammarskjöld, in July 1960, and with the expansion of the UN's peacekeeping responsibilities, Hammarskjöld's successor, U Thant, designated me as his Military Adviser with responsibility for all peacekeeping operations. By the end of 1964 the Yemen, West Irian and Congo operations had ended, and after the withdrawal of the UN Emergency Force (UNEF) in Gaza and Sinai early in 1969, only two UN observer groups remained: in the Middle East and Kashmir. In addition to these, there was a peacekeeping force in Cyprus, and except for an occasional incident, the operation had become more or less routine. This had greatly reduced my work, and early in 1969 my post was abolished. However, my deputy, Lieutenant - Colonel Lauri Koho of Finland, remained in the office of the Under Secretary-General for Special Political Affairs as the Military Liaison Officer. Expertise in logistics and air transportation was retained by the Field Service Operations of the General Services Department of the UN Secretariat by engaging retired service officers with suitable experience.

After the October 1973 Arab-Israeli war, when a second UN Emergency Force was established,[1] a military logistician and an air force transport officer were added to the field service staff. In 1974 Koho returned to Finland and was replaced by Major Timothy Dibuama of Ghana, and shortly thereafter an assistant from Ireland was added to the staff. Subsequently, Dibuama's designation was changed to Military Adviser in the Office of the Under Secretary-General for Special Political Affairs. At the beginning of 1987, he was appointed Military Adviser to the UN Secretary-General in a revival of the appointment I had been the first to hold, and promoted to major-general.

The appointment of a military advisory staff to the office of the Secretary-General has been controversial, to say the least, but this

ix

controversy is part of the general debate related to peacekeeping operations in the UN. The signatories to the UN charter envisaged peaceful negotiations for the settlement of disputes, and if these failed, enforcement action could be authorised. Peacekeeping operations, by military personnel and organised forces, were not envisaged in the charter and although guidelines have emerged, a Special Committee for Peacekeeping Operations, appointed by the General Assembly in 1964[2] has yet to conclude its deliberations. Thus, peacekeeping operations have retained an *ad hoc* character. They must have the consent of the parties involved in the conflict, at least the tacit approval of the permanent members of the Security Council and approval for financing; they must have voluntary contingents; and they must employ its troops in a peaceful role, permitting only the minimum use of force in self-defence as a last resort.

In the early days of the UN, it could manage peace observation operations according to the practice established by the League of Nations. The problems of command, control and management arose when UNEF I was set up to end the Suez war in 1956.[3] The UN operations in Korea, an enforcement action, were turned over to the Unites States to overcome Soviet opposition, thus excluding any involvement by the UN Secretariat. It also obviated the use of the Military Staff Committee provided by the charter. With the change in the Soviet attitude, resulting in support for the United Nations and peacekeeping in particular, the Soviet Union proposed the use of a Military Staff Committee to assist in the conduct of peacekeeping operations; on this the United States and other Western powers have been sceptical, and have yet to respond. Troop-contributing countries have expressed their reservations as they insist on retaining a voice in the management of peacekeeping.

UNEF was authorised by the General Assembly under the Uniting for Peace resolution,[4] placing the responsibility for the conduct of the operation on the Secretary-General. On being asked by the General Assembly to assume responsibility for a military force, albeit to be used in a peaceful role, Hammarskjöld added a military advisory staff to his office and appointed General I.A.E. Martola of Finland as his Military Adviser for UNEF; once these operations had become routine, Martola returned to his country. One military staff officer, Major Benaventura Cavalcanti of Brazil, remained in the office of the Under Secretary General for Special Political Affairs, but after some time he also left.

The role of the Military Adviser at the UN continues to be debated. Some of the permanent missions that are active in peacekeeping have their own military advisers who expect to be kept informed of developments. They wish to see a high-profile UN military advisory staff who can also maintain regular contact with them. Missions without military advisers, unless they have someone with military experience, would just as soon receive memoranda from the UN secretariat and forward them to their own governments to respond to and when they are instructed from home to convey a communication to the UN they ask for a meeting with the relevant UN staff member. Over the years the UN Secretariat has adopted the view that some military expertise is needed, e.g. for logistics, movements, rotation of contingents, record keeping, maintenance of a maproom and briefings. This military staff is preferred to be at the middle level of seniority and is expected to keep a low profile. My view falls somewhere between these two.

A question often asked of me is how I acquired this job. The answer is that I was chosen by Hammarskjöld as a citizen of India, a country which enjoyed great international prestige under Jawaharlal Nehru's leadership. I was a veteran of two wars, the Second World War and the operations in Jammu and Kashmir, and I had commanded a contingent in UNEF and served as UNEF Chief of Staff as well as some two months as acting Force Commander. Although, on leaving UNEF I, I had been promoted brigadier and given command of an independent infantry brigade group at Ladakh, a critical strategic area on India's borders with Tibet and China, Hammarskjöld and Ralph Bunche, Under Secretary for Special Political Affairs, who had given his endorsement to my selection, had evidently forgotten about my promotion because their request to Nehru referred to 'Colonel' Rikhye.

Hammarskjöld had spent Christmas 1957 with UNEF and returned the following year for another visit. He was interested in some innovative ideas for training that I had introduced to improve the performance of the staff and the troops and invited me to visit the United Nations in New York. On the conclusion of my duty in Gaza, I spent a week at UN headquarters meeting Secretariat staff related to peacekeeping and representatives of countries with contingents in UNEF. At a luncheon attended by his senior associates Hammarskjöld asked me to express my ideas on the importance of training peacekeepers for operational missions. Before I left for India, he asked if I would be interested in a UN assignment; I replied that I would but only after completing tenure of my new command and receiving the approval of my government. I returned to New York five months later, soon after the independence of the Congo when its army mutinied, the Belgians intervened, and civil war broke out.

My career with the United Nations was launched when I was selected by the Indian Army Chief of Staff, General K.A.S. Thimayya, to command the second Indian contingent to UNEF. The first contingent was sent hurriedly by air as soon as UNEF was established, with Colonel Sarup Singh Kalaan, a first-rate officer of the Rajputana Rifles, as liaison officer. This was the first experience for the UN as well as the member-states in organising a military force of this kind. There were many management problems to be overcome. Among them was the thorny question of the relationship of the national liaison officers to the Commander. General Burns had held high command during the Second World War, where commanders of Allied formations were directly under their superior Allied commanders, and their national liaison officers only had political functions. Accordingly, Burns placed the contingent liaison officers in a separate category, provided them with minimum essential services in the field and excluded them from his chain of command. This upset most of these officers. The Canadian contingent commander was also commander of the base logistic units, but others from Denmark, Norway, India and Yugoslavia were excluded from the commander's conferences and from his mess. Moreover, they were permitted privileges in the B mess, intended for majors and those of lower rank, as well as field service civilian personnel, including mechanics, clerks, secretaries and security personnel. This particularly incensed Kalaan who was accustomed to being a member of an exclusive officers' mess.

After a visit to the United Kingdom, Thimayya made a stop at Gaza to see the Indian troops and meet Burns. Since they were both Allied veterans of the Second World War, they got along well. In his usual light-hearted vein, Thimayya brought up Kalaan's complaint, to which Burns replied that he hoped to resolve the problem. Thimayya then proposed that because the Indian contingent was the largest in the force, Burns should appoint an Indian Chief of Staff. This too was well received, and Burns said that his choice would depend on the merits of the officer proposed. I had completed almost four years as the GSO1[5] of the 1st Armoured Division, the only one in India at that time, and was due for a change and a promotion. Thimayya had known me from the time I had led the first Indian armour into the Vale of Kashmir to stave off the Pakistani invasion of Srinagar and later when I commanded the Royal Deccan Horse, equipped with Sherman tanks, in the Jammu area during the last phase of fighting that ended in 1948. Eventually he chose me to take the second Indian contingent to Gaza and said that if I did a good job as its commander there was a good chance of my being selected for the Chief of Staff's appointment. He teasingly added 'You'd better be good.' So it seemed that I had made it.

The operation in Jammu and Kashmir was my last war, as I was denied the opportunity to return to India in the aftermath of the Indian-Chinese border war in 1962. When fighting broke out between India and China, I requested U Thant, Hammarskjöld successor, to release me for national service. He reluctantly agreed to send my request to the Indian government but made it clear he intended to inform Nehru that I could not be spared from my UN assignment.

Although fighting ended in a few days, I was keen to return to the army. My UN appointment was temporary and after all I had chosen the army as my career. I realised U Thant's request would prevail and therefore was not surprised when the Indian Permanent Representative, Ambassador C.S. Jha, told me that our government had agreed to U Thant's request for me to remain with the UN. And he quipped, 'Pandit Nehru has many generals he can send to the top of Himalayan peaks, but you are the only one who is wanted on the top floor of the UN secretariat.' Soon after this, the Indian army was expanded and my name was on the list to be considered for promotion. The Selection Board of the Ministry of Defence, on the basis of the report on me for the command of the 114 Independent Indian Infantry Brigade Group in Ladakh, recommended my promotion to major-general to the Indian government. When I received notification of this promotion, I was pleasantly surprised, but it bothered some officials at the UN. I had been asked for first on the assumption that I was a colonel, but I was already a brigadier. Now I was a major-general, a rank usually held by the Chief of Staff of a military observer group or a force commander who carried the UN rank of Under-Secretary. I did eventually receive the rank of Under-Secretary for the duration of my appointment as Commander of UNEF from February 1966 to June 1967, and it seems that my promotion to major-general created a precedent for my successors.

During my UN service and later as head of the International Peace Academy, which is devoted to the development of training and research on peacekeeping and related matters, I have relentlessly urged that a qualified military advisory staff of sufficient size be made available to the UN Secretary-General. This has yet to happen.

This book deals with the UN operations in the Congo from 1960 to 1964, known by the French acronym ONUC. This was the largest peacekeeping endeavour that has existed up till now, and it called for considerable human ingenuity and political skill.

Acknowledgements

This book is an International Peace Academy publication. There are many who helped me to complete it notably the Board of Directors of the Academy who generously gave their support. I am most grateful to the Chairman of the Board, Mr James H. Binger of Minneapolis, Minnesota, for his steadfast support for my writing and my other endeavours related to peaceful resolution of conflicts, and to Mrs Ruth Forbes Young of Downingtown, Pennsylvania, the Founder of the Academy, who has shared my hopes and expectations for a more peaceful world for nearly a quarter of a century.

This book could not have been completed without the efforts of two of my colleagues at the Academy to whom I owe special thanks. Ms Dolores Fenn did pioneering work in the search for documents stored in the UN archives and in coping with first my handwritten drafts and subsequently with my attempts at word-processing. Later Ms Linda Margraff took over these arduous duties and continued her assistance even after returning to her academic studies.

My wife Cynthia helped me in many ways. She had served with ONUC during its early traumatic days. She cheerfully accepted the many hours that I spent in my study on the book and was always ready to laugh at some of our shared and separate experiences in the Congo.

It goes without saying that this manuscript would never have seen the light of day without the patience and editorial contribution of my publisher Mr Christopher Hurst, to whom I am extremely grateful.

This book is dedicated to the memory of my father and older brother, who gave their lives in the service of humanity. My father, Rai Sahib, Dr Madan Lal Rikhye, a North Indian physician and a veteran of the Mespotamia campaign in the First World War and the Chitral campaign after the Russian Revolution, came out of retirement in response to the call of Lord and Lady Mountbatten to senior Indian Medical Service personnel to organise and manage medical services for refugees after Partition and the independence of India in 1947. He died while making his rounds of a tented medical facility. Satinder, my older brother, volunteered for the Royal Indian Air Force shortly after the outbreak of the Second World War and became a fighter pilot. He served two tours of combat duty in the Burma war and returned to India to convert to flying Dakotas for a newly-raised Indian transport squadron. During the partition of the country these aircraft were in great demand by the military and for refugee airlifts and he was killed in an air crash.

This book is also dedicated to the scores of officers and men of the UN peacekeeping operations in the Congo who, like my father and brother, gave their lives in an effort to alleviate human suffering and bring about peace. The memory of these and of others, including the great UN Secretary-General Dag Hammarskjöld who made the supreme sacrifice in the Congo, will always be cherished and should be an inspiration for future generations.

New York, June 1992   INDAR JIT RIKHYE

NOTES

1. Security Council Resolution 340 (1973).
2. General Assembly Resolution 2006 (XIX).
3. General Assembly Resolution 1000 (ES.1), 5 November 1956.
4. General Assembly Resolution 377 (V), 3 November 1950.
5. General Staff Officer (GSO) is equal to Chief of Staff in the US system.

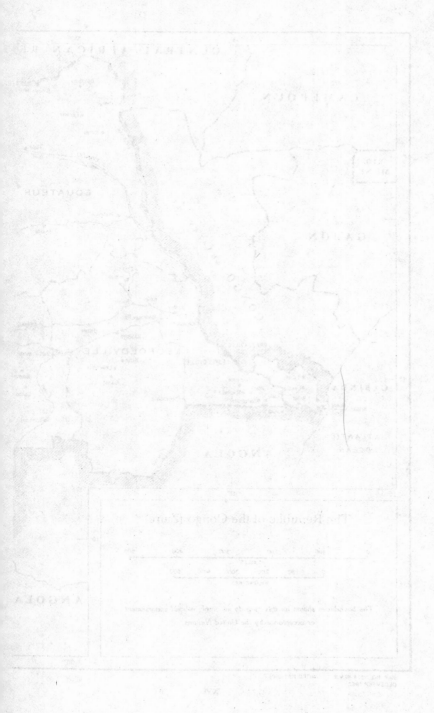

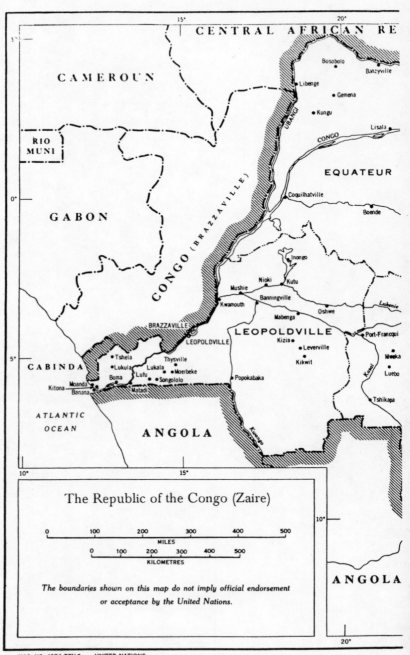

The Republic of the Congo (Zaire)

0   100   200   300   400   500
MILES

0   100   200   300   400   500
KILOMETRES

The boundaries shown on this map do not imply official endorsement
or acceptance by the United Nations.

MAP NO. 1274 REV.2   UNITED NATIONS
DECEMBER 1962

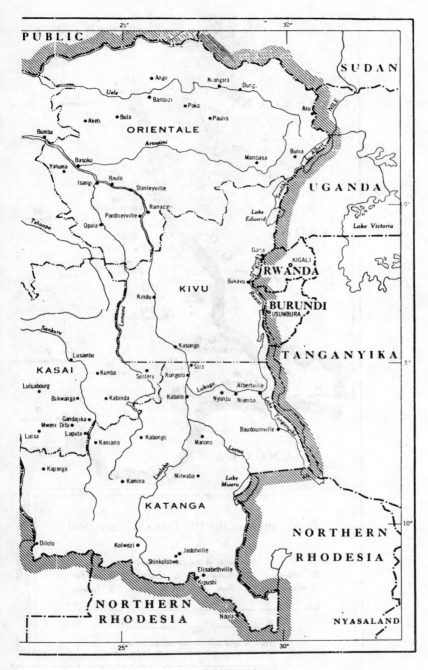

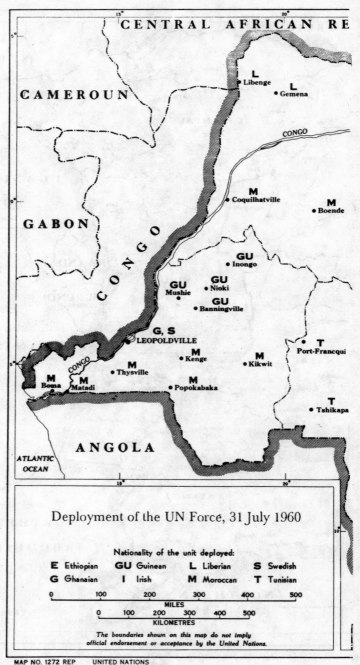

Deployment of the UN Force, 31 July 1960

Nationality of the unit deployed:

E Ethiopian	**GU** Guinean	**L** Liberian	**S** Swedish
G Ghanaian	**I** Irish	**M** Moroccan	**T** Tunisian

0   100   200   300   400   500
MILES

0   100   200   300   400   500
KILOMETRES

The boundaries shown on this map do not imply
official endorsement or acceptance by the United Nations.

MAP NO. 1272 REP   UNITED NATIONS
FEBRUARY 1961

xviii

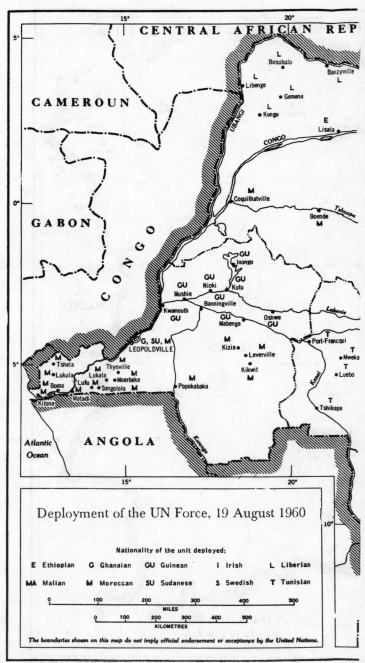

Deployment of the UN Force, 19 August 1960

Nationality of the unit deployed:

E Ethiopian   G Ghanaian   GU Guinean   I Irish   L Liberian

MA Malian   M Moroccan   SU Sudanese   S Swedish   T Tunisian

The boundaries shown on this map do not imply official endorsement or acceptance by the United Nations.

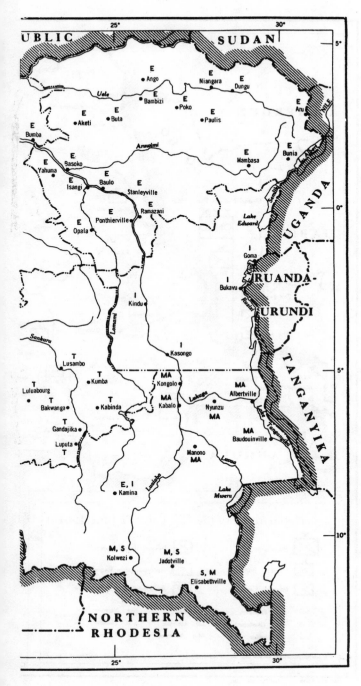

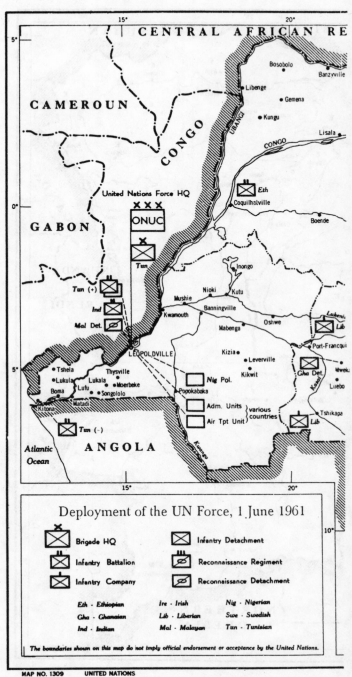

CENTRAL AFRICAN RE

Bosobolo
Banzyville
Libenge
Gemena
Kungu
Lisala

CAMEROUN

CONGO
UBANGI
CONGO

Eth
Coquilhatville

United Nations Force HQ

ONUC

Boende

GABON

Tun

Inongo

Tun (+)
Ind
Mal Det.

Nioki
Kutu
Mushie
Banningville
Kwamouth
Mabenga

Oshwe
Lukeni
Lib

Port-Francqui

LEOPOLDVILLE

Kizia
Leverville
Kikwit
Gha Det.
Mweka
Luebo

Tshela
Lukula
Lukala
Moerbeke
Boma
Lufu
Songololo
Kitona
Matadi

Thysville

Nig Pol.
Popokabaka

Adm. Units
Air Tpt Unit

various
countries

Tshikapa
Lib

Tun (-)

Atlantic
Ocean

ANGOLA

Deployment of the UN Force, 1 June 1961

⊠ Brigade HQ	⊠ Infantry Detachment
⊠ Infantry Battalion	Reconnaissance Regiment
⊠ Infantry Company	Reconnaissance Detachment

Eth - Ethiopian   Ire - Irish   Nig - Nigerian
Gha - Ghanaian   Lib - Liberian   Swe - Swedish
Ind - Indian   Mal - Malayan   Tun - Tunisian

The boundaries shown on this map do not imply official endorsement or acceptance by the United Nations.

MAP NO. 1309   UNITED NATIONS
JUNE 1961

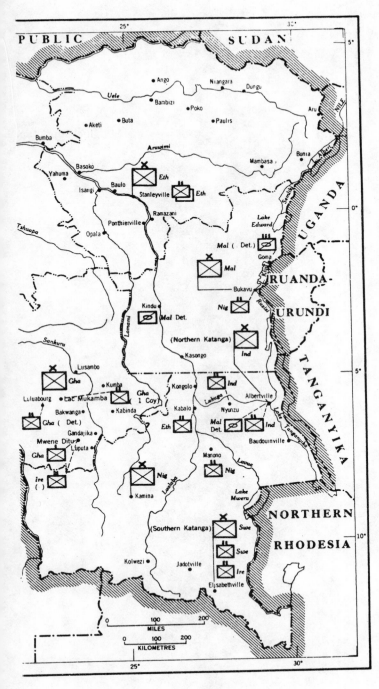

1

BEGINNING OF THE CRISIS

The Belgian Congo became the independent Republic of the Congo on 30 June 1960 (it was renamed Zaïre in 1971). As independence approached all waited to see if the Belgian gamble would succeed. It failed, and a disaster of great magnitude fell on the Congolese, the Belgians and the other Europeans who lived there. The psychological climate, already shaky, became more agitated. Uncertainty and insecurity abounded. The Europeans and the Congolese alike were susceptible to any rumour.

The enthusiasm felt by everyone for independence barely lasted a week. The UN team under Ralph Bunche attending the celebrations[1] were no exception and grew more apprehensive as each day passed. On 5 July, General Emile Janssens, commander of the Force Publique, addressed the Congolese non-commissioned officers of the Leopoldville garrison following the first acts of indiscipline the previous afternoon. He wrote on the blackboard: 'After Independence = Before Independence', and announced: 'The Force Publique continues as before.' These words had a cataclysmic effect on his listeners, and the word soon went around that independence had brought little change to the army.

It was suspected at the time of independence that General Janssens planned to organise resistance to the successor government headed by Patrice Lumumba, and he later admitted this in his memoirs.[2] Similarly, the Belgian resident minister, W.T. Ganshof van den Meersch, was actively engaged in preventing Lumumba's government from fully taking power.

The future of the mineral rich-province of Katanga, in an independent Congo ruled by Patrice Lumumba, became of increasing concern to the Belgians, British, French and United States who had major economic

1

interests there. The Balubas of South Katanga, led by Moïse Tshombe, had their own ambitions, and a secessionist plot was in the course of incubation. Besides, there were notable external elements with designs on the Congo. The Soviets were believed to have sought opportunities in the country with the weakening of the imperialists' position through the Belgian Communist party. In Africa, Sekou Touré of Guinea and Kwame Nkrumah of Ghana, anti-colonial and thought to be radical by the West, who had led their countries to independence after a hard struggle, had thrown their support behind Lumumba. It would have been surprising if Sekou Touré and Kwame Nkrumah had not hoped that the Congo would join the Ghana-Guinea union to give psychological impetus to the embryonic Pan-African state.

On the evening when Janssens spoke to the Congolese soldiers in Leopoldville, troops from Thysville (a garrison town some 130 km away on the road to Matadi), sent to the capital to cope with indiscipline, refused to obey their European officers. The first mutiny in modern times against a force's entire officer corps had begun. The next day, Lumumba tried to halt the action by the troops of the Force Publique by promoting all soldiers one grade, and announced the dismissal of Janssens.

But the mutiny, still unknown outside the military camps, had spread. On 8 July Lumumba decided to retain only a few Belgian officers as counsellors and africanised the entire officer corps. He appointed Victor Lundula commander of the army with the rank of major-general, and Joseph Mobutu chief of staff with the rank of colonel. Lundula, who was now burgomaster of Jadotville in Katanga, had formerly been a medical sergeant - major; and Mobutu, a journalist, had been a civilian clerk. The Congolese Senate changed the name of the Force Publique to 'Armée Nationale Congolaise' (ANC). But panic had already swept the European community in Leopoldville on the nights of July 7 and 8 as the news of violent incidents began to arrive from the Lower Congo. Large numbers of Belgian experts and technicians fled, and many essential services collapsed.

On the morning of 7 July the first assault against Europeans since independence took place at Thysville. At least two, if not more, Belgian women were raped by men of the marauding ANC. Within a week of independence, the Congolese government, with little experience in administration, found itself preoccupied with complaints, demands and demonstrations that had erupted from the first days of the transfer of power. It was now confronted with its most serious problem so far, the unity of the ANC: the very forces of law and order that were so sorely needed by the young republic at its birth were torn by discontent and turmoil. The Thysville incident became the signal for a general uprising against Europeans, which the Congo government could not deal with alone and which looked likely to lead to disaster.

Janssens, who had been officially removed as commander of the Force Publique but was still in *de facto* command, appealed directly to the commander of the Belgian metropolitan forces stationed at bases in the Congo to help him restore order; the latter, after consulting with the Belgian ambassador, Baron Jan van den Bosch, fortunately did not comply with this request. By the terms of the Friendship Treaty concluded between Belgium and the Republic of the Congo at the time of independence, the Belgian metropolitan troops stationed in the country could only be called into action by the Belgian ambassador at the request of the Congolese Minister of Defence, who happened to be Lumumba himself. Any action against Africans by the Belgian troops would unquestionably have set off a calamitous eruption.

The panic caused by the ANC's dissensions, coupled with a wave of strikes, gave rise to an increasing amount of irresponsible and ill-informed talk, by Americans and Belgians among others, of 'UN intervention' with troops, principally to take command of the ANC. Such talk was staved off by Bunche with the explanation that it was the UN's practice strictly to avoid involvement in internal political affairs.

It became evident that the situation was rapidly worsening for the government, which seemingly had no control either in Leopoldville or elsewhere. Active hostility to the Belgians was increasing. On 9 July, there were menacing demonstrations in front of the Belgian embassy where Janssens still foolishly remained; by refusing to leave the country, he had become a focus for anti-Belgian feeling. Congolese troops were becoming drunk in public areas, thus foreboding more trouble. The African population at large was not yet seriously involved in the disturbances, but food shortages through strikes and other disruptions could quickly change this.

Bunche and his colleagues were confined to the Stanley Hotel in Leopoldville where they had been staying since their arrival. On the morning of 8 July rampaging mutineers invaded the hotel and all the guests, including Bunche, were rudely ordered at gunpoint to go down to the lobby. Fortunately, though ruffled, they were not harmed, but they had little idea what might happen in the next few days. For Bunche it was an unforgettable experience.

We should now turn to the food supply situation in the Congo: there could have been unimaginable consequences if the populations of Leopoldville, especially, or any other urban centres had started to feel the pinch of hunger. In Leopoldville this could have happened within a few days. Food shortages and an enormous inflationary potential appeared to have been developing rapidly as a result of interruption to the overall transportation system. The government apparently had no systematic plan to avoid the impending dangers, and indeed may not even have realised them. The ports of Matadi and Leopoldville were reportedly at a standstill. The European pilots were not working, and consequently ships could not be taken into Matadi. River traffic was not functioning due to strikes. The pipeline from Matadi, which was the only source of fuel supply for Leopoldville, still remained undamaged, but it was not working, and the local fuel supply was said to be adequate for a maximum of eight days.

While the effect of the European food processers and planters being evacuated from the major supply regions was not yet clear, the African processers in Leopoldville were starved of raw materials and therefore could not work. Local food prices in the public markets were 150 per cent above normal in the few places that were spot-checked. The inflationary potential grew as pay was raised by as much as one-third in some key sectors. Finally, strikes continued to spread, triggered and encouraged originally by the successful tactics of the Congolese army. It was felt that although the situation was extremely serious, there was a possibility of controlling it with very quick action.

In his report to the Secretary-General, Bunche likened the situation in Leopoldville to a 'powder-keg' but he hoped that the explosion might be averted. Tension was high among Europeans, owing to the shock of disillusionment over the reliability of the ANC. It was felt that this state of virtual rebellion in the force was due to a mixture of its insistence on africanisation, frustration at the failure of many expected changes for the better to materialise after independence, political factors such as the omission from the government of Bolikango people since the force was strongly Bangala, and the general weakness of military leadership.

On 9 July, Ambassador van de Bosch called on Bunche to seek his advice. He said he was under increasing pressure to call in Belgian troops from the bases to protect Belgian nationals, but he could not obtain Lumumba's agreement to this. Bunche strongly advised against any unilateral intervention by Belgian troops, which would have extremely dangerous consequences. Following his meeting with van de Bosch, Bunche got in touch with Hammarskjöld and asked him to consider the possibility of providing the Congo government with UN military advisers to help it replace the existing command of the ANC.

The ambassador met Bunche again the next day, when he outlined his views on the worsening situation for Belgian residents. The army, government and country were disintegrating, his approaches to the angry Prime Minister were futile and there was now mounting pressure in Belgium for direct intervention by Belgian troops. He asked Bunche to advise Kasavubu and Lumumba to accept the Belgian offer to place their troops, under the command of their own officers, at the service of the

Congolese Republic to help maintain law and order. Bunche again questioned whether bringing Belgian troops into action would not disastrously inflame the Africans.

Bunche was aware that the American ambassador, Clare Timberlake, had been urging Kasavubu and Lumumba to seek assistance from the UN in the present emergency, but had apparently not been precise about what form such assistance should take. Timberlake had mentioned a UN force to replace the Belgian troops, a UN commander for the Congolese troops, supported by a UN adviser, and a UN commander for the Belgian metropolitan troops until they could be replaced or repatriated. Bunche thought it unlikely that the UN would assume any kind of responsibility for Belgian troops in the Congo.

Bunche met Kasavubu and Lumumba and the cabinet to discuss the military crisis and the question of what military assistance the UN might be asked to provide. In the final moments, the discussion became more complicated and emotional when the Minister of Justice read out telegrams just received stating that, in contravention of the treaty, Belgian troops had gone into action in Luluabourg.

Both Lumumba and Kasavubu expounded the necessity for africanisation of the army, saying too that they recognised that their military establishment and the police could not avoid deteriorating rapidly under the new regime without considerable assistance from non-Belgians. They realised also that the state would be incapable of maintaining law and order if prompt assistance were not given to the police force. Thus, they asked Bunche to convey their appeal to the UN, without any clear idea of what they wanted or could reasonably expect, except that they needed quick action. They would gladly accept any military assistance the UN could offer and said they hoped that the UN could at least partly meet this challenge.

Bunche conveyed to New York the Congolese government's wish that the UN would provide technical assistance of a military nature, including advisers, experts and technicians to assist it in developing and strengthening the ANC for national defence and to maintain law and order. It wanted as much assistance as possible, as quickly as possible. This, of course, included expert assistance in military organisation and training, but not participation in actual internal policing or in providing 'fighting' men. Bunche, while acutely aware of the difficulties that would face the UN in carrying out the Congolese request, saw that the alternatives were infinitely more difficult, not the least being the near-certainty of widespread unilateral action by Belgian paratroopers if attacks on Belgians persisted.

On 11 July, Hammarskjöld informed Bunche that because matters were so urgent, he planned to take action on the Congolese government's request on his own initiative, without seeking the Security Council's approval. Because the Secretary-General could do this where technical assistance was concerned, though not military assistance, he asked Bunche to get the Congolese government to request 'technical assistance in the field of security administration' rather than 'technical assistance of a military nature'. Bunche reportedly saw Thomas Kanza, the Congolese Minister for UN Affairs, who promised that an official request would be sent to the Secretary-General immediately with the suggested wording.

This request was indeed sent, but for some unexplained reason it reached Hammarskjöld only several days later. Meanwhile, he received a telegram dated 12 July from the President and Prime Minister of the Congo with a totally different request. It read:

> The government of the Republic of Congo requests urgent dispatch by the UN of military assistance. The request is justified by the dispatch to the Congo of Belgian metropolitan troops in violation of the Treaty of Friendship signed between Belgium and the Republic of the Congo on 29 July 1960. Under the terms of the treaty, Belgian troops may only interfere on the express request of the Congolese government. No such request was ever made by the government of the Republic of the Congo and we therefore regard the unsolicited Belgian action as an act of aggression against the country.
>
> The real cause of most of the disturbances can be found in colonialist machinations. We accuse the Belgian government of having carefully prepared the secession of Katanga with a view to maintaining a hold on our country. The government, which is supported by the Congolese people, refuses to accept a *fait accompli* resulting from a conspiracy between Belgian imperialists and a small group of Katanga leaders. The overwhelming majority of the the Katanga population is opposed to secession which means the disguised perpetuation of the colonialist regime. The purpose of the requested military aid is to protect the national territory of the Congo against the present external aggression which is a threat to international peace. We strongly stress the extremely urgent need for the dispatch of UN troops to the Congo.

The request for UN troops came as a complete surprise to Bunche in Leopoldville, since there had been no previous discussion or indication that such an extreme request would be made. The most that might have been anticipated as a result of the activities of Belgian troops was a protest to the UN at the violation of the Friendship Treaty; the request for troops had apparently been made because of the secession of Katanga and various engagements between the Congolese and Belgian troops in the Matadi sector on July 11. Bunche felt that without quick UN action the involvement of Belgian troops would be extended, and before long French military forces would probably intervene from across the river at

Brazzaville.

The situation was rapidly getting worse, and it became obvious that deep fear was spreading throughout the European community and even among the Africans; excitement began to rise to fever pitch and tension was unrelenting. This led Bunche to change his original view of not getting involved militarily, and he reported that he was now inclined to lean heavily on some manifestation of a third presence as the only way to save the situation. The presence should definitely be international and military in character, though not necessarily consisting of fighting men. Speed became the keynote; there must be a quick and impressive 'move-in' by the UN if its effort was to be effective. A request for United States troops was also made by Congolese officials in their desperation since they assumed it would be several weeks before any UN assistance could arrive.

The same day, 12 July, some 4,000 members of the ANC at Camp Leo 2 in Leopoldville were reported to have forcibly regained their arms which had earlier been deposited in armouries. The potential danger was thus greatly increased.

Bunche, assuming the Security Council would approve the proposal for action suggested to Hammarskjöld that a few companies of troops with defensive arms should be sent as observers with one company being stationed in each locality - French-speaking units could be sought from Tunisia, Lebanon and Canada, and also from Scandinavia and Iceland. Several helicopters and light aircraft would be needed to transport observers from one place to another, as had been done in the operations in Lebanon. There should be a company of military police and a number of technicians for operating trains, power stations, oil pumps, and so on. Finally, a military band, as colourful as possible, should be sent to 'trumpet the international presence' and create a favourable psychological effect.

On the morning of 13 July, the Belgian ambassador ordered Belgian troops into action to prevent Congolese troops from entering Leopoldville and, after the arrival of Belgian reinforcements, to cordon off the European neighbourhood's *communes* from the African ones. He handed the Vice-Premier, Antoine Gizenga, a note stating the Belgian intention to activate their troops if certain specific measures, such as the freeing of Europeans who had been arrested, were not taken and order was not restored throughout the territory. His decision to act had followed the arrest of Belgian officers at Camp Leo 2 and the airfield, and he also cited the mistreatment of Belgian prisoners and the raping of Belgian women at Thysville.

In New York, for the first time in the history of the UN, Article 99 of the Charter was invoked and an urgent meeting of the Security Council demanded. During the night and the early hours of July 14, the Security Council considered a report of the Secretary-General[3] on a request for UN action and the request for military assistance addressed to him by the Congolese President and Prime Minister. The Council called on Belgium to withdraw its troops from the Congo and authorised the Secretary-General to provide the Congolese government with military assistance until its own national security forces were capable of carrying out their proper functions. Thus ONUC - *Opération des Nations Unies au Congo* - was set up.

While the Security Council debated the issue in New York, there was no meeting of minds between the contending parties in the Congo itself. The Congolese ministers were trying to make the Belgians lay down their arms, while the Belgians had no compunction about putting on a show of force, for some time at least, even though this was likely to produce a reaction of great bitterness. It was reported too that the Congolese ministers could not take any course without consulting their troops first. Thus, even at this early stage, the way was open for the military coup which actually occurred in September. Bunche reported that he could see no prospect of the Belgian troops returning to conformity with the Friendship Treaty unless the UN in some way made it possible for them to do so.

Within twenty-four hours of the Security Council resolution, the first UN troops, the *Casques bleus,* arrived in Leopoldville. These were detachments of the 9th Infantry Battalion from Tunisia. The advance party of the Tunisian brigade was the first unit to reach the Congo, on the evening of 15 July, and it was immediately deployed in the centre of Leopoldville where tension was high. The rest of the capital and the surrounding area were taken over by the Ghanaian brigade, which arrived the next morning. During the following days, the main body of the Tunisian contingent arrived and was sent to Luluabourg to be deployed in Kasai province. They were followed by the Moroccans, who were immediately despatched to Thysville, Matadi and the southern part of Leopoldville province. At about the same time, the Ethiopian contingents landed at N'Djili airport and were immediately airlifted to Stanleyville and other parts of Oriental province.

Bunche was now finding his dealings with Lumumba, who had a totally wrong notion of the role of the UN troops, increasingly difficult. On 16 July, he had to point out categorically to him that the UN troops who were pouring in were not in the Congo with a political purpose, that they would not fight Belgians or anyone else, and that they would remain wholly and exclusively under UN orders.

On 7 July, in a letter to Bunche, the Belgian ambassador stated that instructions had been given to the Belgian forces in the Congo to limit their possible military intervention to the minimum point compatible with the security of Belgian nationals. In all other matters the Belgian commander had been advised to follow the instructions given him by the military commander of the UN force.

On the morning of 18 July, Major-General Carl von Horn of Sweden, Chief of Staff of the UN Truce Supervisory Organisation (UNTSO) in Jerusalem for the previous three years, took over as Supreme Commander of the UN force. To help him take over and organise the force at its inception, he had been authorised to bring with him a small group of officers also serving with UNTSO in Jerusalem. On the same day, one of Lumumba's secretaries of state told newsmen in the presence of Major-General Henry T. Alexander, Chief of Staff of the Ghana Defence Force and commander of the Ghanaian troops in the Congo (he was on secondment from the British Army), that the UN had failed them, and that if the Belgian troops did not leave the country within seventy-two hours the Congolese government would call for Soviet troops. This was in Stanleyville, where Alexander had been deputed by Bunche to deploy the UN Ethiopian troops and try to calm the fears of the Belgians. Meanwhile, Bunche met the Congolese cabinet, and later reported what had taken place to the Secretary-General.

During his discussion with the cabinet, he had assured Lumumba that Belgian troops, following the Security Council's decision, would leave the Congo when the UN forces arrived. However, Lumumba said he regretted to inform the meeting that, contrary to the decision of the Congolese Republic, Belgium was still sending its troops into the country; and his next move could well be the deliberate incitement of the people against the UN—something which, no doubt, could easily be done with this 'totally unenlightened populace'.

On his return to Leopoldville's N'Djili airport from Stanleyville on the night of 17 July, General Alexander, acting on Bunche's instructions, met General Gheysen and proposed that there should be complete Belgian withdrawal from Leopoldville by the evening of July 19. He pointed out that this would be the only means of avoiding the population's getting completely out of hand as a result of constant incitement by the government. Gheysen recognised that a Belgian withdrawal from Leopoldville would be beneficial psychologically and finally agreed to meet the UN at noon on 19 July to give a definite answer—which would depend on sufficient UN troops being available there.

All the Ethiopian UN troops who had arrived in the capital on 17 July had been sent to Stanleyville the next day and 500 Moroccans were sent to Thysville, the situtation in both places having taken a dangerous turn. Only the Ghanaian brigade remained in Leopoldville. Gheysen now requested consent from the UN for his own troops to undertake a 'rescue action' in four troubled areas in Oriental province (Watsa, Dunia, Paulis, and Yangambi), where hitherto no UN troops had been deployed. Alexander told him that this was not acceptable to the UN, but Gheysen replied with a new proposal that the UN should 'observe any necessary rescue action which would be notified to the UN beforehand'. While Alexander took a favourable view of this, Bunche reported to New York that he did not see how the UN could, even indirectly, be a party to any Belgian military action in the Congo, however strong the justification for it might be.

Lastly, Gheysen requested the UN to obtain a parachute battalion for its force quickly as the only way of reaching remote places in the country. Bunche favoured this suggestion, but realised that it would not be easy to fulfill, and sought the views of the Secretary-General. Hammaskjöld was hesitant, and asked for Von Horn to amplify and evaluate it.

On the Congolese threat to Soviet troops, Hammarskjöld informed Bunche that through Mongi Slim, Tunisia's Permanent Representative to the UN, he had 'animated' the five representatives of African states contributing troops to the Congo to take up the idea of making approaches to Lumumba with their heads of state. He pointed out that as contributing countries, they felt strongly that his criticism of the UN and threat to request Soviet intervention greatly complicated their position and endangered the whole UN operation, which had begun successfully. The Secretary-General told Slim that basically the Congo had to choose—in broad terms—between African solidarity and the Soviet Union on one side, and on the other side the UN and the major powers that fully supported it.

Turning to the ANC, Bunche said that he visited Camp Leo 2 on the morning of 17 July with the Congolese ministers Bomboko and Kanza; and that the Congolese soldiers clearly resented the presence of these ministers and demanded their immediate departure. A riot nearly broke out and the party left.

On 18 July Bunche stated in a cable to New York that while the risks of this UN operation were frightening, they none the less had to be faced and taken. He reported that the Europeans were scared and bitter and expected the worst. The Africans were also scared and bitter, but this was combined with the expectation that miracles would occur such as the instant withdrawal of all Belgian troops, immediate generous supplies of food, and various tangible boons from independence. He shuddered to think of the consequences of an incident involving conflict between UN troops and members of either the African or the European community or, worst of all, with Belgian troops. The ANC understood nothing about the UN, and UN identification-marks were virtually meaningless to them, but Bunche expressed the hope that we would soon give meaning to them. The restoration of the ANC, which had so far caused most of the disorders, was one of the main challenges for the UN.

Also on 18 July, the Council of Ministers invited Bunche, Von Horn and Alexander to a meeting to discuss an 'ultimatum'. The attitude of the Congolese towards the UN was generally friendly, mixed with some misunderstandings and much over-expectation. Bunche bluntly reviewed the realities of this operation, the Congolese attitude in the past few days and the implications of their threat to seek Soviet military aid. Towards the end, Bunche was asked to inform the Secretary-General that the Council of Ministers was not seeking the withdrawal of UN forces. It recognised that the coming of Soviet troops to the Congo could provoke a world nuclear war and only wished that the UN would bring an end to Belgian military actions and that the Belgian armed forces would return immediately to their bases and soon leave the country altogether.

Following this meeting, Bunche, Von Horn and Alexander met Gheysen and Ambassador van den Bosch to discuss the phasing-out of Belgian troops. The UN representatives pressed for a speeding-up of their withdrawal and urged that they should be much less conspicuous while they remained. They also insisted that UN troops would take over as soon as they arrived. The Belgians were reluctant to make significant concessions, but the UN side believed they were beginning to understand the realities of the situation; they assured the UN representatives that their troops were being removed from Leopoldville to the camps in the provinces covered by the Friendship Treaty and that the only addition to their deployment was the despatch of a military engineer company to Matadi to get the port open. The Belgian government only wished to speed up the evacuation of civilians in Leopoldville and its vicinity so that their troops could also be withdrawn in accordance with the Security Council decision. It was a matter of choice for their nationals whether to be evacuated or not.

In the Congo, the discussions between the UN and the Belgian representatives for the withdrawal of Belgian troops from Leopoldville raised three main points. The first was that with the arrival of the Swedish battalion on 20 July the UN European troops would outnumber the Belgian forces in the Leopoldville area. Secondly, the UN could not accept the Belgians' formula that the pace of the withdrawal of their troops could be directly related to the speed of evacuation of Europeans, since this implied that the UN was not in a position to afford adequate protection. Finally, the UN assured the Belgians that the Swedish battalion would control N'Djili airport, that the road to it would be policed by UN African troops, and that the UN would extend its policing activities beyond the existing city lines to areas previously maintained by the Belgian troops by organising its own patrols throughout the city. Bunche and Von Horn pledged that they would request the immediate return of Belgian troops to the area if the situation there threatened to get out of hand. This pledge needless to say was not publicised.

On 19 July, Andrew Cordier, Executive Assistant to the Secretary-General, informed Bunche that in addition to the increase in the number of American aircraft from nine to thirty-three announced on 17 July, he had just been notified that it had been raised further to a total of eighty-eight. This speed-up in airlift capability would of course make it much easier for the UN force to receive - and use - all the troops and equipment provided by the various national contingents. Because of the political dangers, it was desirable to build up the force with all possible speed to 10,000 men, with efficient equipment and adequate supplies.

The main problem now facing the deployment of the forces was their internal movement by air. On this aspect, Bunche said, 'If we had some Dakota aircraft and crews, we could do some rescue work in some of the episodes mentioned by the Belgian Ambassador, but we have to blanket the country to protect all of the 70,000 to 80,000 Europeans.' On 19 July, he reported that the public reaction to the Belgian troops' being withdrawn and security duties taken over by the UN troops had been favourable. A major problem now developing was that every town and hamlet was appealing by cable for UN troops—mainly for reasons of prestige and curiosity! UN headquarters in Leopoldville was being besieged by such requests and in fact Bunche felt that if the build-up of the force continued, it would be possible to use the same tactics throughout the country as in Leopoldville and for the Belgian troops to be able to depart finally from the Congo.

On 20 July, Lumumba formally requested in writing that UN soldiers should replace Congolese as guards at the Palais de la Nation (housing the parliament) because the latter were suspected of involvement in a plot to kill him. Compliance came within the UN's policy of providing special protection to such places as government buildings, embassies, consulates and public works installations, but Bunche reported, 'This request had an ironic touch since he [Lumumba] had just been threatening to run us out of the country. Sitting through such sessions without erupting convinces me that Job had nothing on me! Really!' On the same day in Leopoldville the Ghana contingent put on a foot parade with a military band and a detachment of the Congolese police. This was the first attempt at a joint parade and was a huge success, thus vindicating Bunche's belief, expressed earlier, in the need to create some spectacular psychological effect.

On 21 July the Security Council adopted its second resolution[4] on the Congo. It called for the speedy implementation by the Belgian government of the Resolution of 14 July on the withdrawal of their troops, and authorised the Secretary-General to take whatever action might be necessary to this effect. It requested all states to refrain from any action that might impede the restoration of law and order in the Congo and the exercise by the Congolese government of its authority and undermine the Congo's territorial integrity and political independence. Lastly, it invited the specialised agencies of the UN to give the Secretary-General any assistance he might ask for.

In Leopoldville the UN team began discussions on completing plans for the Belgian military withdrawal to comply with this resolution. The Belgians suggested that the UN relieve their units in eight areas, but that their troops should remain available to respond to immediate appeals for help. There was a NATO store at Banana which they had to guard, and in addition they would remain at the military bases agreed to by the Congo in the Friendship Treaty. The Belgians asked for air landing rights and facilities for supply and movement throughout the country.

Katanga was not included in the Belgians' withdrawal plan, their position being that they were in that province at the request of the local authorities and could only withdraw eventually after consultation with those same authorities. Again, the UN representatives pointed out that in view of the Security Council resolutions their position had to be that Belgian armed forces must withdraw completely from all territories of the Congo, including Katanga; in other words from within the boundaries of the state as it existed at the time of the Security Council resolution approving its accession to UN membership.

Hammarskjöld cabled to Bunche on 24 July the result of his own dealings with the Belgians on this problem. He had told them that, after carefully studying the whole legal problem involved in the resolution on their withdrawal, their Friendship Treaty with the Congolese and so on, he was obliged to demand the withdrawal of their troops both from the bases and from Katanga. An official memorandum setting out the analysis which had led him to this conclusion would be handed to the Belgians the next day, and they could assume that if the conflict between their respective viewpoints remained unsolved he would place this memorandum before the Security Council. He also informed the Belgian government that he could not negotiate the validity of his stand, which he had taken on his sole responsibility and which could be challenged only by the Security Council.

The same day, Hammarskjöld informed Bunche that the Belgians had timidly proposed that UN observers should be attached to their military units at the places where they considered them necessary for the protection of Belgian citizens so that the UN could 'see for itself' what was being done. Hammarskjöld replied that he could accept the idea in principle though based on a different formula. First, the UN should always receive prior information of any such action and be given the opportunity to intervene. Secondly, there was to be no intervention by Belgian troops where the UN was already present except if the UN requested it. And finally, UN advance representatives or groups should be able to visit places where the Belgians were still stationed to evaluate the situation on the spot and the possibility for the UN to take over the task in question itself.

Hammarskjöld felt that the Belgian formulation had the virtue of helping to push the UN operations forward more quickly, although in the exact form proposed it was not acceptable. The Belgian ambassador, faced with Hammarskjöld's reaction, seemed to find himself trapped but he replied that while the dangers of the situation made it impossible for his government to wait, it was prepared to accept the delay involved in referring first to Leopoldville.

On this question, Bunche felt that, ever since their troops had been ordered into action in the Congo, the Belgian authorities had persistently striven to get the UN identified with their military activities. They now made a new and comprehensive proposal. It was that if the UN were to take Belgian troops into their own forces, joint military actions should be undertaken. UN troops should be carried in Belgian military aircraft, Belgian military medical units should be accepted, the UN should give its agreement when notified of intended Belgian actions and should even request such action when it was capable of acting on its own, and lastly it should attach observers to Belgian units to report on any military encounters. Bunche, however, rejected any idea of ONUC collaboration with Belgian troops. Bunche and Von Horn saw no objection to the Secretary-General's formula mentioned above, but considered it unlikely ever to be invoked. As for advance representatives, it was found that nothing of this nature was necessary. The Belgians had already left Stanleyville, Thysville and Matadi when UN troops moved in there, and at Boma and Luluabourg they had agreed to leave as soon as the UN established a substantial presence. The places which the Belgians had previously cited as needing urgent attention were those where neither they nor Americans had a presence and where they wished to send 'rescue parachute detachments with UN observers, if possible'. There were no problems concerning the areas where Belgian troops remained, since the UN was free to enter them. Von Horn said that it would be very difficult for him to provide observers at short notice because of the shortage of competent officers, and besides it would delay the deployment of the UN force throughout the country and thus actually slow down the Belgian withdrawal.

The decisive fact at this juncture was that, except for Katanga and the military bases, the Belgians had agreed to leave every location that they now occupied whenever the UN was able to send in its own troops. No advance parties had so far been sent to any of the places to which UN troops had subsequently gone. But Bunche and Von Horn said that if it would help the Belgians in any way, they would be ready to try to undertake it as a matter of course. Incidentally, the Belgians had never asked the UN into any place where they had troops except when they were on the point of leaving.

On the basis of the plan for withdrawal presented by the Belgians at a meeting on 23 July, Bunche reported that it should not take long for all their troops to be recalled to their bases. It was decided to concentrate on this by moving UN troops to the indicated places as quickly as possible, using the men and planes already available. This would not, of course, apply to Katanga. Bunche also reported his belief, in spite of having no evidence to support it, that the Belgian bases were being used as centres for efforts towards secession, dissension and activities hostile to the central government.

In top-level staff discussions on what functions ONUC would perform in the event of demonstrations or actual riots, the question arose as to whether tear-gas should be used rather than clubs or guns; the implications for and against need no elaboration. Bunche was in favour of having a modest supply of tear-gas canisters and storing them without publicity. They should be used only in dire emergencies and by specially trained units, such as already existed in the Congo in the Moroccan and Tunisian contingents and also the Ghana police contingent. The use of fire-hoses was considered as an alternative, but dropped because of the unreliable water pressures in Leopoldville! This whole question was raised only because it was considered obligatory to be prepared for any emergency or contingency since government authorities in the Congo at this time were almost non-existent.

Bunche reported on 24 July that, as expected, the Vice Premier and some of his colleagues were interpreting the new Security Council resolution as meaning that the Belgian troops would all be out of the country in three to four days. In this, he felt, they would be disappointed, but they could take it that the troops' complete withdrawal would be announced reasonably soon. He warned that they would be extremely bitter and possibly reckless if they got the impression that the Belgians intended to stay on at their bases indefinitely. The potential for the public to be incited on this issue through the radio was all too clear.

It also appeared that Lumumba and other Congolese had selected the Belgian ambassador in the Congo, Jan van den Bosch, as a handy scapegoat. Bunche reported that he was extremely 'visible' in Leopoldville since he had stayed on there long after the breaking of diplomatic relations between Belgium and the Congo. While Belgian troops controlled the city, he was not at any very great risk, but now that they had gone his house was being guarded by UN Ghanaian soldiers. If the Congolese tried to attack him, a possibility that could not be excluded, then the UN would clearly have to take action to protect him. However, if there were an attempt to arrest him, it was less certain what the UN would be expected to do.

This matter was clarified by the Secretary-General. Since diplomatic relations had been broken, the Belgian ambassador had no status in relation to the Congo government, but he did retain a position in relation to the UN. This was because a Belgian diplomatic representative was required to provide liaison in the Congo between the UN and Belgium while its forces were being withdrawn. Thus the Congolese government would have to accept him for as long as this process continued. This did not mean that the Belgian ambassador was in any sense accredited to the UN or had any formal status under UN rules; it was merely a necessary *de facto* arrangement. Against this background, therefore, the UN had to take responsibility for his security and give him adequate protection against possible attack or arrest.

On 25 July, Hammarskjöld outlined the basic structure of ONUC. In the Congo he would have a Special Representative, who would be the top man with political responsibility. This was Ralph J. Bunche. Major-General Carl von Horn was Supreme Commander of the UN Force, and Dr Sture Linner was Chief of Civilian Operations. At UN headquarters in New York the chain of responsibility started with the Secretary-General, and he was assisted by a small group of trusted political advisers which included Andrew Cordier, Heinz Wieschoff and Ralph Bunche. This group also included myself as Military Adviser to the Secretary-General and Sir Alexander MacFarquhar as Adviser on Civilian Operations. It was known as the 'Congo Club'. We will look more closely at its working in the next chapter.

NOTES

1. Bunche, a black American, was Under Secretary-General. The team also included two political assistants, Brian Urquhart and F.T. Liu; Sture Linner, initially intended to be UNDP Resident Representative, and consequently appointed Chief of Civilian Operations; Mario Harrington, Deputy Chief of Civilian Operations; and Bunche's personal assistant, Pauline Lacerte.
2. Emile Janssens, *J'étais le Général Janssens*, Brussels: Charles Dessart, 1961, pp. 219-23. *Fin de la souveraineté belge au Congo. Documents et réflexions*, Brussels: Institut Royal de Relations Internationales, 1963.
3. UN Security Council Document, S/4382.
4. UN Security Council Document S/4387, 14 July 1960.

2

ON JOINING HAMMARSKJÖLD

I reached New York on 23 July 1960 and was met at Idlewild International Airport by Leo Kennedy, a member of the United Nations travel staff, who took me in a Cadillac limousine to the UN building on Manhattan's East River. I was warmly received by the Secretary-General's personal staff and was exchanging pleasantries with them when Andrew Cordier ambled out of his office on his way to see the Secretary-General. He stopped to greet me, and welcomed me back to the UN. Cordier was a hulk of a man and carried his enormous problems on a broad pair of shoulders. He was tremendously patient and could astonishingly spare much of his valuable time to listen to anyone who sought his guidance or help.

Presently Hammarskjöld came out of his office wearing a neat custom-made white silk suit, greeted me warmly with a smile, and, thrusting some cables into my hand, said, 'General, will you please write out replies to these.' He then left me abruptly and returned to his office, with Cordier following him. I stood there overwhelmed and bewildered, not knowing what he was talking about. That was the start of my new job as Military Adviser to the Secretary-General for the Congo operation.

I read through the cables, but could not make head or tail of them, and when Cordier returned to his office, I went in and told him so. He laughed affably, which I later learned was his normal way of handling both simple and complicated situations. He briefly explained what had happened in the Congo. The Secretary-General and he had spent the last few days and nights obtaining military personnel from various countries and making arrangements to have them flown out there. When he finished this summary introduction to the UN operation, he looked at me indicating that now I knew the background and should get on with my job. But I still

Above: UN Secretary-General Dag Hammarskjöld, during a break in a Security Council meeting in New York, with the author, his Military Adviser for the Congo, August 1960. *Below:* Ambassador Rajeshwar Dayal, who replaced Ralph Bunche as the Secretary-General's Personal Representative in the Congo, August 1960. (Photos: United Nations)

did not know where to begin and therefore said that I would be of little use to anyone until I had been properly briefed on the background to the situation in the Congo, current developments, and the aims and objectives of the UN force there.

Cordier said that I would find all that out at the Secretary-General's evening round-up. Meanwhile, I was shown my office which was next to that of Ralph Bunche, who had been sent to Leopoldville to attend the Congolese independence celebrations as the Secretary-General, representative. When the disturbances broke out, Hammarskjöld had asked him to remain there, and following the establishment of the UN operation in the Congo, had appointed him as his Special Representative. He was now our man in the Congo.

At 7.30 in the evening I was called to the Secretary-General's evening round-up. He was already seated at the head of the table, smoking a small cigar, and had a pile of cables in front of him. Cordier sat to his left, and around the table were Heinz Wieschoff, Director of Political and Security Council Affairs and Hammarskjöld's political adviser for the Congo, and Sir Alexander MacFarquhar, a former member of the Indian Civil Service who had put in a stint in the UN Development Programme in Bangkok and been called from there to be the Secretary-General's adviser for the civilian operations in the Congo.

Hammarskjöld picked up one cable after another, asked a few questions of his colleagues, and dictated rapid replies. This occupied a great deal of time, during which cocktails were served. Then at 9.30 Hammarskjöld invited us to supper in an adjoining dining-room. Cables kept arriving from the Congo and were answered almost as fast as they were received. It was past midnight when I returned to my hotel to sleep in a bed for the first time in forty-eight hours.

I never got a chance that day to express to Hammarskjöld the apprehensions I felt concerning my job. However, the next day, while we were going through the same routine, he invited my views on some questions relating to the Congo force. I took this opportunity to say that I was hardly in a position to make any useful contributions as long as I did not understand the situation, did not know the country, and had not examined the situation personally. Hammarskjöld readily agreed to my visiting the Congo and authorised me to travel to any part of the country and spend as much time as I needed to study conditions and developments.

I was due to leave New York on July 27 and started obtaining all possible information connected with my new job. There were some publications available, and I talked to a number of delegates and their military advisers. I found much information in the Technical Assistance Bureau in reports received from their many field experts.

While I was fully occupied with this, Hammarskjöld informed me that he had received a cable from President Nkrumah of Ghana voicing serious disagreement on the conduct of the military operations in Leopoldville. His Chief of Defence Staff and commander of his troops in the Congo, Major-General Alexander, would arrive in New York the next day to discuss these developments, and I was to assist. When I met Alexander, it became clear that this highly trained and experienced officer was unhappy with the political conduct of the military aspects of the operations. More serious, he had already lost confidence in the ability of Major-General von Horn, the newly-appointed Swedish commander of the UN force. Many of the problems raised by President Nkrumah stemmed basically from these issues.

I was greatly impressed by Alexander's intimate knowledge of the situation, his presentation and his recommendations. But as I had already explained to Hammarskjöld, I lacked intimate knowledge of the situation and declined to take any active part in the discussions which followed. Alexander recommended that because of the vast size of the country, the nature of the terrain and communications, the difficulties of supporting a force under these conditions, and the complicated relationship with political superiors, the Congolese government and the local authorities, the UN force in the Congo should be so organised as to have a Supreme Commander responsible for political, logistical and other important issues, while an Executive Commander should be in charge of the actual conduct of the military operations. A third higher military position should be established for a military adviser to the Congolese government. What the proposal actually boiled down to was that Von Horn should be nominated as Supreme Commander and Alexander as Field Commander or military adviser to the Congolese government.

While there was some justification for Alexander's recommendations, the proposals were unacceptable to the Secretary-General politically. The appointment of a British service officer to a high position in the UN command in the Congo was out of the question since Britain was a permanent member of the Security Council, was a colonial power, and had important local interests. Despite his impatience with the set-up in the Congo, Alexander had served the UN well. He left behind a fine group of Ghanaian officers and men, whom he had led during the critical early days. I was sorry to see a none-too-pleased Alexander return to Accra. Thereafter, the UN never found itself eye to eye with Nkrumah over the handling of ONUC (Opération des Nations Unies all Congo).

Alexander also raised the problem of the ANC. He said that with its Belgian officers gone and no available trained Congolese officer corps it was without effective leadership. On his arrival in the Congo with the advance element of the Ghana troops, he had realised that, unless brought under control, the ANC would remain the most serious obstacle to ONUC in carrying out its mission. He had therefore persuaded the acting Chief of Staff, General Maurice Mpolo, to agree to the disarming of the ANC. However, on July 20, Lumumba had told Brigadier S.J.A. Otu, the senior Ghanaian officer, that he would not permit the UN to disarm his army. Lumumba had taken this up with Bunche, who ordered the Ghanaian troops to return the ANC's weapons. Alexander urged that the ANC had first to be re-disciplined and re-trained before being permitted to go around with their weapons. Otherwise they would surely pose a considerable threat to peace.

Hammarskjöld contended that regardless of the merits of Alexander's arguments, the UN had no authority to disarm the ANC. This decision was based not only on the absence of a mandate from the Security Council but also on the fact that if the ANC were disarmed, the UN would have to station troops at every place where the ANC were located. Besides, the UN would have to assume complete responsibility for law and order in the Congo instead of assisting its security forces, whatever their capability might be. This would turn the UN into an occupying power replacing the Belgian troops, whose withdrawal from the Congo was one of the UN's main objectives. It was a dilemma, and Hammarskjöld favoured compliance with international law. It turned out that Alexander's prediction proved correct, and the UN paid an enormous price for rearming the ANC in Leopoldville.

Lumumba had also arrived at the UN on July 24 and during his meeting with Hammarskjöld the UN operation was reviewed. However, there were two major items on the agenda: ending the secession of Katanga and the role of ONUC and aid to the Congo. The latter, though complicated enough, proved relatively easy to discuss whereas the first question proved extremely difficult and started a chain of events and responses from the Congolese and the Secretary-General which augured ill for the future of the Congo and the UN.

A number of events occurred about the time of Lumumba's arrival in New York. Moïse Tshombe, the secessionist President of Katanga, issued an appeal to the Congolese and Belgian governments and the UN Secretary-General for the creation of a confederation of Congolese states, obviously with the intention of thwarting any plans that might be made during Lumumba's visit to end the secession. On the 25th, Lumumba denounced the Belgian-Congolese Treaty of Friendship, which had been intended to be the cornerstone of relations between the two countries after independence. On the 26th, the Congo's Minister of Finance, presumably on the advice of his Belgian adviser, disavowed Lumumba's agreement with L. Edgar Detwittler, a private American entrepreneur, to develop the

Congo's mineral resources, indicating dissension within the Congolese cabinet.

While I was not present at all the meetings with Lumumba, I was included in a working lunch with him and the Secretary-General informed me of the substance of their conversations together. I could make out that Hammarskjöld was not pleased with the trend of these discussions or satisfied with the results. There was, of course, a great difference in the negotiating styles of the two men. Hammarskjöld was skillful and suave and used complicated arguments in scholarly language based on international law and practice. Lumumba was a revolutionary, still fighting, unskilled in diplomacy and unable to distinguish between Hammarskjöld, who had vowed to help newly - independent countries and was a proven friend of the oppressed, and the colonial powers whom Lumumba had fought all his adult life. The main problem was the inability of Lumumba and other Congolese to understand that the UN was not a sovereign entity providing assistance to them. In such an arrangement the recipient and the donor come to an agreement, but where the UN is concerned, the member-states had to agree. Furthermore, it was obvious to Hammarskjöld that he would have to handle negotiations relating to Katanga personally. He made plans to go first to Brussels and then to Leopoldville. Accompanied by Heinz Wieschoff, he left New York on July 26.

I had much to learn from Alexander, and listened carefully to all he had to say before he left New York. At first he had been discouraged by the vastness of the task and of the country. Fear, hate and suspicion had spread everywhere so that the Congolese even feared the UN. But gradually Alexander had come to believe that there was hope that the UN could deal with the crisis. The size of the country and the poor communications required a large UN operation, with a built-in capability for transportation, radio communications and support services. To succeed, this operation had to be speedy and implemented with determination. The ANC needed urgent attention; its re-disciplining and re-training would be the key to the UN's success. The departure of European technicians, officials and executives had to be stopped. And above all, the co-operation of the Congolese cabinet was vital.

With the exception of his recommendations relating to the higher command of ONUC, which surprised me coming from such an experienced man, I found Alexander's other ideas valuable and worthy of serious consideration, particularly his anticipation of ONUC's three major tasks: the withdrawal of Belgian troops and their early relief by ONUC; deployment of UN troops at all centres of the ANC, sharing their barracks and supporting them logistically and administratively; and the setting up of a bilingual team to train the ANC. These were exactly the tasks that I later found needed attention.

He further proposed that ONUC should include a minimum of sixteen battalions. Force headquarters and a brigade of four battalions should be kept in Leopoldville, with a battalion at Thysville-Matadi; a brigade in Luluabourg with a battalion in that city and a battalion each at Banningville, Kikwit and Albertville; a brigade of three battalions in Bukavu with a battalion each at Bukavu-Kisenui, Albertville and Kindu; a brigade in Stanleyville with two battalions in Stanleyville; and a third battalion at Akete-Paulis-Watsa.

I arrived in Leopoldville via Paris, Marseilles and Brazzaville on July 28. The following day, with the assistance of John Olver, the Chief Administrative Officer (a colleague from UNEF days), I was travelling over the heart of the Congo in a chartered Cessna aircraft of Sabena flown by a former Belgian Air Force officer. During the next ten days, we covered some 10,000 miles, dropping in and out of what would normally have been thought inaccessible airfields, used only in emergency.

The pilot and I had little notion of the disturbances, since information available at ONUC headquarters in Leopoldville was scanty, to say the least. We therefore had to reconnoitre the area, judge the situation as best we could from the air, and then attempt a landing. We evolved a drill for this. On reaching our destinations we would circle above 2,000 feet, safe from small arms fire. After a good look and being satisfied that we were not being fired at, we would next circle over the town at less than 1,000 feet. Having ensured at this altitude that there was no firing and that no hostile crowds had assembled, we would make a low circle around the airfield and land if all looked well. My young Belgian friend was not only skillful but showed great courage in taking me to several places which all Belgians and other Europeans had already evacuated. Only once did he decline to land. That was when we flew over an airstrip in Oriental province at normal flying height. I inquired why we were not landing, and he said, 'Commies, I don't care for them'. After all he had done for me, I was hardly in a position to argue.

I had already met Ralph Bunche in Leopoldville. My first meeting with him was on the sixth floor of the ONUC headquarters. This was in an apartment building called 'the Royal', located on a broad tree-lined avenue of large villas and apartment buildings; it was not really suited for offices, but had been selected only because no better premises were available. Bunche sat at the head of a long dining table with his personal staff, at that time consisting of his political aides Brian Urquhart and F.T. Liu and his secretary Pauline Lacerte whom I had first met in Gaza. The scene struck me as extraordinary, since I had never seen such a large-scale operaton being conducted in this way before. Papers, cables, maps and reports, next to empty cans of food, used plates, empty bottles of Coke and

Evian water, lay all over the table. A pile of papers lay in front of Bunche, and he did not like anyone to take any of them away as he might need them at any time. Despite the apparent chaos, nothing was ever lost as Bunche knew exactly where everything was. The room was commonly called the 'snake pit'. The group worked around the clock with little sleep and usually with little food.

Bunche was a greying, heavy-waisted black American in his late fifties. He had received the Nobel Peace Prize for masterminding the ceasefire arrangements and the General Armistice Agreements for Palestine in 1949 after the assassination of Count Bernadotte. He had risen high in the UN through perseverance, hard work and a tactful, kind and generous approach to every situation. During the next few years I was to work closely with him. He had a remarkable degree of political acumen, clear thinking and understanding of complex political-military situations. Meeting him in this room and observing him conduct this major UN operation was an experience in itself.

It was obvious that Bunche was extremely overworked and understaffed. Yet he took the time to explain patiently the latest developments; this, I came to learn, was characteristic of him. ONUC's Ghanaian troops had almost gained control of Leopoldville, and the ANC had been persuaded to return to their barracks. Some Belgian troops still remained at key points in the city and at N'Djili airport, but they were gradually being withdrawn to their local bases. Moroccan troops had moved into the Thysville-Matadi area and appeared to be successful in their attempts to quiet the ANC there. Tunisian troops were at Luluabourg and other places in Kasai. Other ONUC troops were deployed in Equateur and Stanleyville provinces, their resources stretched to the limit. The evacuation of Belgians and other Europeans wishing to leave the Congo was going ahead smoothly.

The secession of Katanga was increasing the excitement and taxing the patience of Prime Minister Patrice Lumumba, his cabinet and the diplomatic representatives of the many governments sympathetic to him. Serious difficulties were beginning to arise between Lumumba and Bunche over the question of the use of ONUC troops to break the Katanga secession, an operation which had not received authorisation from the UN Security Council.

ONUC troops still lacked cohesion and adequate command and control. Although the Force Commander had arrived, he had not been able to take over effective control of his force, especially the operations of the Ghana brigade under General Alexander. Adequate machinery for close integration of the political, military and civilian operations within ONUC had yet to be established. I therefore immediately launched into examining the *ad hoc* organisation of Force headquarters and obtaining information on all the troops which had already arrived in the Congo. The Force Commander Major-General von Horn, whom I knew well from my time in Gaza, had assumed command on July 18. He informed me that he had brought with him ten observers from the Truce Supervision Organisation (UNTSO) in Jerusalem where he had been Chief of Staff before his assignment to the Congo. Lt. Col. John Berthiume, a French Canadian, was acting as his Chief of Staff, and the remaining nine officers held other key appointments on an *ad hoc* basis in his headquarters. This obviously was too unsatisfactory an arrangement to last. I therefore advised the Secretary-General that we should immediately borrow experienced staff officers from UNEF. This would give us time to obtain proper staff for ONUC. Within a few days, ten qualified and experienced staff officers joined ONUC from UNEF units in Gaza. For the establishment of a Force headquarters and its operational and logistics units, I drew heavily on my experience with UNEF, the first peacekeeping force ever established by the UN.

However, any plans to develop the Congo's peacekeeping force organisation and its operational capability required knowledge of the historical background and the circumstances that led to the present crisis. It soon became evident that these were complex, and to understand the situation would require study, briefing and an inquiring mind. While I attended to the immediate problems of the ONUC force, I devoted as much time as I could to investigate the political, economic, social and strategic issues involved so as to be better prepared to undertake my responsibilities.

I had soon gathered enough facts to plan the overall organisation of the ONUC force. However, I felt that I did not know enough of the developments that had led to UN intervention in the Congo, the basis on which troops were deployed and assigned their tasks, and the environment in which they had to operate. Such knowledge was essential in order to fine-tune the force organisation, its future deployment and the definition of operational orders, and to organise the logistical support. I needed a comprehensive picture of the evolution of the crisis that had led to past decisions by the UN and which in turn had involved operations at that time. And in between my work at Force headquarters and Bunche's office, I spent as much time as I could talking with Bunche and his advisers Urquhart and Liu to obtain a clearer picture of the diplomatic intricacies; also with Von Horn, Kettani the deputy force Commander, and Brigadier Steve Otu, commander of the Ghana contingent, who had been intimately involved in the events in Leopoldville. I also read through all the cables in Bunche's office and asked questions on complex issues.

Bunche was anxious that I pitch in with his staff at once. However, Hammarskjöld had told me to return to New York, which according to my understanding was to be my base. So after a few days of briefings and getting myself fully acquainted with developments in the Congo, I returned to New York. But I had hardly settled down in my new office when six or seven days later Hammarskjöld received a request from Bunche for me to be sent back to assist him in finalising the organisation and establishment of the UN Force in the Congo and especially in organising its headquarters. So back I flew to Leopoldville to join Bunche.

3

THE UNITED NATIONS ENTRY
INTO KATANGA

Initially, the question of the secession of Katanga was generally assumed to be part of the problem relating to the Belgian military intervention in the Congo which would disappear with the withdrawal of their forces. In a radio broadcast on 11 August, the Premier of Katanga province, Moïse Tshombe, declared the mineral-rich province 'totally independent from the Congo'. At the same time, he requested economic assistance from Belgium for his *independent* state, and for Belgian troops to deal with the mutinous Congolese troops and help restore law and order. Such a move was not entirely unexpected, since there had been rumblings of a separatist movement even before the Congo became independent from Belgium. Only two days before independence, Congolese officials had flown to Elisabethville to check the movement towards independence. Tshombe was reluctant to share his province's wealth with the central government and was apparently dissatisfied with Leopoldville's offer - to give Tshombe the presidency of his province and a number of cabinet posts for his political party. He had also not received the expected share of the central government's posts for his Conakat party.

In the Congo, Lumumba was insisting on early withdrawal of the Belgian forces. In order not to create a vacuum, which would allow the rebel forces to gain an advantage, the United Nations had to phase such a withdrawal with the ability of ONUC troops to replace the Belgian forces. Accordingly, UN troops were being deployed in the provinces no sooner than the aircraft carrying them touched down at Leopoldville; after refuelling and receiving orders from ONUC, the troops were flown to their

27

Above: Patrice Lumumba, Congolese Prime Minister *(centre),* with UN Representative Ralph Bunche on his left, at a press conference in Leopoldville, July 1960. *Below:* President Kasavabubu *(centre right)* with Colonel (later General) Joseph Mobutu on his right, reviewing troops in Leopoldville, January 1961. (Photos: UPI/Bettmann)

intended destination. At a meeting in Stanleyville on 18 July with General Henry Alexander, acting UN Commander, Lumumba had issued an ultimatum to the UN to remove Belgian forces from the country by midnight the next day; if this were not done, he would call on Soviet troops for assistance. The same day, the Congolese parliament called on the Belgian forces to withdraw within twelve hours. The following day, the lower house decided, in a second resolution, that diplomatic relations with Belgium could be broken by a specially-convened session of both houses. However, the senate voted the same day to reject the idea of Soviet military intervention in the Congo that Lumumba was threatening to request.

In the absence of a clear mandate from the Security Council, it was explained to me in my early meetings with Hammarskjöld's advisers that the force had three tasks: first, to remove the threat to international peace and security by arranging the withdrawal of the Belgian forces throughout the Congo; secondly, to assist the Congolese government in the restoration of law and order; and thirdly, to assist in the training and reorganisation of the ANC. However, it was clear to us that ending the secession of Katanga was one of the problems that had to be dealt with. The UN could not accept the secession for a number of reasons. For example, the basis of Congolese independence was the *Loi fondamentale*, which was accepted by all Congolese leaders, including Tshombe; the newly-independent Congo had signed a Treaty of Friendship and Assistance with the Belgian government (it had not yet been ratified); the UN had admitted the Congo to membership, including Katanga and all the territories inherited by the new state on its independence; and lastly, the Security Council had agreed to assist the Congolese government. Accordingly, in his dealings with Tshombe, Hammarskjöld was careful not to give any indication that might be misrepresented or in any way blur his position.

The threat of intervention in the Congo by troops from the Soviet bloc or indeed from any other state, and the urgent need to consider developments in the Congo crisis, had led to an extraordinary session of the Security Council on 20 July. In arranging this meeting, the Council decided to ignore a request from Lumumba for a postponement to enable him to participate. Hammarskjöld told the Council[1] he had informed Tshombe that the UN had to regard the Congo as a single entity in the light of its earlier recognition of the new nation for membership in the world organisation. He also informed the Council of his plans to visit the Congo for an on-the-spot study of the situation and for consultations with the Congolese leaders and UN officials.

In his report on ONUC, Hammarskjöld said, 'We have got off to a most promising start, but we have in no way rounded the corner.' The Force had been brought to its planned strength of 10,000, but it might have to be expanded. He asked the Council to clarify further the role of the UN troops in the implementation of its appeal for the withdrawal of the Belgian forces from the Congo. In the meantime, he had arranged to send General Raymond Wheeler, who had supervised the clearing of the Suez Canal after the 1956 war, to the Congo to organise the reopening of the river port of Matadi, and Dr G.S. Candau, Director-General of the World Health Organisation, to assess the Congo's health needs. After a lengthy debate, including acrimonious exchanges between the Congolese representative Thomas Kanza and the Soviet First Deputy Foreign Minister, Vasily V. Kuznetsov, on the one hand, and the Belgian Foreign Minister Pierre Wigny, on the other, the Council approved a resolution by Ceylon and Tunisia[2] that called on Belgium to implement the withdrawal of its troops and authorised the Secretary-General 'to take all necessary actions to this effect'; and requested 'all states to refrain from any action which might tend to impede the restoration of law and order' or 'undermine the territorial integrity and the political independence of the Republic of the Congo.'

This resolution essentially dealt with enhancing Hammarskjöld's ability to press the Belgians to speed up their withdrawal, and to prevent foreign intervention in the Congo's internal affairs, especially any which might affect the law and order situation. It also, for the first time, provided authority for the Secretary-General to help maintain the territorial integrity of the Congo. However, the Council did not set any time-limit on Belgian withdrawal. The Belgian Permanent Representative urged delay in their troop withdrawals; whereas the Soviets, led by Kuznetsov, had introduced their own resolution - which they later withdrew - in which they designated Belgium as the aggressor and demanded total withdrawal of its troops within three days.[3]

It was becoming evident that the operation in the Congo had become a victim of the Cold War and that Hammarskjöld would face many pitfalls in his task. The Russians had already objected to the presence of the US Air Force personnel stationed at N'Djili airport; these were essential ground personnel for the troop, food and supply airlift. Confronted with such problems, Hammarskjöld had advised Bunche in the Congo to ensure that United States assistance to ONUC must in no way be allowed to become mixed or confused with any action by the US Air Force that might be perceived as collaborative between the two NATO partners, the United States and Belgium. Such early indications of Cold War influences only proved a warning of more, and much worse, to follow.

After the Security Council meeting, Hammarskjöld set out to plan the implementation of the resolution. He decided to go to the Congo with a stop in Brussels, but postponed his departure in order to receive Lumumba at the UN. This was the stage at which I joined Hammarskjöld's staff. In between his many meetings, with Lumumba among others, his staff met him to report and discuss developments in the Congo, our conversations with delegates, and press reports, and to hear the gist of his discussions. If instructions or information had not already been sent to ONUC on urgent matters, then cables were drafted at the evening round-up. When he did not have a dinner engagement—something which he now avoided as much as possible—he sent for sandwiches, and we worked through most of the evening and often late into the night. On these occasions he managed to look remarkably fresh and exuberant the next morning. I was to learn later that among his many ways of relaxing, such as writing and listening to classical music, he invariably took a brisk walk every night, however late the hour.

I worked out my own ways of keeping up with him. I took some morning exercises, gentler than I was used to as a young brigadier on operational duty in India, and a short siesta after lunch. One day the executive office's administrative officer, Mrs Grace Lodge, asked me if there was anything I needed in my office, and so I replied that I would like a sofa to rest on. To my surprise, she looked shocked. When I had first arrived, she had asked what sort of secretary I needed. Since I had never been asked such a question before, I said jokingly that I preferred a blonde, and she had left my office then with the same look. What with my request for a blonde secretary and now a sofa on which to rest, she was clearly troubled about my character. However, she complied with both my requests and eventually tolerated my attempts to introduce some levity into our tense lives.

While I was involved with the visit of Lumumba and talks with General Alexander, already described, I was busy gathering information about the Congo, learning details of ONUC and preparing to leave for Leopoldville. After stopping in Brussels to urge the Belgians to speed up their troop withdrawal, Hammarskjöld had arrived in Leopoldville ahead of me. When I met Bunche after my arrival, Hammarskjöld was busy with Sture Linner of Sweden, chief of ONUC's civilian operations. I joined him at lunch together with Bunche and his team, including Brian Urquhart, F.T. Liu and Pauline Lacerte, a secretary whom I had first met in Gaza. ONUC headquarters was located in a modern, seven-story apartment building that was not really suited for offices. There was a Greek restaurant on the ground floor, which had somehow continued to function through the chaos and was now being kept going with UN patronage. We all had our meals there. Hammarskjöld, who enjoyed informality on missions, happily joined the staff at these meals, and the staff took great pleasure in having him among them. Personal touches like these, and his responses in meeting people at all levels, made him a popular leader.

During these meetings with the Congolese ministers, led by Vice Premier Antoine Gizenga in the absence of Lumumba, Hammarskjöld tried to explain that his plan called for the least possible disturbance to law and order and to the country's economic life. He emphasised that after the withdrawal of the Belgian forces, the Congo would have to face up to its more serious internal problems. The UN could not interfere in those problems, and that applied to Katanga as well. Furthermore, Katanga, so vital for the economic life of the country, required due consideration of the interested Europeans and therefore careful negotiations were needed. The Congolese responded with a demand for immediate action to end the secession of Katanga and for withdrawal of all Belgian troops. Hammarskjöld appealed for patience. He assured the Congolese that the 22 July Security Council resolution covered Katanga, but pointed out that he needed time to complete his negotiations. This appeal was in vain.

Lumumba continued his North American tour, and while in New York sent a protest to the Security Council against the Belgian government and the government of Katanga province. On 1 August Moscow Radio reported that Hammarskjöld was 'supporting the Belgian aggressors, who are becoming more brazen. This is understandable since behind them are not only the NATO colonial powers. The UN Secretary-General Hammarskjöld, staying on in Leopoldville, is supporting them by his more than conciliatory position.'

Realising the total obsession of the Congolese government with the question of Katanga, Hammarskjöld dispatched Heinz Wieschoff to Brussels on 31 July with a personal message for the Belgian Foreign Minister, Pierre Wigny, advising him of the seriousness of the situation in Leopoldville and urging his government to declare its intention of withdrawing its forces from Katanga. Once that declaration had been made, Hammarskjöld would then make arrangements for a peaceful deployment of the UN troops in Katanga and for the security of the Europeans.

While we waited to hear from Wieschoff, turmoil in the Congo continued unabated; the country seemed to possess inexhaustible ability to produce complex new situations. In Leopoldville, the well-led and well-trained Ghanaian troops had restored order. ONUC preferred to restrict the ANC to their barracks where they could do least harm, but on 1 August, when unrest broke out among the industrial workers demanding their monthly wages, ONUC agreed to the Ghanaians' recommendation that they be joined by the ANC and Congolese police to deal with the demonstrations. Such a move was expected to satisfy the Congolese government, which had been complaining that ONUC had *disarmed* their troops but let the Belgian forces continue their *occupation* of the interior. When order was restored, the Ghanaians and the ANC withdrew to their barracks, leaving the Congolese police to enforce the existing curfew after 6 p.m. The return of the Congolese security forces on to the city streets alarmed the Europeans, but was received well by the Congolese authorities and by most of the diplomatic corps.

Wieschoff returned on 2 August and reported that the Belgians felt that neither they nor the UN should interfere in the affairs of the Congolese people, and that Tshombe represented a political force in the Congo which should receive due consideration. The message, in short, was 'Hands off Katanga'. Having made the correct move towards the Belgians - who had now shown that they refused to co-operate - Hammarskjöld decided to dispatch UN troops to Katanga on 6 or 7 August. Bunche was to go on ahead to Elizabethville and make arrangements for their peaceful entry. It was neither possible nor permissible for UN troops to consider fighting their way into Katanga, and therefore the co-operation of the Belgians - who had not only their troops there but also advisers who influenced Katangese leaders and led the Katanga gendarmerie—was vital if the UN were to succeed. Before leaving New York, Hammarskjöld had already asked ONUC to prepare plans for the entry of its troops into Katanga. ONUC was thin on the ground, and thus it was a question of priorities; troops would have to be spared for the critical task. The Swedes were chosen to be the first to move, to be followed by Irish and Moroccans. Their airlift and logistical arrangements were well in hand, and there was little that I could add to the preparation.

Tshombe had made clear his position by declaring that the UN troops were not welcome in Katanga and that he would 'regard UN intervention as an act of aggression', to be opposed by force. On 3 August Hammarskjöld made a move to placate the Katangese: he issued a clarification statement[4] emphasising that the UN troops were not under the orders of the central government and that under no circumstances would they be a party to internal conflict. Initially, Hammarskjöld had chosen only European troops, but later as a compromise the UN spokesman was permitted to announce that Swedish and Ghanaian troops were detailed to Katanga to assuage the Africans, particularly the Congolese. Subsequently Moroccans, intended to reduce European anger occasioned by Lumumba's intimacy with Nkrumah, replaced the Ghanaians. Preparations were also under way for Bunche to leave the next morning.

Before the end of the day, there were ominous signs of what Bunche's mission could expect. Tshombe threatened a shooting war to bar UN entry. When ONUC declared that it intended to go ahead with its plans, he retorted: [5] 'They will have to fight their way in', and ordered mobilisation of what was believed to be a reserve of about 200,000 men. Tshombe was known to have 500 loyal soldiers under Belgian officers; there were also 15,000 Belgian civilians in Katanga, and presumably some of them would be available as volunteers and probably as mercenaries. The UN now had a total of 11,000 men in the Congo; its strength lay not in its numbers, but in its ability to rally international support for its actions, based on Security Council authorisation.

There was also reaction from the central government to Hammarskjöld's plan to send Bunche to Katanga. Gizenga informed Hammarskjöld that Bunche should be accompanied by three Congolese ministers and twenty Ghanaian soldiers. Hammarskjöld reminded him that he had already rejected the same proposal at his meeting with the Congolese cabinet. He emphasised that Bunche was on a UN mission and that this could not be combined with other elements. The next day Gizenga withdrew his request.

Through all such distractions, Hammarskjöld and Bunche carefully prepared the mission. Both were aware of the personal and political risks involved in the venture, but were determined to proceed. I watched and listened to them with admiration, realising that they had the stuff that made great men, which indeed was what they both were. Bunche, a veteran of UN peace missions, showed no trace of anxiety but only calm and caution, as he meticulously tried to anticipate problems that might arise during the day. Careful as they both were, they decided to put on record the Secretary-General's precise instructions to his deputy in the form of a letter dated 3 August.[6]

It was almost daybreak when Bunche left the Royal with his party for N'Djili to board an aircraft for a flight to Elisabethville. The rest of us turned to other chores, but with the mission to Katanga very much on our minds. Since there was no way for Bunche and ONUC to communicate, we simply had to wait for his return. He did, however, arrange a code-word that he proposed to send through Belgian channels to indicate whether UN troops should come to Katanga or not.

Bunche was received on his arrival with courtesy, but he made little headway in his talks with the Katangese leaders, especially with the Interior Minister, Godefroi Munungo. That evening, Tshombe played a trick by announcing without Bunche's consent that the decision to send UN troops to Katanga had been cancelled. Bunche felt that there was an element of bluff in the warnings and threats of dire consequences if the UN intervened in Katanga, yet he was convinced that they were all fearful of Lumumba. The next morning the arrival of the second UN plane with civilian experts caused a commotion. The two high-level Belgian officials with Tshombe, Ambassador Robert de Rothschild and Count d'Aspremont-Linden, interrupted his meeting with Bunche in a state of great agitation. They said that preparations were being made to prevent the landing of the UN plane, which was believed to be carrying military personnel in civilian clothes, and they asked Bunche to order that the plane be diverted to Kamina. In spite of assurances that there were no military personnel aboard, Munungo ordered the plane to be kept at one end of the runway and refused to allow the passengers to disembark. This was enough to convince Bunche, who had spent a sleepless night trying to assess Tshombe's intentions, that UN troops would not be able to land in Elisabethville without bloodshed. He sent the code-word to Hammarskjöld to postpone the move of UN troops, and immediately flew back to Leopoldville.

Receiving Bunche's message, Hammarskjöld instructed Cordier in New York to call an urgent meeting of the Security Council to consider developments in Katanga. Without waiting for Bunche to return, he took a special flight to New York. He told me to remain, since he planned to come back. He hoped to obtain a better mandate from the Council to speed up the withdrawal of the Belgians and enable him to introduce troops into Katanga. Besides, he wanted me to continue assisting Bunche and to finish planning the reorganisation of the UN force, including its headquarters.

Before leaving, he issued a statement[7] that after Bunche's consultations in Elisabethville he had called for a meeting of the Security Council to consider the situation. It emerged from Bunche's report that the local authorities in Katanga were indicating that they would oppose UN entry by force. As such, entry by the UN would only be possible if it resorted to force. He added: 'Such an initiative by the United Nations Force is against the principles established by the Security Council for the operation of the Force and against the conditions on which various contributing have agreed to send units to the Force. In the circumstances, the Secretary-General has intrusted the supreme commander to cancel the sending of the UN military units to Katanga on Saturday, 6 August 1960. Further instructions will be given after the consideration of the matter by the Security Council.'

Unlike Gizenga in Leopoldville, Lumumba, while travelling in Africa, had praised Hammarskjöld for his decision to send UN troops to Katanga, but when the UN postponed its entry, he attacked both Hammarskjöld and Bunche for their failure to act and for refusing to take members of his cabinet with the UN to Katanga.[8] There were other critics, notably the Soviet Union, which had not let up their attacks against Hammarskjöld. The political environment, already complex, was worsening. In a memorandum to the President of the Security Council,[9] the Soviet Union for the first time blamed ONUC for failing to enter Katanga, for the alleged disarming of the ANC, and for including European contingents in the Force. It stated that if such shortcomings continued, the UN command should be replaced by a new command that would be prepared to take the right kind of action to deal with Katanga. On 6 August, Nkrumah offered armed assistance to the Congo if the UN could not cope.[10] The following day Lumumba requested the Security Council to send a group of observers from the Afro-Asian countries[11] to ensure the withdrawal of the Belgians from the Congo, including Katanga.

On his return to New York, Hammarskjöld began preparing for the Security Council meeting. A two-day delay to enable a Congolese delegation to arrive allowed him more time for consultations. On 6 August he issued his report to the Council[12] saying that he had received assurances from the Belgian government that its troops were already being withdrawn to their bases and repatriated to Belgium. However, on the question of Katanga, the Belgian Foreign Minister had said that his country's troops were there at the request of the Katanga authorities for the safety of individuals; they were not there to interfere in internal affairs. However, in the view of the Belgian government, there was law and order in Katanga, and life was normal; secondly, the Katanga authorities had called for a reconstitution of the Congo as a federation; and furthermore there were many European technicians who were maintaining the economic life of the region. They were resolved to leave if there was any danger of anarchy raging in Katanga as in other parts of the Congo.

Hammarskjöld had informed the Belgians and the Katangese that the UN troops were under the sole command of the UN; that they were not permitted to interfere in internal affairs and therefore could not be used to impose any particular political position; and that the UN military were not permitted to act except in self-defence. Thus, the entry of the UN troops was intended to be peaceful, and they would be deployed to assume security responsibilities as they had done elsewhere in the Congo.

The report elaborated the events before Bunche's departure for Katanga, what occurred there, and the circumstances that led to the postponemnt of entry by the UN troops. In view of the opposition by the Katangese, including open threats of force, entry by the UN military units could only be achieved if they too resorted to the use of force. He reiterated the principles governing the operation of the Force described in his first report, and commended by the Council in its Resolution of 22 July, one of which was that military units would be entitled to use force only in self-defence. This statement was amplified by the following interpretation: 'Men engaged in the operations may never take the initiative in the use of armed force, but are entitled to respond with force to an attack, including attempts to use force to make them withdraw from positions they occupy under orders from the commander.' Thus the Force was not entitled to take the military initiatives and action that would have been necessary to implement the Council's decisions.

In asking for the Council's instructions, Hammarskjöld made a number of points. First, its resolution applied to the Congo as a whole, and he was acting accordingly. Secondly, it was clear that the objectives of the

Council could not be achieved without the use of force, for which he did not have authority. Thirdly, if the Council wished to maintain those objectives, it should either change the character of the Force, which appeared to be impossible both for constitutional reasons and in view of the commitments to the contributing countries, or resort to other methods that would enable him to carry out his mandate. And fourthly, the main problem in the Congo was not the question of Belgian withdrawal but an internal one. Hence the question of the UN's assumption of security responsibilities in Katanga, and whether this would be done under the control of the central government or independently without influencing the internal political outcome, was of great importance to the leaders of Katanga.

In closing, Hammarskjöld asked the Council to clarify its views and lay down rules for operations that would effectively separate the questions of peaceful and democratic development in the constitutional field from any questions relating to the presence of the UN Force. He urged speedy action because the achievement of a solution in the Congo was 'a question of peace or war, and when saying peace or war I do not limit my perspective to the Congo.' He directed his remarks especially to the Katangese to assure them that the UN would not hamper their negotiations for the future of Katanga within the Congo, and to make clear that the Europeans' best and most realistic hope for the future was to adjust to the changed circumstances, and work in harmony with the people among whom they lived and wished to continue living.

The Council had two draft resolutions before it. One, by the Soviet Union, would order the UN troops to use *any means* to remove Belgian troops from Katanga and the Congo. In presenting it, Kuznetsov, the Soviet First Deputy Foreign Minister, charged that the UN had disarmed Congolese troops and yet failed to carry out its mandate to replace Belgian troops and allay public unrest. Hammarskjöld spoke out against the Soviet resolution and denied the charges made by Kuznetsov. He said that the UN would not 'help Congolese people by actions in which Africans or Congolese kill other Congolese'. The Soviet draft was withdrawn before the vote.

During the debate, the Congolese Foreign Minister, Justin Bomboko, alleged that the Katanga government's refusal to admit UN forces was the result of 'an opposition created and maintained by the Belgian government'. The Belgian Foreign Minister asserted that Katanga would admit UN troops as soon as it had received assurances of UN intent, and that Belgian forces would be withdrawn as soon as the safety of Belgian nationals was assured. The United States delegate, Ambassador Henry Cabot Lodge, said that the UN must not become involved between Congolese and Katanga authorities, but that its troops should enter

Katanga speedily to permit the Belgian troop withdrawal.

The second draft resolution was presented by Ceylon and Tunisia, and adopted on 9 August[13] by a concurring vote of the Soviet Union, with France and Italy abstaining. It made

(a)   a renewed demand for the speedy withdrawal of Belgian forces from all parts of the Congo, including Katanga, and their replacement by UN troops;

(b)   a declaration that the entry of the UN troops into Katanga was necessary for the full implementation of this resolution; and

(c)   a reaffirmation that 'the UN Force in the Congo will not be a party to or in any way intervene or be used to influence the outcome of any internal conflict....'

With his hand considerably strengthened, Hammarskjöld made three quick moves. He obtained assurances from Pierre Wigny that the 1,700 Belgian troops in Katanga would leave and that the Belgians would use their influence with the Katangese authorities to secure the admission of UN troops; he cabled Lumumba, assuring him that there would be early compliance with the Council resolution; and lastly, he cabled Tshombe announcing that he would arrive in Katanga province on 12 August with two Swedish infantry companies of ONUC under his exclusive command. He would be accompanied from New York by Wieschoff and from Leopoldville by General Ben Hammou Kettani of Morocco, the ONUC Deputy Force Commander, and myself. He explained that the troops would have only the right of legitimate self-defence in the event of their being attacked, which he ruled out as inconceivable. Tshombe had already sent a cable to Hammarskjöld saying that he was ready to negotiate the entry of UN troops into Katanga, and Hammarskjöld had replied that there was no question of conditions being attached to any agreement and that he hoped Tshombe would accept the obligations contained in the Council resolution. In his reply to Hammarskjöld's cable of 10 August, Tshombe agreed to receive him with due courtesy.

In Leopoldville, while we prepared the Swedish troops and Field Service personnel for the trip to Elisabethville and awaited Hammarskjöld's arrival, there was great excitement in the African residential area unconnected with the events in New York. Within hours of Lumumba's announcement on 10 August that he would take drastic measures against anyone trying to break away from the central government, an influential group of the Abako party, led by the Congo's President Joseph Kasavubu, came out in favour of giving more autonomy to the young republic's six provinces. When Lumumba's supporters tried to break up a meeting of Abako, fighting broke out. Lumumba rushed to the scene and was beaten up. The Ghanaian troops immediately threw a cordon around Lumumba, and the Congolese police isolated the area of rioting. In another development in Kasai province, Joseph Ngalula, a leader of the Baluba people, announced that he had informed the UN Secretary-General of the establishment of a provisional mining state in Kasai province with himself as its head.

Hammarskjöld left New York on 11 August, briefly stopping in Accra to meet Nkrumah, a close ally of Lumumba, whose troops were playing an important role in ONUC. Soon after arriving in Leopoldville, he joined discussions with Bunche and others, including the political, military and administrative staff involved in the preparation of the move and those who were to accompany him. Bunche was to remain behind and see Lumumba after Hammarskjöld had left for Katanga; this was intended to avoid last-minute dramatic situations, since Lumumba was expected to insist that he, or at least some members of his cabinet, should travel with the Secretary-General.

The choice of Swedish troops was good and made sense under the circumstances - some of us referred to them lightheartedly as Hammarskjöld's own tribe. But what was even more important was that they had come from Gaza where they had gained experience in dealing with complex situations like the one we expected to encounter in Katanga. I certainly felt at ease with the thought of their being ONUC's vanguard in that province. The unit was well-led and fully prepared for its assignment. Every man thoroughly understood his job, and I reported to Hammarskjöld that I was more than satisfied with their readiness. The choice of Kettani was also wise. He was from a moderate African country, which enjoyed close links with both Europe and the United States. He had great political acumen and was the most battle-experienced and decorated senior officer in ONUC. He was in his sixties, and during the Second World War had led Free French troops in the later campaigns in Western Europe. I am not sure that Hammarskjöld was aware of Kettani's soldierly qualities, but apart from his nationality, he chose him because he was responsible for training and reorganising the ANC, into which it was intended eventually to integrate the Katanga gendarmerie. It was also hoped that Moroccans would replace Belgian military instructors along lines similar to what had been achieved to some degree with the ANC.

We took off at 8 a.m. on 12 August in the UN Force Commander's white Convair aircraft, with a Swedish crew. There were also some Swedish troops aboard, but the remainder followed at brief intervals in four DC-4s. After a flight of nearly five hours, we arrived over Elisabethville and contacted the tower to obtain clearance for landing. Airport control told the pilot that only the plane carrying the Secretary-General could land and that the one carrying the the Swedish troops should turn back. I was given this message by the navigator of our plane, which I immediately reported to Hammarskjöld in the hearing of Wieschoff and others. They all paused to think. Hammarskjöld then said, 'Our troops must go with me.' He turned to me, and asked, what I thought. Realising that the success of the Secretary-General's mission to Katanga was contingent on his ability to arrange the entry of the UN troops, I said that it he went in without the troops, Tshombe might not agree to accept out troops later. If he insisted on arriving as planned, there was the possibility that Tshombe might block other aircraft once our plane had landed, or he could even refuse us permission to land. However, I did not think he would take the risk of turning the Secretary-General's plane away if he insisted on the Swedes accompanying him. Besides, there was always the risk that we might be fired at, but surely they would not fire at the Secretary-General. I said he should insist on landing with the troops, or alternatively go back. Without another word, Hammarskjöld said, 'Tell them that I will land with the Swedish troops or I will leave.' The others concurred by their silence. It was obvious he had made up his mind and only wanted confirmation.

I followed the navigator to the crew cabin and listened as he conveyed our reply to the control tower. The tower replied that Major Guy Weber, Belgian military adviser to Tshombe, was by his side and would only permit the Secretary-General's plane to land. I asked the navigator to ask Weber to speak to me on the microphone, and when he was listening, I said, 'This is General Rikhye, Military Adviser to the UN Secretary-General. Mr Hammarskjöld has instructed me to ask you to immediately convey to Mr Tshombe that he insists on landing with the two Swedish companies, otherwise he will turn back.' I had to repeat the message for him to understand it fully. He told me to wait. We did, somewhat tensely and in silence while the plane continued to circle around the airport at about 2,000 feet. Down below we could see a crowd, including a lot of soldiers, milling around with their guns at the ready. Shortly afterwards, Weber responded with Tshombe's reply, which was to agree to our demand. We touched down a few minutes later, and I insisted on being the first to disembark to get a quick look at the situation. The crowd waiting on the tarmac looked like a normal collection of people laying on a ceremonial reception.

Hammarskjöld was greeted by Tshombe and Munongo, and several Katangese followed, along with a host of Belgians. The Belgian military were everywhere. There was a guard of honour, commanded by Belgian officers. A military band struck up with some unfamiliar music, which we presumed must be Katanga's national anthem because of the many flourishes. We later learned that it was *'Vers l'Avenir'*, which was indeed Katanga's unofficial anthem, the official anthem *'La Katangaise'* being incomplete due to the sudden death of its composer. To Hammarskjöld's embarrassment, Tshombe stopped in front of Katanga's flag. He was relieved when the band stopped and we were ushered into our cars for the ride to the Union Minière guest house, where we were to stay.

First to call on Hammarskjöld were the Belgian representatives, Ambassador de Rothschild and Count d'Aspremont-Linden: they had come to impress upon him the achievements of Belgian assistance to Katanga against the background of the chaos following the Congo's independence and to praise Tshombe and his government. They cautioned Hammarskjöld not to attempt to dismantle an orderly administration lest the Congo suffer great economic harm. Rothschild was a suave professional diplomat, whereas Aspremont-Linden was highly emotional and almost broke down as he pleaded for the avoidance of another chaotic situation, which he predicted would follow if the UN insisted on the early departure of Belgian military advisers and experts. Hammarskjöld did his best to assuage their concerns, but reiterated the points he had already made to Belgians, Congolese and Katangese alike.

Later, Hammarskjöld met Tshombe and members of his cabinet to whom he again stated his position on Katanga. At the end of this meeting, he stated in a communiqué that they had discussed problems arising from the Council resolution of 22 July and 9 August, and given special attention to the practicalities for the deployment of ONUC troops in Katanga. There was mention of the principle of non-interference in internal affairs that applied explicitly to the activities of the UN Force. Tshombe gave out his version, which of course was more favourable to his position.

Besides the normal internal security needs of the province of Katanga, there were extensive and widely-scattered mining installations and ancillaries. The Union Miniere, the major industrial complex, had its own security apparatus that met its needs within the industrial area. However, security against external threats was the responsibility of the police and the Force Publique - or had been up till the time of its mutiny. The industrial security organisation had worked closely with these bodies. After secession the police and Katanga gendarmerie were reorganised under Belgian officers, mostly the same as had served in the province before independence, and the previous security arrangements were restored.

The railways in Katanga needed special attention. The whole transportation system in the Congo had been established for the benefit of Belgian agricultural and mining exploitation. It was a typical arrangement designed primarily to meet the trading needs of the colonial power rather than serve the interest of the country and its inhabitants. On the Congo river, seagoing vessels could ply upstream as far as Matadi, above which the river was navigable by shallow-bottomed boats as far as Oriental province. The country's transportation system relied primarily on this river and its tributaries; roads and small railway systems connected with the river traffic. A railway line, starting at Port Francqui on the Kasai river, ran through Kasai to Katanga, passing through Elisabethville, and then via Ndola and the Rhodesian system all the way to South Africa. At Tshilongo, 250 km north-west of Elisabethville, there was a branch-line west to the major mining town of Kolwezi, continuing to Dilolo where it joined up with the Benguela railway, thus providing access to the Atlantic. At Kamina, the largest Belgian air base, about 300 km. north from Tshilongo, a branch-line went north to Kabalo and ended at Kindu, a river port at the eastern end of the Congo river. From Kabalo there was a rail connection to Albertville, a port on Lake Tanganyika; this route connected, via the lake and the Tanganyika railway, to Dar es Salaam on the Indian Ocean. (See map, page 244).

It was out of the question for the UN to guard this extensive network and therefore we would have to examine carefully where our troops would be needed most. Obviously, Elisabethville presented a major challenge. The city, with its government and mining installations in and near the airport and its communications centres, must be kept under the UN's control. Besides our own installations, guards would be needed for essential services and perhaps for VIPs. There was also the question of guarding opposition leaders; we had already been made aware of the need to guard Tshombe's opposition, the Balubakat, an organisation of the Baluba people, in Jadotville. They were present in all the other large towns and at the mining installations, but their numbers were highest in the north, where trouble was anticipated. Tshombe had not regained control over most of the north, and once he resumed efforts to assert his authority throughout the province fighting could ensue.

At this juncture, I only wished to be able to assess broadly the requirement for troops and their likely major tasks. I concluded that Katanga required a separate area command which would have to be somewhat independent to enable us to respond to its needs. While I considered its future organisation, I asked for ONUC's views about their troop and logistical requirements. I was confident that Kettani would have some good advice for the Force Commander when he arrived.

On the following day, some dissident Balubas from North Katanga arrived to present an anti-Tshombe appeal to Hammarskjöld, but on orders from Major Weber the Katanga police dispersed the group and arrested several of them. The police had thrown a smoke bomb and charged the gathering with sticks. I gently chided Weber for the undue use of force by his police, and left it at that. In the mean time, we received word that trouble was brewing in Jadotville, and with Hammarskjöld's approval

I set off with a UN security officer to examine the situation. On arrival, I found that the northern Balubas, the Balubakat, as opponents of Tshombe's Conakat party, were a constant target for harassment and physical attack, and that we would therefore have to provide protection for them as a priority. On my return, with the consent of both Hammarskjöld and Kettani, I ordered the Swedes to send a platoon to Jadotville, and this was done the next morning.

Hammarskjöld, Kettani and I discussed the ONUC set-up for Katanga. Ian Berendsen, an experienced UN political officer from New Zealand who had accompanied Hammarskjöld from Leopoldville, was made head of the ONUC office with the title of Officer-in-Charge ONUC, Katanga. Adequate field service staff were provided for communications and support. A Katanga area command was to be established pending acceptance by Von Horn, who was to be responsible for Katanga and Kivu provinces.

The entry of UN troops into Katanga was planned to enable ONUC to deploy its troops rapidly in Elisabethville, Kamina, Jadotville, Kolwezi, Manono, Kabalo and Albertville. The Irish from Kivu were to go to Albertville; the Malians from Leopoldville and the Ethiopians from Kasai to North Katanga; the remaining Swedes from Leopoldville were to join their two companies already at Elisabethville and Jadotville; and the Moroccans were to go to Kamina and the western mining towns. With the help of a new staff, who had started to arrive at Force headquarters, a complicated troop movement plan, converging on Katanga by road, rail and air, had been drawn up, and it worked smoothly when Hammarskjöld ordered the move for the following day.

Von Horn agreed to set up a Katanga area command with the few staff officers he had brought with him and to send to Leopoldville for Colonel H.W. Byrne of Ireland to assume command. He then sought a private meeting with Hammarskjöld, and after about half an hour emerged from the living-room of the guest-house, saying he was on his way to make his official calls. I walked in to continue my work with Hammarskjöld only to find him red in the face and showing very uncharacteristic signs of agitation. He thrust a paper into my hand and said, 'Carl has no idea what this operation is about. Here . . . he has given me this list of what he wants. He wants to build an army. Really! Really! I told him I was not going to start an armament race now'. He went on: 'He also wanted better administrative support and has put it on this list. Will you discuss this with him and take care of it?' Hammarskjöld then turned to more important issues: the withdrawal of the Belgians and the growing conflict among the Balubas. There was a large refugee camp near Elisabethville, and the problems had already begun.

Von Horn later approached me to discuss his talk with

Hammarskjöld. He said he had recommended five or six infantry brigades, at least one squadron of tanks, two reconnaissance units, several field and anti-aircraft regiments, and an air element composed of reconnaissance and fighter planes and sufficient squadrons to maintain a thoroughly adequate airlift for Katanga. He had warned Hammarskjöld that the people in New York (i.e. the UN Secretariat) had no concept of the requirements in the field and were therefore giving him the wrong advice. Von Horn had anticipated that ONUC could be at war with the Katangese, for which we were not prepared, and he was not confident that the UN could command adequate logistical support from New York. This, on top of there being no clear orders from New York, would make it difficult for ONUC to defend itself. Von Horn said he was surprised at Hammarskjöld's reaction; surely I, as a battle-experienced man, would understand the needs of ONUC in Katanga and support him.

Knowing how badly out of touch Von Horn was with military reality, I thought a little education would not do him any harm. I asked if he realised just how many troops he had asked for, and the weapons, transport, supplies and maintenance that would be needed to keep them in the field. His troop requirements added up to two infantry divisions, with artillery and other supporting arms and services. The ONUC force in Katanga would then be equal to an army corps of 30-40,000 men. Leaving aside the logistics problems in the field, we already had to import food for about 15,000 troops by sea and air, and that quantity would have to be at least doubled. Then I pointed out the problem of moving these troops into Katanga. The available US Military Air Transport Service aircraft were able to bring in perhaps 500 men with their equipment per day. Therefore sixty days would be needed to move the troops he wanted, at a cost of hundreds of millions of dollars. Lastly, I asked him where he would get these troops from as we were already nearly drying up the acceptable countries. The remaining few would not give us more than a few thousand. I finally said. 'Dag has already given you his reply, and there are my views. Forget it, Carl'.

Von Horn had now shown his hand. Previously Hammarskjöld had only heard about his limitations from others, but now he knew them straight from the horse's mouth. He realised that his compatriot was a liability and hoped that I would deal with him and keep the military operations going. Shortly afterwards, he endorsed the military aspects of our plan. There was not much else to discuss with Von Horn now and so, leaving Kettani with him, Hammarskjöld and I left for Leopoldville, making a brief stop at Kamina.

The Secretary-General decided to establish a special group to plan for the takeover of Kamina and its future use. By its Treaty of Friendship with the Congo Belgium was allowed to retain troops at the three military bases of Kamina, Kitona and Banana after Congolese independence. Of the three bases Kamina was the largest, and had excellent flying facilities. But because the presence of Belgian troops and the potential use of military facilities by secessionist Katanga posed a serious threat to the Congo and the regime as a whole, Hammarskjöld had insisted in his discussions with the Belgians, and they had agreed, that these bases be handed over to the UN's care. Back in Leopoldville, Lumumba had kicked up a row at being excluded from the UN's Katanga venture. Immediately on arriving, Hammarskjöld wrote to Bomboko, the Foreign Minister, that he would like to report to the central government on the implementation of the Security Council resolution of 9 August. A bitter exchange of letters followed between Lumumba and Hammarskjöld. First, Lumumba responded to the note Hammarskjöld had requested Bunche to deliver personally to him on 12 August, before leaving for Katanga. He wrote that he disagreed with Hammarskjöld's interpretation of the Council resolution. The first resolution on Katanga required the UN 'to provide the Government of the Congo with such military assistance as may be necessary'. Thus the UN was not neutral, and was required to place its resources at the disposal of the Congolese government. UN troops could therefore be used to subdue the rebel government of Katanga, and the government could call for UN services to provide transport for civilian and military personnel and protect the representatives of his government who had been sent to Katanga.

Lumumba also took issue over the role of ONUC. He charged that Hammarskjöld's interpretation that ONUC's role was only to arrange the withdrawal of the Belgian forces was improper. The UN was required to assist the Congolese government in pacifying the country and in restoring law and order. Lumumba then attacked Hammarskjöld for failing to consult him before leaving for Katanga and acting in a way that gave the impression that his government did not exist. Furthermore, the assurances that Hammarskjöld had given to Tshombe, which Tshombe amplified in his statement to the press, were clear evidence that the Secretary-General had made himself party to Katanga's conflict with the central government and that the UN was being used to influence the outcome. He added that it was incomprehensible that the UN should have connived with the Belgians to exclude African troops from being sent to Katanga. Lumumba concluded his letter with five demands:

(a) that the task of guarding all the airfields of the Republic should be entrusted to the ANC and the Congolese police in place of the UN;
(b) that troops be sent to Katanga from Morocco, Ethiopia, Mali, Tunisia, Sudan and Liberia, as well as Congolese troops;
(c) that aircraft be kept at the disposal of the government of the Republic for the

transportation of Congolese troops and civilians engaged in restoring order throughout the country;

(*d*)   that all arms and ammunition distributed by the Belgians in Katanga to the partisans of the rebel government, whether Congolese or foreign, should immediately be seized and put at the disposal of the Republic, since they were the property of the government; and

(*e*)   that all non-African troops be withdrawn from Katanga immediately.

Hammarskjöld replied on 15 August that Lumumba's letter contained requests contrary to his interpretation of the Council's resolution. He felt that there was no point in discussing them then; he would report to the Council requesting it to take a stand on the position he had taken. In his reply, Lumumba added   nothing new to what he had said previously. However, in his third letter written on the same day, he made a personal attack on Hammarskjöld, charging that he had sent troops from Sweden because of his country's affinity with the Belgian royal family. This was a reference to Queen Astrid, the mother of King Baudouin, who had been a Swedish princess. He stated further that Hammarskjöld had only decided to send African troops to Katanga after he, Lumumba, had publicly denounced him for only sending Europeans. Furthermore, not only had Hammarskjöld failed to stop in Leopoldville to consult his government, but he had delayed the UN's arrival in Katanga by making a twenty-four-hour stop in Brussels to consult with the Belgian Foreign Minister. In view of all these developments, Lumumba wrote, 'the Government and people of the Congo have lost their confidence in the Secretary-General of the United Nations. Accordingly, we request the Security Council today to send immediately to the Congo a group of observers representing the following countries: Morocco, Tunisia, Ethiopia, Ghana, Guinea, the United Arab Republic, Sudan, Ceylon, Liberia, Mali, Burma, India, Afghanistan and Lebanon.' The task of these observers would be to ensure the immediate and entire application of the Security Council resolutions. Lastly, Lumumba requested Hammarskjöld to delay his departure for New York to enable a Congolese delegation to travel with him on the same flight.

The crisis in relations between the UN and the Congolese government, and in particular between Hammarskjöld and Lumumba personally, came on top of the difficult relations that already existed between Lumumba and Bunche. This brought the UN operations to a most critical stage. There was little to be gained from continuing an acrimonious exchange of letters. The Congolese had not responded to Hammarskjöld's initial suggestion for a meeting, but the present atmosphere was not conducive to a useful meeting anyway. Thus Hammarskjöld left the same day, reaching New York on 16 August. The Congolese did not fly with him, and were asked to make their own arrangements for their delegation as there was enough time for them to travel by scheduled airlines. I left for New York two days later to implement plans that I had completed for the reorganisation of ONUC.

Difficulties between Lumumba and the UN had emerged at the very outset of the Congo operations, the primary cause beign Lumumba's lack of understanding of the UN system. He expected it to act like a powerful state, such as France, when providing assistance to countries with which it had entered into agreements. He did not realise, either at the beginning or later, the limitations on the UN and the process required to have its actions approved. The first to fall foul of Lumumba and his cabinet colleagues was naturally Bunche, the Secretary-General's Special Representative in the Congo. Then Hammarskjöld faced a similar situation when Lumumba came to the UN in New York. There was no common ground between them, and at the meetings in New York their relations became extremely shaky and only worsened with the developments that led to the first UN entry into Katanga.

In New York, seasoned statesmen like Mongi Slim of Tunisia and Alex Quaison-Sackey of Ghana tried to moderate this revolutionary fighter in his dealings with Hammarskjöld and others at the UN, but with only slight effect. The stark fact was that Lumumba was inexperienced in international diplomacy and indeed in the conduct of government. In negotiations he was like an angry bull who would see red on every side and charge at it relentlessly. I myself saw him lose more friends and gain more enemies than any other leader who ever came to the UN.

The UN's entry into Katanga was made possible by Hammarskjöld's skillful diplomacy and sensitive management of the operation. It would have been impossible for the UN to have gone into Katanga with Lumumba or any member of the central government without the use of force, for which the UN had no authority and its members no will. It was possible to appreciate Lumumba's ruffled feelings at being left out of the first move into Katanga, but his refusal to see the UN Secretary-General on his return from Katanga was not only a serious diplomatic *faux pas*, but an insult both to the office of the Secretary-General and personally to Hammarskjöld, a man who was received in the capitals of member-states in a style often beyond the writ of normal protocol. Hammarskjöld was thus absolutely right not to waste more time in Leopoldville but to return to New York to deal with his responsibilities relating to the Congo, irrespective of the behaviour of its misguided prime minister.

Apart from the grave problem of relations with Lumumba, the Katanga operation was a great success for Hammarskjöld and brought him well-deserved accolades. He took great political and personal risks in achieving the peaceful entry of troops into Katanga. However, there were other critics besides Lumumba, notably the Soviet Union. On 11 August, *Pravda* stated that the UN Secretary-General had 'voluntarily agreed to surrender the forces he led into Katanga's capital, Elisabethville by directing them to stay in their barracks till further orders'. It added: 'Each day the behaviour of the United Nations' Secretary-General, Hammarskjöld, is growing ever stranger, if not to use a stronger word.'

Lumumba had taken the lead in the opposition to Hammarskjöld's policies, which soured their mutual relations and caused Bunche to request his recall to New York. Even worse, Lumumba triggered off a chain of events which led to the worst crisis in the UN's history, his own political ruin, and finally his death. It brought renewed chaos in the Congo, and caused the break-up of the new state and terrible suffering and loss of life for the Congolese. This is not to mention the heavy sacrifice of lives ONUC had to pay in remedying the situation. The entry of the UN into Katanga proved not to be the end of the crisis in the Congo, but only the beginning.

NOTES

1. SG/935, 20 July 1960 or Security Council, 877th Meeting, para. 3ff.
2. UN Document S/4405, 22 July 1960.
3. S/4402 SCOR, 15th year, 877th meeting, para. 176.
4. UN Press Release SG/939, CO/36, 3 August 1960.
5. *New York Times* report, 25 July 1960, and Associated Press, 3 August 1960.
6. Unpublished UN document.
7. UN press release, 5 August 1960; *New York Times* published UPI Report, 6 August 1960
8. *New York Times*, 5 August 1960. This speech was given in Morocco.
9. UN Document, S/4418, 6 August 1960.
10. UN Document S/4420, 6 August 1960.
11. UN Document S/4421, 7 August 1960.
12. UN Document S/4417 and Addendum, 6 August 1960.
13. UN Document, S/4426, 9 August 1960.

4

THE UNITED NATIONS FORCE: ORGANISATION AND ROLE

On my first visit to the Congo, I had to consider an organisation for the UN Force and its headquarters and define its operational role in clear and simple words. My visits by plane to many important places in the Congo had given me a good understanding of the terrain and local conditions, and the state of communications by road, river, rail and air. I had also gained an understanding of the political environment and the operational conditions prevailing in different parts of the country.

On deploying its troops, ONUC had not followed any set plan but, as was to be expected, had responded to demands to replace Belgian troops for security assistance wherever the UN was most needed. The advance party of the Tunisian brigade, which was the first unit to reach the Congo on the evening of 15 July, was immediately deployed in the centre of Leopoldville where tension was high. The rest of the capital and the surrounding area were taken over by the Ghanaian brigade, which arrived the next morning. During the following days, the main body of the Tunisian contingents arrived, and was sent to Luluabourg to be deployed in Kasai province. They were followed by the Moroccans, who were immediately despatched to Thysville and Matadi, i.e. the southern part of Leopoldville province. At about the same time, the Ethiopian contingent landed and was immediately airlifted to Stanleyville and other parts of Oriental province. The Force headquarters, being a part of ONUC headquarters, was at Leopoldville, and used N'Djili, the city's main airport, some 15 miles away, as the main air base. As more troops arrived they were flown in to remote areas either to replace the departing Belgian troops or in response to new outbreaks of disorder.

The establishment of the command and control of the Force followed a similar *ad hoc* pattern, with unforeseen consequences for future operations. Initially, with only the Ghanaian and Tunisian troops available in the Congo and Von Horn, the designated Force Commander, yet to arrive, it was natural for a Ghanaian commander to take temporary charge under the authority of Ralph Bunche. But instead of Brigadier S.T.A. Otu, who had arrived earlier with a special mission sent by Nkrumah to assist Lumumba, or Brigadier Joe Michel, the Ghanaian Brigade commander, it was General Alexander who was to fulfill this function. He had accompanied the advance elements of the Ghanaian troops and assumed command. It was an odd arrangement, but it obviously had the approval of Nkrumah and was therefore acceptable to the UN. Thereafter, because the UN had no military command structure of its own, it allowed Alexander to provide that need as a practical temporary arrangement. Consequently, while all arriving contingents received their directives from Bunche, it was Alexander who executed them, in spite of being outside the UN's command structure. Regardless of his qualities as an experienced senior military officer, a chain of events was unwittingly set in motion that left the position of the Force Commander lacking stability throughout the Congo operations.

Alexander already wore two hats: he was simultaneously commander of the Ghanaian troops in the Congo and army Chief of Staff back in Ghana. Thus he reported to two superiors, Bunche in the Congo and Nkrumah in Ghana. While wearing his third hat as acting ONUC Force Commander, he was required to be solely responsible to the Secretary-General through Bunche. Alexander's position was equally questionable from the viewpoint of troop-contributing countries, whose troops were under his orders; his position as a Ghanaian officer seconded from the British army inevitably seemed anomalous. One only needs to consider the position of the Moroccans and Tunisians with their experience of French colonial rule and of the Ethiopians who were used to serving under Haile Selassie. Apart from Alexander's Ghana connection, his British nationality ruled out the possibility of his being considered for the Force Commander's post.

On July 15, Alexander made an agreement with General Gheysen, commander of the Belgian metropolitan forces in the Congo, and General Mpolo, acting Chief of Staff at the ANC, for the peaceful disarming of the ANC. Accordingly, he proceeded to disarm the ANC in Leopoldville. This action and his forceful personality had aroused the admiration of the Western press, which had dominated reporting from the Congo. Such favourable reports aroused the ire of the Congolese who were already none too pleased with the disarming of the ANC. Only a few days earlier, the Belgians had dropped paratroops and flown more of their troops from the Kamina base to put down a mutiny in Katanga by the ANC men who were loyal to the central government, and had disarmed them. The similarity between these actions later led Lumumba to accuse the UN of collusion with the Belgians, and it did not take long for Lumumba to protest to Otu and Bunche. In time it became clear that whereas Alexander's initiative might have been commendable in another political environment, in this case it began the deterioration of the UN's relationship with the ANC. Faced with the urgency of remedying the UN's military command structure and with no news from Von Horn in spite of the delicate issues involved, Bunche recommended to Hammarskjold that Alexander be appointed acting Force Commander for the time being.

Bunche had no soldiering experience, but he had learned to deal with military officers while acting as a mediator in the Middle East. He had been responsible subsequently for the operations of UNTSO from New York, and it was he who supervised the establishment of UNEF, the first peacekeeping operation involving military contingents. In addition to looking after this force from New York, Bunche had visited the UN troops several times in the Middle East and built up a reputation among the military of the troop-contributing countries. Furthermore, he had Brian Urquhart as one of his two political aides. Urquhart had served with the British parachute troops during the Second World War, including a tour of duty on the staff of the airborne corps dropped at Arnhem. Thus there was no lack of understanding of the military needs and how best to meet them. What was still lacking was a general in uniform who could devote all his time to his job and a command and control apparatus to handle the Force, which now totalled approximately 11,000. The eventual removal of Alexander from command caused the temporary loss of a general in uniform, but without any serious lowering of efficiency; and there were many obvious political gains.

After receiving Lumumba's protest, Bunche became aware of the grave consequences of disarming the ANC. Despite the opposition by Alexander, Bunche had insisted that the ANC's weapons be returned. Neither Alexander nor Von Horn when he assumed command had the political imagination to consider the consequences of disarming the ANC. Indeed, it was the divided ANC that eventually fuelled the splitting of the Congo. If the UN were to apply the practice of disarming the undisciplined ANC, should it also have disarmed the Katanga gendarmerie, or for that matter the Lumumba loyalists in Oriental province? Should the UN have forcibly dealt with Mobutu's coup, which was only supported by a couple of battalions at the most?

Alexander and Von Horn failed to understand the UN role in the Congo, which was to help the Congolese and train them to assume their own responsibilities. There were some 24,000 men in the ANC and if they were to be disarmed, the UN would have to replace them. Alexander and Von Horn only saw the immediate task and did not think about the long-term impact of disarming the ANC, whom they looked upon, at least for the time being, as opponents. This action developed the first serious split between the Congolese and the UN.

Included in the responsibilities of ONUC assistance to the Congolese was the restoration of law and order and the training of the ANC. The fact that dissident ANC troops were largely responsible for the disorder and violence presented ONUC with a dilemma as to how best to restore order quickly. Disorderly elements of the ANC were removed to their camps, and disarmed when it became necessary. Thereafter, the ANC could be retrained until it was in a suitable state to return to its tasks. This was the pattern of behaviour of colonial powers when dealing with dissidence, opposition or revolt by their colonial troops, and this was what the Belgians had done in the Congo both before and after independence. And this was how Alexander used the UN troops, forgetting that the UN had not replaced the Belgians as the new colonial authority. By disarming the Congolese troops, he inflicted on them the worst dishonour that could befall any soldiers—instead of expecting them to work with the UN and allowing the UN to train their forces in the future.

The rapid and effective deployment of UN troops to critical areas and the early withdrawal of the Belgian forces was due to Bunche's vigorous management of the operations, supported by Urquhart and Liu. Back in New York, it was Cordier who often arranged by telephone and personal persuasion for the African and other troop-contributing countries to prepare their troops quickly for the airlift to the Congo. Cordier was also in continuous contact with the United States Permanent Mission to the UN, and in fact more often directly with the Department of State to obtain aircraft and essential supplies and matériel for the Force in the Congo. In these efforts he was assisted by David Vaughan, the American Under Secretary-General for Administration, whose Field Service was responsible for providing ONUC with radio communications, security and administrative support in the area of operations. As I became more familiar with the nature of ONUC, I was amazed to learn what had been achieved by so few with so little in so short a time.[1]

On 18 July, Von Horn arrived in Leopoldville and assumed command of the Force. It had taken him seven days to travel from Jerusalem, a journey which should have taken no more than twenty-four hours had he chosen to travel in a commercial aircraft; commercial airline connections were regularly available via Brussels, Paris and Rome to Leopoldville or Brazzaville, which were linked by a regular ferry connection across the Congo river. On 12 July, UN headquarters had asked Von Horn to ready six military observers for duty in the Congo. The following day Hammarskjöld told him by phone to send the team and that he should also leave for the Congo, since he was required as Military Adviser to Bunche. Furthermore, if the Security Council authorised a peacekeeping force, he was to be its commander.

By his own account[2] Von Horn had, on his own initiative, doubled the number of officers from six to twelve, and added communications personnel from the Field Service. What he did not mention in his account was that the cargo for transport included personal belongings, consumer goods (Jerusalem had become a peaceful post, at least in appearance and environment) and, above all, a UN-provided official Buick limousine. A four - star plate had been fixed to each of the fenders by an over - zealous staff officer on the assumption that Von Horn was to carry the title of *Supreme Commander*, ONUC, and as such would be equal to a four-star general. Being unaware of the load requirement of Von Horn's entourage, the Field Service in New York chartered a SAS commercial aircraft, which proved on arrival not to be large enough and also developed mechanical trouble. Having despatched a very rude signal to New York and vented his frustration by phone to Cordier, Von Horn called the US Military Attaché in Tel Aviv for help in obtaining an American military aircraft. With the obvious approval of the UN Secretariat, a C-130 arrived in the early morning of 17 July to collect the party from Amman and carried it to the Congo, arriving there at 2 a.m. on 18 July.

No one was able to explain to me how Von Horn came to be called Supreme Commander and promoted to Lieutenant-General. This designation does not appear in any of the UN command charts, although it was in fact used even by Hammarskjöld in some of his earlier statements. Perhaps it was intended to protect him from professionals of the ilk of Alexander, or was it assumed that each of the contingents, some of them the size of a brigade, warranted such a title? The fact that the ANC was headed by a major-general and that there were senior-ranking Belgian generals in the Congo might have been another factor. Whatever its cause, it did not help the man or his image. The UN Force in the Congo was to be bigger than UNEF, but it was not intended to be a major military force. It was to operate in a large country, yet there was no need for separate commands with their own resources. I soon discovered that there were two groups of persons who referred to Von Horn in this grandiose style: his immediate staff, who were the loyal group that he had brought from UNTSO to bolster his image; and the Field Service, who had also given him the derogatory nickname 'El Supremo' because, consistent with his record with UNTSO, he was already unfortunately engaged in full-scale war with that service. Realising the harm his inflated title would cause, I attempted to remedy the situation by making it clear that in future

organisational charts and communications from New York his correct title
was Force Commander.

When assigned to UNTSO, Von Horn was a senior colonel in the
Swedish army equal to brigadier (a rank Sweden had not yet introduced,
although it did so subsequently). The Swedish government authorised
him to wear the badges of a major-general, but did not promote him till
many years later after his retirement. However any attempt to compare
rank structures and seniorities between armies is misleading because of
different practices and standards. Therefore, for all practical purposes
Von Horn was a major-general in the UN system, and as the Force
Commander was equal to Bunche's rank of Under-Secretary but junior to
him in seniority. His immediate subordinates were Alexander, a major-
general in the British Army; Kettani, the Deputy Force Commander and
a Moroccan major-general; and Iyassou, an Ethiopian brigadier-general.

I was a substantive brigadier and held the rank of Director Grade 2,
one step below an Under-Secretary in the UN system at that time. Thus
Von Horn was senior to me in the UN hierarchy and that was what
mattered as far as I was concerned. However, by virtue of my appointment, I was not his subordinate; somewhat like a chief of staff at the next-
higher echelon of command, I often had to convey what the Secretary-
General expected of him. Such an arrangement was not new to me since
it was based on a long tradition and on my own experience. I had served
as a GSO 1[3] of the armoured division in India as a lieutenant-colonel,
where the three formations were commanded by brigadiers. It was my job
to follow up on the orders issued by the commanding general and in his
absence from headquarters to interpret his policies into orders. It was no
different in UNEF, with eight national contingents with commanders
invariably older than myself, and with more seniority: in the absence of
the commander, I acted for him.

I had first met Von Horn in Gaza in 1958, soon after he was
appointed Chief of Staff of UNTSO, in a vacancy left by Burns's
appointment to UNEF. He came over to EIMAC (Egyptian-Israeli Mixed
Armistice Commission) which was a part of UNTSO but under Burns's
operational control. In addition, he was paying a visit to the Swedish
battalion. Thereafter, he visited Gaza often to enjoy the officers' mess life,
and like any soldier enjoyed watching guards, drill and the men's sports.
He was soon a popular visitor to other messes besides the Swedes, and was
always included in celebrations of special events. UNEF had managed to
bring peace and quiet to its area of operations, and the social life of the
officers and soldiers was built around meals and life in their messes. Indoor
games and good conversation over drinks broke the monotony of the
routine life and brought some humour into the loneliness of life away from
families. Carl von Horn fitted well into this life-style, and, like others in

Gaza, I enjoyed his company. During one such evening of conviviality he shared with me his hope of commanding UNEF one day. I never gave the matter another thought. Some months later he told me that he had asked the Secretary-General to consider him for the command of a UN force whenever an opportunity arose, but I let that one pass too.

Von Horn had just turned fifty-seven when he arrived in Leopoldville. He had joined the Swedish Horse Guards at eighteen, but tiring of the ceremonial life he graduated from staff college and joined the general staff. After various appointments he found satisfaction in Movements and Transportation when he was assigned to the railway movements. Although Sweden was neutral during the Second World War, it still had to protect its borders, which gave Von Horn experience in moving large numbers of troops by train and running road transport between Sweden and Finland while the latter was involved in a life-and-death struggle with the Soviet armies. Experiences such as these made him the natural choice for the assignment to assist Count Folke Bernadotte in his Red Cross work in the repatriation of prisoners of war. At the end of the war, he served as military attaché in Norway and held regimental and divisional commands.

Although Von Horn lacked operational experience and had never seen action, he did have a number of assets that could be useful to him in his new task. As a Swede, he was from a traditionally neutral country, like the Secretary-General. He had spent some three years with UNTSO familiarising himself with the UN system and peacekeeping diplomacy. He was tall, looked well in uniform and had a good command of English and a smattering of French. Hammarskjöld and Cordier both asked me, separately, 'to help Carl'. I had become well acquainted with him in Gaza, and in spite of what the civilian administrative staff had said in the past and more recently in New York, I intended to do as they asked, but it turned out to be more difficult than I had anticipated.

During my very first meeting with Bunche, after his initial briefing on the Congo operations, he told me in a few words of his difficulties with Von Horn who, he said, was being stubborn on operational and, particularly, administrative questions. He had failed to attend Bunche's staff meetings, since he claimed to be busy elsewhere. The absence of the military at these meetings had led Bunche to make decisions which later proved to be unwelcome to Von Horn. Bunche hoped that during my visit I would be able to arrange better co-ordination between the political, military and administrative branches of ONUC headquarters. At the same time, he asked me to assist him with military advice that he was not able to obtain from Von Horn.

John Olver, Chief Administrative Officer (CAO), had met me at the airport on my arrival in Leopoldville. We had been colleagues in UNEF, and with his laconic sense of humour he gave me a fascinating account of the early days of ONUC and the problems with 'El Supremo'. When I called on Olver the next morning to arrange for a charter aircraft for my travel through the Congo, he had a lot more to say about Von Horn and the team that had come from UNTSO. Olver called in his deputy Virgil de Angelis and Sam Feiffer, who was in charge of accommodation and transportation. At the end of half an hour, I realised that we had a serious problem on our hands which I would have to deal with, however unpleasant it might prove to be.

Typically, the military wanted the best housing, the best cars and a higher *per diem* daily subsistence allowance than the rate received in Jerusalem. Pressed by his UNTSO colleagues, as I was told, Von Horn had made these issues of greater priority than the arrangements for his troops. I was already familiar with the *per diem* arrangements. They were fixed in relationship to local costs and had nothing to do with hardship posts. Besides, the rates applied to all UN personnel entitled to *per diem*. This was another point of dispute with the military, since many preferred to receive *per diem* instead of the centrally organised messing and housing. But the administrative staff were opposed to this because it encouraged cheating; military personnel, taking advantage of their connections, might continue to receive their supplies from their units without payment while getting the *per diem* allowance at the same time. I quickly decided not to lose much time on such matters, but to leave them to the administrative branch to handle.

Von Horn gave me a warm welcome when I called on him. As I expected, he had a lot to say about the civilians. He was not satisfied with the administrative support and felt strongly that he should have his own Chief Administrative Officer. There had been such a position at UNTSO to look after a few hundred military observers; now he had nearly 11,000 men in the Force, and there would soon be still more. The Force should have a separate administrative organisation which would be more concerned with the military needs, instead of the present arrangements whereby he felt the Force received short shrift. He urged that I should recommend such a change to the Secretary-General and he expected me to support him.

Even though I had hoped that Von Horn would not raise the question of *per diem* for UNTSO officers, to my dismay he did. Indeed, it took up most of our time, and so far we had not discussed any part of his operational role. I listened in silence and concluded by saying that I would take up this matter in New York. I did ask about operations but he had little to say other than how well the men were doing and how little their work was appreciated by the civilians. He then returned to talking about the appalling conditions the troops were operating under, i.e. no decent accommodation, hard rations and what little they could procure locally. He repeatedly talked about the poor administration and reminded me that I should attend to it as a priority. I ended the meeting by informing him of my travel plans and that we would be seeing each other each time I returned to Leopoldville to discuss my observations before reaching any conclusions on the organisation of the Force.

My next meeting was with the military staff, starting with Lt. Col. John Berthiume of the Canadian Van Doos Regiment. He was acting Chief of Staff and, together with an operational officer, a Briton with the Ghana Brigade, he briefed me on the troop deployment, operations and logistics. There were no military logistics in the Force yet, and therefore the units in the field were left to their own ingenuity and whatever the Chief Administrative Officer (CAO) could do. Local procurement had been authorised, and while the situation was not the best, there was no emergency. What struck me most was that nearly every UNTSO officer I had met expressed the hope that I would arrange an increase in his *per diem*. This continued to disturb me, for I had never yet experienced a situation where, in the face of an emergency, headquarters staff officers had expressed so much concern for their own welfare instead of urging me to improve the conditions of the troops in the field. I had little intimate experience of observer groups, and so I wondered if the behaviour of such officers was different or if it was something I had yet to learn.

During the next few days, it became abundantly evident to me that the military were not properly integrated at ONUC headquarters. Neither Von Horn nor his UNTSO team had understood their mission and where they fitted into the overall pattern of the UN operations. Von Horn told me that soon after he had arrived, he had asked for an operational directive and was shown a long paper drafted by Bunche. The paper included comprehensive instructions for operations, which Von Horn felt were legalistic and incomprehensible at lower command levels. He told Bunche that this paper was of little use to the Force.

In the case of UNEF, Burns had helped draft an operational directive before the arrival of the troops and their deployment. Had Von Horn arrived immediately, he could have assisted Bunche in preparing such a directive. However, Von Horn had shown little interest in joining Bunche and his aides in discussing events and deciding future actions, so I had to find a way to get either Von Horn or a reliable qualified military representative to attend Bunche's meetings. Kettani was not only too senior, but he was also engaged in establishing rapport with the ANC and the Congolese authorities to arrange the training of the Congolese troops. Iyassou, the Ethiopian Brigade commander, was well qualified, but would have to be brought from Stanleyville. Bunche was agreeable to this arrangement, but I had yet to discuss it with Von Horn.

The dozen officers who had come from UNTSO and some British officers borrowed from the Ghanaians - some twenty officers in all - had met the urgent need to establish an advance Force headquarters. Their commander was comfortable working with them, and he had confidence in Berthiume, the acting Chief of Staff. But I was disappointed with the staff; they were doing their jobs well enough, but they had failed to establish the environment of a Force headquarters. Although at that time I did not have access to their service records, it was apparent that many of them had had no previous staff experience in the jobs they were performing, and their staff work was disappointing, to say the least. I found most of them unsuitable and decided to recommend their return to Jerusalem.

Replacements were needed immediately and only UNEF could provide them in a hurry; that is, if General Prem Singh Gyani, its Commander, could spare them and their individual governments would agree. We would also have to rely on Gyani's selection since no one remained in Gaza from my time there. But he could be relied on; after all, he had held several operational commands, the last being that of an infantry division, and he had served as commandant of the Indian Defence Forces Staff College. However, more staff would be required at ONUC and they would have to be obtained from troop-contributing countries.

An organisation for the UN Force had already emerged, based on operational requirements and the geographical division of the country into provinces. After Leopoldville, the provincial capitals were the next to call for UN troops. Each of these had a good airfield where US aircraft had landed to disembark troops after their flights from their home countries. The United States had only agreed to provide an external airlift, and therefore the UN was responsible for all internal movement. At this stage, ONUC did not have this ability, so it ensured that the unloading points of the external airlifts coincided with its troop deployment needs. Any deployment beyond the provincial capitals had to be arranged locally with available surface transportation.

The UN's large-scale civilian operations were also based on provinces, with their headquarters at the provincial capitals. A small advance administrative team was added to each to support the troops and the civilian teams. As demands for operational commitments for troops and for greater assistance to the government arose and the local political situation became more complex, Bunche had to post an ONUC representative in each province.

I found the organisation of the troops in the field rational and far-sighted. Leopoldville, Oriental and Kasai provinces had a brigade of troops each, and I therefore recommended that they be named area commands. The troops in Equateur province were from more than one contingent and were too far apart to be made into a cohesive command considering the absence of internal air capability at the time. Furthermore, a cohesive command was only useful if its commander could coordinate its operations and influence its conduct with administrative support and reinforcements. Since this was not the case at present, I recommended that each contingent operate directly under the Force headquarters.

The city of Leopoldville was already a separate area command and should remain so because of the heavy demands for security by the Congolese authorities and ONUC's own requirements. The air base was also located there, and was operating centrally under Group Captain Fred Carpenter, a colourful and able Canadian. This was the best arrangement and should continue.

The UN Field Service communications had established preliminary radio links, providing telex service between Leopoldville and the provinces where our troops and civilian experts were deployed. Also, in other towns where UN personnel were present, if the local telephone and telegraph facilities were not working, UN experts were sent to make them operational, and had succeeded in several places in doing so. Last but not least, UN teams had restored air control communications at airfields used by ONUC.

The organisation of the Force signal communications presented some difficult problems. The Congolese (at least, those who were educated) spoke French, as did a large part of the Force. Only Canada could provide bilingual military personnel and so of necessity the signal communications would have to be built around a Canadian unit. Fortunately, Canada had given its consent to assist in this respect, but it could only spare a small unit. In evolving this organisation, I relied on the UN communications as the framework between Force headquarters, area commands and other provinces. The Canadians were to provide communications forward of this network to units and sub-units at distances beyond the range of infantry unit radios.

Our most important need was for an efficient staff. I would have to rely on troop-contributing countries, but it would be difficult to integrate different staff systems. At UNEF, a combination of the British and American systems had been evolved and it had served satisfactorily. I decided to use the same basis now. The French-speaking African contingents had already told me that they had few staff-trained officers to spare and I was therefore obliged to ask for more bilingual officers from the others. Canada could help and I knew that India had a growing pool of such officers, although they might not have sufficient ability in speaking French. Generally, I would have to rely on Canada, Ireland, India, Pakistan and the Nordic countries.

The UN had no other types of troops besides infantry units and formations. Even the brigade-size troops included no more than a few support personnel. At Force level, there were few other than staff personnel. Thus the entire network of supply, services, signal communications and air supply had yet to be organised. Estimating that the size of the Force would be approximately 15,000, I worked out a detailed table of organisation. In doing so, I had to take into consideration the availability of troops from acceptable countries. Hammarskjöld had wisely opted for African troops at the top of his list. Ghana had sent a small hospital with its brigade, but we could not expect it to stretch its resources further in this area. I had hoped to get some flying crews from some of the African states, but not ground staff. The Nordic countries could supply us with all the technical manpower we wanted, but their recruiting practices for the UN made it difficult to raise more than a limited number. In any event, we asked them to find the men for maintenance and repair of vehicles, weapons and instruments, organised as teams to work separately or in conjunction with other contingents. The Canadians and the Nordics also provided aircrew as well as technicians and ground staff for the air unit.

The UN's system of administrative and logistics support for peacekeeping operations had evolved continuously since the first time a mission had been placed in the field. Before UNEF, the General Services in New York had undertaken the responsibility for support of the UN observer and other missions by creating a Field Service. However, UNEF's peacekeeping operation was different from the military operations of a state or group of states in that the UN had no military units of its own and therefore no military support organisation. Thus it had to call on troop-contributing countries to send contingents which would be self-contained and self-reliant for a limited time. It then called on other states to assist in providing, on an *ad hoc* basis the contingents for essential supplies, emergency rations, and ground and air support. Meanwhile, the UN Field Service was building its own supply resources until it could assume this responsibility. But the need for logistics support for the forward units still remained, requiring special arrangements. For this I turned to the UN member states to provide military logistical support in the field.

A novel pattern of administrative and logistical support for peacekeeping operations emerged. The UN Field Service assumed responsibility for the higher echelons of the armed forces down to Force level. From here onwards, the Force was responsible, except that, apart from limited powers given to the military, all local purchases, hiring of local civilians, renting of housing or services and financial matters remained with UN officials. This arrangement was necessary to ensure that the UN administrative and budgetary requirements were met by UN civilian staff, who were not subject to such frequent rotation as the military, and who were also bound by UN rules and regulations. Indeed, it could not be done in any other way. These matters became points of friction between the military and UN staff because the military bridled at control by civilians, forgetting—or more often ignorant of—the fact that they would be subject to similar controls if they were themselves ever responsible for these matters in their own forces.

At UNEF, Burns's or my differences with the Chief Administrative Officer were no different from what we would have experienced in our own respective civilian defence headquarters dealing with our civilian counterparts. The fact was that few officers had that kind of experience and they came to the UN with false expectations. Force commanders were not intended to be little Caesars, but were subject both to the regulations of their national military and to the arrangements that operated in an alliance,—specifically, in a UN peacekeeping force. Like any other commander, I had learned to argue and hotly contest benefits for my troops and it was always easier if one could educate the administrative staff by preparing them, softening them up and emphasising the importance of one's recommendations for the success of an operation. Too often, however, senior military officials fought for the wrong cause - for benefits for a few, even for themselves. It was no wonder that they were always frustrated. Somehow I had to weld the Field Service and the military in the Congo into an integrated operation - for its own success, and for the welfare of the military personnel.

We would have to turn to India and Pakistan to provide the bulk of the services. Both fielded large armies based mainly on the Second World War pattern, and which should meet our requirements. I was not quite sure how the contingents would agree to operate together. To make it easier, I proposed that each would provide a full service: India the supply (rations, petroleum products) and Pakistan the ordnance (clothing, office supplies, spare parts) and their respective officers would head these services at Force headquarters. We also asked both to provide hospitals, but only India did so. I planned to include other Asian contries for troop contributions, but realised that we could not count on them for logistics personnel. We could, however, ask many of them for an aircrew. I also asked Latin American countries to provide some staff and aircrews. Since Hammarskjöld was eager to involve some of the East European countries in the Congo, we asked them to provide air and ground crews, as well as logistics personnel.

Equipped with my outline organisation chart, I went to see Von Horn. After a quick look, he said that he hoped I would do the best for his Force. We then addressed the question of personnel to fill the staff slots. I was ready with the details and gave him my frank assessment of his present staff and the basis of my recommendations. As expected, he disagreed with my evaluation of the capabilities of his staff, but accepted it since I was only recommending that they be sent back to UNTSO in Jerusalem. At this point, he again reminded me not to forget to take up the issue of the *per diem* of his staff. As for his acting Chief of Staff, Berthiume, he was adamant that he should remain. I decided that this was a suitable opportunity to explain the complex nature of the operation and the importance of the political and, consequently, the security realities.

We agreed to adjourn first for a quiet lunch at the restaurant near the zoo, which he had found very agreeable. We went there often during the next few months to discuss ONUC affairs in seclusion because it was seldom frequented by UN personnel or the press. I took this opportunity to explain to him that the mission given me by Hammarskjöld was to help him and Bunche work together for the success of the UN operation in the Congo and so above all we must address ourselves to improving co-operation. I summed up what both he and Bunche had told me and then came to the point I wanted to make. I said, 'Look, Carl, this is a very complex political-military operation. Unlike UNTSO, it is a large military operation which will decide the future life of a young nation. Ralph (Bunche) and you cannot run this show on separate tracks. You have to put your acts together. You are the Force Commander, but Ralph represents the Secretary-General. Now, you are not going to let Dag down, so what are you going to do to work with the civilians?'

He understood my point and assured me that he liked Bunche and would never let Hammarskjöld down. Then he added, 'But you know these civilians can talk for hours. I have other things to do and you know it is a waste of time to sit through endless, boring meetings about constitutionality, international law and politics. I should have my own political adviser, like I had Vigier in UNTSO. Now, there was a man who had everything at his finger-tips; he could explain things in a few minutes and make his recommendation. It was easy to understand, and then I could make my decisions. He was so good that I always agreed with him - why don't you recommend that to Dag?'

I told him that his idea would not work because of the different nature and size of the operation. In UNTSO he had been the senior UN representative, whereas here it was Bunche. UNTSO was a military observer operation established as a result of political negotiations - the process of negotiation in the Congo had only just begun. The withdrawal of the Belgian forces, which was about to be completed, required special efforts by the Secretary-General in New York and Brussels, and in the Congo by Bunche. In addition, there was the assistance to the Congolese government and the restoration of law and order—again being arranged by Bunche—which demanded complicated negotiations because of the many factions involved and the problem of the ANC. All these tasks, and what one could anticipate of the future, were beyond the role of any Force Commander under similar circumstances. I concluded by saying,. 'Carl, you have to accept the predominance of political considerations and you have to look to Bunche for guidance. But, of course, it is you who have the troops, and not the civilians. I can understand your unwillingness to attend Bunche's meetings, therefore you must have a good staff officer to attend on your behalf.' This brought me to the question of the Chief of Staff.

I explained my reasons for suggesting Iyassou for that post. He did not object to Iyassou acting as a liaison officer, but insisted on retaining Berthiume. When I pressed my arguments, he agreed to the appointment of Iyassou, a man he liked and respected, but he still wanted Berthiume as deputy Chief of Staff. Iyassou, I said, was a gentle person who would never be able to manage Berthiume; therefore, I did not believe such an arrangement would work. Besides, the senior UN staff did not have confidence in Berthiume because he was fraternising too much with the Belgians and had virtually assumed the role of their advocate at ONUC. Most of the information leaks from ONUC were, rightly or wrongly, believed to have emanated from him. Accordingly, I advised Von Horn that he should let Berthiume return to Jerusalem. Surely, he replied, he had the right to ask for one staff officer by name. He was relying heavily on Berthiume and wanted to retain him, and so I suggested that he keep Berthiume on his personal staff as his Military Assistant, to which he agreed.

We now turned to the administrative support of the Force. I told Von Horn that according to his wishes I had looked into the possibility of creating a separate UN administrative support for the Force, but had found no way in which it could act independently of the CAO. Therefore, it was better to leave the arrangements as they were and organise the military staff so that they related well to their civilian counterparts. As Commander, he would thus deal with his own Chief Logistics Officer who in turn would deal with the civilians. This satisfied Von Horn, but he urged me to have the new staff posted as quickly as possible.

The next morning, I took up the organisation of the Force first with Olver and then with Bunche. They both agreed but commented, rightly, that an organisation could only work if the people involved *wanted* it to work. They said, 'We want you here, Indar.' I told them I was flattered by their confidence, but could best serve the interests of all concerned by remaining in New York.

Hammarskjöld was pleased with my plans and the guidelines that were their basis. After receiving his approval on 11 August I sent several cables to my office in New York instructing them to send letters of request to the countries concerned. Gyani generously agreed to assign a number of key staff and we had the approval of their governments. These officers were then flown to Leopoldville within a fortnight.

Once the machinery was set in motion, I could devote more time to the operations. In addition to Major Bonaventura Cavalcanti of Brasil, Colonel Gus Bowitz of Norway had joined my staff in New York; however, my staff were overwhelmed by the many instructions I had sent them and it was evident to me that I should return to UN headquarters to implement the reorganisation of ONUC and discuss all aspects of the operational role with Hammarskjöld. With his approval, and the reluctant agreement of Bunche, I left Leopoldville for New York.

I had not even been back there a week before Hammarskjöld sent for me to his office. He held a cable in his hand which had obviously been addressed to him personally and he said to me, 'Indar, I am afraid I will have to send you back to Leopoldville. I want you here, but from what Ralph Bunche tells me, he needs you urgently with him. I cannot take any risks with the operation in the Congo, and if he insists that he wants you back there, I am afraid I will have to ask you to return immediately. I don't really know what is happening, but he seems to be having a lot of problems with Von Horn.' I was greatly concerned over the organisation of headquarters and the services for ONUC, so I said, 'I will go to Leopoldville as you wish, but I am in the middle of making arrangements for the organisation of headquarters and the services for the UN force. Gus Bowitz is a highly qualified officer, but would you please tell Andy Cordier to help him during my absence?' Hammarskjöld replied, 'Don't worry. We will take care of it.' And, with his typical shy smile, he extended his hand and wished me a good trip. I was in Leopoldville twenty-four hours later.

On arriving there I learned from Bunche that he faced two major problems, one new and the other old. His new problem was Lumumba and his old problem, which by now was chronic, was Von Horn.

From the time of the UN entry into Katanga, the UN's relations with Lumumba and the Congolese authorities had taken a turn for the worse. On 16 August, in a show of force and to display his authority over the return of ANC soldiers held by the UN and ONUC administration, Lumumba had declared martial law and ordered his troops into the city of Leopoldville. Consequently, the ANC were all over the city and had arrested UN personnel, including two officers. These were later released on Bunche's personal intervention. On 18 August, 200 Congolese soldiers were sent to the airport to seize control of it from the UN. On their arrival, they beat a Canadian officer unconscious and manhandled seven other soldiers on the suspicion that they were Belgians. While the UN command prepared to take the airport by force with Ghanaian and Sudanese troops if it became necessary, Iyassou, the newly-appointed Chief of Staff, obtained the agreement of General Victor Lundula, the commander of the

ANC, and his Chief of Staff, Colonel Joseph Mobutu, that except for six men the ANC would be withdrawn from the airport and the UN would continue to be responsible for the security of this vital installation. However, the atmosphere in Leopoldville was charged with hostility between the UN and the Congolese. The troops were on alert and the ANC and the Congolese police were present throughout the city.

During his visit to Leopoldville, Hammarskjöld, had been able to obtain a basic agreement from the Congolese government for the UN Force.[4] This agreement made the UN operations possible during the months of crisis through which that government was to pass. By its terms, the Congolese government agreed to act in good faith, ensure freedom of movement for the force in the interior and accord the requisite privileges and immunities to everyone associated with the activities of the Force. They agreed to explore jointly the functioning of the Force, and the Congolese would facilitate its tasks. For its part, the UN agreed to act in good faith in accordance with the UN Charter and the Security Council resolutions concerned and it was prepared to maintain the Force in the Congo until its task was completed.

The Congolese had become so nervous about a possible response from the UN that on 17 August Lumumba's personal guards arrested two UN security officers who had delivered a letter to Lumumba from Bunche. The officers resisted the arrest, whereupon one of the Congolese soldiers aimed his rifle at them. A UN Ghanaian guard at the Prime Minister's residence intervened and saved the two from being killed. However, the Congolese insisted on keeping them in custody. News of the arrest of our colleagues was brought to Bunche when (as usual) he was at work after dinner and having a discussion with the rest of his staff, including myself. After a quick consultation, Bunche asked me to go to Lumumba's residence to obtain their release. Liu accompanied me to help with the French interpretation and George Ivan Smith, the UN spokesman, came too.

It was a strange situation. The UN was guarding the Prime Minister and his household, including his ANC guard, but our security officers were in the hands of the ANC. On arrival at the house, I found that we were in control, but we had to be infinitely careful to avoid any action that could possibly harm our men or result in shooting in the Prime Minister's home. As we entered, the Ghanaian soldiers saluted smartly. I saw a slouchy Congolese soldier, and, impressed by the Ghanains' turnout, shouted at the ANC guard, 'Why can't you stand to attention?' Since he could not understand what I said, I repeated 'Attention!' and Liu repeated the same word with French pronunciation. The Congolese soldier came to attention. Then I said, 'Call the guard,' and Liu repeated *'Appelez la garde!'* The soldier obliged, and five or six other Congolese soldiers joined him to form a line, all standing to attention.

Ivan Smith said, 'Let us get our boys.' I replied, 'Yes, get them to the car quickly while I inspect the guard.' As I checked the guard, I could see our men moving out of the guardroom towards the car. Liu was doing marvellously with proper military commentary, leaving me to wonder where he had acquired it.

It was now time to leave, at which point our two men told us that their identification cards, personal papers, money and personal possessions had been taken from them. Liu asked the Congolese about them, and one offered to take us to the ANC camp where they were being kept in an office.

Since things had worked well so far, we decided to take the risk and go to the camp. It was almost midnight when we arrived; we were taken into a room where there was a sleepy officer in charge, reeking of beer. When Liu introduced us and explained the purpose of our visit, the young man was so overwhelmed at the sight of a general that he grabbed my hand and kissed it, with saliva dripping from his mouth. At least, that was better than a show of violence. He told Liu that he had never been close to a general, let alone spoken to one, and assured us that he would hand over all the belongings of the UN men. He opened his cupboard and offered us all the contents - which included the belongings of other innocent victims! We thanked him, and after friendly handshakes left the camp for our headquarters. I was glad to have brought our men safely back, but had been saddened to witness the hopeless performance of the ANC, who were so inexperienced and whose political leaders did not deserve their positions of authority. The Congolese needed proper guidance and surely the UN could help them.

After consultation with Hammarskjöld some days earlier, a policy decision had been made to return the ANC's weapons, which were in the custody of the UN troops in Leopoldville. Force headquarters had held on to the weapons, believing that if they were returned to the ill-disciplined ANC, there would only be more violence. The question of the return of the ANC weapons had come up following Bunche's unpleasant meeting with Lumumba after Hammarskjöld had left for Katanga. When he returned to ONUC headquarters, Bunche sent for Von Horn and insisted that the weapons be returned immediately to the ANC, but Von Horn refused to comply. Bunche then used his capacity as the Secretary-General's Special Representative in the Congo to go over the Commander's head, and issued orders for the return of the weapons directly to the troops concerned. He was promptly obeyed.

As for Bunche's other problem, relations between him, his political aides and his administrative staff on the one hand and Von Horn on the other had worsened. Two incidents had occurred while I was with

Hammarskjöld in Katanga but after our return to Leopoldville. Because of Hammarskjöld 's and Bunche's preoccupation with problems relating to Lumumba, Bunche had neither the time nor the desire to mention them - not even to me, who was so closely concerned. Only because his relationship with Von Horn had grown so bad did Bunche press Hammarskjold to send me back to Leopoldville to assist him in dealing with the problem.

The first of the two incidents related to the administrative organisation of ONUC. Von Horn had mentioned to me his idea of having a CAO for his Force, as he had had in UNTSO and UNEF. I had advised him against it because the situation in the Congo and the role of the UN there were different. The Force was only part of the overall ONUC operation, which had another component, namely the civilian operation. The UN had established a centralised administration to take care of both. The civilian experts and the gradually increasing civilian assistance programme covered the same area as the troops. To avoid duplication, an integrated system was the best solution. In any event, a separate CAO with the Force would not have been able to function without turning for assistance to Oliver, the CAO of ONUC. Having failed to persuade Bunche and me to agree to his having his own CAO, Von Horn decided to send a cable to David Vaughan, the Under Secretary for Administration at the UN, through Cordier.

In a conversation I had with Von Horn after returning to Leopoldville to deal with the problems of his relationship with the political and administrative staff at ONUC, he explained that he had sent this cable to New York for two reasons: first, he wanted to express his views to Cordier and Vaughan for reconsideration at a higher level, and secondly, he had suspected for some time that his cables to New York were being censored by Bunche. The first was understandable to me but the second was not, because all communications to New York were cleared with Bunche and Von Horn knew this as well as anyone else at ONUC. There was another problem with the cables from the Force Commander: they were drafted in military terminology by a Swede and a French Canadian, who could not write English as well as they could speak it.

When the duty communications officer received this particular cable, he showed it to his chief Walter Baumgarden who, after reading the contents, took it to Bunche for approval. Normally, after correcting the draft, Bunche or one of his aides would have authorised its despatch, but in this particular cable, Von Horn had written 'I cannot conceal from you the fact that the administrative contribution here in spite of all personal ambitions and efforts is NOT, repeat NOT, up to standard and therefore on the 29th day of operations jeopardising its success ... it is my duty NOT to conceal from you *never have so many people managed to produce so few results in so long a time.*' He then went on to comment on the administrative issues and ended by asking for Jan van Wijk, who was then serving in that capacity with UNTSO and had gained his confidence, to be appointed as his CAO.

When he learned the next morning that his cable had not been sent, Von Horn called Baumgarden and proceeded to dress him down in parade-ground fashion. Baumgarden could only find De Angelis to complain to, who in turn took up the matter with the General. The burly De Angelis appeared and made his point before the Force Commander in his usual cool manner. In response, Von Horn ordered De Angelis to stand up straight and take his hands out of his pockets when talking to a general. All this, of course, ended up before Bunche.

Bunche told Von Horn that he could not tolerate the critical remarks in his cable and if it were sent he, Bunche, would have to resign. Von Horn retorted that he could not accept censorship of his communications and that he too had come to the meeting prepared to resign. This implied that the Secretary-General would have to choose between accepting Bunche's resignation and removing Von Horn from command. Obviously, Von Horn could see who would be the winner and loser in this argument and quickly added that surely they were not going to present Hammarskjöld with two resignations. There the matter ended for a while, but unfortunately it was only the prelude to what followed a day or two later.

I began my work to establish smoother relationships between the military and civilian staff by having a good talk with Iyassou, and came to the conclusion that he was a good choice, but that he would require a good, loyal deputy. Such a person had to be a gifted military writer, an experienced staff officer and, if possible, someone with previous UN experience. Iyassou would have to deal with contingent commanders, and national liaison officers, and meet Congolese officials and foreign ambassadors, as well as their military attaches. The Deputy Chief of Staff should be able to run the headquarters and keep close to the political and administrative staff. I thought of Colonel Justin McCarthy of Ireland who had served with distinction as the Chief Operations Officer of UNOGIL, and mentioned his name to Iyassou. With his consent, I discussed the matter with Von Horn, who remembered McCarthy and thought well of him, and after obtaining Bunche's approval, I sent a cable to Hammarskjöld recommending that he request McCarthy from the Irish government. Dublin responded favourably and McCarthy was installed in his new new job within a week.

I did not expect the Force headquarters to become entirely effective with the arrival of Iyassou and McCarthy, but I did expect that the presence of two experienced officers, both skilled diplomats and soldiers, would facilitate Bunche's work and improve relations with the administrative staff. Therefore, all I could hope to achieve for the present was to calm the situation at headquarters and follow up on Bunche's directives to the military myself. Realising that I could be helpful, Oliver had given me an office on the same floor as his own. He and De Angelis also offered me the spare room in their apartment at the Royal, which I gladly accepted. This provided us with many opportunities to discuss the needs of the Force, and for once the administrators began to get the kind of attention that they wanted in order to plan and provide the required support for the troops.

I spent some time with Bunche, who needed to discuss several military-related questions. These were not only military matters, but political issues with security overtones. Unquestionably, Von Horn had failed him in this respect. At this stage, I was not sure whether he lacked the ability to provide this kind of assistance or if he merely could not work well with Bunche. I also had to find out if Von Horn was too busy to spend the necessary time with Bunche, bearing in mind that in any case he was bored by long political discussions. However, I would not be able to come to a conclusion on this until the organisation of the Force was completed. I would also have to consider if Von Horn, or any commander, could afford to spend an hour or two in the morning and again in the evening with the UN mission chief. However, it was abundantly clear to me that the Special Representative of the Secretary-General in the Congo must have access to such continuous advice. If I did not come up with a suitable arrangement, I would probably end up spending more time in the Congo. Yet in New York the situation was essentially the same: Hammarskjöld required a military adviser at his side, and my staff was not able to assume this role in my absence.

I spoke with Iyassou at least once a day and visited the troops in and around Leopoldville. It was amazing that the UN mission was actually being carried out, mainly due to the determined leadership of Bunche, supported by his political and administrative aides, the ability of the senior contingent officers and the quality of the troops who were able to operate in the most difficult circumstances. On returning from these visits, I checked in at Bunche's and my own office to deal with my own work, and then usually attended a diplomatic or officers' reception to meet other people.

I often dined with Von Horn and briefed him on the day's events, consulted him on matters under consideration in the political or administrative offices and expressed my views frankly on the operational aspects of the Force. We both welcomed these occasions as we had a lot in common and not only talked business but also relaxed.

After the first evening or two together, I was surprised that Von Horn had not yet implemented the arrangements on which we had agreed.

Since he was out visiting the troops, I asked Iyassou if Von Horn had briefed him on matters that we two had discussed and that he had to do for the day: these included some important questions concerning the training of the ANC which should have been passed on to Kettani. Iyassou said he had seen the General in the morning, but had not been given any instructions. When I met Von Horn that evening, I asked what had happened. He mumbled some excuse and then said that he had no objection to my passing on to Iyassou the results of our discussion. Already somewhat mellowed, he looked affably at me and said, 'You know, Indar, you should have been my Chief of Staff. And what a fine team we would be.' I was not flattered. I suspected that he could not remember the details of our conversations by the next morning. That was the beginning of my talking directly to his staff, at his own request and with his full blessing.

Bunche had made up his mind by now that he could no longer be useful to the Secretary-General as long as he stayed in Leopoldville. His problems with Lumumba had reached a critical stage. Every utterance of Lumumba's was an attack on the UN; he called for the removal of all white UN troops, he expressed little confidence in the Secretary-General or his representatives in the Congo, and he had started to look actively for assistance elsewhere. The Soviets had sent 100 trucks for aid to the civil administration, which, with their approval, had been delivered to the ANC. In Kasai, Albert Kalonji had declared the independence of the mining-rich area of Bakwanga; he had obtained the assistance of some Belgian and other white soldiers to head a group of ANC men who had joined him against the central government. Lumumba had ordered Lundula and Mobutu to despatch ANC units from Luluabourg to end Kalonji's secession. In the other provinces, fearing new attempts at secession, Lumumba had ordered arrests of suspected spies; thus a witch-hunt was on, accompanied by beatings and unprovoked attacks on many innocent persons. The stage was set for the long civil war that followed.

Lumumba had also looked to Africans for help. He had called a high-level meeting of representatives of African states in Leopoldville on 30 August and had sought military assistance as well. He already had Nkrumah and Sekou Touré of Guinea willing to make their troops available to him to end secession in various parts of the country. The Egyptians expressed their support for establishing an African command, and on 18 August King Mohammed V of Morocco also announced his complete agreement with the others on forming an African command to support the unity of the Congo and avoid attempts to split the country.

Despite these moves, the African states remained committed to dealing with the crisis in the Congo with the UN's help and recognised that such an objective could best be achieved by Hammarskjöld. The fact that the Soviet Union had accepted Lumumba's request for direct assistance had introduced another compelling factor. Hammarskjöld now began a desperate struggle to save the Congo from collapse and anarchy. His primary objective had been to persuade the Soviet Union, together with the other big powers, to support the UN's efforts in the Congo. He had to stop the Soviets from giving reckless encouragement to the fiery and temperamental Lumumba; for this he had to rely on the Africans.

The Security Council was to meet on 21 August; to my surprise both Bunche and I received instructions from Hammarskjöld that I should return at once with information on the latest developments in the Congo to help him with the presentation to the Security Council. Since no scheduled airline flight was available for several hours, Oliver drove me to the airport about midnight. He spoke to the liaison officer of the US military air transport command, who said a C124 could be put at my disposal for a flight to their air base in Tripoli, Libya, where the rest of my flight would be arranged. My plane left within an hour, and eight chilly hours later we reached Tripoli.

I was greeted by a colonel and his wife and taken to their home for a shower and a meal. Hours later I was on another C124 flying to a military airfield near Paris. On landing some five hours later, I was escorted by US military police and rushed to Orly in time to catch the afternoon Air France flight to New York. Some nine hours later, I was seated behind Hammarskjöld in the Security Council chamber.

The debate was in full swing and Hammarskjöld wrote a number of crisp questions for me to answer. I wrote brief replies. Within an hour, he asked for the floor to present a report on recent developments. In his opening remarks, he said 'Mr President, I have just received some important information on the developments in the Congo.' He paused and slightly turned his head towards me, then continued. Although the diplomats and the press were aware of my sudden return and presence, I appreciated the covert signal of acknowledgement for my dash from Leopoldville.

After a number of postponements, the Security Council meeting had begun on 21 August, the day of my return to New York. The Africans faced a dilemma, since they did not wish to take sides between Hammarskjöld and Lumumba in the dispute between them over Katanga. The Soviets, the day before, charged in a letter to the Secretary-General that his inclusion of Canadians in ONUC (Canada being an ally of Belgium in NATO), contrary to his own commitment to the UN, was the cause of the Congolese reaction which had resulted in the beating of Canadian personnel. Such accusations against Hammarskjöld made the Africans even more cautious since they wanted to avoid being caught up in the East-West ideological battle. They were also embarrassed by Lumumba's behaviour, which had resulted in arrests and manhandling of

ONUC personnel.

Bearing in mind Lumumba's suggestion for an African command and the Soviet proposal for a group representing troop-contributing states to have a daily meeting with Hammarskjöld and the Congolese government,[6] Hammarskjöld proposed setting up a Congo Advisory Committte of troop-contributing countries, along the same lines as in UNEF.

It seemed unlikely that the Council would respond positively to this request by the Secretary-General for an endorsement of his policies, and it concluded its session in the early hours of 22 August without taking sides over Lumumba quarrel with him. However, statements by Council members gave enough indication that they had generally rejected Lumumba's complaints against the UN and endorsed Hammarskjöld's authority for directing ONUC operations.

After my return from Leopoldville, Hammarskjöld's preoccupation, besides the Security Council, was with organising ONUC's leadership. His first choice as Bunche's replacement was Rajeshwar Dayal, then serving as India's ambassador to Pakistan, and no stranger to the UN, having served in UNOGIL in 1958. He was expected to arrive in New York in early September and after a few days' consultation would join ONUC. Bunche had urged his early arrival, and Hammarskjöld warned me to be prepared to return to Leopoldville to assume acting charge of the mission until Dayal arrived. Since it would only be for a week or so, I did not hesitate to agree.

By now Hammarskjöld was well aware of the difficulties between Von Horn and the UN senior staff. Before leaving Leopoldville to come to New York for the Security Council meeting, I had another talk with Bunche about Von Horn. While Bunche had reluctantly agreed to allow me to return to New York, he expressed concern about the handling of the Force. For the first time, I said to him that Von Horn was not a suitable choice and that we should tell this to Hammarskjöld. He paused to think, and then said that if we raised this question there would be problems; I understood that these would be with the Swedes and with other governments. Hammarskjöld was already faced with criticism of the command of the peacekeeping force by Lumumba, by some of the African states and by the Soviets, and to admit at this stage that Von Horn was a poor choice would only exacerbate the opposition.

In New York, as soon as I found a moment with Cordier, I gave him a brief account of the leadership problem at ONUC. I ended by suggesting, 'Andy, why can't you send Carl back to UNTSO?' He responded with his short nervous laugh and replied, 'Dag will have to keep him in ONUC for the time being. You have to take care of Carl for now.'

There were other factors, but I had no doubt that Hammarskjöld's decision, given at our regular meeting that evening, that Cordier would now go to Leopoldville to visit ONUC and assume acting charge to enable Bunche to return was in consequence of my conversation with him about the unsuitability of Von Horn. The visit would provide Cordier with an opportunity to look at the higher UN leadership questions and advise Hammarskjöld. Turning to me at this meeting, Hammarskjöld said words to this effect, 'I want you to go to Leopoldville, but to help Carl. The military are going through hard days and they have a difficult task ahead. You are needed there. Cordier will return after Dayal has taken over, and Dayal will need your help too. You know what is on my mind and you are well acquainted with the Congo situation. You will have to remain there until Dayal has settled down and the Force operations are satisfactory.'

I returned to my office, where Bowitz and Cavalcanti were waiting, and stunned them with the news of my new mission. We worked through most of that night and the next day on what they had to do in my absence, which would possibly be for several weeks. Fortunately communications between Leopoldville and New York by telex were satisfactory, and we had already learned to use them effectively for our work.

I left for Leopoldville that evening for my third visit and mulled over my assignment during the flight. I looked forward to working with Cordier and then Dayal, but hated the thought of virtually having to run the UN Force with Von Horn present. My personal relationship with him was still good, and I had to avoid letting the goodwill between us burn out. I had either to quit or urge his replacement before we reached that point.

I had no expectations of replacing Von Horn myself. I strongly felt that the Force Commander should be carefully chosen and should have commanded at least a division in the field and preferably have had some UN experience. I had yet to command a division, and in any event, I never considered for a moment that an Indian would be acceptable in such a position now that Dayal was to lead the mission. In India before I came to New York, a visiting friend, Sir James Lindsay, had asked me about my future plans. I said that I intended to take early retirement from the army and seek a career in the private sector. He asked if I had any civilian job in mind, and I told him about an offer made me by Pat Williamson, chairman of Williamson and Magor in Calcutta, one of the largest tea estate management companies. Pat had been in my regiment during the war and we had become friends. In the 1950s, when the Indian government had insisted on the Indianisation of foreign-owned companies, Pat had taken in two of my younger brothers to work on the gardens, and asked me to join him in Calcutta.

I had forgotten about this conversation with Lindsay until I received a letter from him in New York, offering me a post on his staff. He was chairman of Metal Box in Calcutta, and planned to groom me as his successor. He inquired how soon I could leave the army and the UN to join him.

This was a tempting offer, since I was on a short assignment with the UN and had no idea how long I would be with the Secretary-General. C.S. Jha, India's permanent representative, was also eager to know my future in order to inform our Minister of Defence, Krishna Menon.

My new assignment to ONUC provided the opportunity for me to ask Hammarskjöld how long he intended to retain me. He replied that I was very valuable to him and that he would need my services for a while longer. Then he showed me a letter he had recently written to Prime Minister Nehru, asking for Dayal to be released to head the Congo mission. He had written that he hoped his venture to replace key personalities from the Secretariat who had been sent to the Congo would succeed so that they could return to take up their regular work again. He obviously had people like Bunche in mind. His letter continued: 'We have made some beginnings, one of which is the recruitment of Brigadier-General Rikhye. We are very happy to have him on our senior staff. He has already made an outstanding contribution under difficult conditions. I thank you most warmly for your undertanding and kind assistance; I know that the sending of Rikhye from his previous assignment in Assam (he meant Ladakh) was a real sacrifice, showing the generosity of your approach and your interest in what we are trying to do.'

This was very flattering. I thanked him for his confidence and encouragement, as well as that of his senior colleagues, while I was carrying out a job that was new to me. This was obviously not a suitable time to leave the UN or think in terms of retiring from the army, and I wrote to Lindsay accordingly.

NOTES

1. For troop contributions, see App. C.1, p. 329, below; for their deployment, see page.....
2. *Soldiering for Peace* (New York: David McKay, 1967), pp. 140-8.
3. General Staff Officer, equivalent to Chief of Staff.
4. UN Document, 5/4389/Add. 5.
5. UN Document S/4450, 21 August 1960.
6. UN Document S/4453, 21 August 1960.

5

FORCE COMMANDER IN ALL BUT NAME

I returned to Leopoldville on 27 August after completing my fourth flight across the Atlantic within a month. I was delighted to be greeted at the airport not only by my UN administration colleagues but also by members of the Indian Contingent who had recently joined ONUC in response to my efforts to organise the Force. Brigadier Harminder Singh, Commander of the Indian contingent, and Lt. Col. N.N. Madan, Chief Logistics Officer at Force headquarters, were among the group. Harminder and I had served together in 7 Light Cavalry during the Jammu and Kashmir operation and were students at the Staff College together. He was a cool, tactful and able officer who would serve the UN and India well.

Madan, known as Nanna, was an exceptionally well qualified logistics officer and had apparently been chosen in response to my urging Delhi to send the best, in the light of the situation between Von Horn and the UN administration. Nanna and I had first met when he was in training at the start of the Second World War, and our friendship had endured over the years. He looked somewhat like the Hollywood actor Ronald Colman, had remained a bachelor and was very popular with women. He had two other assets which he used with discretion. First, he was reasonably well-off and entertained with style. This gave him a playboy image, which he enjoyed because his rakish façade concealed an excellent mind. And secondly, he was a first cousin of Prime Minister Nehru, a fact he was careful never to mention. As we greeted each other I asked, 'Hey, are we going to lick the logistics problem?' Laughing loudly in his usual style, he replied, 'You bet!' Having been apprehensive about returning to Leopoldville to run the UN Force in all but name, I began to feel somewhat comforted.

Above, left to right: U Thant, UN Secretary-General in succession to Hammarskjöld; the author; Ralph Bunche, UN Under-Secretary for Special Political Affairs. New York, November 1961. (Photo: United Nations) *Below:* Conor Cruise O'Brien, UN Representative in Katanga *(left),* with Moise Tshombe, 'President' of Katanga, September 1961. (Photo: Black Star)

Early the next morning I was in Bunche's office, where we were joined by Cordier and Galo Plaza, a former President of Ecuador and member of the three man UNOGIL mission to Lebanon in 1958, to whom Hammarskjöld had entrusted the task of arranging the transfer of the Belgian military bases of Kamina, Kitona and Banana to the UN.

Bunche planned to return to New York the next day, and we therefore had a lot to discuss. Relations with Lumumba had not improved. On 26 August he had declared that he hoped Hammarskjöld would honour his promise to bring about a Belgian troop withdrawal by 30 August and that if the Belgians had not left by that day, 'we will know who committed sabotage.' On the role of the UN force, he commented they had been invited solely to drive the Belgians out of the Congo and would have to withdraw after accomplishing that aim. He added, 'We do not want another occupation.' Our life with Lumumba was going to be no easier than before.

The situation in Kasai had suddenly deteriorated. Furthermore, there were indications that Lumumba had ordered an invasion of Bakwanga on 24 August. There was already severe fighting between the traditionally hostile Lulua and Baluba tribes, which had broken out soon after the declaration of independence. The UN's Tunisian troops had succeeded in bringing about a semblance of peace between them, but after the declaration of secession by Bakwanga, the fighting had resumed. The arrival of the Congolese army had only added to the chaos and the suffering of the people. Albert Kalonji, leader of the break-away state of Bakwanga (also called the Diamond State after the mines), was not able to obtain the desired support from Katanga because of Tshombe's own problems in the north of his province. As expected, Tshombe and Kalonji signed an agreement on 25 August to estabish a common defence plan and an economic and customs union.

Having been denied the use of the UN troops to dictate his terms, Lumumba finally fulfilled his threat to resort to aid from the Soviet Union. The Soviets provided an airlift starting on 25 August and ground transportation to the ANC on 27 August. Lumumba had also declared, as we have seen, that he wanted the UN troops to leave as soon as the Belgian forces had departed, equating UN troops with a new 'imperialistic colonialism'. However, the mandate of the UN Force in the Congo, unlike that of UNEF in 1956, was laid down by the Security Council. In addition, it had tasks other than ensuring the withdrawal of the Belgian troops. Thus Lumumba alone could not dictate the future role of the UN, but he could make its operations difficult and hazardous, and already seemed to have done so to some measure.

Cordier, Plaza and I, having just arrived from New York, considered our respective tasks and how we could best coordinate them. Cordier was going to take over immediately from Bunche. He also intended to call on important Congolese leaders and meet key foreign envoys. Plaza, assisted by General 'Spec' Wheeler,[1] would start gathering information from the Belgians on their military bases, and intended to visit the military staff and Von Horn. We agreed to meet in the evening for a round-up.

I started with Von Horn. He had received a cable from Hammarskjöld defining my mission, namely that I was placed temporarily at his disposal. I therefore asked how I could assist him. He said I should continue to do what I had done in the past, and asked me especially to help in establishing the newly-arrived staff. He then turned to his favourite theme of administration. Now that there was a military logistics staff, I said, they should deal with the UN administration. I intended to spend a good deal of time with them to shake them down and help settle the logistics units which had arrived. He was disappointed at not having his own CAO, and said that he expected me to ensure that the 'civilians' delivered.

When I asked how he wanted me to relate to the command structure, he said, 'Look, Indar, you are Dag's military adviser and here to help me while you still have to do your own job. We have already worked out a good arrangement. You tell me what the civilians want, we can discuss how best to do our job, and then you tell my staff what we have agreed on.' I answered that it had worked well in the early days, but he now had his full staff. I would be pleased to ensure that his staff knew what he had agreed to, but he had to arrange for one of his senior staff to attend the meetings of the head of our mission. I then suggested that he nominate McCarthy for the job, who was already dealing with the political staff but not on a regular basis. He agreed. I wanted such an arrangement so as to avoid issuing orders directly to the staff myself because I wished to remain outside the chain of command and staff of the Force.

After calling on Iyassou, who had a string of contingent commanders and liaison officers waiting to see him, I met McCarthy and his operational staff for a briefing. His Chief Operations Officer was an Indian gunner, Lt. Col. A.K. Mitra, whom I had met briefly when I was an instructor at the Senior Officers School, Mhow, Central India. In the intimate life of the Indian Army I had heard only good things about him. The Deputy Chief Operations Officer was from the Pakistan Armoured Corps, Major Ejaz Azim, 13 Lancers. He had a post-independence commission, and we had never met before, but his commandant at the Academy had been my own first squadron commander in 6 Lancers, Brigadier Francis Ingall. Mitra and Ejaz became a formidable team, and we became close friends.

The ONUC force was about 15,700-strong and was expected to reach 17,000 within a few weeks when an Indonesian battalion of 1,000 and a company each of Malayan and Guinean troops arrived. More logistics units and air crews were also due. The deployment of the troops was: 2,390 Ethiopians in Oriental province; 2,390 Ghanaians in Leopoldville; 740 from Guinea and 510 from Egypt in Equateur; 1,370 Irish, with a battalion each in Kivu and Katanga; 570 from Mali in North Katánga; 3,220 Moroccans in Leopoldville, Thysville and Katanga; 390 Sudanese in Matadi; 580 Swedes in Katanga; and 2,640 Tunisians in Kasai. Besides the headquarters at Leopoldville, several administrative units had arrived: a supply unit and a hospital from India, ordnance and a transport unit from Pakistan, and air and ground crews from a number of countries to fly and maintain about sixty chartered, leased and UN-owned aircraft.

I was conferring with the military staff on 7 August when a duty operations officer came in to report that a US Globemaster carrying a Canadian signals team had been attacked by ANC troops on arrival at Stanleyville airfield the previous day and the team badly beaten. They were rescued from the local prison by the Ethiopian troops and kept at their brigade hospital overnight. The American captain and the Ethiopian commander had decided that the aircraft transporting the injured should return to Leopoldville the next day to avoid further incidents, because the Congolese had mistaken the French-speaking Canadians, some of whom were wearing their para wings, for Belgian paratroopers. The plane was expected to arrive at N'Djili airport in about an hour. I hurried to inform Bunche, and he suggested that I go to meet it. He said that ONUC had made arrangements for the security of N'Djili with the Congolese and that the ANC were only permitted a token presence. Concerned that our entire airlift by the United States could be prejudiced and that the news of this incident would be badly received in Canada, coming only a few days after another incident at N'Djili, he was anxious to avoid anything further happening of the same kind.

Accompanied by a French-speaking staff member and a UN security officer, I rushed to the airport and arrived just as the Globemaster plane had landed. As we suspected, the ANC had learned via the air control radio network about this plane carrying 'Belgian paras'. A Congolese officer was moving towards the unloading ramp of the aircraft and from somewhere, contrary to the agreement between the Congolese and the UN, some forty ANC soldiers materialised. Our Ghanaian troops on duty at the airport were also moving towards the aircraft. Eventually, the Ghanaians, by cajoling and shoving the Congolese, placed themselves betweent the aircraft and the ANC. A young Ghanaian officer kept urging me not to worry because his troops had a friendly relationship with the ANC troops present and would be able to handle them.

An ONUC Indian medical team was on hand, and entered the aircraft first. There were two stretcher cases—Capt Elvert L. Mott, USAF, and Corporal Glendon Kavel of the Royal Canadian Signals—who were carried out. Then followed the walking injured, who caused a stir among the Congolese. One of them said '*Les paras belges*' and raised his rifle at the wounded. I was already angry at the sight of our innocent soldiers and airmen who had come to help the Congolese and received only beatings and injuries in return. I went for the man who had his rifle pointed at the injured and with my best soccer kick, knocked the rifle so that it clattered to the ground. Watching my reaction, the Ghanaian officer ordered his men to turn around and forced the ANC away from the aircraft by shouting and yelling at them in French and Lingala.

My car had been followed to the airport by the press, and they were all over the aircraft when it arrived. It took me only a moment to recover from my violent response, which seemed to have worked. Not only did my action leave me stunned, but it had the desired effect on the ANC and made the Ghanaians act more forcefully. When I turned around to see who else was there, I saw a journalist taking pictures. I turned on him and said, 'Now surely you were not taking a photograph of me, were you?' He stopped dead, fearing that I might use my left foot on his camera, and then he grinned and said 'Oh no, this one is not for publication. I am with you, General. But I would like to write it up.' I agreed and shook his hand in mutual understanding that we each had a job to do in our own way. He kept to his word: there was a description of the incident in *Newsweek* but no photograph, which could have done great harm. I promised myself never to lose my cool in the Congo again—one could never calculate what the effect might be.

On my way back to the Royal, I decided to visit the Ghana brigade and see the commander, Brigadier Joseph Ankrah. They were doing a good job in the capital, and I was also able to commend the young officer at the airport to his brigade commander. My car carried a radio, and the Ghanaians were warned of my visit. When I met Ankrah, he reported that the ANC and the Congolese police were all over the city in a threatening demonstration of force, trying to give the impression that the local people were antagonistic to the UN. Ankrah had placed his army and police units to check the Congolese in a determined demonstration that the UN would not tolerate a repetition of what had occurred a few days earlier. At least on the surface, the situation was calm. I asked what kind of trouble he expected. He replied that there were several possibilities: a number of ANC soldiers from tribes whose political leaders were opposed to Lumumba were likely to mutiny if encouraged; the Abako party could stir up trouble in the African quarters of the town; and there could be demonstrations of public anger at their economic afflictions. He had kept an adequate reserve of his troops and police in readiness to respond to such eventualities.

My next call was on Kettani. Of all the senior military officers in ONUC he had the best political understanding of the situation in the

Congo. However, as a traditional military man, he kept aloof from it. When in a talking mood he could be eloquent, and luckily he was on this particular day. Apparently, what got him going was my asking if he envisaged being able to start serious training of the ANC. He replied that the Congolese had two choices: to let the ANC become a rabble, which they were close to being already, or to make it an effective instrument of government. The training of the ANC had to be dealt with in two ways, from top to bottom and from bottom to top.

At the top were the Congolese leaders. They were busily engaged in their struggle for survival, politically and personally, and therefore had no time to learn matters relating to the use of security forces. In any case, it was not practical while the present political crisis lasted to take them away for training. The senior-level Congolese officers had all been dragged into politics and, together with many of the more junior officers, enjoyed politics more than going to the barracks to work with their troops at training. That left the junior officers and the men who had expressed their desire to train.

Kettani had some 300 instructors spread over the camps in Leopoldville, Thysville and Kasai. He also had a team in Katanga. He added with a note of pleasure that some of the majors and colonels had expressed interest in being trained if it were possible to send them abroad. He knew that a number of Western embassies' military attachés had been sounding out the Congolese officers. However, he cautioned that the promise to go abroad would divert the interest of the Congolese away from working with his teams. It was obvious to me that the competition among countries for their own schools to promote their own political interests would be considerable and would affect Kettani's efforts. At the same time, the UN must accept that the Congolese would receive excellent training at these schools and therefore, in principle, should support such efforts.

On 23 August Lumumba asked Bunche for the services of Kettani in the reorganisation of the ANC, and because Kettani was already engaged in this task, Lumumba's request at this stage seemed to be related to his plan to send the ANC to Bakwanga. Kettani would need to perform an overnight miracle to improve their quality by the time the ANC were ordered to invade Bakwanga two days later.

Kettani and Ankrah both appreciated the UN's management of operations. They were given their roles when they first arrived, and whenever they ran into problems, which were generally political, these were resolved by Bunche or his aides. Equally they had no complaints over the logistics support for their troops. They were conscious of what conditions were like in the country and appreciated what was being done for them. Besides, both had regular air connections with their own countries for support. I was glad to hear this, since these views were contrary to those expressed by their Force Commander.

I returned to the Royal for a meeting on administrative and logistics questions. Madan had gathered his service staff, the Indian senior medical officer and supply officer and the Pakistani ordnance and transport officers. A representative of the ONUC air force and De Angelis, the Deputy CAO, were there. The UN administration had already established a network of local supplies and transport by road, river and rail, and UN representative in each province was available to assist over housing and other local facilities. The contingents ran their own mail service at that time, and each unit had its own small 'PX' general purpose store. All the major contingents had their own welfare stores and movies. Madan and his military staff were now engaged in establishing a military logistics network such as accompanied the troops in normal military operations. This was a challenging and by no means easy assignment which would need careful planning and time to place the organisation on the ground. It was not somethig that a single CAO on the staff of the Force Commander could accomplish because, not being trained in military systems, he would not even have known where to begin. I left Madan and his colleagues, wishing them good luck and assuring them that for the coming weeks they would receive my priority attention.

Bunche, Cordier, Plaza, Linner and I had an evening round-up, which was quickly got over as we all had more to do. I was to have my usual evening session with Von Horn over dinner and said I would inform them of his reactions to what I had been able to do during the day. I duly met Von Horn in his office at the Royal and we then drove out to the restaurant near the zoo in his official limousine with its four stars. He had begun to wear three stars on his shoulder patches. He prided himself on his Guards background and when inspecting or visiting troops was in the habit of noticing a missing button or an unpolished brass. Now he himself was improperly dressed. He was wearing unauthorised badges of rank, because only his own government could authorise his rank and certainly no such authority had come past me. Furthermore, while he wore three stars his car carried four stars. I resisted the temptation to pull his leg because I did not envisage smooth sailing ahead with him.

He was more tired than I had ever seen him. He said the climate was affecting him as well as the difficulties of his job, i.e. problems with Bunche and then the UN administration. We enjoyed our food and wine and I was able to apprise him briefly of my day's work. But he was not much interested and said more than once that I could do whatever was necessary in keeping with the Secretary-General's wishes. He was sorry to see Bunche leave, but thought that it would be in the best interests of ONUC. He got on well with Cordier and looked forward to working with him. He wanted to know about Dayal, but my previous acquaintance with him was limited to a brief period, and therefore could not be very informative.

We had little to say on our way back to the Royal where I was to be dropped. He had a busy social life, meeting senior commanders and staff as well as being invited by embassies who wanted to learn at first-hand about ONUC operations. Besides, under Berthiume's lavish care, a Canadian army chef and a well-stocked Flagstaff House[2] were beginning to have an apparent effect on the General's health—I had been informed that he took a rest after lunch, which was not unusual for anyone who had served in the Middle East, but I couldn't help but say to him that he should take care of himself. He reminded me that he had been due to go to Sweden on leave but had to come to the Congo instead. He was also concerned about his wife, who was in poor health.

Bunche, Cordier, Urquhart and Liu were already busy discussing their day's work and drafting a cable to Hammarskjöld. Finally I was alone with Bunche and Cordier and told them that Von Horn was tired and, as I thought, unwell. I said that he was not being well served by the coterie of staff around him, who should protect instead of indulging him. I was asked if I could improve this staff, but answered that Von Horn would never agree to a change. There were more pressing matters for Bunche and Cordier to attend to than Von Horn. In any case, he was my responsibility and we turned to arrangements for Bunche's departure.

On 29 August, Bunche was winding up his affairs in Leopoldville. He visited the American and Canadian injured in the Indian general hospital, where an American airman told him that they owed their lives to an Ethiopian nurse who had courageously thrown herself on the ANC jeep which was carrying the arrested American and Canadian men to the local jail. After being pushed out of this jeep she had managed to get aboard another one and followed them to the jail, and then warned the Ethiopian brigade commander, who rescued them. It was inevitable that the American and Canadian governments should protest strongly, but the incident also greatly disturbed troop-contributing countries, which were mainly African. By its declarations, Lumumba's government had incited the Congolese against the UN and against whites in general. Thus several governments expressed their concern to Lumumba, urging him to tone down his invective. In his talk with the press before leaving the Congo, Bunche told them, 'Never before has so much patience and effort been required of the United Nations . . . I am a patient man, but my patience has worn thin.'

He also declared that the last of the Belgian combat troops would depart from the Congo that day. Some 1,500 of their technical military personnel were to remain to service the military bases until replaced in phases by UN personnel. The Congolese governemnt declared later that day that the UN had not met its commitments because, they contended.

the withdrawal order applied to all Belgian troops. During my first visit to the Belgian bases I had concluded that the UN must plan an orderly take-over of the bases. Each was like a township, including city services and a variety of technical installations for the support of the military. The Kamina base, for example, had installations not to be found elsewhere in black Africa. The recruitment of suitable personnel by the UN would not be easy and would certainly need time. At a brief meeting of the committee on the Belgian military bases that day, we made plans to visit them, beginning on the following day. As Plaza concluded the meeting, a wag among us quipped that had the UN complied with the Congolese demand to remove all Belgians, the multi-million-dollar bases would have been left to the care of 'God or the bush'.

Reports of the first clashes between the ANC and the Katanga forces at Luputa on Kasai's border with Katanga reached us on 29 August. This was inevitable and was a poor augury for peace in that area. The efforts of our Tunisian troops (about 400 of them) to limit fighting were limited to their own area of deployments; the area of fighting was too large for any effective control. They also proved useful in arranging evacuation of some of the wounded Congolese soldiers to Leopoldville in UN aircraft. There were reported to be far too many dead for the UN troops to cope with.

On 30 August Bunche left for New York and Cordier assumed the responsibilities in the interim as the Special Representative of the Secretary-General in the Congo. The day coincided with the end of the pan-African parley in Leopoldville. The conference, which included influential delegates like Mongi Slim of Tunisia and Alex Quaison-Sackey of Ghana, decided to support the unity and integrity of the Congo and backed the central government without mentioning Katanga; concluded that African aid to the Congo must be in harmony with the UN; exhorted the UN and the Congo to collaborate; and called for an African summit meeting to arrive at a consensus before the General Assembly meeting. It gave its strong endorsement to the UN, and sent notes of thanks to Bunche and through him to Hammarskjöld. In a private meeting with Lumumba, the delegates expressed their disapproval of the beatings of American and Canadian personnel by Congolese soldiers. The support of the African states for the UN was most heartening for ONUC personnel who had suffered arrests, violence and all kinds of indignities at the hands of the Congolese. ONUC needed such encouragement to face the dangerous and difficult tasks that still lay ahead.

I flew with Plaza and his committee on 31 August to Kamina and found the base under siege by the Katanga gendarmerie. Tshombe sought guarantees that the UN would not permit the ANC to enter the base. Irish and Swedish troops were responsible for its security and the Katangese did not think the UN troops could defend it against a Congolese attack. The

ONUC representative in Katanga, Ian Berendsen, issued a statement that the UN would bar the ANC and the Katanga forces from entry to the base. Furthermore, the UN would only permit its own aircraft to land there. This seemed to have calmed Tshombe, but tension in the surrounding African town remained, requiring an alert by the UN troops.

I was somewhat familiar with the base and already had an advanced technical military team to present me with their suggestions. After consulting them and the Irish battalion commander, I was ready with my presentation to the Plaza committee. The Belgian base was primarily used for the training of air crews as it provided almost year-round flying weather. The flying school had to have technical services to give it a degree of self-reliance, in that it could not only service aircraft but could also manufacture some spare parts. The base required security, which was provided by the army, and the latter in turn required logistical support. A parachute establishment was located there.

In order to save on Belgian technicians and support personnel, the base employed a large number of civilians and thus the Belgians and local labour, together with their dependants, made up a sizeable town, a typical military camp or cantonment. Now, in accordance with the needs of the UN, all the Belgians had to be replaced and the locals retained. Accordingly, I decided on a minimum number of military personnel for essential duties and to provide support and maintenance facilities for the UN air unit—and of civilians to keep the base going. If any additional personnel were hired for such responsibilities, this would relate to the planned use of the base for the UN's civilian operations. Plaza and others hoped that the base with its technical facilities, the best in that part of Africa, could be used to establish a technical training institution, and worked on plans to develop these ideas into a reality. The other two bases, Kitona and Banana, were of use only to the military. I thought they could also be useful to Kettani for the training of the ANC: he could bring the Congolese here away from the politics of the capital, instill some discipline and train them. After quick visits to the three military bases, I hurried back to Leopoldville.

The pace of developments in the Congo was rapid and the military arm of ONUC was badly blunted by the growing ineffectiveness of its Force Commander. I had only made a beginning in settling the staff so that they could work together. Madan and his logistics team were getting on well with the UN administration, but there was much to be done before they could be welded into an effective team. General Burns had succeeded in achieving this with UNEF. In ONUC the Force Commander, from the moment he arrived, had declared war on the UN administration and, when he failed to get his way over anything, washed his hands of that part of his responsibility and never failed to say 'I told you so' when anything went wrong or was not good enough. If, having picked up the Force Commander's bat, I played well, he would get up and take the applause.

I did not like this arrangement of command because it was totally out of keeping with my upbringing. Besides, it would not be long before the staff, and later the troops, would find out who was running the show; his personal staff were likely to be the first to complain, and that would upset Von Horn. Besides, if he had any sense of dignity and honour, he should resent my position. Although I would often remind myself to be cautious and avoid stepping on his toes, there were occasions that required action, and I could not reach him because he was not available.

In Von Horn's order of priorities, taking ceremonial parades on the arrival or departure of units and contingents had a high place. Usually a reception followed each such occasion, and considering the numbers of arrivals and departures it kept him very busy. Added to it were the official calls to make and receive, the round of diplomatic and military receptions and dinners, and hospitality to be returned. Perhaps the seeds for General Alexander's suggestion that there be a 'Supremo' and a separate field commander lay in his anticipation of the higher-level military of ONUC incurring such obligations. In any case, there was not much time left to see the Force Commander unless one followed the circuit or saw him for a meal in the evening, which I did as often as possible. Regrettably, some decisions could not wait till dinner-time and had to be made on the spot. The staff at headquarters found me available to explore courses of action, discuss matters with the political staff, rush to see a Congolese official if needed, and consult the embassy staff concerned. In the days that followed, there were critical developments demanding quick decisions, and I made them without qualms.

The invasion of Bakwanga ordered by Lumumba had further divided the government and added more distance between him and Kasavubu. The call to the Soviet Union to provide an airlift for the ANC invasion, in addition to the use by the ANC of the Soviet trucks intended for civilian use, had raised a storm in Leopoldville, heightening the existing political crisis. The news of fighting in Bakwanga was bad. Some 1,200 ANC had succeeded in capturing the town after bitter fighting, but nearly 200,000 Balubas were around the town continuing to fight. While the Balubas were engaged in combat with the ANC, it did not deter them from continuing their battle against the Luluas. Our garrison of 400 Tunisians was protecting the Europeans and the UN personnel. We required a large internal airlift capability, which we did not have at that time, to respond to fighting on such a scale. The Congolese gave no quarter in this terrible war. They took no prisoners and hacked off the arms of those they had killed to show as war trophies. The ANC lost about thirty men, and while it was difficult to estimate Baluba killed, the local Belgian doctors estimated the number at about 1,000. There was no doubt in my mind that the UN could not stand aside and allow the massacre to continue.

Obviously dissatisfied with UN assurances that we would not permit the central government's troops to enter the Kamina military base, Tshombe renewed his threat to put the base out of action. The Katanga leaders feared that it was too lightly held by the UN, and we received reports that Tshombe had slipped in a group of political activists and some forty gendarmes. The 33rd Irish battalion of about 400 men was responsible for the base, a number that in my view was sufficient. However, at the suggestion of Ian Berendsen, the ONUC representative in Katanga, I agreed to the move of 100 Swedes from Elisabethville to Kamina as a show of force. It was also an insurance against any designs that Tshombe might have had on Kamina.

Our reports from there did not indicate any undue concern for its security against any threat from the tribes residing outside the base. They did, however, state that the Belgians were tardy with their troop withdrawals. This was reported to New York and on 31 August Hammarskjöld lodged a protest with the Belgian government for failing to comply with its commitments. Walter Loridan, the Belgian ambassador to the UN, in a letter to the Secretary-General, had said that all Belgian troops in the Congo were to be withdrawn by 29 August 'with the sole exception of some members of 1st Paratroop Battalion who are in transit in Albertville'. This referred to a small guard of Belgian vehicles which were waiting for a boat to take them across the lake to Usumbura. In fact 400 parachute troops, 120 airfield guards and 50 men at the flying school were still at Kamina. Loridan blamed the delay on the lack of air transport which the Belgians had hoped the United States would provide in their aircraft on UN airlift duty empty returning.

Shortly after Hammarskjöld's protest was made public, the Soviet Deputy Foreign Minister, Kuznetsov, called on the Secretary-General to protest against the continued Belgian presence in the Congo (in fact, his visit was more concerned with the Belgian civilian technical presence). The Soviets called for the removal of all such personnel and stated that the UN should consider providing the manpower immediately on a temporary basis.

By the beginning of September, the city of Leopoldville, which had never been short of panic and rumour, was abounding in talk of a coup against the government. Such rumours always conveyed the prejudices of the groups responsible for them. Central to such gossip were the three Congolese leaders: Kasavubu, who was about to oust Lumumba with Western help; Lumumba, who planned to overthrow Kasavubu assisted by Nkrumah, Nasser and the communist countries; and Mobutu, who had suddenly emerged as the dark horse who was going to get rid of all the politicians and establish a military-type dictatorship. The Western embassies appeared to be among the prominent sources of such gossip.

Lumumba's relations with the West, which had been delicate from the very start, were now at a crucial stage. His declarations against the UN and against Hammarskjöld in particular, his radical leanings in international relations and more recently his reliance on Soviet assistance to the ANC in defiance of UN resolutions, which had called for all assistance to the Congo to be channelled through the UN, had brought these relations close to breaking-point. The presence of fifteen Soviet transport aircraft at Stanleyville airport alarmed the West and caused serious concern to the UN. The Soviet embassy in the capital kept silent and therefore it was difficult to predict how these aircraft might be used in the future. Lastly, the bloody civil war being waged in Kasai, with reports of all sorts of atrocities by the combatants, had horrified Congolese and foreigners alike. The thought of it spreading to other parts of the country was frightening—and it might well do so. Somehow this had to be stopped. At ONUC Force headquarters I warned Iyassou and McCarthy to prepare adequate reserves from wherever they could muster them and have aircraft ready to meet new emergencies.

On 3 September, in a conversation with Cordier at the end of the day, I learned that Kasavubu had in mind a remedy to resolve the current leadership crisis. He intended to dismiss Lumumba under the constitutional authority vested in him and dissolve parliament. Kasavubu asked for ONUC assistance in arresting some leaders, presumably including Lumumba, but Cordier refused to involve the UN in any way in these plans and warned Kasavubu that such actions could lead to disorder. Cordier had then consulted Hammarskjöld by telex, and he gave me a summary of their exchange which is more fully reported by Urquhart in his *Hammarskjöld*.[3] There was a danger of disintegration of authority. The UN was responsible for maintaining law and order within the framework of its mandate, but Hammarskjöld cautioned that even a hypothetical discussion of any possible moves now would make the UN party to possible internal conflicts.

Liu was present at my meeting with Cordier, and the three of us talked for a while on the likely impact on ONUC operations if Kasavubu went ahead with his plans. Leopoldville was at the centre of the stage on which such a drama would be enacted, and that was where I should concentrate my attention. The Ghanaians were thoroughly reliable and well-led. Their commander Ankrah, while conscious of his President's politics, was determined to carry out his mandate under ONUC orders. I said that I would speak to Otu and Ankrah the next day and give a hint to ONUC senior staff of likely coming events. I also decided to speak to Kettani since we might need his troops as well as his advice.

The next morning, after a quick word with McCarthy, I saw the Ghanaians and Kettani. As I expected, they were on top of the situation. They too had reduced likely events to three possibilities. The first was that Kasavubu might overthrow Lumumba either by assassination or by political moves, or by encouraging the population of Leopoldville (largely favouring Abako) to demonstrate or even riot to promote conditions favouring the removal of Lumumba. The second was that he would remove Lumumba forcibly with the help of Mobutu by first encouraging demonstrations by ANC troops from tribes opposed to the MNC. And the third was that Lumumba might cause his supporters to riot due to the poor economic conditions; these could be blamed on the foreigners, who were still in control, and on Kasavubu and his coterie of friends who could be accused of being agents of Belgium and the West. However, Otu, Ankrah and Kettani were not yet aware of Kasavubu's latest moves. I therefore told them to be prepared for any of the three likely events. Kettani said that in his meetings with Lumumba and ANC leaders he had cautioned them against continuing the war in Kasai and urged a disengagement. He had the impression that General Lundula was complying loyally with Lumumba's orders whereas Mobutu was having second thoughts about their misadventure.

On 5 September, Cordier was kept busy visiting Kasavubu, who confirmed his intention of dismissing Lumumba and other Congolese leaders. At about 7 p.m. Cordier sent for me to say that Kasavubu had decided to go ahead with his plans. Just over an hour later, Kasavubu announced on the radio that he had dismissed Lumumba and six of his ministers and called on Joseph Ileo, President of the Senate, to form a new government. He pledged to end the civil war and appealed for calm. After the broadcast, a letter was delivered from Kasavubu to Cordier asking the UN to take over responsibility for the maintenance of law and order throughout the country and to close the airfields to all but UN traffic. About half an hour later Lumumba came on the radio and in a highly emotional speech, which he repeated a number of times, declared that Kasavubu was no longer the head of state. A Haitian UN expert, Jean David, had offered Cordier his services in helping to reconcile Kasavubu and Lumumba, which Cordier accepted with some hesitation. David shuttled between the presidential palace, Lumumba's residence and the Royal but had little success.

I realised that Kasavubu had an experienced and skillful Belgian adviser, A.J. Bilsen, and furthermore that the Western ambassadors had urged him to act against Lumumba just as they were pushing Mobutu into precipitous action. But Kasavubu's actions were so close to what the UN desired that it seemed to me he could not have acted on the advice of the Western embassies alone. It looked as if there was a UN connection somewhere—which many in the international community also believed. I was not privy to any such arrangements, but was uncomfortable with developments. However, the opportunity to take steps to end the civil war in Kasai overcame my discomfort. Besides, I was responsible for military matters and political decisions were not my province. Cordier, who was extremely concerned at the possibility of destructive clashes between opposing factions in Leopoldville, had asked me to ready troops for the closing of the airports to prevent any further troop movements to Kasai or by the Stanleyville pro-Lumumba ANC to Leopoldville or any other place. We had also considered the possibility of closing the radio station in the capital.

Although Cordier had kept up his relations with Von Horn, it was more out of form because he dealt with me on all matters of substance. Cordier had told Von Horn of his plans but he turned to me to weigh the odds. Later that night he decided to close the airports, and I passed the necessary orders to the troops through the Force staff. I went to sleep in the early hours of the morning, pleased that the closing of the airports would facilitate our ending the civil war but somewhat bewildered at the turn of political events which I felt did not bode well for the future of the Congo or the UN. After a short nap I went back to Cordier's room. He was already up and talking with his aides. He turned to me and asked that I order the immediate closing of the radio station. I left his office and went to the Force operations room, where I found Mitra and told him what Cordier wanted. He looked at me quizzically and asked, 'You want me to order our Ghanaians to take over the radio station and close it? What if Lumumba wants to use it?' 'The radio will be closed to all, Lumumba or Kasavubu or anyone,' I replied.

There were two or three other staff officers at work who had stopped what they were doing to listen to our conversation. I knew that Mitra with his awareness of political considerations was thinking several steps ahead, of the consequences of closing the radio. Realising that some of the younger officers were present, he did not pursue the questions that I could see in his eyes. He looked at me and said, 'Very well, Indar. If you want the radio station closed, so it will be.' He then turned to his staff and said 'You have heard what the General wants. Let us go to work, chaps. Get me Colonel Ankrah on the phone.' I left him to do his job.

The closing of the airports had a salutary effect on the nature of fighting in Kasai, but the closing of the Leopoldville radio proved controversial and politically dangerous for the UN. Before the end of the day, Kasavubu, who had access to the radio in neighbouring Brazzaville through his friend President I' Abbé Fulbert Youlou, was broadcasting from there. Lumumba had no such access and had therefore been silenced. The UN was thus open to accusations of favouring Kasavubu, whom the West supported, thereby raising another political storm.

In New York, Hammarskjöld had been in consultation with his advisers and with key delegates. He was determined, as were most of the advisers, that the UN should remain out of the Congo's internal squabbles. He had told Cordier that even a hypothetical discussion of Kasavubu's planned actions 'would place us in a most exposed position', but then added, 'If you have to go ahead, time may be more important than our comments.' He was being realistic in his approach in that there are developments in the field which influence decision-making and often do not allow time to think comprehensively or stay abreast of events so as to influence their course. However, Hammarskjöld's instructions to Cordier were couched in language which was typical of him. Having lived through many days in Leopoldville and read through Hammarskjöld' instructions, it was my understanding that Cordier was not being told that he had to give a positive 'no' to Kasavubu's plans. Whatever was going to happen would happen. Cordier was told, 'We maintain law and order under UN rules, not being a tool for anyone . . . Even a hypothetical discussion of possible moves . . . would make us a party to possible internal conflict.' There was not even a hint to Cordier that he should convey to Kasavubu his own expressions of concern at any likely breakdown in law and order, nor had Hammarskjöld said anything about his own concern or that of the UN over the possible consequences.

After Kasavubu's actions, Hammarskjöld sent specific instructions to strengthen Cordier's hand in dealing with lawlessness. Cordier had spoken to Von Horn and enjoined me to be sure to instruct the staff that the troops might have to use force in legitimate self-defence. Accordingly, our troops were at maximum alert. However, the UN's main problem was to identify a legitimate Congolese authority. Under the Congolese constitution, the Head of State had the authority to remove the Prime Minister, provided he had the document of dismissal countersigned by one other cabinet member, which in this instance was the case. However, the Prime Minister did not have any constitutional powers to dismiss the President, as Lumumba had attempted to do.

Kasavubu's request to Cordier for personal protection could legitimately be granted under the ONUC mandate and assisting in the maintenance of law and order was legitimate too, but the closing of airports and the radio station required an ONUC judgment on the spot as to whether it was necessary due to the existence of a grave emergency. As it turned out, it was relatively easy explaining the closure of the airports, relating the action directly to ending the civil war in Kasai, but it proved difficult to justify the closing of the radio station, especially when the only person being denied a voice to speak to the people was Lumumba.

Besides the political shenanigans, most of us in ONUC were concerned with the possible behaviour of about 4,000 ANC troops in military camps in Leopoldville, who were ill-fed and had not been paid. Kettani had advised Cordier that the UN should provide the back-pay and rations in order to stave off any involvement of the ANC in the political crisis. Accordingly, Cordier requested 1 million dollars, which Hammarskjöld authorised, to be paid by Kettani to the ANC. On 9 September a meeting of the ANC commanders of Leopoldville, Luluabourg and Stanleyville was held under Lundula and Mobutu to discuss pay and administrative matters. In the meantime, Lumumba was ordering the ANC to attack and seize N'Djili airport from the UN, but the ANC decided against taking any action—since the UN was expected to provide them with their pay and rations. Later in the day Kettani informed Lumumba of the UN's intention to assist with pay and rations and, after obtaining his official approval, handed the money to senior ANC officers. Thus the threat of action by the ANC was averted.

As could be expected, there was a political storm in Leopoldville. Some of the embassies were pleased and others displeased at the UN's actions, each side being anxious to draw the UN officials to its own side. I was one of the main targets of their attention because they wanted me to influence Hammarskjöld and Dayal; knowing Hammarskjöld's instructions to Dayal, I did my best to keep detached from the debate around me. Dayal had reached Leopoldville on 5 September in the middle of the crisis and was briefed by Cordier on the current developments. He sat through Cordier's meetings with the staff, puffing at his pipe and listening, but no sooner were we alone than he almost exploded. He had been given no inkling of actual developments at his briefing in New York and was totally taken aback to find himself as the designate Special Representative of the Secretary-General in the Congo, arriving not to take over a running operation with Cordier only temporarily in charge, but an operation involving ONUC in what was obviously a major crisis. In these circumstances a smooth take-over was impossible, and he became a helpless witness to events which would cast a pall over the future of ONUC and had serious implications for his future role.

Naturally, he was wondering if it would be wise for him to take over his duties at such a time, but knowing his background and his enormous experience of diplomacy, I said that we should soon know what the effects of recent events would be on developments in the Congo. Hammarskjöld had selected him for good reasons, which had been further highlighted by the current happenings; he was the best man to do the job and was needed there. It was obvious that Dayal relished the challenge, but he was most uncomfortable with the direction events were taking and their effect on

ONUC's mission. He concluded our brief conversation by saying that he intended to watch the situation and would suspend his decision whether or not to remain.

Three other events became of concern to ONUC. First, an Ilyushin aircraft carrying Lundula from a visit to Stanleyville was not allowed to land at N'Djili airport. Secondly, Kamitatu, the President of Leopoldville province, who was on a visit to the interior, was unable to return to the capital by air. And lastly, Kasavubu asked the Public Prosecutor to issue a warrant for Lumumba's arrest on the grounds that he had incited the public to commit acts of violence, so creating conditions that could lead to the overthrow of the 'lawful and established authority'. On 7 September the Congolese Chamber of Deputies annulled the actions of Kasavubu in dismissing Lumumba and of Lumumba in declaring that Kasavubu was no longer a valid President. The Senate debated this issue as well but did not reach a decision till the next day, when it declared the dismissal of Lumumba void. However, Kasavubu in turn declared the resolutions by the two chambers void on the grounds that decisions he himself had made as Head of State were not subject to parliamentary approval.

Cordier's actions had led to considerable controversy. The West had lauded the removal of Lumumba, but the Socialist states were appalled, and the developing countries, including many troop-contributors, were dismayed at ONUC's response to the Congolese manoeuvrings. It was already evident that Dayal would have to dampen the fires which he had had no hand in setting alight, although some were to connect him with recent developments. Besides, Dayal said to me that his position lacked both responsibility and authority; he could not have arrived at a worse time, but he could not run away now. I told him he was the only man who could extricate the UN from the present crisis with dignity and that he must take over. He was well known for his courage in the face of adversity and, as I expected, he decided to take up the challenge. It was time for Cordier to depart, as Hammarskjöld had conveyed in his communication to him and to Dayal. The change-over took place on 8 September.

On the same day Antoine Gizenga, Lumumba's deputy, added more fuel to the fire by calling on the People's Republic of China and other pro-Lumumba governments for aid. Hammarskjöld sent a protest to the Belgians for sending arms to Katanga on 7 September in violation of UN resolutions, and two days later received the explanation that some light weapons requested by the Force Publique before 30 June 1960 had been mistakenly sent to Katanga. Meanwhile, Lumumba had embarked on a new campaign against the UN, accusing it of interference in the Congo's internal affairs. On 11 September, he tried to enter the radio station but was prevented from doing so by the Ghanaian troops in charge of security there. The next day Mobutu arrested Lumumba, who was later released by Congolese soldiers.

On 8 September the representative of Yugoslavia had asked for an urgent meeting of the Security Council, claiming that a situation which threatened world peace had arisen in the Congo because of external support for the secessionists and the attempt to overthrow the legal government. Such actions, he said, had been facilitated by the practices of the UN command which, under the appearance of non-intervention in the Congo's internal affairs, had created great obstacles for the central government in the exercise of its authority over the whole territory of the Republic. The same day, Lumumba asked the Security Council to meet in Leopoldville so that its members could see for themselves the situation allegedly created by the interference of the UN authorities in the Congo's domestic problems.

On 9 September when the Council met, the Soviet Union repeated this demand that it should meet in Leopoldville. The demand was rejected. In a statement to the Council, Hammarskjöld said that he assumed responsibility for the actions of his representatives in the Congo, claiming that they had acted impartially during the constitutional crisis and that the emergency measures concerning airports and the radio station had been necessary to ensure the operation of ONUC in fulfilment of its mandate. The UN force faced a difficult situation in south Kasai, where the ANC seemed to have broken away from its commanders, and there were extremely serious developments in Katanga. It was not only Belgian assistance to Katanga but also external assistance from others to the central government which had cast a blight over the whole situation in the Congo. The Council's aims could only be achieved if all external assistance were channelled through the UN. Hammarskjöld emphasised the dangers created by the Congo's financial bankruptcy, adding that the effectiveness of UN assistance depended on law and order being maintained and the country's political leaders showing a sense of responsibility and making efforts to solve their domestic problems peacefully.

In the Congo, Kasavubu and Lumumba had formed rival governments and their representatives had arrived and asked to be invited to the Security Council meeting. The Council members generally were of the view that if an invitation were to be given, only one delegation could be selected and the mere act of selection would amount to interference in the Congo's internal affairs and must therefore be avoided. The debate in the Council continued, and Hammarskjöld began to realise that no substantive action was likely to emerge. He therefore instructed Dayal to negotiate with the rival leaders in Leopoldville on the reopening of the airport and the radio station.

Tension in Leopoldville was acute and a spate of new rumours was circulating. The increasing activity among parliamentarians in support of

Lumumba caused Kasavubu to suspend parliament on 14 September. Meanwhile we were watching the situation anxiously because either of the two leaders could incite his youth party members or ANC units to take violent action. That evening Mobutu, on one of his frequent visits to the ONUC offices at the Royal, asked to see Dayal. There was nothing unusual in this request since he often called on Dayal to discuss his concerns over developments in the country. I was usually present at these meetings, and was again that evening. But as he sipped his drink, Mobutu quietly told Dayal that he had decided to neutralise Kasavubu and Lumumba as well as parliament to allow them time to reconcile their differences. The army would fill the vacuum—temporarily, as it did not intend to take over. He would make an announcement on the radio at 8.30 p.m. It was already after 8 o'clock.

Although taken by surprise, Dayal recovered quickly and warned Mobutu of the danger of the army entering politics. But Mobutu insisted that his action was only intended to provide time for the leaders to reach an agreement; it would not be a military coup. I was no less surprised than Dayal; the two of us had discussed the chances of a military coup, knowing how intensely the Western embassies were wooing Mobutu. Mobutu and I had spent many evenings discussing the army's role in a newly-independent country and the pitfalls of military rule. He had given me the impression of being a true patriot who was more than a little bewildered by the rapidity of independence and the heavy responsibilities thrust upon him. He was politically sensitive: following a stint as a civilian clerk in the army, he had continued his education and become a journalist. He had joined Lumumba before independence and held him in great regard. Although Dayal was more sceptical, I was prepared to believe Mobutu when he claimed that he did not intend to assume power for himself, at least not at that time.

Dayal looked at me for a response, but it was clearly a political affair and therefore not for me to react on this occasion. With dignity, and politely yet firmly, Dayal advised Mobutu that at times of crisis a commander should be at his command post, and it was best for him to do likewise. Extremely embarrassed at having a military coup in the offing and its leader actually in his office, Dayal hurried Mobutu to the elevator and bade him farewell. We returned to Dayal's room to hear our recent visitor make his announcement—which, however, had apparently been taped in advance. We worked late sending cables to Hammarskjöld and considered the consequences.

Mobutu could rely on the loyalty of some troops from Equateur province, where he came from, but otherwise he had little influence over the ANC. Already several days ago, he had moved with his family into a safe house next to General Kettani. Within a few days of his coup he requested from Dayal an apartment in the Royal for the safety of himself and his family, and was reluctantly provided with it. As ONUC had anticipated, Mobutu's coup was no cure for the ills of the Congo and only further exacerbated them.

In spite of the dramatic developments and changes at the level of UN leadership, I had kept up a steady round of consultations with the Force staff and made myself available to provide advice and direction. There were three rivals for power in Leopoldville—Kasavubu, Lumumba and Mobutu—and in addition Gizenga had raised Lumumba's flag at Stanleyville, Kalonji ruled in Bakwanga, and Tshombe was engaged in consolidating his power in Katanga. Faced with these developments, it was important that I review the mission of the ONUC forces and prepare them for the anticipated tasks.

The operations of the Force were in compliance with the general principles set by the Secretary-General and authorised by the Security Council (S/4387 of 14 July 1960). The principles were based on the experience gained through previous peacekeeping operations and in response to the unique needs of the Congo situation (S/4389). Hammarskjöld first based the reasons for United Nations intervention in the Congo on the explicit request of the Congolese government, whose lack of control over the instruments for the maintenance of law and order 'created a situation which through its consequences represented a threat to peace and security' (S/4389, para 5). The UN was to assume a responsibility belonging to the national authorities, but ONUC was to remain impartial in internal conflicts and under UN command (S/4389, para 7). The UN and the Congolese government would later sign an agreement that constituted another of the basic principles promulgated by the Secretary-General in future peacekeeping operations; this guaranteed the UN troops freedom of movement within their area of operations and all facilities they needed for access to that area in order to accomplish their task successfully. This agreement instituted a policy of 'good faith' regarding the purpose of the Force within the Congolese territory. The UN was also to be guided by this policy of 'good faith' in the interpretation of the purposes of the force (S/4389, add. 5).

When considering the composition of the Force, Hammarskjöld took into account the views of the host government. However, following past experience, countries with special interest in the situation and the permanent members of the Security Council were excluded from the list of participants. Military assistance should come mainly from sister nations in Africa, which quickly demonstrated their willingness to help. Hammarskjöld appealed to the Council's permanent members and other Western states for supplies, specialist personnel and aid in the airlifting of troops and materials. He turned to neutral countries, Ireland and Sweden, to provide contingents including infantry, logistical and technical personnel, and air and ground crews; and Switzerland, whose laws did not permit the use of its troops outside the home territory, to provide personnel to assist in training the ANC. India and Pakistan had already provided logistics units and Canada the air transport unit and army signals regiment.

The ever-expanding requirements in the Congo led the Secretary-General to seek additional troops. Hammarskjöld asked the Socialist and Asian countries to provide military units and Latin American states to provide air crews. The East European states expressed their willingness to assist, but only under the proviso of Article 43 of the Charter.[5] Yugoslavia, which had provided troops for UNEF since it began, agreed to supply air crews for transport aircraft.

At ONUC headquarters the organisation of the Force was proceeding with vigour. Regardless of the negative views of Von Horn, Olver and later Habib Ahmed, a Pakistani, the new CAO built with Madan an administrative and logistical machinery that I thought was a remarkable achievement given the circumstances. To appreciate the size of the task, one has only to consider the vastness of the Congo and its sparse lines of communication, the climate, the diminishing local resources and the diversity of the troops in the Force. While every contingent had an important role to play in building this organisation, the main burden fell on the logistics units provided by India, Pakistan and the Nordic countries. The Indian and Pakistani staff, with the help of the UN administration in the Congo and New York, supplied the leadership. My expectations in relying on such arrangements were more than justified because from the available and acceptable countries able to provide contingents, only India and Pakistan had the logistics personnel and facilities available to meet our needs in the Congo.

The organisation of the ONUC Air Transport Unit offered another challenge. Luckily, Air Commodore Fred Carpenter, commanding officer of the Canadian Air Transport, who had flown the Canadian signals and other personnel into the Congo, was lent by his government as Air Adviser. He took the first steps in organising an air headquarters to control military aircraft that were chartered from Sabena and other companies outside the Congo; these took their instructions from the Air Staff. The US Military Air Transport Service had established an advance headquarters at N'Djili, and they required co-operation and support. Carpenter assumed all these functions and performed a great service to ONUC during the difficult early days of its build-up.

Bill Carr succeeded Carpenter and took over the organisation of the air transport just as the member states had begun to respond to the Secretary-General's requests for air personnel. The UN air base was established at N'Dola (not to be confused with the town of the same name on the Copperbelt) close to N'Djili. Some of the countries had only provided flying personnel, and therefore the ground crew for maintenance, loading and air control were a precious asset. The available local facilities were stretched to the limit within a few days of the ONUC operation beginning. The diversity of the available ground technicians made supervision difficult, yet no risks were acceptable where the flying fitness of the aircraft was concerned. Carr put together a remarkably efficient air unit with a high safety record.

I considered the building up of the administration of ONUC an essential prerequisite for good operations, and Ahmed, Madan and Carr were free to see me or call for me at any time. Luckily we did not have to work all the time, and like any good organisers they could arrange good parties at which we could relax and have some fun. Carr and some of his staff shared a house which had a pool, and his Sunday lunches became notable social events. Madan kept up socially with the civilian and military personnel of ONUC in Leopoldville and took care of visitors. He also enjoyed good relations with the diplomatic corps and Congolese officials. At his periodic parties one could appreciate the variety of his associates and friends, usually heavily weighted in favour of beautiful women.

While the situation in Leopoldville greatly concerned us, we could hardly ignore developments around the country. The events in Oriental, Kivu, Kasai and Katanga provinces caused us alarm, whereas Equateur province had remained calm. The Liberian battalion was the first to enter that province and set up its headquarters at Libenge on the northern side of the Congo river. Libenge was an important economic centre, as well as the centre for Congolese refugees to escape to Congo-Brazzaville. The Belgian troops had left immediately after the arrival of the Liberians and soon thereafter the units established posts at Gamena, Banzyville, Bosobolo and Zongo. The Moroccans were responsible for the province south of the river with their headquarters at Coquilhatville. The situation in Kasai required more troops, and the Liberians were moved there, being replaced in North Equateur by the Egyptian parachute battalion which had arrived earlier in Leopoldville. As the situation in the Congo improved parallel to the arrival of ONUC, the movement of refugees diminished, obviating the need to monitor their movement. Therefore, the Egyptian battalion headquarters was moved to Lisala with a detachment at Bumba.

Both sides of the Congo river were calm until the ANC at Coquilhatville heard of payments being made to the ANC at Leopoldville and mutinied, demanding pay and a bonus. This was followed by a mutiny of the police and raids by the soldiers on the post office in the vain hope of finding money there. Prompt action by the Moroccans brought the situation under control.

In Oriental province, following the removal of Lumumba, his deputy Antoine Gizenga had escaped to Stanleyville about the middle of September. His arrival triggered off a struggle for supremacy within the ANC, between pro-Mobutu elements and those who continued to profess loyalty to Lumumba and had the backing of Gizenga. The outcome of this struggle remained uncertain for a few days until Gizenga gained more support and established firm control over the ANC with the help of General Lundula. As was the case elsewhere, the ANC soldiers had received no pay and here too they looted and marauded at will. First, from a humanitarian point of view, to protect the civil population from the marauding soldiers and, secondly, to prevent further deterioration of the ANC's morale, the UN agreed on the recommendation of the ONUC Chief of Staff, General Iyassou, to pay 370,000 dollars to the troops, just as it had done in Leopoldville. The payment was made subject to good behaviour by the Congolese troops.

In forwarding Iyassou's recommendation to Hammarskjöld, Dayal and I were only too well aware of the political concerns of some of the member-states. When ONUC obtained Hammarskjöld's permission to pay the ANC at Leopoldville, states sympathetic to Lumumba implied in their comments that these payments had strengthened Mobutu's hand, thus enabling him to carry out his coup against Lumumba. According to a telegram sent by Hammarskjöld to Dayal, even Nehru had misgivings over this payment, which were shared by Nkrumah and Nasser.[6] Hammarskjöld had asked for a report from the Force Commander since his deputy Kettani was involved, and in his report Von Horn stated that although a payment of 1 million dollars had been authorised the ANC had only accepted 100,000 dollars. The purpose of the UN command was to persuade the ANC soldiers to appear for training and thus to keep them off the streets. Who had paid the rest to make up the dues to the ANC in Leopoldville remained a mystery to us. It was rumoured that the Belgian advisers told Mobutu not to accept any more funds from the UN, because the Belgian government had already compensated its departing nationals, and that Mobutu had been paid by the mining interests; also that he was being paid by the CIA. While we never did find out the identity of the donor, I felt certain then, as I have since, that the money paid to the ANC, other than the open UN payment, was intended to influence the Congolese troops to further that donor's interests.

The collapse of the Congolese administration after independence left a trail of murder and looting in Kasai province. Whereas the ANC had mutinied and gone on a rampage in Luluabourg, the ancient hatred between the Luluas and Balubas flared up again, resulting in some of the worst tribal clashes in the recent history of Africa. The first available troops the Tunisian brigade which had started to arrive in Leopoldville - were sent by ONUC to Kasai to restore law and order. Led by Colonel Lasmar, who was among the best of their officers, the Tunisians began moving into Luluabourg on 22 July; they persuaded the ANC to turn over their weapons for custody in their camps, and brought an end to the lawlessness in the city within a few days of their arrival.

The existing animosity between the Luluas and Balubas had been further fuelled by the political machinations of the Belgians: they provided political and military support to Kalonji, the Baluba leader, thus helping him to form the so-called Independent Mining State of South Kasai. Belgian interests in the diamond mines in Bakwanga were the motivating factors behind these moves. Savage tribal warfare had erupted in Tshikapa, the seat of the diamond mining company Forminière. Lasmar moved an infantry company to this town, evacuated the sick and wounded from the hospital, and arranged to relieve the Belgian troops for their immediate departure. At the same time he deployed his troops in the key provincial towns to restore law and order.

One of the foremost tasks facing the UN troops in Kasai was restoring rail communications, which were vital for the resumption of economic activity. UN troops established guards at all key points and provided escorts for trains, enabling the railways to start operation on the Port Francqui-Katanga line. Meanwhile, encouraged by the calm which the UN had restored, the Balubas entered into an alliance with the Bashiokas and Bampendes, while the Luluas continued to dominate the provincial assembly, where they were in the majority. These tribal political alliances soon led to the creation of the Mining State of South Kasai. Kalonji later declared himself a king.

The severity of inter-tribal fighting created a serious problem for the UN troops, whose role was to intervene with its presence and end internecine fighting or lawlessness by the ANC or mobs. Our troops, of course, were authorised to use force only in self-defence and no more than the minimum required. Indeed, most contingents were reluctant to use any force at all if they could avoid it because they understood the circumstances of the Congolese. The fact that the ANC was without effective leaders and that the political leaders were inexperienced and had strong tribal affiliations was much too obvious for even the simplest of the soldiers to fail to understand. Besides, UN troops were strongly motivated by their officers in the important role of pacification of the country and no one wished to become involved in a fire-fight with Congolese civilians or military. The UN had no enemies and was in the Congo to assist the Congolese, not to fight them. It had to assist in the restoration of law and order, help the ANC to assume its responsibilities and then get out as soon as it could. The UN's determination not to use force, contrary to what the Congolese had experienced with their recent Belgian masters, was seen as weakness, and it was not long before the Congolese began to show a lack of respect for the UN troops. When the latter acted firmly the Congolese opened fire, wounding a number of Tunisians and other UN personnel.

I visited the northern provinces and Luluabourg, and had a particularly lengthy discussion with Lasmar on this subject since he had by this time taken the most casualties. In Kasai the presence of the UN troops had not entirely prevented tribal killings, pillaging and other barbarities; these could only be prevented by vigorous action which would in turn expose the UN troops to Congolese fire and result in casualties on our side. The tragic fact was that we were operating in a country where moral values tended to be misconstrued to suit particular motives. The UN troops carried the responsibility of ensuring the security of life and property for *all* inhabitants, and such a conception could never be understood by the Congolese, who invariably accused the UN troops of siding with their enemies. Inevitably, this led to clashes and to the UN suffering casualties. In time, we were to learn that the Congolese were not alone in their misconception of the role of the UN troops because many external interests who considered themselves superior to the Congolese in their human and moral concerns also expected the UN troops to act in support of their self-serving interests.

Since my days in Gaza I had remained convinced that the UN guidelines in the exercise of the right of self-defence were the best for UN peacekeeping forces. However, I remained equally convinced that the usefulness of organised military units in peacekeeping required them to act as armed military units in the face of harassment, including the use of force against them. Therefore, peacekeeping forces had to defend their posts, their personnel and their equipment and have the freedom to move to enable them to carry out their tasks. However, the exercise of the right of self-defence had to be controlled and kept at a minimum level, and when this was not enough, diplomatic and military contacts would have to be established to end the clash. In the early days of our operations in the Congo, Hammarskjöld and Bunche often heard me express my views on the subject but had not yet entirely given their consent. Dayal, with his vast experience in dealing with rioting and lawlessness, was more understanding but asked me to interpret the guidelines within Hammarskjöld's view that great restraint had to be used by UN troops in exercising the right of self-defence. I gathered that Lasmar had similar instructions from his government, because he kept repeating that Tunisians were not in the Congo to fight. Yet he remained unhappy with the UN's inability to minimise risks involved for his troops.

Lasmar's task was not made any easier when in mid-August, on Lumumba's insistence, weapons were restored to the ANC in Luluabourg.

In reaction, Kalonji announced the formation of a South Kasai army under Major Crèvecoeur, a former Force Publique officer from Belgium. The ANC units sent by Lumumba had joined those at Luluabourg in an attempt to invade the Mining State and Katanga. Without any form of logistical support or any money, these troops merely added more turmoil to the existing chaos brought about by tribal warfare. They stole food, pillaged, raped and killed. Most of the ANC were too busy ensuring their own survival at the cost of the local population and never crossed the Kasai provincial border, but with their withdrawal from the frontier area the Kalonji forces saw their opportunity and began to expand their area of control, causing more fighting. At Leopoldville we decided to reinforce the Tunisian brigade with the Liberian battalion. The Liberians took up duty along the railway line, enabling the Tunisians to move more troops to cope with the growing threat from Kalonji's forces.

After the arrival of the Irish battalion in Kivu province early in August, the situation there was brought under control. The move of Stanleyville ANC troops through the province led to some clashes which were effectively controlled by the UN Liaison Group established under the colourful Colonel Mollesward. He was a Swedish version of Colonel Blimp, rotund, short and monocled. But he had a lot of UN observer experience, was fearless as well as charming, and had been given responsibilities relating to North Katanga about which we shall say more later.

In anticipation of an invasion of Katanga by the ANC, our troops in the province, who were posted at all important population centres, were redeployed to block entry into Katanga from Kivu and Kasai; also, the flying of all aircraft other than the UN's was banned. To keep the frontier under surveillance, a UN observer group was formed under Mollesward with headquarters at Elisabethville, and he established four field stations to cover the main entry points into Katanga. Tshombe's Belgian advisers were not to be outdone, and moved a gendarmerie unit to Bukavu. The gendarmes then attempted to arrest some local political opponents of Tshombe, and trouble began. Clashes broke out in Bukavu and there were incidents in the Luena-Bukama area. These were brought under control by the UN troops, and some 800 refugees from Bukama were returned to their homes.

At Manono it was the Europeans who were being harassed by the Baluba, and the second Irish battalion, which on its arrival had been located at Albertville and had secured the airport, was asked to assist in their evacuation. Reinforcements from the Swedish battalion at Elisabethville were flown to Manono and the Europeans were evacuated in the same planes to Albertville and then by steamer across Lake Tanganyika and beyond. Some 1,000 Baluba gathered at Albertville and demanded that some of the Europeans be handed over to them. The Irish troops had a strong position around the airport and while they held their ground firmly, their commander parleyed with the Balubas. Finally the Europeans were allowed to depart.

The Force headquarters staff, its area commands and sectors, the logistics and air transport were working well. And I could say that I had helped Dayal to deal with the complex political and security situation.

NOTES

1. He had been Deputy Supreme Commander, South East Asia Command, under Lord Louis Mountbatten in the Second World War.
2. Colonial name for the army commander's residence.
3. Brian Urquhart, *Hammarskjöld* (New York: Harper & Row, 1972), p. 441.
4. Ibid., p. 446.
5. All members of the United Nations, in order to contribute to the maintenance of international peace and security, undertake to make available to the Security Council, on its call and in accordance with a special agreement or agreements, armed forces, assistance, and facilities, including rights of passage, necessary for the maintaining of international peace and security.
   - Such agreement or agreements shall govern the numbers and types of forces, their degree of readiness and general location, and the nature of the facilities and assistance to be provided.
   - The agreement or agreements shall be negotiated as soon as possible on the initiative of the Security Council. They shall be concluded between the Security Council and Members or between the Security Council and groups of Members and shall be subject to ratification by the signatory states in accordance with their respective constitutional processes.
6. Rajeshwar Dayal, *Mission for Hammarskjöld: The Congo Crisis* (Princeton University Press, 1976), p. 99.

6

WITH DAYAL IN LEOPOLDVILLE

Mobutu's declared coup further exacerbated the already confused political leadership crisis in the Congo. This and the controversy over the role of ONUC in closing the airports and the radio station in Leopoldville were the dominant issues when Dayal assumed his responsibilities as the UN Secretary-General's Special Representative. Although Dayal had reopened the airports and the radio station, Cordier's past actions, in spite of being intended to facilitate the maintenance of law and order, had made ONUC's role controversial and impaired its acceptability. ONUC dealt carefully with Kasavubu and Lumumba, who were both clamouring for recognition by the world organisation. But now the Army Chief of Staff had joined in the fray. This was not an entirely unexpected move by the second most senior officer of the ANC because a rumour that he was likely to do so had circulated in the diplomatic community for some days beforehand. I, for one, was incredulous that even if the mild-mannered, scholarly-looking Mobutu, who talked like Hamlet about his country's political crisis, was serious about what he had declared he would do, he could possibly think of using such a rabble as the ANC, which had been on the rampage ever since independence, as his power-base for governing the country.

In spite of the august position he had assumed for himself, Mobutu continued to visit the ONUC offices to call on Dayal and the military staff or to see me. He remained close to Kettani, who kept a paternal vigil; he and his family remained under the protection of the UN's Moroccan troops. He met his Belgian advisers at the ANC offices and kept his usual diplomatic contacts. Although I sensed that much was going on of which the UN was unaware, we could only base our judgment on available valid information and what we could learn as a result of our overt inquiries. Some diplomats, especially friends of Lumumba, warned us of the manoeuvres by the Belgians, Western intelligence agencies and the military attachés at the American, British and French embassies, but they were unable to support their contentions from any reliable source. While we could not ignore such possibilities, we could hardly base our actions on their information in coping with the crisis before us.

I had come to know Joseph Mobutu well. We had met almost daily, and Dayal, Kettani and the ONUC military staff also saw him frequently. Dayal spoke French, but although I had studied it, I could not converse and needed an interpreter. Mobutu often came to my apartment in the Royal and later to a house near the river to which I had moved. Sometimes he brought his wife, who only spoke Lingala, and his daughter on whom he doted. I had little difficulty in establishing a comfortable personal relationship and like my other colleagues at ONUC I tried to impress on him the importance of sustaining a constitutional government in the Congo and the important role of the army within such a framework. Kettani had regaled him with his views on the ills of military takeovers in the Arab world, and I had talked about the 'banana republics' and military dictatorships in South America. Apparently other influences prevailed. However, I believed that his intervention had been patriotically motivated because there appeared no other way of resolving the conflict between Kasavubu and Lumumba. At this stage I was also convinced that he only intended the ANC to take over for a limited time. Dayal did not entirely accept my point of view and so Kettani, Iyassou and I tried all the harder to hold Mobutu to his promise that he would hand over power to a civilian government as soon as the two political leaders could settle their differences.

Major B.M. Ghorpade of the Indian Armoured Corps was the deputy Chief Liaison Officer, ONUC, the Chief being Brigadier Otu of Ghana. Ghorpade was a French interpreter and ONUC relied on him for dealing with the ANC. Of princely origins, he had a style of dealing with the Congolese that had gained him their confidence. I had instructed him to stay close to Mobutu and report on the goings on.

Shortly after Mobutu's declared coup Ghorpade spent a long evening with him, and Mobutu asked him to convey to the UN his personal views on the current political crisis. He said that he intended to stand by his decision to maintain strict neutrality in relation to the crisis. The ANC was reluctant to pursue fratricidal warfare on the Katanga front and he had ordered a ceasefire, notably in Bakwanga. But because Katanga and the Kalonjists were not aware of the change, they had continued fighting. He asked the UN to persuade Tshombe and Kalonji to order a cessation of hostilities against the ANC; he also sought the UN's good offices in settling the matter of the ANC's food and finances. He assured us that any assistance provided by the UN would not be used against secessionist elements.

Ian Berendsen in Elisabethville and Gustave Duran, our admirable political officer in Kasai, were advised to convey Mobutu's ceasefire pledge to both Tshombe and Kalonji. Similar instructions were sent through Force headquarters to UN troops in North Katanga, Oriental and Kasai to get ANC units and rival forces to end the fighting. Also, the Force Commander and Kettani were instructed to assist in the preparation of ANC rolls to make it easier to issue food and pay.

On 15 September Lumumba, while trying to rally the support of the ANC troops at Camp Leopold, was attacked by Baluba soldiers who were angered by the massacre of their people in South Kasai by ANC troops whom he had sent there to end the secession of Bakwanga. Earlier that morning Mobutu had called a meeting of the officers and men in the camp to explain his actions. Lumumba had joined in and addressed the meeting, but the Baluba soldiers became increasingly hostile and threatening, finally forcing Lumumba to seek shelter in the Ghana officers' mess nearby. Colonel Joseph Ankrah, the Ghana Brigade commander, immediately reinforced his guard and sought Dayal's help to stave off an attack by the Baluba soldiers on the mess. Dayal requested Kasavubu to persuade the Balubas to return to their barracks, but Kasavubu declined to help as he had already approved the issuing of warrants for Lumumba's arrest.

Accompanied by Mitra, I joined Ankrah at the mess. Lumumba was in a room surrounded by hostile Baluba soldiers who were shouting at him, kicking and slapping him, and tugging at his clothes and his hair. This was in spite of the ring of Ghanaian soldiers who were doing their best to protect him using their bodies as shields to keep the Balubas from tearing him apart.

Ankrah told us that earlier he had been shuttling between Lumumba and Mobutu, who had remained in the ANC camp, to reach an agreement that would calm the situation. Lumumba agreed to Mobutu's conditions for allowing him to meet Kasavubu and Ileo, but this did not satisfy the soldiers. As word spread of Lumumba's presence in the Ghana officers' mess, more ANC soldiers arrived there from their camps in the city. Ankrah had his troops ready to meet a possible assault, but he rightly wished to avoid such a situation. He needed help, so Mitra phoned the operations room to have the UN standby troops put on alert, and I called for more UN security officers to reinforce Sergeant Victor Noble, who usually accompanied me alone on my visits to the Congo, and had become engaged in keeping the anti-Lumumba ANC away from the Prime Minister. Late in the afternoon, Ankrah and I decided to send an urgent radio message to the Ghanaian guard commander at the President's house to inform Dayal, who was there seeing Kasavubu, that the situation was critical.

Dayal arrived at the mess within an hour and told us that Kasavubu had prevaricated to the end. Ankrah briefed him on the situation in the mess and on the deployment of his troops. Despite the pressures of the day, Ankrah was calm and had kept his usual dignity, concluding quietly: 'Mr Dayal, we have to get Lumumba out quickly, otherwise fighting is going to start at any minute and we will have a bloody mess on our hands.' Standing tall among us, Dayal was puffing on his pipe as he listened to Ankrah. After thinking for a moment he replied, 'All right, take me to him.'

Ankrah led the way. Noble and another security officer had managed to gain control of the door leading to the room where Lumumba was being held. The two then stood before the crowd of angry soldiers, containing them by their sheer will. An opening was made for us to pass through. Noble let us in and as we made our way past the Congolese solders, Lumumba came forward to greet Dayal, warmly thanking him for coming. Dayal was a skillful diplomat with great charm, yet when he concentrated on a problem his powerful eyes and hawklike nose made him appear formidable. As he shook Lumumba's hand he turned round and gave what I called the 'Dayal look'; he held everyone's attention. On that occasion I witnessed another quality in Dayal which he had obviously acquired during his long service in the distinguished Indian Civil Service to which he had belonged before India's independence. As a magistrate and judge and later as a senior administrator, he had dealt with riots and lawlessness. I was glad he was with us at this critical moment. The situation demanded personal courage and toughness, but also a sharp mind and decisiveness. Dayal demonstrated them all. He sat down and proceeded to extract promises from Lumumba that he felt would be of help in dealing with the constitutional crisis. These he was able to obtain, but as events were to prove, the initiative had already passed out of Lumumba's hands —something that neither Lumumba nor Dayal knew then.[1] Dayal had nearly concluded his talk with Lumumba when Ambassador Andrew Djin of Ghana arrived. Djin immediately began to harangue the Ghanaian officers for holding Lumumba in the mess and for failing to provide him with adequate security. Suddenly Lumumba got up and picking up the same refrain began to berate Ankrah, claiming that he had come to the mess to make a telephone call but instead had been forcibly detained.

This proved too much for Ankrah to bear. He had had no food or drink all day and was both physically and mentally fatigued with the responsibility of saving Lumumba's life, and now Lumumba had turned on him. He shouted at Lumumba, calling him a rat, and threatened to leave at once with his Ghanaians. Djin had continued shouting all this time. Dayal finally put an end to the drama by telling Djin that the accusations against Ankrah were unfair and that Ankrah and his men, along with his UN colleagues, had gone to great personal risk to save Lumumba. He ordered Djin to leave the room immediately: if he did not comply, Dayal would leave with the UN Ghanaian troops and leave Djin to cope with Lumumba. At this Lumumba embraced Dayal, thanking him profusely and complimenting Ankrah on what he had done. While Ankrah still shook with rage, the Ghanaians hung their heads at Lumumba's shameful turn-around.

When Djin realised that Dayal meant what he had said, he withdrew. Dayal now turned to us and said, 'Let us get Lumumba out of here quickly.' We agreed on a plan in which he and the rest of the UN party would leave by the front door, drawing the attention of the Balubas, while Ankrah would remove Lumumba by the back door. The ruse worked and Lumumba went into hiding for a few days, probably at the Ghanaian embassy which was heavily guarded by our Ghanaian contingent.

The day was not to end without further excitement. Late that night the Soviet ambassador, Yakovliev, called on Dayal to inform him that the Congolese President had requested him to close his embassy within twenty-four hours and that thereafter diplomatic immunities would be withdrawn. Yakovliev asked for an aircraft to bring Soviet aid personnel from Stanleyville, which Dayal agreed to provide the following morning. When asked what was to become of the Soviet transport aircraft on loan to the Congolese, the ambassador said that they were to be withdrawn. At Dayal's request, he agreed to leave all the medical supplies being used for the aid programme run by their doctors. These supplies were turned over to the Ethiopian troops for their hospital in Stanleyville where, in addition to attending to their own troops, they cared for the civilian population.

In New York, criticism of ONUC had intensified. Many African and Asian countries were shocked and angry at its failure to respond when Mobutu carried out his coup. Members of the Western group had remained silent. The closing down of the Soviet and other East European embassies in the Congo added more weight to the existing view that the Western states had had a hand in encouraging Kasavubu and Mobutu to bring this about. V. A. Zorin had replaced Kuznetsov as the Soviet Permanent Representative to the UN, and during the debate in the Security Council that began on 9 September he was harshly critical of the UN and made scurrilous attacks on Hammarskjöld.

When it became clear that the Council could not act, a special session of the General Assembly became unavoidable. This was scheduled to occur immediately before the 15th General Assembly session that was due to open in the third week of September, and many important world leaders were expected to arrive in time to take part. With a major commitment by

India to ONUC, Nehru had announced his participation. He had already written to Hammarskjöld questioning the UN's handling of the Congo operations and asking what ONUC was doing if the constitutional process could be so easily subverted. Hammarskjöld asked Dayal for his comments, which he could use in his reply to Nehru. Dayal felt that it was essential for Nehru to be informed of the realities of the Congo situation. He expected Krishna Menon, the vituperative Indian Defence Minister and frequent leader of Indian delegations to the UN General Assembly and other international events, to attend the special session, and therefore it was important for Nehru to be briefed so that he could give Menon his instructions in time. Hammarskjöld was so pleased with the lucidity of the report that he wanted to issue it, with some modifications, to the UN. Dayal demurred and discussed the matter with me. It was an honest statement of the facts and put the blame squarely where it belonged, namely on the Congolese leaders. However, we agreed that any published report would have to use restraint in describing the role of the Congolese leaders, and therefore a UN-style report was released instead.

Dayal's first report as Special Representative of the Secretary-General to the Congo was issued on 20 September [2] in time for the opening of the special assembly. In spite of its restraint, the Congolese leaders did not like it, and the champions of Kasavubu and Mobutu found it equally distasteful in that it exposed their heroes. The report covered all important aspects of ONUC's operations from its inception. It briefly described the circumstances that led to the establishment of the operation, its difficulties and its achievements. An account was given of the political instability in the Congo and the problems of non-intervention by the UN. Dayal wrote: 'This [the UN's] extensive programme, viewed against the background of a comparative absence of any governmental organisation, bulks even larger. This situation imposes on the United Nations operation an increasingly grave responsibility to weigh its every action, and to impose on itself the most careful restraint in order to ensure that its presence promotes, and does not retard, the political development and independence of a new state.'[3] He re-stated the Security Council directive[4] that ONUC should not in any way interfere in the internal affairs of the Congo. It was a difficult task to begin with, but it became more complicated when three groups were claiming authority, each wanting to use ONUC to promote its own interests. Using the entry of the UN's troops into Katanga as one important case in point, he drew attention to the mistaken notions of the central government under Lumumba, who first wanted to use the UN's air transport and other resources for the invasion by his troops and later threatened to wrest control of the airports by force and deny them to the UN.

The political crisis that surfaced on 5 September had added new problems of a complex nature. Dayal stated: 'In such a situation ONUC has maintained with scrupulous care an attitude of strict neutrality, avoiding any action which could be interpreted, even remotely, as influencing the political balance.' However, the UN was in the Congo not as a mere observer, but had a heavy responsibility in maintaining law and order and assisting the civil authority. In the absence of such authority it had to decide carefully on its actions so that they would not appear one-sided. In spite of these difficulties ONUC's military and civilian operations had accomplished a great deal, though there was much still to do.

The report concluded: 'There is still time for the Congolese leaders and people to take stock of the situation, to put an end to factional and party strife, to reconcile political and sectional interests and to embark on the path of national unity.' And on the essential character of the mission he gave this summary: 'This mission is in the Congo to help but not to intervene, to advise but not to order, to conciliate but not to take sides.' He urged the political leaders, before it was too late, to make a wise choice. Only then would it be possible for the UN to utilise its resources fully to enable the sovereign republic of the Congo to take its rightful place in the world community as a stable, self-reliant and prosperous state.

At the Royal, we had correctly anticipated the reaction to Dayal's report. It would be lauded by those who had the true interests of the Congo at heart and derided by all the self-servers. The Congo had many true patriots, but they had not yet risen above their tribal or factional loyalties. Mobutu was among the few who could think beyond those limited bounds, but at that time he had only a small constituency of support. He was almost totally dependent on his Western backers who could drop him as quickly as they had taken him up up if he proved unreliable. With the active help of his Belgian advisers—former Force Publique officers who had moved to Brazzaville and were always present in his house—Mobutu started a series of consultations with ANC officers from around the country to solicit their loyalty. In return he assured them regular pay, logistics and other essential services. In time his power-base grew.

While, as anticipated, there was little applause from the Western powers, the members of the UN, and especially of the Congo Advisory Committee, showed tremendous interest in the report, and the need for a further, more comprehensive one had become obvious. The task of preparing such reports had been eased by the addition of a support staff for Dayal to conduct his affairs. Bunche's two political aides, Urquhart and Liu, remined to facilitate the change-over; John McDiarmid, a senior and experienced administrator, was appointed Executive Director to coordinate the military, civilian and administrative branches of ONUC; William Cox, an able legal adviser, remained; and Habib Ahmed, a Pakistani, had already replaced Olver as the Chief Administrative Officer. Sture Linner,

Chief of Civilian Operations, and Von Horn, Force Commander, completed the team. With the exception of the last, the team was a good one, and to make up for the 'lame duck' I was to stay on in the Congo indefinitely. While I enjoyed the excitement of being in action with Dayal and the troops, I realised that the job for which I was brought to the UN was not being attended to as well as it should have been.

I shared an apartment with McDiarmid at the Royal, but was hardly ever there, being constantly on the move visiting troops. I refused to take part in any ceremonial other than turning out the guard at unit headquarters, an age-old tradition which required no diversion of the unit's energies. I insisted on seeing troops at their tasks, basically relying on the commanding officer and the national liaison officer for information, yet maintaining direct communication with the ranks below. I ate with the troops, saw them at work and play, and did what a field commander or a senior-level visitor should do. I only relaxed this rule by sometimes accepting meals in the officers' unit or contingent mess. I knew, from my own experience as a contingent commander in Gaza, the pride with which the officers and the men entertained visitors; regardless of the circumstances such occasions were always turned into national culinary feasts. These functions were also useful because in the relaxed atmosphere of an officers' mess a shared meal created personal bonds between the higher command and the units in the field and I would leave with a better understanding of how the unit operated and what had to be done by higher echelons of command to make its task easier.

When in Leopoldville my routine was to join Dayal in the morning at about 7.30 a.m. He had already read the night cables and dealt with some of them. By 8 o'clock his staff meeting was under way and usually ended within an hour. Depending on what was the most urgent task of the day, Dayal would continue working with those involved in it while the rest would go to their respective branches to brief their staff and issue the day's orders. Now that the military staff had McCarthy and Mitra, one of them would attend and return to the operations room to implement necessary orders and brief Von Horn when he came to the office. I would then see a string of visitors, diplomats, service attachés, contingent liaison officers, Habib or his staff, and the military staff, especially the logistics branch which was determinedly building up its services under Madan's watchful eye.

The welfare staff of the administration had been busy, and organised an institution for meals, drinks and indoor games. We had access to an outdoor swimming pool, riding stables, a golf course and tennis courts. McDiarmid, an outstanding tennis-player, organised several afternoon games with De Angelis and Bovay from the administrative staff and McDiarmid and myself as partners. The several officers' messes kept up their social circuit. Some of us were involved in the diplomatic and official Congolese hospitality. All these social contacts were useful. Von Horn and I kept up our dinners at the zoo restaurant, but less frequently.

Often Dayal would send for me to join him when he was meeting ambassadors or political leaders. There was hardly a discussion which did not have security implications involving the operations of the UN force. Dayal and I talked things over at meals when I joined him and Susheela, his wife, who had arrived in Leopoldville in the last week of November. Besides her great abilities as a hostess, Susheela, brought up in a distinguished industrial-political family, was sophisticated in international affairs. I had met the Dayals first when they were my quests in Gaza in 1958, and became aware then of Susheela's diplomatic acumen and how well the two worked together. Whenever possible we took long walks together. We talked incessantly about current events and the task before us, and thus I understood what was in Dayal's mind in a way that greatly helped me in the task I had to perform, just as I had learned to understand Hammarskjöld and Bunche. Like those two, Dayal took pains to discuss and explain issues so that I might better understand the diplomatic process because my experience in Gaza had been different from what the UN was called on to do in the Congo. For my part, I brought my military experience to their talks, so ensuring that military considerations were part of the decision-making process.

Meanwhile, both Kasavubu and Mobutu were consolidating their respective positions. On 20 September Mobutu declared the installation of a Council of Commissioners made up of university graduates under the presidency of Justin Bomboko, Lumumba's Minister of Foreign Affairs, as a caretaker government till 1 January 1961. Nine days later Kasavubu endorsed the Council. Although the division of responsibility between him and Mobutu was not clear, it seemed that there was an effort to activate a co-ordinated operation, presumably through Belgian advisers whom they shared.

The much-heralded 15th Session of the General Assembly opened on 20 September attended by a galaxy of world leaders. After the customary opening of the Session with a message from Emperor Haile Sellassie of Ethiopia, the US President Eisenhower in his address supported Hammarskjöld's conduct of the Congo operation and called for all possible assistance to the young nation to be channelled through the UN. Tito criticised the colonialists but was moderate about ONUC; Nkrumah strongly supported Lumumba, while refraining from criticism of the Secretary-General. On 23 September, Khrushchev made his notorious speech attacking the colonial powers and Hammarskjöld, and called for the replacement of the Secretary-General by a troika consisting of representatives of East, West and non-aligned nations. In a masterly statement before the General Assembly on 26 September, Hammarskjöld spoke of the importance of the international organisation to the middle-sized and small states. In defence of his own role he said, 'I would rather see that office [the Secretary-General's] break on strict adherence to the principle of independence, impartiality and objectivity than drift on the basis of compromise'. The Assembly rose and gave Hammarskjold a thundering ovation. But the Congo operation remained at the centre of the East-West conflict in spite of efforts by him and many UN member-states to isolate it from that conflict.

At Leopoldville difficult days lay ahead, but less so than what our colleagues faced in New York. As the Special Representative of the Secretary-General in the Congo, Dayal was the field extension of Hammarskjöld's operation and consequently he too was caught up in the storm that raged in New York. His first report had soured some Congolese, as well as other Africans and some West Europeans. As he himself wrote, 'Among the foreign envoys in Leopoldville I happened to know the trio who represented the Western great powers. Clare Timberlake, who presided over the US Embassy, had formerly been Consul General in Bombay... Ian Scott of Britain had belonged to the Indian Civil Service ... The French Ambassador, Charpentier, was a diplomat of skill and finesse ... My expectations, however, were soon to meet disappointment, as the international issues seemed so intricate and the prejudices and pre-dilections of the envoys too ingrained to allow them to relate their activities to the disinterested activities of the United Nations.'[5]

Dayal's daily visitors included an increasing number of diplomats and politicians who tried in every possible way to woo him to their own political views. I too was not spared, and had to take my share of listening to their diatribes. Besides the three Western ambassadors mentioned above and the Ghanaian ambassador, the Egyptian and Indian diplomats were most active. The Indian chargé d'affaires, Attar Rahman, had served in the army, was a keen hunter and had established easy rapport with the UN military just as he had with the diplomatic community. He was junior to Dayal in the Indian foreign service, but he and I were more or less contemporaries.

Taking advantage of the presence of nearly a brigade-sized Indian contingent, I had given its commander, Brigadier Harminder Singh, the additional function as commander, Leopoldville area, with responsibility for the administration and security of the ONUC military staff and the logistics units. These duties gave Brigadier Singh and his Indian succes-sors some additional interesting responsibilities which they appreciated. Thus Rahman had the commander of the Indian troops, several Indian staff officers in ONUC, Dayal and myself to deal with. Only Dayal and I were not part of the Indian chain of command, although both of us were in Indian service on temporary assignment to the UN. After early exchanges, Dayal arranged for Rahman to show him his communications to India to ensure that they were factually accurate, especially with regard to ONUC operations. This and Dayal's special reports gave Nehru an accurate picture of events in the Congo and greatly improved India's ability to engage in constructive dialogue with the UN.

Ambassador Morad Ghaleb of Egypt was a medical doctor by training who had become a confidant of Nasser during the revolution. As a prominent member of the 'Panch Sheela' group of five nations (China, Egypt, India, Indonesia and Yugoslavia), which were the precursors of the Non-Aligned Movement; and as the representative of a powerful Arab and African state which at that time had a contingent in ONUC, he was active in the diplomatic drama being enacted in the Congo. Other Arab diplomats with large contingents, i.e. the Moroccan and Tunisian, kept a lower profile but were available to help ONUC and their own contingents. Because of my association with UNEF, Morad believed that I would be sympathetic towards Egyptian policies and expected my support. Had the Egyptian ambassador understood ONUC's role and the framework within which Dayal and I operated, many of the problems which arose concerning the operations of the Egyptian troops could have been avoided.

While we had to listen patiently to what our visitors had to say, we also had to continue dealing with our many other tasks. The scale of fighting in Kasai and North Katanga was becoming critical, and therefore at ONUC we discussed the possibility of ending the fighting. Dayal and I began to consider my making another visit to the area and what the chances were of my being able to negotiate a ceasefire. In North Katanga the parties involved were the Balubas, supported by the Stanleyville ANC, and the Katanga gendarmerie. In Kasai we had to deal with Kalonji's forces on the one side and the ANC and Lulua tribesmen on the other. The latter situation appeared the easier of the two, and so I began working with the force staff in developing plans and instructions for the Moroccans to arrange a ceasefire. Fighting in North Katanga was more complex. Katangese forces had been moved to the north only after Belgian advisers had assumed their new role. The operation was conducted by them to help Tshombe reassert his authority over an area where the writ of the Balubas prevailed. Thus Dayal's strategy of reducing, if not entirely eliminating, the Belgian advisory factor would facilitate a solution of the problem in North Katanga as well.

The coup against Lumumba had encouraged his political foes and provided new opportunities for them to increase their authority. Thus Tshombe felt that the lack of support for the Balubas from the centre provided an opportunity for him quickly to repress the Baluba dissidence. His forces renewed their efforts to gain greater control over towns and communications, and this led to a new wave of fighting. Sporadic clashes occurred between the Balubas and the gendarmerie involving a considerable loss of life. These clashes took place mainly in the Luena-Bukama region. They were triggered off by the arrival of the gendarmerie platoon at Bukavu on 2 September when it attempted to arrest some local inhabitants and met with opposition. Some 800 Balubas immediately sought refuge with the UN troops, returning to their homes once order was restored.

Because of the involvement of Belgians in support of Tshombe, the Europeans at Manono were being harassed by the Balubas, who were also interfering with the flight operations at Manono airport. An Irish company was already at Manono and was reinforced by more troops from the Swedish battalion at Elisabethville. ONUC evacuated Europeans in its returning aircraft. On 15 September a crowd of 1,000 Balubas demanded that the UN hand over some Belgians to them. ONUC troops refused, and threw a security cordon around the airfield, and after long negotiations persuaded the Balubas to leave.

In spite of the removal of Lumumba's government by the middle of the month, ANC elements ordered by Lumumba to invade Katanga from Kivu had reached the line of the Luika river inside Katanga, and an exchange of fire had occurred. The UN's Mali troops, following the ANC, persuaded them and the Katangese to stop firing. Mollersward arrived on the scene and negotiated a ceasefire and a neutral zone of 30 km. on both sides of the river, which would be free of rival troops and patrolled by ONUC.

Understanding that the invasion of Kasai and Katanga by Lumumba did not have the approval of Kasavubu and Mobutu, Dayal and I, separately and together, directly and indirectly, brought every possible pressure on the two coup leaders to withdraw the ANC from the two provinces. Happily, on 18 September, Mobutu agreed to order an end to the fighting with Katanga, and the next day the ANC received orders to withdraw. We were ready with UN assistance, including aircraft to return the Congolese forces to their permanent camps. On 23 September, Kasavubu ordered the ANC to withdraw from Kasai and asked for UN assistance to transport them, which was readily given. However, the withdrawal created new problems. The ANC had, as usual, not received their rations and pay. Therefore they had resorted to pilfering and violence as they passed through inhabited areas. We had to authorise the issuing of essential rations and some money to keep them under control until they could be removed from the area on assurances that they would return to their permanent bases. The removal of the ANC from Kasai and Katanga brought the civil war to an end.

Dayal and I agreed that the end of fighting between the ANC and

South Kasai-Katanga provided a suitable occasion for me to visit Kalonji and Tshombe to make arrangements that would prevent it recurring. Tshombe was pleased at the developments and accepted that Moller-sward's observers should continue to watch Katanga's borders. The situation in Bakwanga was complex and dangerous. When the ANC had first arrived unexpectedly, they had occupied Bakwanga and, true to their usual style, had massacred many civilians and looted shops and houses. On their departure, the balance of power tilted in favour of Kalonji's volunteers, who did not withdraw and attempted to advance towards Luluabourg. This move had to be blocked by the UN.

Kalonji's forces, which were based on Gandijika, had a total of about 5,000 troops. His officers were Belgians, Rhodesians and South Africans. Initially, he had Belgian Air Force helicopters with their markings painted over; the air crew were probably Belgian servicemen in civilian clothes. I attempted to land at Gandjika, but had to agree to give up the attempt when my crew said that the airfield was not suitable.

The bulk of the Kalonji forces were concentrated along the railway line towards Luluabourg. They were spread from Gandjika to Mwene-Ditu and Luputa and were attempting to group with another column approaching Bakwanga from the south. Our Tunisian brigade had troops deployed to protect the European compound in Bakwanga, the two airfields and the power station. The Liberian battalion was in the Mwene-Ditu-Luputa area.

My meeting with Kalonji went well enough, but he moved little on the question of his white officers and refused to confine his forces to a limited role of police duties. So I flew back to Elisabethville to talk to the Belgian technical mission. Rothschild was away in Brussels and so, accompanied by Ian Berendsen the ONUC representative in Elisabethville, I met the second senior officer and other members of the Belgian mission. I asked the Belgians to use their influence in arranging the withdrawal of their officers and Katanga 'volunteers' from Kalonji's forces and to stop giving logistics aid. Now that the ANC had withdrawn from the so-called Mining State of South Kasai and UN troops were in effective control there, the Belgians agreed to my proposals concerning Kalonji's forces. But they demurred over asking Tshombe to recall his 'volunteers'. I said, 'How about disarming the volunteers and retaining them as police in training?' The Belgians accepted this.

On receiving my report from Elizabethville on the progress of my talks on South Kasai, Dayal cabled Hammarskjöld suggesting action at all possible levels to support my efforts. He was going to take up the question of British 'volunteers' with Scott, the British ambassador.

Kalonji had reached an agreement with Kasavubu and Mobutu to respect the ceasefire in South Kasai, and a no-man's-land controlled by the

UN, was established. Mollersward's team would include one representative each of Kalonji and of Leopoldville. Lastly, Dayal asked Hammarskjöld to continue pressing the Belgian Foreign Minister to co-operate.

By the end of September, after his return from Belgium, Rothschild was behind our effort to keep peace in South Kasai. He said that the technical mission was likely to be withdrawn and return to Brussels, to be replaced by a few advisers. Colonel Gillet, Kalonji's 'Chief of Staff', and Crèvecoeur suggested that the UN assume responsibility for Kalonji's forces because if the remaining three Belgians and one Briton left Kalonji his troops would cause chaos. The UN advised that Kalonji should only use his men for police duties and that our Tunisians would keep a watchful eye.

On 8 October, the Secretary-General requested the Belgian government to withdraw all its military, paramilitary and civilian personnel who had been placed at the disposal of the Congolese government. On the same day he asked Dayal that either he or I should meet Tshombe and personally deliver a letter from him calling for the number of Belgian experts employed by Katanga to be reduced, and to arrange a ceasefire in North Katanga. It was decided that I should be the one to see Tshombe. I had already met him a few times, first when accompanying Hammarskjöld to Katanga to introduce UN troops there and later when concluding arrangements for the organisation of ONUC's Katanga area and the future of the Kamina Belgian military base. Furthermore, as I was responsible for military matters in the Congo and was therefore dealing with the problem of fighting in North Katanga, I had visited the area in this connection too and met the political leaders, including Kalonji.

There was a more sensitive political concern that led to my selection as the negotiator. Both Hammarskjöld and Bunche had run into difficulties with the central government after their visits to Katanga. Dayal wished to avoid this happening again, and was more comfortable to have me visit Tshombe. Already, I had learned to alternate my two hats—as an emissary of the Secretary-General and as his military adviser—to advantage. Since Kasavubu, Mobutu and Lumumba were all interested in ending the fighting in North Katanga for one reason or another, little opposition to my assignment was to be expected from the three who claimed to be the central authority. Nor was any problem expected from Tshombe since a visit from the Secretary-General's representative would only enhance his status. Dayal informed Hammarskjöld that arrangements were in hand to send me to Elisabethville within the next few days.

At first glance my two tasks—delivering Hammarskjöld's letter calling on Tshombe to reduce the number of Belgians employed by his government and negotiating a ceasefire in North Katanga—appeared to differ from each other but they were in fact closely interrelated. The

Katanga gendarmerie and police had Belgian advisers. Hammarskjöld, under the urging of the UN member-states, and Dayal, whose efforts to develop a UN technical assistance programme were thwarted by the Belgian civilians in the Congo, were calling for the removal of Belgians from the central government because they were much more than mere advisers; they were engaged in the day-to-day political events and influencing vital decision-making. Hammarskjöld wanted to reduce, if not eliminate, direct Belgian interference in the daily life of the Congo, and this also applied to Katanga where the Belgian presence was a major obstacle to any attempt at reconciliation between Katanga and the centre.

The effect of Belgian involvement in the fighting in North Katanga became obvious from the brutal manner in which the Katangese security forces dealt with the Balubas; clearly this was something they were allowing, if not encouraging. The Belgians had made their choice of supporting Tshombe and they were therefore opposed to the Balubakat, the political organisation of Balubas in Katanga, who opposed him. Yet another related reason for urging the removal of Belgian security advisers was that they were basing their operations on their past colonial experience when dissent and disorder were dealt with harshly. In contrast to the past, the actions of the Katanga gendarmerie and its Belgian officers were now under the watchful eye of the international diplomatic community and the press, which were no longer prepared to tolerate the violation of international norms.

I decided to deal with the Belgian factor first and then with the fighting in North Katanga. Once I was able to start discussions, other tasks could be taken up as well. The place of our meeting was pre-determined by the fact that Tshombe was the *de facto* leader of Katanga and thus, as the representative of the Secretary-General, I would have to go to him. Not only that, but the negotiations would have to be conducted at his residence; however I hoped that the venue of the meetings could be changed if I invited him for a meal to the residence of the ONUC representative in Elisabethville, a rented Union Minière house.

Tshombe was a sophisticated man. He had entered his father's successful business and married the daughter of one of the traditional rulers of the Luandas, a tribe which had been divided by the colonial powers so that different groups lived in Katanga, Tanganyika, Northern Rhodesia (Zambia) and Angola. Those in Katanga were Tshombe's political power-base, and he enjoyed influence in the neighbouring states through Luandas residing there. Accompanied by Ian Berendsen, who could also assist in interpretation, I decided to pay a courtesy call on Tshombe soon after my arrival. He was flattered and introduced me to his older children. The eldest, a daughter, had finished school and was at the point of deciding on her college education. She was interested in diplomatic training, which led to a good discussion of the comparative benefits of attending regular college first, as Berendsen and I had done, or attending the French Institute of Administration, the cradle of French-speaking administrators and diplomats. Tshombe appreciated the discussion, was relaxed, and shared a few laughs. This augured well.

I had to deal with four centres of authority. First there was Tshombe himself with whom it was possible to negotiate on a fairly reasonable basis, and Munongo, his Minister of the Interior. Secondly, there was Ambassador Rothschild, an able diplomat, whom I had met before. The basic negotiations between the Belgian government and the UN were in the hands of the Secretary-General, but it would be important to have Rothschild's support in dealing with the Katangese and the Belgian security advisers. Then the Katanga gendarmerie and the police would have to be dealt with in two ways: Tshombe would have to be convinced that the actions of the Katanga security forces were doing him more harm than good, and the Belgian officers would have to be convinced that the gendarmerie and police had taken on a responsibility beyond their capacity and that their reprisals were fuelling instead of curbing the tribal conflict. Lastly, the Baluba leaders would have to be persuaded to show more restraint in dealing with the guerrillas, especially the *'jeunesse'* the young gangs. On the basis of past relations between the UN and the Baluba leaders, nothing but full co-operation was expected from them: ONUC had helped to save the lives of many of them, given them protection in Elisabethville, and organised a refugee camp.

After being briefed on recent developments in the area and consulting with Berendsen, Henry Byrne (Commander Katanga Area) and Mollesward (chief of the UN observers in North Katanga), I decided on the steps I would take in the negotiations. It would be necessary to assure Tshombe that a ceasefire agreement in North Katanga was both a UN and a local affair and not intended in any way to influence the overall question of Katanga's relationship with the centre. He had to be convinced that his gendarmerie had fuelled the fighting and that a ceasefire would permit the Katanga civil administraton to resume its functions. Then I had to convince Rothschild that the Belgian and other foreign civilians would be safer under UN protection and offer assistance in their evacuation if that was desired. Finally, the Balubas had to be assured of their security and that they would be humanely treated by the provincial authority.

I decided to see Rothschild first; this was because once I had persuaded him to agree to my approach, I could ask him to help me persuade Tshombe and the Belgian experts, who were former colonial officials. Only the Belgian government could promise their nationals future employment or compensation on being repatriated. Furthermore, only Rothschild could promise Tshombe alternative means of assistance for the future. I was glad to find Rothschild amenable; obviously the Belgians had been persuaded through Hammarskjöld's efforts to co-operate with the UN. Also persuasive was the fact that the Katanga administration—including its security forces now bereft of the pre-independence Belgian chain of command notwithstanding the efforts of a handful of advisers—had proved incapable of coping with the problems. Rothschild virtually admitted that he could not rely on the provincial authority, implying that the Belgians needed the UN to take care of their interests.

Rothschild said that he was withdrawing his mission and leaving immediately. I was invited to his farewell party, and arrived in time to hear him declare that Nehru and Nkrumah considered the presence of the Belgians in Katanga an act of neo-colonialism. He was surprised at this attitude, he said, since India and Ghana both provided examples of close collaboration with the previous rulers. Tshombe, who was present, showed his anger at Belgium's unilateral withdrawal of its mission, and strongly attacked its colonial policy and failure to recognise Katanga as an independent state. I left the reception with the pleasant feeling that the chances of my negotiations succeeding had greatly improved.

Rothschild and I had agreed that I should meet the Belgian military advisers and discuss security issues with them before talking to Tshombe. At this meeting, which Byrne also attended, Tshombe's military adviser Major Guy Weber raised a number of issues, such as the deployment of UN troops, their numbers and role. He asked how we were going to deal with the Baluba 'rebellion'. The UN method of peacekeeping operations was explained to him, but he had difficulty in understanding our system of avoiding the use of force, and did not think it would be possible for the UN to cope with the 'terrorists'. When it became evident that his beliefs, based on experience as a colonial officer, were unchangeable I switched to trying to convince him of our ability to influence the Baluba leaders, many of whom were already under our protection, pointing to the large number of troops available to us in Katanga and our ability to respond to incidents by the use of our air transport. Rothschild clinched the discussion by saying that his government would support the UN's efforts to restore law and order in Katanga, and that it in turn would expect us to meet our responsibilities.

To allow time for Rothschild to see Tshombe and for Tshombe to talk to his military adviser, Berendsen and I used the interval to review what we had done to keep abreast of the situation in North Katanga and, not the least important, to talk with Baluba leaders who were living under UN protection in a camp at Elisabethville. With Berendsen's help I explained to them again and again that our success in persuading Tshombe to agree to a ceasefire would depend on their full co-operation.

We assured them of our continued protection, but they had to persuade their men to stop fighting. It was for the UN to deploy its troops to próvide security in the area. We received their assurances of co-operation, and they asked for our assistance to return to North Katanga, to which we agreed; it would be helpful to us if the leaders returned to establish their authority over the young fighters. I expected opposition from Tshombe to our transporting Baluba leaders to the north and that I would have to allay his misgivings.

I found Tshombe mellowed when I went to see him. He argued on two issues that were central to the question of Katanga's secession, the same issues relating to the role of the UN in the Congo that he had taken up with Bunche and subsequently with Hammarskjöld when they were in Elisabethville. At every available opportunity he had sought clarification on the UN's role in the Congo, namely that ONUC was in the Congo at the invitation of the central government and therefore acting on its behalf. Carrying this point further, Tshombe argued that by its efforts to end the fighting in North Katanga, the UN was interfering in the internal political affairs of the state because the Balubakat was opposed to him and favoured the central government. Tshombe knew the UN's point of view and I concluded that he was taking up these points to reassure himself that there was no change in UN policy on Katanga. When he heard my assurances, it was easy to persuade him to go on to the arrangements for the ceasefire. He agreed that I should work out the details with his advisers and return to him with our plans.

While the fighting in North Katanga was caused by the political rivalry between the Luandas and the Balubas, the antagonism between the Balubakat and the gendarmerie had grown during the past few weeks because of the harsh and brutal measures the gendarmerie had adopted in repressing lawlessness. The locals retaliated by adopting almost identical measures against the gendarmerie. It was therefore essential to separate the two parties and introduce a third party between them with the ability to maintain order. The UN was suitable for such a role, but it had to gain the confidence not only of Tshombe but also of the Belgians. At least three, if not four, infantry battalions would be needed to take responsibility for North Katanga. Byrne, with his headquarters in Elisabethville, had about the same number of troops deployed in the south: they had an extremely difficult task and had also to maintain liaison with the Katanga gendarmerie and security forces at the capital of the province, which considered itself an independent state. Byrne was also in command of the troops in Kivu. All these troops numbered about 8,000 covering an area about 1,000 miles from north to south and 800 miles from east to west. The need to reorganise the command structure of ONUC troops in Katanga and Kivu became obvious to me.

After a meeting with Byrne and other unit commanders, I decided to separate Kivu and place it under a Nigerian battalion which had recently arrived in the Congo. The Irish unit which it relieved was sent to North Katanga. Thus there would be two Irish units in the north, and it was best for them to be commanded by Byrne; I arranged for him to move his tactical headquarters to Albertville to be closer to the area of conflict. I appointed Colonel Juhlin, the commanding officer of the Swedish battalion, to be Deputy Commander Katanga Area, with responsibility for rear headquarters (logistics and administrative support for Katanga) and troops in the South Katanga sector.

The North Katanga sector included the Pweto-Mitwaba road; the Mitwaba-Mukulakulu road, running across the Parc National de l'Upemba; the Mukulakulu-Milamboo road (by the Lubudi river); then the North and Northwest as far as the Katanga-Kasai border, including Kaniama but excluding Kamina. To facilitate control I subdivided this area into two neutral zones. Of these Zone A was to include Kabalo, Kyunzu and the Nyunzu-Niemba-Manono road but to exclude Kangolo in the north, Albertville and Pweto in the east, Mitwaba and Malemba-Nukulu in the south, and Kabongo and Kaniama in the west. Zone B was to include Kanondo-Dianda-Bukama-Luena, but exclude Lubudi.

Having first reorganised the ONUC troops in the area, I was able to bring Tshombe's Belgian security advisers into our discussions. Although they were reluctant, I insisted that the gendarmerie be neutral in the two neutral zones, but I agreed that they could remain in their camps. This made the Belgian officers feel easier; they were now convinced that the UN was not against them. I also agreed to the gendarmerie remaining responsibile for areas outside the neutral zones provided they did not act aggressively, and that the neutral zones should return to local administrative authority as soon as conditions improved.

Armed with a plan agreed to by both the Belgian advisers and the UN, I went back to see Tshombe on 18 October and he readily accepted it. It was time to celebrate, and Katanga Area headquarters arranged a worthy meal attended by Tshombe and his personal advisers. I wondered if Tshombe had as much to be happy about as we did in the UN because, whether he realised it or not, the agreement was a major concession on his part. The UN had succeeded in establishing that his secessionist government had failed to establish control over much of the north, in spite of Belgian aid; that the UN was the best third party to assist in restoring law and order; and that the UN was carrying out its task impartially. Since we had assumed responsibility in the north, only the southern part of Katanga now remained under Tshombe, while ONUC was assisting the rest of Katanga and the other provinces to maintain administrative authority and thus bring the newly-independent Congolese state under symbolic unitary control. Not the least important aspect of agreement was that with it the curtain had at last fallen on Belgian attempts to maintain some form of residual colonial control over mineral-rich Katanga.

While I was engaged in negotiating a ceasefire agreement with Tshombe, Mobutu arrived in Elisabethville, reportedly seeking Tshombe's support for his regime. After they had met, Mobutu said, 'Tshombe is with me also vis-à-vis the UN.' This meeting, as soon became evident, had little impact on events in the Congo.

I flew back to Leopoldville hoping to devote some time to military staff matters, but instead arrived just in time to join Dayal in dealing with a new crisis. Some of Lumumba's supporters had been rather active, and in order to establish his authority Mobutu ordered several arrests. Kamitatu, the provincial president, opposed this high-handedness and sought UN assistance. Dayal responded by ordering strong UN preventive action and in a show of force UN troops established a strong presence in the city and showed that they were prepared to prevent Mobutu from acting improperly. Mobutu turned up at the Royal, accompanied by a large group of officers to convey the strength of his support. He spent several hours visiting Dayal and other UN officials and left complaining to the press that the UN wanted him to quit politics. The fact was that neither Mobutu nor his officers had much control over their men. Let loose on the city, the ANC were back to their ways of breaking windows and beating suspects. ONUC, after its painful and costly efforts to restore order in the city, was determined not to allow this.

In New York, Hammarskjöld was being spoken of as one who had either helped or hindered Lumumba while he in turn tried to persuade the General Assembly to allow the UN to get on with the job of providing the civil servants, engineers, doctors and teachers the country needed so badly. In a statement to the Assembly, the Soviets were milder in their criticism of Hammarskjöld's role than they had been previously; they could not ignore that it was the UN that had saved Lumumba from Mobutu's marauders. However, this fact was never acknowledged by the growing string of Mobutu's admirers. Some Western commentators were predicting a shift in Hammarskjöld's policy towards the view of India, Ghana and Guinea, but the views of these states varied somewhat because the latter two expected the UN to be actively engaged in support of Lumumba and assist in his return to power, whereas India merely maintained that Lumumba was the Prime Minister and was closer to Hammarskjöld's views on the role of the UN.

Hammarskjöld consulted the key statesmen involved in the situation—Nehru, Nkrumah and Sekou Touré—and after harmonising their views arrived at a solution, which he then cleared with that group before implementing it. Besides his Congo staff team, he relied on Frederick

Boland, the Irish President of the General Assembly, Mongi Slim of Tunisia and Claude Correa of Ceylon, both on the Security Council. He dealt with the troop-contributing countries through the Congo Advisory Committee, but with the United States and the Europeans directly and with the help of Cordier and Bunche. He used various intermediaries for his contacts with the Soviets and their allies.

Dayal's role was crucial. He had been selected as an outstanding diplomat, with experience at UN headquarters and with the UN observer group in Lebanon, and was a highly respected senior official in India itself. As a good administrator and leader, Hammarskjöld consulted him as he had consulted Bunche and various heads of mission in formulating and implementing policy. Naturally, Dayal preferred to avoid any development likely to prove unfavourable to India. But he would always view problems from the UN's viewpoint first, and if the solution conflicted with India's interests, he would discuss it with Hammarskjöld and suggest modifications that would not prejudice the UN's interests. Failing that, he could suggest approaches to India to persuade it to alter its view to bring it closer to the UN's. There was always a solution because over the Congo the UN and India were agreed as to the basic goals.

India's role in New York assumed new importance. Khrushchev made the front pages in the newspapers by banging his shoe on the table and denouncing the Secretary-General in the General Assembly, but it was Nehru who dominated diplomacy relating to the Congo. Throughout his life, Nehru had fought for democracy, freedom, constitutionality and international law, and thus he did not side with the Western states that wanted to override these principles in their support for Kasavubu and Mobutu, just as he opposed the Soviets over their insistence that the UN should throw in its weight behind Lumumba in his bid to regain authority. This was also the position of the UN and thus the policies of India and the UN coincided. Since the Soviets had attacked the Secretary-General, that was reason enough for the West not to do likewise. But the attitude of the Western powers towards India began to change and they chose Dayal as their target.

There were already enough differences between Dayal and the Western diplomats in Leopoldville over the UN's refusal to allow Mobutu a free hand in dealing with Lumumba and his supporters, but now these diplomats wanted to persuade him not to press for the removal of Belgian advisers. Yet the presence of these advisers was preventing UN experts from operating. As General Janssens cynically told the ANC, ' "Before independence" equals "after independence" '. The UN could play no part in this charade: it was they who had restored law and order, provided security, supplied food and economic wherewithal and the funds to help the newly-independent Congolese state, so how could they possibly allow the Belgians to regain control of the country in another guise? On this question there could be no common ground between Dayal and the Western diplomats. In time this disagreement was to grow.

Hammarskjöld, being in full agreement with Dayal on this, pressed ahead by demanding early action from the Belgians. In addition to the note on this question that he had already sent to the Belgians, he sent two others on October 14 and 19. In the first he reminded them that on 13 October, in reply to his note of the 8th, he had been informed that all Belgian technicians had been withdrawn from Katanga excepting a small technical assistance mission. However, Dayal had reported that in Katanga there were still 114 Belgian officers, eleven other ranks and fifty-eight police officers. It was also reported that all key civil and security positions in Katanga were either held by Belgians or under their control.

In the second note Hammarskjöld wrote that there were reports that in the self-styled Autonomous State of South Kasai, Colonel Crèvecoeur, wearing Belgian uniform, was training the local forces, and the medical officer of Forminière, a Belgian, was the chief medical officer of the military units. It was also reported that a Belgian businessman was transporting military equipment from Katanga to South Kasai. The Secretary-General raised questions concerning reports that an office had been opened in Brussels for recruiting personnel for the Congo. He ended: 'Belgian experts have seriously hampered the implementation of the UN technical assistance programme . . . It is clear that their employment . . . by the Congolese authorities, and the activities of these experts, which are often directed against the UN, cannot fail to give rise to serious disputes, especially in view of the unstable political situation at present prevailing in the Congo.'

The last week of October saw further attempts by Mobutu to strengthen his position. He left Leopoldville for a visit to the north and ordered the Thysville garrison to come to the capital. He claimed that this was intended to prevent an attempt by Lumumba to rally African opinion to his side for a counter-coup, but I had reason to believe that his advisers had told him to do this in case the UN troops, who were being gathered for a UN Day parade on 24 October, might instead be used to end his bid for power. The Leopoldville garrison, joined by reinforcements from Thysville, did what they were best at: they put up road-blocks, fleeced their own people of money, got drunk, beat up a few people and generally displayed their muscle. Working with Dayal, I tried hard to persuade Bomboko and the remaining ANC officers to send the troops back to their barracks.

At about the same time, reacting to the UN's pressure to remove Belgian advisers, the Katanga regime called for the removal of Ian Berendsen from Elisabethville and moved troops into the city. Our warnings went unheeded. We had enough troops in both Elisabethville and Leopoldville to make it clear to the respective local authorities that they should not trifle with the UN, and when all attempts at persuading them to reduce their forces in the cities and cease their confrontation with ONUC went unheeded, Dayal allowed me to take appropriate action. The Tunisians had replaced the Ghanaians in Leopoldville, and under their able and tough Colonel Lasmar they seized control of all vulnerable points including entrances to the city. The Ghanaian police, who were there to assist the Congolese counterparts but in fact did most of the work, were out in strength. Bomboko and Mobutu were warned to keep their troops under control and order their return to barracks. We took similar action in Elisabethville, using Ethiopian and Swedish troops. When it became clear that we meant business, the ANC in Leopoldville and the gendarmerie in Elisabethville were reduced to their normal levels.

On 28 October, the Belgian government replied to Hammarskjöld's three notes dealing with their experts in the Congo. It argued that there were no UN resolutions prohibiting any government from providing technical aid to the Congo if requested; further, there was nothing in any resolution that called for the withdrawal of Belgian officials working for the Congo. The Belgians claimed that the Congolese government had the right to ask for technical assistance and therefore the UN could not question it. Lastly, there were 2,000 Belgian technicians in the Congo so the UN could hardly claim to be able to replace them with the 200 available. The only positive statement was that the Belgians were willing to send a representative to New York to discuss this matter.

In Leopoldville Kasavubu had realised, like Tshombe, that the Belgian advisers were essential in enabling him to remain in power. He found an easy ally in Mobutu, who was angered by constant reminders of the misconduct of his troops, in asking Hammarskjöld to recall Dayal: several Western diplomats encouraged Kasavubu and Mobutu to do so although their governments had not reached that point in the course of its normal policy-making.

I, as well as Dayal, was meeting the press and had become acquainted with a few reporters. The journalists of the English-language press did not even pretend to hide their antagonism to Dayal, in which they were influenced, at least in part, by Western diplomats. At this time ONUC was preparing a new report by the Special Representative of the Secretary-General, and Dayal was devoting great care to it. He and I had frequently given background briefings to the press before a major press release, but despite our efforts most of the Western press had lately made only negative comments about ONUC. Dayal and I thought the next report would be important and that it would therefore be useful if we divulged some of its key sections in advance. Dayal deputed me to do this and a briefing was arranged accordingly. When it was over, one of the reporters asked if my remarks were part of the report. When I said that they were, to my great surprise I was asked by more than one of them why I was sharing this information ahead of the report being officially released. When I reminded them of the past practice of doing this, I was asked if the embassies had the same information. I said they had, but not in the precise words I had used. One of them, apparently acting as spokesman for the others, folded his notebook and said, 'Thank you, General. We won't be filing your briefing—we will wait for the official report.' They then walked out leaving me bewildered. Someone had done a good job on the press.

After their disastrous military intervention, the Belgians were attempting to repair the damage done to their relations with the Congolese. It seemed to me that their policy was based on the hope of retaining Congolese friendship—combined with respect for the country's independence—and continuation of technical aid. This approach ignored the fact that their historic role as the country's former colonial masters made them the last Western state that should have been involved in seeking to prop up politicians of their choice or meddling at all in the country's confused political environment. Our troops in South Kasai now reported a renewal of fighting—a predictable development because of reports that Kalonji was training his troops and acquiring arms. The four whites with Kalonji had masterminded a plan for the Balubas to invade South Kasai. Tribal fighting had resumed and Kalonji's forces led by the whites were involved in providing support to the Balubas. In a surprise operation, our troops swooped on the Kalonjists and apprehended Captain John Roberts, a mercenary of British origin, and three 'businessmen'. Roberts admitted to having led a Baluba reprisal raid, and two of the so-called businessmen were identified by their consulates: they were Raul Swaenen, a Belgian, and Rubens Ballardi, a Brazilian. After consultations with the consulates, they were released and put on flights to Europe.

Our Liberian and Ghanaian troops, interposing themselves between the Balubas and Kalonjists, reported that the latter were well armed with Belgian NATO-type weapons. Kalonji had violated the ceasefire agreement, and Tshombe, by permitting weapons and foreign personnel to move through his territory, had violated the North Katanga neutral zone accord that I had negotiated with him: the UN's protests and warnings for preventive action were conveyed to both men. The prompt effective measures taken by the UN troops in Kasai had a salutary effect.

At the UN in New York, while the Congo Advisory Committee was discussing the dispatch to the Congo of a Conciliation Commission composed of Asian and African representatives, the Western embassies were busily engaged in finding new ways of strengthening Mobutu. The

Americans, British and French offered training for ANC personnel, and the first batch of eleven officers went to the United States. Mobutu, like many Congolese who took the Belgian paratroops as their model, was keen to have a similar unit. The Congolese had asked the UN for assistance in para training and accordingly we had arranged for the Moroccans to provide it. The paras had become 'Mobutu's Own', to which he posted officers and men loyal to him. It was from this unit that he chose the eleven to go to the United States. I was pleased with this arrangement, hoping that these officers would return more professionally oriented and inspired.

Hammarskjöld was anxious to learn from Dayal how soon the Conciliation Commission could go to the Congo. Dayal had doubts about the advisability of an immediate visit, but decided to check the political mood in Leopoldville. Kasavubu and Mobutu both suspected that the Commission was a disguised attempt to return Lumumba to power, and publicly rejected its good offices. Dayal decided to visit Kasavubu and asked me to see Mobutu. Our visits were pleasant enough, but we found both of them firm in their opposition to the Commission. Dayal accordingly advised Hammarskjöld that it could face a hostile reception and that its visit was therefore not timely.

Dayal's report was ready to be sent to New York. Its publication was likely to raise a storm, a fact which, together with the Conciliation Commission's future activities, indicated that Dayal might well be asked by the Secretary-General to visit New York to assist him with the Congo Advisory Committee and the General Assembly; Hammarskjöld had been through some difficult days and could do with his help. As he had expected, Dayal received a summons to leave for New York, which he did on 2 November, the day his report was released.

Dayal's main points were that the coup by Mobutu intended, by his own declaration, to neutralise the political crisis between Kasavubu and Lumumba, and that the ANC, instead of providing security, had become the major fermenter of lawlessness. The day-to-day business of the administration was to be conducted by the College of Commissioners, the new group empowered the country's administration, who were selected from among students, who were among the few educated people available, and who had brought along their Belgian teachers as their advisers. These advisers hindered the work of UN experts who, regardless of the obstacles placed in their way, had to attend to administration to keep the country going.

In describing the law and order situation, Dayal said that the incursion of the ANC into Leopoldville had resulted in incidents reminiscent of the mutiny earlier, and required ONUC to stretch its resources to cope with it at a time when its troops were largely deployed in the provinces. The ANC's activities in Leopoldville had influenced the conduct of ANC units in the provincial capitals, and only strong action by the UN troops had restored law and order in the cities. The threat from the ANC had not receded, and a large number of UN troops had to be kept in the cities to keep the peace. Another complicating factor was the violent advent of bands of lawless youths of various political persuasions who were taking advantage of the prevailing disorder. They too had to be dealt with, and this, in addition to the situation in North Katanga and South Kasai, was putting a heavy strain on ONUC troops.

Dayal concluded that there was an opportunity in the present situation to try and achieve the unity and integrity of the Congo if only individual, party or factional interests could be subordinated to national interests. The UN operation, for its part, was sparing no effort to prepare the ground and create the conditions necessary for fruitful political activity.

NOTES

1. UN Document S/4531, 21 September 1960.
2. *Ibid.*
3. *Ibid.*
4. *Ibid.*
5. Rajeshwar Dayal, *Mission for Hammarskjöld: The Congo Crisis* (Princeton University Press, 1966), pp. 43-4.

7

ACTING CHIEF OF UN MISSION

I was appointed Acting Special Representative of the UN Secretary-General in the Congo on 3 November during Dayal's absence in New York. Dayal had suggested to Hammarskjöld that either Linner or I should be left in charge. Linner was senior to me, but Dayal felt that because I had worked closely with him and was better informed on political and security matters, I was the more suitable candidate. Linner and I had got on well together and I knew that because of the demands of running the civilian operations, he would in any case expect me to take care of political and security matters if he were chosen to head the mission. I told Dayal that I would be perfectly happy to work for Linner, but finally Hammarskjöld's choice fell on me.

I was somewhat concerned—and so was Dayal—as to how Von Horn would react to my appointment as his superior, he too being an Under-Secretary. As long as we had kept up the charade of Von Horn being the Force Commander, he was not overmuch concerned how I managed the operations of the Force. This of course was not the case with his personal staff, who had gradually lost authority to the highly—qualified staff recently appointed. 'El Supremo' was no longer taken seriously; he had in fact become a figure of fun and therefore Dayal began to discuss the problem in a lighter vein. Eventually he said to me, laughing, 'This is a military matter. You deal with it.'

I decided to play my role with a low profile so as to cause the least ruffling of feathers at ONUC headquarters and among the diplomatic community who would have yet another Indian to deal with. To avoid making Linner or anyone else feel that I had taken on the airs of being the boss while Dayal was away, I used the 'Chief of Staff' practice which

130

allowed that officer to run the show in the name of the Commander. In that way I ran the operation for Dayal. Instead of a daily meeting of all heads of the UN in the Congo, I started the morning with a smaller meeting of the military, political, public information and legal staff. Then I visited Linner just before his meeting with his branch chiefs and the UN agencies, after which I met the administrative staff. McDiarmid did the co-ordination as before, and since he knew much more about the UN system than I did, I relied on him to work with the civilian and administrative operations. This seemed to work well. I also made myself available to the senior - level UN staff at any time, as I had done before Dayal's departure.

During my first call on Linner we discussed my new assignment. Not only did he not resent it, but he felt that it was correct for me to take over for a few days. We talked about Von Horn and Linner said that we both knew his problem: he was sensitive on questions of position and therefore I needed to handle him with care. I went straight on to see Von Horn as I felt that I had to do what I could to maintain our relationship. He received me politely enough but he appeared less affable than usual. He was very pale and his eyes seemed sunken; obviously he had had another heavy night. I explained to him how I intended to conduct myself while covering for Dayal, assuring him that that the arrangements we had made concerning military matters would continue and that I would come to see him whenever necessary. Furthermore, we would continue to meet for dinner as often as possible; lately, due to my travels around the country, such meetings had been less frequent. However, I would keep him informed as often as was needed and consult him on military matters as before. He looked no happier when I left. My only consolation was that he was never at his best on the 'morning after the night before' —which was why I preferred to see him in the evenings when he was mellower.

As we expected, Dayal's report had caused something of an explosion in Leopoldville, just as it had in New York. President Kasavubu, in spite of having the support of his tribal group, the Bakongo, many of whom lived in the city as well as in the interior, depended on Mobutu for military support, but Mobutu was only now building his power-base in the army assisted by Belgian advisers and supported by the West. He could not entrust his own and his family's safety to the ANC, not even his own parachute regiment, and so depended on the UN for protection. Yet while having little control over his troops who, given an opportunity, would behave badly he was hailed by the Western press as the Congo's 'strong man'. Meanwhile Lumumba, ousted by Kasavubu and with Mobutu out to arrest him, languished in the Prime Minister's residence under UN protection. The stark reality was that there was no authority at the centre capable of governing.

The UN's efforts to maintain law and order were being thwarted by the Western-backed Kasavubu and Mobutu, who aspired to rule the country. On the other hand, Lumumba's supporters wanted their man returned to power. As Chief of Staff and self-appointed head of the ANC, Mobutu had ordered the Congolese army to return to Leopoldville's African *communes* or townships to establish his and Kasavubu's authority, thus causing a renewal of violence which the UN had worked so hard to prevent. This was a reversal of the situation from the earlier days when UN troops were first invited into the Congo by the government to help it contain a mutiny of its own soldiers and protect the civilian population, including Belgians and other West Europeans. Now Western countries supported the Congolese leaders who were sending the same troops, whose nature and training had not changed, to establish their control over the civilian population. It seemed that the West had encouraged such a move, knowing there was little risk to their own nationals and being largely unconcerned about Congolese life and property, which suffered most from the ANC's depredations. The UN, under its mandate and in the absence of any recognised civil authority, had to confront the ANC to keep order. This confrontation angered not only Mobutu but also his Western supporters. This seemed strange to us at that time.

Events in the Congo and their international political ramifications had led to a reassessment of strategies in New York and Leopoldville. Hammarskjöld and Dayal had exchanged views by telex, of which I was fully apprised. At ONUC, with the help of my advisers, we kept developments under constant review. The sad thing was that the UN, which had intervened in the Congo with the intention of isolating the Congolese crisis from superpower rivalry, was now the primary victim of that rivalry. Frustrated at the slow pace of the UN's efforts to deal with the Katanga secession and convinced that its hands were being tied by the Western powers which were backing the Belgian backers of Tshombe, Lumumba had decided to invade Katanga with what little of his forces he could muster. He obtained Soviet aircraft and used Soviet trucks donated for civilian aid to transport his troops. The West, never much pleased with Lumumba's leftward leanings or with his rhetoric, chose this moment to encourage his ouster. First there was the 'constitutional' coup by Kasavubu, but since he had no troops at his command, a coup by Mobutu followed. In spite of the fact that Mobutu had hardly any control over the ANC except for perhaps a couple of units, it did not take long for him to order the closing of the Soviet-bloc embassies. The situation was now ripe for Khrushchev to enact his drama in the General Assembly. The Western powers were now openly siding with the coup leaders; they did not wait for the Congo Conciliation Commission to begin its work but succeeded in having Kasavubu's delegation to the UN appointed by the General Assembly's Credential Committee. Because of the East-West divide, the

UN Secretary-General and ONUC still had their original mandate but no generally recognised authority in the Congo to deal with, except for the President within the framework of his limited responsibilities under the *Loi fondamentale*. Since there were no Soviet-bloc diplomats left in Leopoldville, we at ONUC had to deal with the often angry poundings at our doors of the Western diplomats.

Belgians had returned to many key posts after their earlier hurried departure, and this was a serious obstacle preventing the UN technical advisers from functioning properly. The appointment of the College of Commissioners had brought in a large body of their former teachers as advisers; Katanga relied on several hundred Belgian advisers and after the proclamation of independence by South Kasai, Kalonji also had a number of them. It was not that the UN had any personal prejudice against the Belgians, but their interference in internal politics was intolerable and a violation of technical assistance norms. Besides, they kept the UN experts out of the offices of their wards. Here the UN was definitely on a confrontation course with Belgium, a matter which would have to be resolved.

In his last report Dayal had singled out Mobutu and his troops on the one hand and the Belgian advisers on the other as the two major factors contributing to instability in the Congo. Therefore it was not surprising that Mobutu and the Belgians should charge Dayal with favouring Lumumba. However, what was more surprising was that the United States rejected the UN version and called on Brussels to join the UN in aid to the Congo. The latter was exactly what the UN desired, but the United States' rejection of Dayal's report relating to the role of Belgian advisers was clearly politically motivated.

A review of the military situation indicated that no serious incidents had been reported recently from Equateur, Oriental and Kivu. However, in Kasai and North Katanga fighting and highhandedness by the Kalonji and Tshombe forces were continuing. Dayal had encouraged Joseph Sendwe, the Baluba leader, to travel through his tribal area to pacify his people. Both Kalonji and Tshombe had spoken favourably of Sendwe's efforts, but in spite of this Kalonji's troops and Tshombe's gendarmerie had resumed their enforcement actions, resulting in a renewal of fighting in the neutral zone. Both secessionist leaders were relying on Belgian military advisers and arms-dealers. The situation was so serious that on my first day as the Secretary-General's Acting Special Representative I had to send a protest to both leaders with a request to them to stop the violation of the ceasefire agreements and co-operate with ONUC.

The Irish battalion at Albertville had posts to guard the railway system in North Katanga and each day a few men would leave these posts to perform this duty. On 8 November, an eleven-man Irish patrol was ambushed by rebellious tribesmen near Niemba, west of Albertville. There were only two survivors, one of whom had survived by feigning death until found by UN troops, while the other was only found after an intensive helicopter and light aircraft search. I ordered the two, Joseph Fitzpatrick and Thomas Kenny, to be flown to the Indian Army's general hospital in Leopoldville where the treatment was the best available anywhere in the Congo. The tragedy was that the attack had been made by Balubas whom the Irish were trying to protect from the marauding Katanga gendarmerie. The explanation given to the Irish unit was that the Balubas had 'received strong witchcraft'. Be that as it may, ONUC continued to pay a heavy price in human lives for their help to the Congolese, who often turned to bite the hand extended to them.

I did not like the situation in Leopoldville and insisted on keeping the UN troops on their toes. The supporters of the rival leaders kept up their unceasing political manoeuvrings to further their respective causes. The diplomats were at it too. The ANC was visible in the city, which was like a tinderbox that could ignite at any time, and daily I would warn my colleagues in the Royal to remain vigilant and inform me immediately of any new developments. It would be difficult, if not impossible, to prevent incidents, but we could respond quickly to control them. As we feared, it was the ANC which started the next round of incidents.

On 6 November, in a road accident, a city police car killed a Congolese soldier. Other soldiers standing nearby opened fire and killed the policemen. They then ran to their barracks clamouring for the death of police who were protecting the provincial President, Cleophas Kamitatu, a powerful opponent of Mobutu. UN troops were already deployed in the city and were able to regain control quickly. However, the rivalry between Mobutu and Kamitatu had intensified, and a couple of days later, Mobutu accused Kamitatu of attempting a pro-Lumumba coup to oust him. He told the press that two army officers of Kamitatu's Bambala tribe were involved, and exhibited weapons seized from them and from soldiers loyal to them. Mobutu accused the UN of having a hand in what he called a plot to overthrow him and replace him with Lumumba; it had sought to trick rival Congolese units into fighting as an excuse to disarm his forces and reconvene the pro-Lumumba parliament which he had suspended two months earlier. He charged that Kamitatu was the instrument of the UN in the alleged plot. Mobutu concluded his press conference by saying, 'These Indians who run the United Nations here are doing everything they can to bring Lumumba back to power and turn the Congo into a Soviet state.' He declared that he was anti-communist and that 'so long as I live, the United Nations action aimed at creating a Soviet Congo will not succeed.' He also declared that he would 'never again meet' Dayal, and he failed to show up at a scheduled meeting with me. The ONUC spokesman's comment was 'sheer nonsense'. I was then asked for my comments. What was there to say?

The situation in the Congo was confused—it was also, sad to say, tragicomic—and no Congolese authority existed. The UN had tried to fill the vacuum by using its troops to keep peace and its police units to keep public order in Leopoldville. In addition, its experts and the resources of the agencies were saving the economy from ruin. But there were limits to its ability to use both the power of the gun and its political and economic clout. The UN could not take sides and prop up a particular Congolese leader. It had no mandate to do such a thing; anyway the division of views within the organisation prevented it from doing so. In this sense the UN could be likened to the Congolese because in its own way it too was split by 'tribal' loyalties.

Under these circumstances the ANC was chosen by the Western powers for the only 'quick fix', but it had changed little since independence and its mutiny. In fact the past weeks of disorganisation and indiscipline had made it worse. The army had no central loyalty, and training was conspicuous by its absence except for a few cadres working with the UN Moroccans. Corporals and sergeants became self-appointed officers, some even taking the ranks of colonel and brigadier-general. It was an army with no privates since Lumumba had promoted them all to the rank of lance-corporal. It would take years of peace to train this army to assume responsibility for internal security.

After my first few weeks in the Congo, I was hopeful that the UN could assist in training the ANC, and in the interim provide security assistance. However, I came to learn that it was a country so split by factionalism, political demagogues and rival aspirants that such a task would be foredoomed to failure. Clashing national interests and different ideas on how the country should be run, especially among the Africans, and the open rift between the Socialist and Western states on the question of who should lead the new state, had locked the world organisation into a kind of negative policy. We had to turn all our attention to resolving the political crisis and meanwhile ONUC had to continue with its efforts to keep peace and provide emergency assistance. The news that the General Assembly had established a Congo Conciliation Commission at this time was encouraging.

The Congo remained at centre stage in UN deliberations for the coming weeks, with Kasavubu in the lead role. He went to New York as Head of State of the Congo to address the General Assembly, which later recognised him as such. In the mean time, the campaign against Belgian attempts to regain influence through its technical assistance programme was gaining momentum. Encouraged by the United States, the Belgian government declared that an arrangement with the UN concerning its technical assistance to the Congo should still be possible, and despatched its Foreign Minister, Pierre Wigny, to discuss this idea in New York. The UN could not ignore the fact that during talks preceding the Congo's independence, the Belgian government had offered aid worth $50 million a year for five years and 10,000 technicians. Congolese leaders like Kasavubu and Tshombe had indicated their preference for Belgian advisers which was not shared by all. The Belgians knew the country and were used to the climate and many of them were willing to serve there. As has been mentioned earlier, no one in the UN was against the Belgians as such, but only against those who wished to restore Belgian predominance. I had little doubt that this question could be resolved.

Kamitatu had publicly criticised Kasavubu's trip to New York and said that the Congo would become a 'second Algeria' if the world organisation supported him. Earlier, his party newspaper had carried a picture of Lumumba with a message that the former Prime Minister 'would soon be installed'. During the night of 10 November, Mobutu had Kamitatu picked up from his residence: word of his arrest spread among Bambala and Mungongo tribesmen, and the next morning they demonstrated in front of the Royal. Mobutu's soldiers appeared in order to deal with them, but shortly afterwards the tribesmen were joined by Kamitatu's police. Expecting just this sort of clash, I had approved of our military being placed on alert; ONUC troops had reinforced the normal guard at the Royal and they now interposed themselves between the opposing sides. Some of the demonstrators—there was by now a full-scale riot—had moved to Mobutu's headquarters. To avoid a clash between Mobutu's troops and Kamitatu's sympathisers ONUC interposed its troops between them too.

Rioters in front of the Royal threw stones and some engaged in hand-to-hand fighting, which caused a few injuries. I was busy discussing how to reach Mobutu when I heard some firing from the direction of our car park. One could not see it from the Royal balconies, but the operations room soon reported that a few warning shots had been fired by the UN guard at the rioters who were quite out of hand.

I eventually managed to speak to Mobutu by phone and urged him to release Kamitatu, but he assured me that Kamitatu was safe and in fact being kept in his house as his guest. They had differences which had to be sorted out. Mobutu put Kamitatu on the telephone and I spoke to him. He said he was well, but what else could he say under the circumstances? I told him I would continue with my efforts to have him released, and pressed Mobutu again to release him before we ended our conversation.

A few hours later Kamitatu was still at Mobutu's house and I had our liaison office call Mobutu to say that I was on my way to see him. Mobutu received me properly, but was not very forthcoming about releasing

Kamitatu. I mentioned that his arrest would raise a number of legal and constitutional questions and went on to point out that his release was necessary because it had led to rioting, which could resume and involve Mobutu's troops. This would lead to intervention by ONUC! I believed that Mobutu understood what I had left unsaid. He said he would decide soon, and I was glad when Kamitatu was later allowed to return to his house. In a joint statement the two leaders said that they had reached agreement to assure collaboration between the ANC and the provincial police. At the UN we doubted Kamitatu's commitment to such an arrangement since it would strengthen Mobutu and weaken Lumumba.

In New York, after the establishment of the Conciliation Commission for the Congo, the UN secretariat started to develop its plans: it had in mind the restoration of the parliamentary system. This was opposed by Kasavubu and Mobutu, and their view was supported by the United States and the other Western powers. The Belgian Foreign Minister Wigny, angered by the attitude of the Afro-Asian states which had endorsed Dayal's last report, particularly as it related to Belgian advisers in the Congo, criticised Dayal and asserted that the UN operation was a failure. He protested against attempts to portray Belgium as the villain in the Congo tragedy and warned that his country would leave the UN if they continued. The United States was disturbed at this development, and while maintaining different views from the UN on its operations in the Congo, issued a rebuttal of Wigny in which it backed the UN's efforts. The US spokesman told the press on 15 November that his country would 'continue to do all it can to promote the objectives of peace and welfare for which the United Nations was asked to lend its assistance to the Congo'.[1]

Kasai and Katanga continued to demand my attention. Despite all the UN's effort's to keep peace there, Kalonji had threatened that his 'voluntary' army would be called upon to liberate his tribesmen in North Kasai unless the UN halted their persecution by other tribes. He was referring to the Balubas, Lulas, Kaniokas and others. I replied that the UN had received assurances from the tribal chiefs concerned that they wanted to preserve peace and I therefore warned Kalonji against taking any precipitous action. Further east, new fighting had broken out at Luenga near Albertville in Katanga. The UN could not relax its vigil.

Every year, on 14 November, the Belgian Congo had celebrated the 'Day of the Congolese Soldier' to commemorate the role the Congolese troops played in the First World War. The idea of repeating the celebration this year was raised and Mobutu had accepted it with enthusiasm; the occasion would give him an opportunity to show his strength and thus enhance his prestige. Besides, a parade was always good for the troops' morale. Viewed from the Royal, it had its advantages but it might spark off an incident if the opposition chose to demonstrate. An attempt to stop the parade would bring us into an open conflict with Mobutu, and the Western embassies would side with him. Yet there were risks in letting Mobutu go ahead with it.

Knowing that Von Horn loved parades, one of his personal staff had suggested to him that in order to show our goodwill a UN contingent should participate, and the General had become quite enthusiastic. There were many angles to this question and I was therefore reluctant to give my approval straight away before we had had some time think through the possible consequences. Would our participation be taken as a sign that the UN was supporting Mobutu? Realising that many contingents in Leopoldville would baulk at the idea of taking part in such a parade, who should be asked and would agree without fuss and consultations with their government? What weapons should our contingent carry? I would of course have to obtain Hammarskjöld's consent.

My advisers were in favour of our participating, and we thought that if we did take part we should have a mixed contingent to avoid representation by a single nationality, and that the troops should carry personal arms. But there would be a mobile standby unit available to deal with any incident. What finally made me agree was the suggesion that by participating we would have our troops right alongside the ANC to cope with an incident if it occurred. On this basis Hammarskjöld gave his approval.

It turned out to be an orderly occasion, well organised by Mobutu's Belgian military advisers. The ANC could march well and its armoured cars went past the saluting base without a breakdown. The Western press were all over the place and questioned me and several other UN military officers. It was a good parade and we said this to the press. I anticipated that Mobutu's admirers would use any compliment from the UN to his advantage, and I was not disappointed. One report stated: 'The Congolese Army staged an orderly parade . . . that earned the praise of United Nations officials. . . . They [senior UN officers] congratulated the colonel [Mobutu] on the discipline and efficiency shown by his troops.' The report added: 'Their [the UN's] plaudits were in contrast to the scathing criticism of the Congo Army contained in a recent report to the United Nations by Rajeshwar Dayal, the Secretary-General's special representative in the Congo. Today's parade was clearly aimed at disproving Mr Dayal's charge that the Army lacked discipline.'[2]

The laudatory comments by his supporters had given Mobutu more confidence, although he had done little to improve the quality of his troops. Meanwhile, Nkrumah at the UN and his envoys in Leopoldville were desperately trying to revive Lumumba's political fortunes. At the Ghana embassy in Leopoldville the ambassador, Andrew Djin, and the minister at the embassy, Nathaniel Welbeck, made no secret of their activities in support of Lumumba since Mobutu's coup. A showdown was inevitable and the first act in this drama began on 16 November with the arrest of an embassy secretary, Lovelace Mensah. Mobutu alleged that Mensah was carrying a considerable sum of money (reported to be CF27,000, equal to about US $540) destined for Lumumba, as well as documents concerning a projected invasion of the secessionist Katanga province by Lumumba forces. This action was linked to attempts by the Katanga Baluba leader, Mwamba Ilunga, who had taken refuge in Stanleyville to form a Baluba province in North Katanga. The documents, it was alleged, also mentioned Antoine Gizenga, a prominent supporter of Lumumba with Communist sympathies who had moved to Stanleyville after the coup.

Welbeck, as chargé d'affaires at the Ghana embassy in the absence of Djin, acknowledged that Mensah was delivering mail, including a letter from Gizenga, to Lumumba at his residence when he was arrested by the ANC. On learning of Mensah's arrest he immediately contacted ONUC and asked for our intervention. I had to know more facts before deciding what we should do and asked our legal and field security staff to make inquiries.

Two days later, the Kasavubu/Mobutu-appointed acting Commissioner of the Interior, José Nussbaumer, announced the expulsion of the Ghana ambassador (who was due depart anyway no later than 21 November), and added that till then Mensah would remain under army surveillance. He also announced that the UN Conciliation Commission,[3] which was already opposed by Kasavubu in New York, would not be permitted entry to the Congo. Nussbaumer praised the ANC and threatened to use it to prevent the entry of the UN commission. This double announcement required different approaches by ONUC. The first concerned the expulsion of senior embassy staff by a regime which was unrecognised, and the second was a declaration by the same regime to prevent, by force if necessary, the entry of a UN organ.

Kasavubu had written earlier to Nkrumah asking him to recall Djin and Welback and this had been rejected. On 19 November Mr Ndele, the Commissioner in charge of security, requested a meeting with me to discuss the Ghana embassy affair. Since I had arranged to see Mobutu at that hour, I asked Cox to see Ndele on my behalf, and Cox advised him against expelling the Ghana diplomats. I too advised Mobutu against taking such an extreme step. Nussbaumer said in a press statement that day that the expulsion of an African embassy was indeed a drastic step, and the UN had advised the College of Commissioners against it, but after consideration they had decided to press ahead. Welbeck told the press that he was awaiting instructions from Nkrumah and meanwhile if

Mobutu's regime forcibly attempted to evict him there would be 'civil war'.

The Congolese Foreign Ministry confirmed the expulsion order the following day but retracted a statement by Nussbaumer that relations with Ghana had been broken. Meanwhile, I had received my instructions from Hammarskjöld. Accordingly, I conveyed them to the Congolese and authorised the issuing of a press statement that the UN would accord the Ghanaian embassy the same physical protection that had been given to the Soviet and Czechoslovak envoys when Mobutu requested them to leave after his coup in September; also that the embassy premises were inviolable and the UN would protect that status. I concluded by saying that the relations between Ghana and the Congo were the concern of the two of them only.

I called a meeting of our senior staff—McDiarmid, Cox, Berthiume, Iyassou and Mitra—and after detailed discussion of possible developments and the courses open to us for coping with the emerging crisis, ordered the military to reinforce the Ghanaian civil police guard at the embassy with Tunisian troops who were on garrison duty. My staff and liaison officers went to the Ghana embassy and advised Welbeck against the use of force. They also took action to cool the young Commissioners. As was expected, my Western callers urged me to support Mobutu, while others insisted that the UN defend the Ghanaians. The only silver lining on the darkening clouds ahead was the assurance from the Ghana contingent, conveyed to me by its liaison officer Steve Otu, that I could count on their loyalty and obedience to UN decisions.

I already knew of Kasavubu's letter to Nkrumah asking for the recall of the senior Ghanaian diplomats. On 17 November, Commissioner Nussbaumer had called on the ONUC staff to insist that Welbeck must leave, saying that Kasavubu had declared in a letter to Nkrumah that Djin, Welbeck and Botsio were *personae non gratae*, but the letter had been returned by the Ghana Foreign Ministry with a note pointing out that it had not been signed by a competent minister. Subsequently, on 19 November, Welbeck informed us that he had heard of Kasavubu's letter to his President on the BBC but had had no communication from Accra; also on that day, the Congolese Chief of Security, Ndele, called on ONUC to advise Welbeck that he must leave. Following this, Captain Pongo of the Congolese security served notice at the Ghana embassy that Welbeck was to depart within forty-eight hours. Welbeck phoned to tell me of this development and of his determination to stay. He had apparently been drinking, as he spoke loudly and incoherently.

Since Otu was in disfavour at his embassy for loyally serving ONUC and had disregarded demands to act bilaterally to support Ghana's political objectives, a harassed young British officer serving with the

Ghanaian army had been scurrying between the Ghana embassy and our headquarters. Although Welbeck had even sought his counsel, there was little that this officer could do beyond sending a cable to Alexander. Welbeck was determined to stay to meet the Conciliation Commission and give them what he called his evidence; he said he would be willing to depart after that. I knew that the Indian and Egyptian ambassadors, Ghaleb and Rahman, had been in touch with him, but I had not been able to contact either of them to find out what had transpired. My last attempt to obtain news from Welbeck by telephone had produced a declamation from him that 'blood must be shed and I am personally going to make Mobutu walk behind me through the streets of Leo like a dog and I am going to die to liberate Lumumba.' Meanwhile ONUC was guarding the Ghana embassy and its residential area.

ONUC liaison staff had arranged for Mobutu to meet me at the Royal. Because of tensions over Welbeck, Mobutu conveyed some hesitation over seeing me in the UN's den and it was suggested we meet instead at Von Horn's residence. Von Horn offered to host a lunch, which was agreeable to both Mobutu and me. This was a cordial affair and Mobutu reiterated his desire to improve his army and that this was his main task. He backed off from my efforts to make him definitely admit that he was going to remain above politics. Colonel Bombozo of Thysville had already taken his troops back from Leopoldville to his garrison.

In my round-up cable to Hammarskjöld, I said that I had learned that Bomboko had met Kamitatu and assured him that he would use all his influence to keep the army out of politics. This was an encouraging sign. On the other hand, Colonel Justin Nkokolo, the commander of Leopoldville garrison and Mobutu's deputy, seemed to have been easily influenced by the three Western military attachés into supporting a military dictatorship under Mobutu. I believed Mobutu was still vacillating between his idealistic view of serving his country as a true patriot by remaining out of politics and grandiose ideas of what he would do for it—and for himself—if he became a military dictator. I therefore believed that it was possible for him to be persuaded to remain neutral if we could nullify the influence of those who wished to see him in the latter role. This , in my opinion, could be achieved first and foremost by dealing with him from a position of strength, i.e. from the military point of view. We had achieved an adequate concentration of troops in Leopoldville and made a discreet show of force at every possible opportunity, preferably without getting into a direct clash with the ANC. Secondly, we had to handle him with tact, give him the necessary support to reorganise his army with training and new equipment, and not adopt any measures that would undermine his authority as Chief of Staff.

I had already asked Mobutu to facilitate our administrative arrangements for the Conciliation Commission. I again raised this matter, and he readily agreed to look into it. He himself started the conversation on the present political crisis and said that since the removal of Lumumba as Prime Minister his declared target of arriving at a political solution was not very far off. I suggested that he should assist the Conciliation Commission, which after all was being sent by the UN whose sole aim in the Congo was to help the Congolese. After discussing it for a while, we agreed to resume our conversation the following day.

As for Welbeck, Mobutu assured me that he was being well-treated, but insisted that he leave the country within forty-eight hours in keeping with Kasavubu's wishes. I again asked that Mensah be released, at which Mobutu said that the man had been allowed to sort out his personal affairs, visit the Ghana embassy and see his family in the African quarter. However, he could not release him, since he had been a resident of Leopoldville for the past fifteen years and was considered a criminal. He had decided that Mensah should be expelled and put on the plane taking Welbeck to Accra.

On returning to the Royal after sending my report of the meeting with Mobutu to Hammarskjöld, I turned to other matters. The ANC and the gendarmerie in Stanleyville had nearly started a battle among themselves. After an exchange of a few shots which had slightly wounded one man, the Ethiopian Brigade was able to arrange a truce. Gizenga had come to our headquarters there for assistance and was under our protection. Discussions about releasing certain detained members of parliament and ANC officers were proceeding smoothly, and the Ethiopians told me that the College of Commissioners would be invited to send some representatives to Stanleyville to finalise arrangements. But I advised the Ethiopians not to encourage this move and instead suggested to Mobutu that he send one of his officers to Stanleyville to arrange a settlement, to which he agreed. It seemed to me better to keep the College out of it, and have the issues decided within a military context.

The situation in North Katanga continued to make me anxious, but it was encouraging that the newly-arrived Nigerian Brigade had been moved to the area; I felt confident that once they and their essential equipment and vehicles were in place we would be able to sort out the mess. Meanwhile, Tshombe was touring the area and adding fuel to the fire. He had so far been to Albertville and Kongolo—in Kongolo, forty armed volunteers had arrived from Conakat and another forty were expected. At Kabalo the airstrip was occupied by members of Balubakat, the Baluba political organisation in Katanga, who were demanding that all Belgians leave town. At Kabongo too the airstrip was occupied by the members of Balubakat and the situation still remained serious.

Ian Berendsen had returned from his visit to Luena. He and the

Moroccan commander had agreed that our present directives should be enforced rigidly to improve the situation. They warned the leaders of 'Baluba Jeunesse', the Balubakat youth group, to abide by ONUC's orders for a neutral zone, and when an armed group of fifty of them managed to enter the European quarter, they were surrounded and immediately disarmed. For the moment, despite the precarious conditions, the coal mines remained open, and we were providing additional protection to enable the railways to continue operating.

Lumumba telephoned me to report that his car had been confiscated and his driver beaten by the ANC and that his servants were afraid to go out of the house for fear of the ANC. I telephoned Mobutu about this, and he assured me that he would take the officer responsible to task; also, that he had given specific instructions that the movements of Lumumba's servants, of doctors who were attending his family and so on, must not be interfered with. I sent an operational officer to check on this, and he reported back that Lumumba was satisfied.

The Yugoslav chargé d'affaires called on me during this time to exchange views. He believed that the College of Commissioners was consolidating its position and that there were moves to persuade Mobutu to carry out another coup to make Bomboko Prime Minister. While he generally accepted my view as to how to deal with Mobutu and the ANC, he felt that nothing should be done which would improve Mobutu's political chances. He was not sure whether Mobutu had any political ambitions, but feared that if his position with the army was further consolidated he might be used as a weapon by powers who were determined to keep Lumumba out of power. I had sounded out Mobutu about the future of the College: he said he had created it to get the administration of the country going and prevent it from falling into further chaos. The College was there for that purpose alone and had no other political purpose. If this was true, the Conciliation Commission would have to contend with the individual ambitions of those in the College who, having once tasted power, would be unwilling to give it up.

In my last cable to Hammarskjöld at the end of a long day I said that we were doing all we could to maintain quiet in Leopoldville and that so far our efforts had been fruitful. I hoped it would remain like this, which should make the task of the Conciliation Commission much easier. The College had put out a special communiqué to the effect that Nussbaumer's declaration about preventing the arrival of the Conciliation Commission at N'Djili airport (see p. 139, above) had been misconstrued by the press and did not have the authority of Mobutu and the College. At lunch, Mobutu had confirmed this and assured me that there would be no interference with the Conciliation Commission.

The next day a sober Welbeck called on me to say that he would leave, but had to wait for a Ghanaian aircraft that was due two days later to take him to Accra. Although the Congolese security men, backed by the ANC, were pressing for Welbeck's departure that very day, the UN was able to persuade the Congolese to agree to a twenty-four hours' postponement. Otu, meanwhile, had informed me that General Alexander and Richard Kwashi, the Permanent Secretary of the Ghanaian Foreign Ministry, were due to arrive in Leopoldville later that day to arrange Welbeck's replacement and return to Accra.

By now I was alarmed at the increasing tension centred around the Ghana embassy and in the diplomatic community. ONUC staff and I received phone calls and visits from Western diplomats urging us to tell Welbeck to leave and avoid a showdown with Mobutu. It was evident that they wanted to see the hated Welbeck removed ignominiously. The Afro-Asians were divided, but at best expected ONUC to thwart any attempt to violate the Ghana embassy. My personal view was that Welbeck should leave although I had no answer as to whether Mobutu's College of Commissioners had the constitutional authority to issue such an order. The hard reality was that Mobutu and the College were the *de facto* authority and controlled elements of the army and the security in the capital. If we could not arrange Welbeck's departure peacefully, there would be an explosion. Meanwhile the fuse was burning rapidly.

I was in frequent contact with Hammarskjöld, Dayal and Bunche in New York, and because of the heightening crisis it was necessary for me to establish open telex conversation in addition to sending coded cables. My colleagues in New York were mainly concerned over the impact the Welbeck crisis would have on the impending visit of the Congo Conciliation Commission to Leopoldville; inability to control it could have ill-effects all round. I told Hammarskjöld that ONUC had been placed in a most embarrassing situation and that efforts to create a peaceful climate for the Conciliation Commission to begin its efforts were being weakened by one man, Welbeck. I said that we were heading for a definite clash with the ANC. Hammarskjöld replied that he had doubts about the wisdom of a show of force on our part; this might lead to clashes, which had to be avoided. He thought it should be possible for ONUC to achieve a psychological effect on Mobutu without the risk of an armed conflict. He immediately spoke to Bomboko, who was with Kasavubu in New York, and who agreed to have a cable sent by Kasavubu to advise Mobutu to exercise restraint and to repair his relations with ONUC.

The only psychological tool I could use in my dealings with Mobutu was simply to talk with him and urge restraint. Later that day I called on him and emphasised the importance of avoiding a clash between the ANC and ONUC; I assured him that the UN would find a way out of the Welbeck predicament, but we needed time. We were in the Congo to assist and not to fight; we had to protect the embassies, just as we guarded him and his family along with other Congolese leaders and diplomats. Over champagne, which seemed to flow in abundance, Mobutu assured me that he would co-operate. I left him somewhat comforted yet unsure of his ability to control his men.

On returning to the Royal, I was informed that two members of the United States embassy staff had narrowly escaped being lynched by a Congolese crowd. The military attaché Colonel Dannemiller, his wife, Chief Warrant Officer Clyde St Lawrence and Frank Carlucci, Second Secretary, had been driving to N'Djili airport when a Congolese cyclist was knocked down by their car and killed. A crowd gathered immediately. The Dannemillers were able to escape in a bus going to the airport, but St Lawrence and Carlucci were beaten and attacked with knives. Carlucci was saved by a Congolese and managed to get into a bus, while St Lawrence ran to escape the crowd. Shortly afterwards another embassy car which Miss Alison Palmer, a vice-consul, was driving to the airport met St Lawrence, who was bleeding from his wounds, and picked him up. Both injured Americans were taken to the Indian Army's general hospital. From our experience it was clear that not only did the Congolese have no organised police force to cope with such incidents but that the near-lynching of diplomats left them unmoved.

On 21 November, the morning reports gave no indication of lessening tensions. Lasmar came to report that the situation around the Ghana embassy was still grave, but that everything possible was being done to avoid a clash. He politely asked whether I could arrange Welbeck's departure from the embassy. I had indeed considered offering him hospitality at the Royal, but there was a difficulty, namely that Thomas Kanza, formerly Lumumba's representative to the UN and a bitter Bakongo opponent of Kasavubu, had taken refuge there, causing angry exchanges between Mobutu and ONUC. To have invited Welbeck to be our guest as well would have strained our relations with Mobutu too severely at this critical stage. My ONUC colleagues, including the Ghanaians, advised me not even to raise such a possibility with Welbeck, because he would not only refuse but would consider it a ruse to get him out of the embassy. I shared Lasmar's concern, but could do little to relieve his anxiety.

I had been reliably informed that Welbeck had received instructions from Accra not to leave Leopoldville and immediately reported this to Hammarskjöld. I said that the UN could not help being involved in this affair although it was entirely between the Congolese and Ghana, because we had assumed responsibility for the protection of the Ghanaian embassy and its personnel, particularly its ambassador. We had succeeded in averting that morning's clash merely by taking advantage of the present friendly atmosphere between Mobutu and ourselves. Mobutu had conceded another twenty-four hours' grace only because of a direct personal request from me. The Congolese were determined to expel Welbeck and had told ONUC that, because he had not behaved like a gentleman in refusing to comply with Kasavubu's orders to leave, they would be obliged to resort to methods which they did not normally like to use. I added that we were heading for a definite clash with the ANC and therefore asked for instructions how to cope with the new development, i.e. Welbeck's order to remain.

At about noon Nussbaumer and Pongo called on Welbeck to leave within twenty-four hours, but when he declined to sign a document agreeing to do so they warned him that he must leave by 4 p.m. that same day. I reminded the Congolese authorities that ONUC had to protect the embassy against any incursion or act of force against the person of the chargé d'affaires. The only news providing some relief was given to me by Captain Peel, Ghana's British liaison officer at ONUC, that General Alexander and Richard Kwashi were due to arrive at 5 o'clock in an RAF plane. I hoped they were coming with a mandate from Nkrumah to review the situation and, if necessary, take Welbeck back with them to Accra.

The Commissioners had been in constant touch with Linner and had several meetings with Cox and Berthoud. They told me that Nussbaumer was losing his cool: in the afternoon he and some other Commissioners were brought to me by Linner and each made a long speech, arguing that they constituted a sovereign government and had ordered the removal of Welbeck and two other Ghanaians under the authority vested in them. I repeated the UN position, which did not question bilateral relations between the Congo and Ghana, but emphasised that the embassy was inviolate and that no diplomats could be removed by force: since the matter of Welbeck was under negotiation, we should allow time for a conclusion to be reached. The Commissioners were undeterred and continued to express their views at great length. They were a group of nice young men, ardent and anxious to do their best for their country. They had arrived well primed by their Belgian advisers, and I wished I could have explained to them some of the realities of international politics. Unfortunately, I had a lot else on my mind.

I received a cable from Dayal in New York. He had just met Bomboko and Cardozo and informed them of the developments over Welbeck's forcible expulsion and pointed out what grave dangers could arise if there were armed conflict between the UN and Congolese troops over this incident. He took the line indicated in the instructions sent to me by the Secretary-General. Bomboko referred to the letter Kasavubu had sent to Nkrumah early in October and the reply from the Ghana Foreign Ministry questioning the validity of the action proposed on the ground that

Bomboko's countersignature on the letter, asking for the removal of seven Ghanaian diplomats, was not valid. Bomboko said that Welbeck had invited the trouble he was in, but agreed that a clash between the UN and Congolese forces would be undesirable. He was informed that some firing had actually taken place, for which he expressed regret. He promised to inform Kasavubu of developments and to have a telegram immediately sent to Mobutu asking for restraint and for the repairing of relations with ONUC. Dayal gave Bomboko the news, which he welcomed, that Alexander would be taking Welbeck out of the country that night.

Von Horn was away from the office more and more, and most of the time could not be reached at his home. If he was taking umbrage at my elevated role I could understand why he was absenting himself, but knowing him as well as I did I suspected that he was ill and hiding it from his colleagues. I knew he enjoyed an early aperitif and dallied over his meals so that when his afternoon nap was included a good deal of time could be lost. But it was more than that, and his personal staff were so silent that even Iyassou, the Chief of Staff, had no inkling of what was up. On this particular day Von Horn had arrived late at the office and left early; when I tried to reach him at his house, I was told he could not be reached. I could have called on Kettani, the Deputy Force Commander, to assume responsibility by informing Hammarskjöld that Von Horn was absent, but wanted to avoid the rumpus this would create. Iyassou, always cautious, did not wish to assume any responsibilities but was always willing to do what I asked. Thus at this critical hour I was holding the fort for Dayal and the figurehead Force Commander was absent.

As the meeting with the Commissioners groaned along, I had to leave the room several times to listen to military reports, read cables from New York and send our own reports, take phone calls from ambassadors who insisted on speaking to me, and direct the political and military operations. I was grateful to Linner who patiently helped me with the Commissioners. Late in the afternoon, Nussbaumer declared that the Commissioners had waited long enough and would proceed to remove Welbeck. They then turned up at the embassy with a ticket for a commercial flight that night which Welbeck refused to accept. On finding him both adamant and well-defended, they retired to consult their advisers and Mobutu. Later they returned to the Royal to force my hand.

I had to leave the Commissioners to have a telex conversation with the Secretary-General in which he expressed his views on the embassy crisis and gave me some more guidelines. They were as follows:

1. A diplomatic move of the kind envisaged had to be taken by the head of state and not by any other authority anticipating his decision.
2. The decision of Kasavubu, when it had been taken, should be communicated to the Ghana government according to the normal rules of diplomacy.

3. To the UN's knowledge, it was unheard-of except in war for a *non-grata* declaration on some diplomatic representative to be implemented by the use of military force. The consequences would undoubtedly be very grave, both where international respect for the Congo was concerned and in practical action.

4. If the President made the decision indicated by the Commissioners, the Congolese authorities should use the presence of Ghana's Foreign Office Permanent Secretary to negotiate the matter in an orderly way; in that context they should withdraw the troops and cancel all threat of the use of force, maintaining the maximum of international diplomatic decorum.

If this were done the UN protection would simultaneously be reduced to the minimum needed for the normal maintenance of law and order. We were insisting only that in this matter of the expulsion proper procedures should be followed. The UN would not stand in the way when the procedures being followed were correct.

The Secretary-General was trying to contact Kasavubu and would let me know immediately he had talked with him. In the mean time I should at once inform Mobutu and the Commissioners of this initiative on our side, expressing the firm expectation that absolutely nothing would be done by the Congolese to pursue their line of action until their contacts with me and of course with Bomboko at the UN had produced the desired results.

I returned to continue the marathon discussion with the Commissioners with a stronger hand, but again had to break off the meeting to receive Alexander and Kwashi. I had been anxiously awaiting their arrival and it did not take them long to understand how important it was that Welbeck should depart immediately. They left me to communicate with Accra from Otu's headquarters and make the administrative arrangements. Meanwhile, I went back to the Commissioners and told them that arrangements were in hand to remove Welbeck. Nussbaumer made another long statement and the others followed. Then at about 7.30, while one of the Commissioners was still droning on about African nationalism and its evolution in the Congo, we heard firing. Minutes later an operations officer came up and reported that fighting had erupted at the Ghana embassy between the ANC and the Tunisians. Lasmar and Nussbaumer immediately left for the embassy to stop it. I had a call put through to Mobutu and was told that Colonel Nkokolo, the garrison commander, was at the embassy and Mobutu was waiting to hear from him. I urged Mobutu to call for a ceasefire and told him that I had sent Lasmar to stop the Tunisians from further fighting. Within about half an hour the fighting had subsided.

Alexander and Kwashi rejoined me at the Royal and suggested that they take Welbeck to Accra as soon as they could get him out; they had already alerted their aircraft at N'Djili to be ready to take off at an hour's notice. Meanwhile, my staff were in touch with Mobutu, who said that the use of force had been contrary to his orders; his story was that two Ghanaian policemen had opened fire first. I suggested to Mobutu that it would be preferable if we could meet immediately at the Royal as it was impossible for me to leave my command post. He sounded shaky and scared of the Tunisians who had their billets along the road where his house was, and suggested that he await the return of two ANC officers whom he had sent to the scene of the incident.

The telephone rang again and it was the Tunisian chargé d'affaires who said that he was reporting to his government immediately that his contingent could not continue to protect a diplomat to the extent of their being involved in a battle with the Congolese, causing casualties to both sides, when the diplomat had been declared *persona non grata* by the head of state. I persuaded him to visit me before he finally sent his cable.

I sent for Mitra, the senior operations officer, and asked him if he had succeeded in contacting the Force Commander: he said he had personally phoned several times but Von Horn was not available. I told him to get the General's ADC on the phone for me immediately. The ADC kept repeating that the Force Commander was not available. Was he unwell? Was he at his house? I could not get a satisfactory reply. I told Mitra to send an officer to the house, and the officer returned saying that the ADC had not allowed him entry and told him that the Force Commander was not available.

By 10 p.m. there was only sporadic rifle fire—the ceasefire seemed to have held. I decided to accept Alexander's offer to remove Welbeck and went with him to see what was happening and try to end the shooting. When we reached the embassy at about 10.30, there were numerous ANC troops milling around and firing in every direction. We left the UN car and began on foot but when we encountered scattered and haphazard firing from the ANC, we hit the ground and crawled forward in the dark. The ANC were firing at the Indian hospital's ambulance car, which was searching for and evacuating the wounded. There was also some unauthorised movement of UN cars that had come to see what was happening. Finally, at about midnight, I told Alexander that we seemed to be on a wild goose chase, as we could not see anything and there was uncontrolled ANC shooting in every direction. It was better to go back to the Royal and attempt to get through early the next morning in case matters had not been resolved by then. Besides, I had to report to New York.

On the drive back to the Royal I stopped at the Indian hospital to praise the staff for their bravery and their efforts to save lives. I was shocked to learn that Colonel Nkokolo had died and that his body was in the hospital mortuary. A Tunisian was also dead and six were under treatment for wounds. Nkokolo's death would cause problems for the UN as he was a popular officer and a good soldier who could have been useful in restraining Mobutu.

The Secretary-General was anxious to know the details of the fighting and how it had broken out. I realised that he and I would be under strong pressure from the Western embassies that had endorsed Mobutu and his Commissioners' action over the removal of Welbeck, because it was the action of the UN in preventing it that had led to the fighting.

McDiarmid had sent Cordier in New York a comprehensive report on the events by telex while I was trying to get through to the Ghana embassy. The Secretary-General wanted confirmed details. It was 1 a.m. in Leopoldville but only 8 p.m. in New York and thus early enough for them to get their reports out. The shooting had not yet stopped, and the situation was confused - I would know more after daybreak. However, I urged the Secretary-General to press Accra to remove Welbeck before any more harm could be done.

The ceasefire was finally enforced at about 7 a.m., and all troops, including the ANC, withdrew from the embassy as agreed, leaving a detachment of Ghanaian police as before. At 8.30, Alexander went there together with a UN officer and an ANC escort. There was no incident *en route* and with the addition of Welbeck the party immediately left for the airport. A slight delay was caused in their departure as the Congolese authorities insisted that Kwashi, who was to have been left behind as acting chargé d'affaires, should leave on the same plane as his papers were not in order. Alexander complied, and the aircraft left for Ghana.

The ANC, meanwhile, had put up some roadblocks and so prevented our staff from reaching the Royal. In several instances UN cars were confiscated and their special plates removed. A number of our people had been detained since the previous night, and while some had been released Colonel Berthiume and about fifteen others were still held in Camp Leo. We were in touch with Berthiume by motorola, and it appeared that they were being treated satisfactorily. The chief of the ONUC air force, Air Commodore Chapman, and others were virtually confined to their houses. We had received reports of searches of UN houses and of incidents where our people had been manhandled. I visited Mobutu to console him on the death of Nkokolo and he assured me he had given orders for the immediate release of all UN personnel in detention.

Nussbaumer had requested a meeting with me that morning, but as I had already arranged to see Mobutu, I asked Linner and Berthoud to see him instead. The purpose of the visit was, of course, to explain and justify his actions the day before: he insisted that he had dealt with Welbeck with the utmost correctness throughout. He repeatedly asked us to secure the testimony of the Tunisian officers who had been at the embassy; he said that tension had been created in the area by ONUC, which had put thirty Tunisians around the house at a time when there were only four Congolese soldiers there and Welbeck was not under any threat. This, he claimed, was the sole cause of the incident that occurred later. Nussbaumer ascribed the responsibility for this action to me personally, and even questioned my motives in the use of troops from Tunisia whose government was normally an ally of the Congolese. When Nussbaumer insisted that Welbeck had been treated properly according to diplomatic usage, Berthoud pointed out that the armed attack against the embassy of a country with which one maintained diplomatic relations was unprecedented in diplomatic history. However, Berthoud added that what was important now was for Nussbaumer immediately to take all steps in his power to release every one of the UN personnel who were detained by the ANC or other Congolese authorities. Nussbaumer agreed but on condition that he was given the reasons why we had seen fit to reinforce our guard at the Ghana embassy at a time when Welbeck was not in any personal danger. It was again explained to him that the immediate release of all UN personnel should be unconditional. Nussbaumer accepted this point and indicated that he would act immediately, but again sought credit for his pacific attitude the day before, claiming that he had been instrumental during the evening in obtaining the release of Colonel Berthiume from Camp Leo, a statement which Berthiume's continued detention seemed to belie.

In the mean time, I returned to ONUC headquarters and briefly saw Nussbaumer to insist on the immediate release of all UN personnel, saying that their detention could not be connected with the military events of last night and would only harm the position of the Congolese authorities. Linner, who joined us, asked Nussbaumer to consider the possibility of making a radio appeal to calm the population of Leopoldville and help to relax tension. Nussbaumer unconvincingly agreed. It was clear that he felt concern over what might be the international reaction to the Congolese action against Welbeck. I said unequivocally that they would be accused of committing violence against the person of a diplomat. I also enjoined on him the necessity of ending hostilities against ONUC.

Mobutu and senior officers came to the Indian general hospital at about 1 p.m. to take away Nkokolo's body. I had posted an ONUC liaison officer there, who took the opportunity to demand on my behalf the immediate release of all UN personnel from detention and the removal of the ANC from the entire Parc Hambise area, where the Ghana embassy was. Mobutu, accompanied by the liaison officer, visited the camps and arranged for the release of our people. Meanwhile, a Malayan patrol went to the Parc Hambise area and found that the ANC troops had already been withdrawn. Mobutu was attempting to pacify his men, who would have appeared from the previous night's incidents to be virtually in a state of war with the UN. He said to the liaison officer, significantly, that all the incidents should be treated together and not as separate issues.

In the morning I received a cable from Hammarskjöld saying that he was 'deeply shocked by the performance of Mobutu's ANC. This may have the most serious political repercussions and influence the whole position of the UN. In the circumstances I request you, as soon as you can piece the main facts together, to cable a full report covering all relevant aspects of the incident, including your own experiences and the story about the ambulance, for circulation as a report in course of Tuesday.'[4]

I had requested McDiarmid, with the assistance of Cox, Berthoud and Mitra, to draft a report on the incident for the Secretary-General, and was being pursued meanwhile by the press in Leopoldville to issue a statement. This, with the help of my colleagues and Fletcher, the ONUC information officer, I prepared, and read out at the press briefing. I said that the UN profoundly regretted the loss of life resulting from the previous night's events and was distressed at being involved in a clash with the ANC. I mentioned that I had expressed my condolences to Mobutu on Colonel Nkokolo's death. The UN did not contest the decisions of the head of state concerning the acceptability of any diplomat in the Congo, but had responsibilities to prevent an assault on an embassy in violation of international agreements.

Cordier informed me by cable that '. . . the General Assembly meeting concluded that night with a point of order from Bulgaria demanding a report on the incident.' He stressed the explosive nature of the situation, and that our report would play an important role in the final stages of the ongoing debate. Thus it was important that the report should not only be factually correct but that any judgements expressed should be cautious and solidly based. My colleagues had a draft report ready for me to go over by that afternoon and we telexed the final text to the Secretary-General before the end of the day. We had three different accounts of the incident, and without extensive verification it would have been difficult for me to comment on how accurate each one was. Since the report was required urgently, I decided to present all three versions.

According to Mobutu, Nkokolo had arrived at the Ghana embassy with four men to see Welbeck when the UN troops opened fire. Nkokolo and his men had all been unarmed. The report of the Tunisian guard commander was that his soldiers had taken their positions in the embassy garden when forty Congolese soldiers arrived and were deployed facing them on the opposite side of the street. By 6 o'clock the Congolese had surrounded the embassy, including the Tunisians, with a battalion supported by two half-tracked armoured carriers. The Tunisian and

Congolese officers met at the embassy while their seven officers were meeting at ONUC headquarters to resolve the crisis. At 7.30, Nkokolo arrived with two civilians (probably Sûreté officers) and declared in an angry voice that he would attack the embassy in a quarter of an hour and take it by force. A little later he made as if to enter the embassy and the Tunisian officer told him that he could go in alone and unarmed. Thereupon Nkokolo struck the officer with his cane and one of the civilians held him as Congolese soldiers set upon him and knocked him down. A civilian ordered the Congolese soldiers to open fire at the Tunisians; they fired several volleys and the Tunisian officer in charge was wounded. The Tunisians returned the fire. The wounded Tunisian officer pleaded for a ceasefire, but in vain.

A number of independent witnesses said that firing began on the ONUC side but only in response to a mass charge by the Congolese led by Nkokolo. Nkokolo, who led the charge, was hit by a machine-gun burst and died instantly. Opening fire in self-defence was the authorised ONUC procedure and, if the Tunisians' account of the episode was accurate, they had acted correctly.

As things gradually returned to normal, I contemplated the consequences of what had happened. I had little doubt that Welbeck had stretched his diplomatic privileges in a despicable way. On the other hand, the Congolese had been absolutely wrong in threatening force, and their subsequent use of it was not only contrary to established diplomatic practice but had clearly not been needed. The resulting attitudes of the diplomatic missions in Leopoldville was ominous. Instead of working together under the doyen of the diplomatic corps, the embassies were sharply divided. Several were behind Mobutu and the Commissioners in their desire to be rid of Welbeck, since he was as much an annoyance to them as to the Kasavubu-Mobutu group. What became evident to me was that the UN could no longer count on some of the states which had professed their support for its efforts to cope with the Congo crisis. When the chips were down, self-interest predominated.

The incident had sadly confirmed that in spite of Mobutu's assurances to the contrary he had not gained control of his troops. Nkokolo had probably acted independently or perhaps primed by his Western military advisers. I prefer not to think that there might here been duplicity on the part of Mobutu. Nkokolo's death and the fighting between the UN and the ANC destroyed the aura of respect for ONUC among the Congolese troops. There had been a military confrontation, and most of the resulting casualties had been on the UN side. The ANC had not been humiliated as they had been by the Belgians, or disarmed as they had been by the UN when it first came to the Congo. These consequences helped to enhance Mobutu's prestige and served the interests of the Western embassies. It also marked the start of a process of reducing the authority of the UN, which, in contrast to earlier days, was now desired by the West. Dayal's reports, the actions of the Secretary-General and ONUC's activities were seen as too independent of Western influence. These had to be curbed, and ONUC kept on a tight rein.

While the Western diplomats openly blamed the UN for causing the fighting and gloated over our limited ability to act against the ANC. The Afro-Asians had different views; they wished that I had acted more forcefully and dealt with Mobutu once and for all. My explanations of ONUC's mandate made no difference to their attitudes. Even the Indian chargé d'affaires, Rahman, said to me, 'You still have a chance to be a hero in India. Why did you stop the military operation when you had the capacity to put an end to Mobutu and send the ANC back to their camps? You can still do it, and I promise I will see that you receive the highest award from India.'

I looked at him, not crediting what I had just heard, and replied that he could not be serious. He said with even greater enthusiasm that he was serious. 'Come on, Indar. You have plenty of guts. Fix Mobutu now.' Whether Rahman was serious or not, my only escape from this dialogue was to laugh and say again that he could only be joking. I said he must surely know my instructions, and how closely Hammarskjöld consulted India.

Ghaleb was the next to see me. He anticipated, rightly, that the Commissioners would act next against him. He too, like Welbeck and Djin, had been active in supporting Lumumba; he duly received his marching orders and left quietly. At the same time, Nkrumah decided to withdraw his embassy and the civil police unit which had played an invaluable role in the city.

23 November became the last day in my current assignment, as Dayal was due back the next day. Security was impossible at his house, which was on the river in Parc Hambise, because the ANC had begun to use boats, and therefore we arranged temporary accommodation for him and his wife at the Royal. At my staff meetings we attempted to compile all the information that was readily available to enable him to get into the saddle quickly. I was certainly glad to have him back.

On the day of Dayal's return, Nussbaumer gave a press conference. Well primed by his advisers, he was still trying to explain his own actions and those of the Congolese soldiers in connection with the Ghana embassy incident for which he laid all the blame on Ghana and on me. He claimed that Nkokolo was killed by two bullets which were heard coming from the enclosure where the Ghana police were stationed. Quoting from a report by a Tunisian lieutenant, which he interposed without making it clear when he was doing so, he claimed that Welbeck had at first agreed to leave without being forced, but because of my orders to send troops to the area to protect him, his attitude had stiffened. Nussbaumer further made the charge that Mobutu denied granting a twenty-four-hour delay in the expulsion, contrary to my statement transmitted through the Ghana liaison officer, and that the 'stupidity' of the orders given was further shown by Colonel Lasmar's 'ultimatum' to me to the effect that if interference with the expulsion order did not stop by 11 p.m., all Tunisian troops would be withdrawn from the area. Nussbaumer claimed that they had not withdrawn only because it was physically impossible for them to do so in the dark while the firing continued. He also said that steps would be taken against diplomats from two other countries in several days, after making sure there would be no repetition of the 21 November incident.

He stressed that the Congo was not at war with the United Nations and that these regrettable incidents would fade into the past. He wondered whether the UN presence was still needed. The UN had been involved in friction on various occasions with the Belgian and Congolese armies, and wished to stay in the Congo now because of the good pay and good conditions. In some respects, of course, UN assistance was needed but 'all these generals and all these contingents' certainly were not.[6]

After Dayal and I had read the report on Nussbaumer's press conference, he looked at me, through a cloud of pipe smoke. As he got up, he put his hand on my shoulder and said, 'You should be punished. You deserve a drink.'

NOTES

1. This Commission was established by General Assembly Resolution 1600 on 15 April 1961, and Jaya Wachuku, Nigerian Minister of Foreign Affairs, was appointed chairman. The Commission decided to visit the Congo immediately.
2. *New York Times*, 17 November 1960.
3. *New York Times*, 17 November 1960, pp.
4. Cable from Secretary-General to Rikhye of November 1960, No. 3635.
5. Cable from Cordier, New York to Rikhye of 22 November 1960.
6. Cable to the Secretary-General from Dayal of 24 November 1960, No. B-1503.

8

ARREST AND MURDER OF LUMUMBA

Incidents involving seizure of UN personnel and vehicles by the ANC had continued since the Ghana embassy occurrence, in spite of Mobutu's assurances that they would be stopped. Bomboko had achieved new prominence on being named by Kasavubu and Mobutu as Chairman of the College of Commissioners. In any event, in the absence of a constitutional government and as a former minister [a role he continued to perform], Bomboko was well known to ONUC, was accessible, as was the President: in effect he was the only civilian official with sufficient experience to be able to deal competently with the UN.

Dayal's immediate task after his return from New York was to assure a measure of security for UN personnel and establish a *modus vivendi* with Mobutu and Bomboko. Working through our military liaison staff and directly with Bomboko, we managed gradually to get the road-blocks removed and the pressures on ONUC were eased. However, Mobutu remained alienated from the higher echelons of ONUC although Kettani and his Moroccans were able to retain their contacts with him. It was rumoured, and later confirmed by Kettani, that Mobutu was considering assuming authority over the national government, but had so far avoided doing so by establishing the College of Commissioners with Bomboko as its head. Kettani informed Dayal after a private talk with Mobutu that the latter had chosen to refrain from such a step since he did not think the time was suitable. In any case, ONUC's task was not made any easier with a government in Leopoldville which did little for the administration of the country and with an army led by its Chief of Staff who had almost no control over his troops and who had to rely on the UN for his personal safety.

My first concern since Dayal's return was with his security and that of his wife Susheela. He received many verbal and written threats to his life, and some of his opponents did not even spare Susheela and phoned threats to her at the Royal. Some Congolese troops, believing that Dayal was living in his allotted house in Parc Hambise on the Congo river, attempted to approach it by boat but were turned back by the UN guard. Captain Gilbert Pongo, of the Congolese *Sûreté*, a familiar though unwelcome visitor to the Royal, called a number of times, brandished his pistol and threatened to kill Dayal. It needed the utmost restraint on the part of our staff to deal with his wild declarations and ease him out of our headquarters.

In consultation with McDiarmid and Habib Ahmed, our Chief Administrative Officer, I worked out a plan with the field security and the ONUC guard commander for the security of the Dayals, who were both very brave and did not want to be cut off from their responsibilities. They made our task easier by their co-operation and warning us of their movements in good time; in addition my work usually called for me to be by Dayal's side and we were often invited to the same social events, so I could personally keep a constant check on their security arrangements. It is to the credit of the UN Field Security that nothing untoward was ever allowed to happen.

My second concern was Von Horn. I had by now most of the facts relating to his absence during the Ghana embassy incidents. The two ADCs, who had been at the house with him on the day the shooting broke out, when called on to explain the circumstances to their respective national contingent commanders stuck to the story that they first gave to the Chief Operations Officer, which was that the General was unwell and was resting. Although I had enough information to refute the version of the ADCs, I decided to let them alone since, after all, they were covering for their General and repeating what they had been told to say.

I had spoken to the Force Chief Medical Officer Colonel B.L. Kapoor, a reputable Indian surgeon, who said that Von Horn had been under the care of a Canadian medical officer. When I questioned him on the nature of Von Horn's illness and whether the Canadian doctor had attended him on the day of the shooting, he became silent; I pressed him for a reply, but Kapoor pleaded that I should not ask him any more questions about Von Horn. When I insisted on being informed, he said that the Canadian doctor had reported to him on the General's condition and asked him to promise not to pass this information to anyone else. I was first aghast, then angry. I reminded Kapoor that he and the Canadian doctor were both military medical officers, and that in any force, whether Indian, Canadian or Nordic, the medical history of a serving soldier is part of the official record and available to his superiors. I wondered if Von

Horn's Military Assistant, Berthiume, who was a Canadian, had exercised his influence over his national contingent doctor. Kapoor had to concede that the normal military practice was as I had stated, but he was in honour bound not to reveal any information since it was 'between two doctors'. I told him to return to his office and tell the Canadian doctor that if he did not agree to my being informed on the state of the General's health I would have to take up the matter with the Canadian government for his violation of military practice.

Kapoor returned later that day. His Canadian colleague had reluctantly agreed to reveal that Von Horn was under treatment for hypertension and that on the day of the shooting his blood pressure had increased alarmingly. He was given medication and a sedative and ordered to rest in bed. When I asked if the General's illness was caused by over-indulgence or by the shooting in his neighbourhood, Kapoor looked at me blankly and said, 'You know the General better than we do.'

I now had sufficient information to begin the process of getting Von Horn removed. Not only was he inept in the command of the large Force, with its responsibility of maintaining law and order, but he had also failed the command at a critical hour because of his inability to withstand mental stress. I had to find a qualified commander for the UN Force very quickly.

Like Bunche, I had come to the conclusion that the usefulness of my remaining in the Congo was now limited. The Ghana embassy incident and subsequent days had lifted the veil from what was gradually becoming known: that I was in command of the force in all but name. Von Horn's recent behaviour had blown the myth created about him by us and by himself, and it was time for ONUC to have a new commander and for me to return to New York where I could be more useful. I had shared my thoughts with Dayal, but he cautioned me to go easy because Von Horn enjoyed Cordier's confidence from his time with UNTSO and when he was with Cordier in Leopoldville; also Hammarskjöld would find it awkward to remove a compatriot. But Dayal had established good contacts with the UN military and in a few days he also concluded that Von Horn should be replaced. In recommending this to Hammarskjöld he emphasised the effect of the climate on the General's health. However, Hammarskjöld, never a man to delay important decisions, showed a hesitancy we had not seen hitherto.

In early December, Major-General Sean McKeown, Chief of Staff of the Irish Army, came to the Congo to visit his troops. As a matter of routine, I had asked the Irish contingent commander to obtain a copy of his *curriculum vitae* for my information: he had done all the right things in command, staff and at schools, working his way up the ladder to the top assignment in his country. He was in his early fifties and seemed a suitable candidate for the ONUC command.

I briefed Dayal about McKeown, and then both of us saw him a number of times during the next few days and again after he returned from visiting the Irish units in Katanga. We came to the same conclusion that he was our man. Before he left the Congo, Dayal asked him if he would be interested in the UN command: he said he would and was flattered at being asked, but did not think his government would release him before the end of his tenure.

Dayal recommended to Hammarskjöld that he appoint McKeown as Commander of ONUC and request Ireland to make him available immediately. With the strong support of Frank Aiken, the Irish Foreign Minister, McKeown was made available to take over ONUC. However, concerned at reports from the Irish staff at ONUC headquarters and other senior officers that I was in fact the man in charge of the military operations, McKeown had asked me before returning to Dublin to explain the higher set-up of the UN operation in the Congo. He asked if I intended to remain in the Congo. I realised what he was implying and replied that when he took over the command I would return to New York to do what I was really supposed to do and that he could count on my full support. He was visibly relieved. On completion of the arrangements for a new commander, Hammarskjöld informed Von Horn in a politely-worded cable that he was needed in Jerusalem and should return to his appointment as Chief of Staff, UNTSO. Von Horn was visibly relieved, and if he had any qualms over his hasty departure from ONUC he never showed them. As was his style, he plunged into the ceremonies of his departure and began his round of farewells. He was due for leave, and in a few weeks he took off for a holiday in Sweden before resuming his appointment in Jerusalem. Recent events had led to my being identified with Dayal's actions and as Hammarskjöld's adviser I was recognised as his man in the Congo. The incidents between the ANC and the UN had shown that I could not be influenced by the divided diplomatic community. I had implemented the decisions of the Secretary-General and UN resolutions, and because the Western embassies regarded these as contrary to their interests I was out of favour with them. They had found it easier to persuade Von Horn, and especially his personal staff, to agree to their suggestions: on a number of occasions the latter had made statements to the press sympathetic to the Western view and contrary to Hammarskjöld's policies. Some of the diplomats for whom I was a thorn in the side openly sympathised with Von Horn's staff when their authority over ONUC operations was reduced. Several Western military attachés had raised the question of my role in the Congo and their concern increased when I took temporary charge of the mission in November.

A British military attaché pointedly asked me, when I was acting head of the UN mission, why as a professional military officer I had taken over political functions, which were contrary to the excellent Indian military tradition of being non-political—he was, in fact, conveying the disquiet of his embassy at my temporary elevation into the realms of diplomacy. I told him, as I often reminded my own countrymen, that our military traditions were largely inherited from the British. The old Indian Political Service had been responsible for diplomacy and been recruited from the military as well as from civilian services.

Since independence India had forged many new practices. The Neutral Nations Repatriation Commission, provided by India and sent to Korea to repatriate prisoners of war, was headed by a serving soldier, General Thimayya. After the police action in Hyderabad, General J.N. Chaudhari, the commander of the troops, was appointed as the military governor. Many distinguished retired military officers were appointed as state governors or ambassadors and some were active in politics. In a democracy the civil and security forces are two sides of the same coin and there should be no separation. It was my belief that no service officer could aspire to a higher command or a staff position in a democratic state without understanding the political processes, thus becoming what my colleagues in the Congo now called a 'political General'. I was proud, not ashamed, of my unique experience in military-political leadership.

President Kasavubu returned in triumph from New York and on his arrival was cheered by thousands of Congolese. Dayal and I, as well as the diplomatic corps, were present at the airport to receive him. The UN General Assembly's recognition of him on 22 November as the Congo delegate had given him a new status. Unquestionably, he was the only recognised Congolese leader. When he had left for New York earlier in the month, none of the UN senior staff had seen him off. Even Mobutu was irritated by his presumption in representing the Congo; now Mobutu was present with his para-commando battalion and an army band.

To the amazement of many diplomats, and certainly those of us from the UN, Kasavubu emerged from the Belgian aircraft wearing a resplendent white military uniform as Commander-in-Chief of the ANC. His sword, which was either too long for his short stature or could not be buckled at the last minute, was carried behind him. He was greeted by Mobutu with a salute and then led to the receiving line of Congolese dignitaries and diplomats.

There was a state dinner that evening at the President's house which Dayal attended. It had rained heavily during the night, and I had gone to bed late after an enjoyable evening with some of the ONUC staff. The next morning I was awakened early by the duty officer, who reported that Lumumba had disappeared from his house during the night. The Moroccan guard had seen a car arrive there at 10 p.m. but it was only in the early hours of the morning that they realised the house was quiet, entered and found it empty. In the past Lumumba had left his house to visit the African quarter and we were not sure if he had done this again, but this time he would have had to elude his UN guards and the ANC troops surrounding his house. Dayal had also been informed, and we immediately sent for Kettani. He had nothing new to add, but by this time it seemed that Lumumba had indeed disappeared.

While Dayal contacted those diplomats who had called on the Prime Minister most frequently to see if they had any knowledge of his movements, I gave instructions to the Force staff to place units on the alert and send our reliable police personnel into the African quarter for information. The liaison staff were told to establish immediate contact with the ANC, the *Sûreté* and the military attachés—particularly the American, British and French who had an extensive intelligence network.

Dayal and I discussed what Lumumba might be up to. A couple of days earlier he had asked Dayal for an aircraft to carry the body of his stillborn child for burial in Stanleyville. Dayal had refused for the reason that an aircraft could not be spared, even for such a purpose, but he had other valid considerations too. Gizenga had already declared that the legitimate government of the Congo, with Lumumba as Prime Minister, was established at Stanleyville, and therefore a UN aircraft provided by Dayal for Lumumba to fly to Stanleyville would have had obvious connotations. Regardless of the possible slurs by the West on Dayal's intentions the flight could only have been allowed at grave risk to the UN's efforts to unify the country. Lumumba could not have obtained a civilian aircraft because these were controlled by the Belgians, and in any case the ANC would have blocked its departure. Therefore, Lumumba might now possibly be attempting to reach Stanleyville by road or river and if this were the case we would probably not hear anything more until he arrived there.

We glumly reviewed the dangerous political consequences there would be if Lumumba succeeded in reaching Stanleyville and the near-certainty that it would lead to an intensification of the civil war with dire effects on ONUC operations. We told the press what we knew so far and categorically denied the charge that the UN had assisted Lumumba in his flight. If the Moroccans had assisted him in any way, then what was the ANC's so-called élite commando unit doing around the house and around the UN guard?

In New York the UN budgetary committee was discussing the financing of the Congo operation. The Soviets had already refused to pay their share and on 29 November they demanded that the UN withdraw its troops to prevent its going bankrupt. They again accused Hammarskjöld of bungling, and opened a new drive to bring the Congo question before the Security Council. The United States, determined to support the operation, waived about $10 million of the $14 million cost of the airlift and supplies contributed by them. Furthermore, it made a voluntary contribution of $3-4 million to reduce the shares of countries with limited funds. These contributions were in addition to the special assessment to cover the cost of the operation. Senator George D. Aiken, the US representative on the committee, said that the offer was a tribute to the UN soldiers who had already given their lives to ensure the success of this historic effort. This seemingly made little difference to the Soviet delegate, Aleksei A. Roschin, who accused the Secretary-General of jeopardising the financial structure of the UN and of having already taken money illegally from the regular budget and threatened technical assistance aid and development programmes by borrowing from their special funds. The UN was already embroiled in a political crisis, but it now faced a financial one.

After the Nigerian brigade had arrived, I arranged for a reorganisation of the troops in North Katanga. There had recently been savage tribal fighting, resulting in much killing. One Nigerian battalion was flown to Kamina and it made sense to me to send it by road from there to Manono, but the motor convoy was attacked with bows and arrows by rebel tribesmen before it got there. Our troops reported fourteen tribesmen killed with no casualties on their side. I was also concerned about new tensions in Kabalo. The Baluba leaders had warned the UN not to protect the Katanga police or the whites. There was considerable movement of pro-Lumumba troops in the area, causing Katanga security forces to react.

On Kasavubu's initiative, a meeting of the Congolese leaders was held at Brazzaville on 29 November. Gizenga had agreed to attend, but because of Lumumba's escape he did not do so. Tshombe's attendance was also in doubt, but eventually he appeared. At the meeting Kasavubu proposed a round-table conference where they would all meet at an acceptable place. Optimistic statements emerged from Kasavubu's entourage, but Tshombe expressed different views before his departure for Elisabethville. He asserted that the Congo could not be ruled from Leopoldville and that the present military regime of Mobutu, who was also at the conference, was a temporary administration. Tshombe spoke repeatedly of 'the states of the Congo', thereby indicating that he regarded Katanga as on an equal footing with the Republic of the Congo. He had met a delegation from Stanleyville, which he did not name, but he would have nothing to do with Lumumba because, he said, 'one cannot deal with a madman.'

There were frequent pro-Lumumba demonstrations in Stanleyville, invariably followed by the harassment or arrest of Europeans. The UN troops intervened on each occasion and obtained the release of those illegally arrested. On the basis of a rumour that unauthorised individuals had recently arrived in the city to engage in espionage, the local authorities ordered a check on the identity cards of all Europeans, and fifteen were detained for having incorrect documentation. It was reported to us that during the check the Europeans had been mistreated and beaten and Brigadier Otu, ONUC Chief Liaison Officer, accompanied by an operations officer, Major Ejaz Azim, were dispatched from headquarters to investigate and facilitate their release.

The ONUC team met Salamu, the District Administrator, and General Lundula and interviewed the European detainees—which revealed that some Europeans had been manhandled, but not to the extent reported to us in Leopoldville; this treatment had only been meted out to those who refused to show their identity cards. The Congolese had also been annoyed by the arrogance of the Belgians who, according to Otu, 'still suffered from their colonial complex'. One had even called a Congolese a monkey, which had led to his being beaten severely. Otu was able to post a UN guard inside the jail and subsequently obtained the release of the detainees. Otu had also been asked to smooth relations between the Ethiopian Brigade and the UN's Chief Civilian Officer. This was one of the few occasions in the Congo operation when civilian-military relations had to be mediated by a higher authority. Of course, there were problems between the civil and military wings, but they were no different from what normally occurred in a multinational force. Both Otu and Ejaz Azim were outstanding officers, and they did not take long to establish harmony and proper coordination.

With Lumumba probably heading towards Oriental province, I viewed the role of ONUC in Stanleyville as critical, as it already was in Elisabethville. The UN had an advantage in Stanleyville since we were familiar with Gizenga and Lundula, just as they had learned to have a degree of confidence in us. In the coming days we would need to draw on our Stanleyville assets to the full.

On 1 December, Kasavubu called for the withdrawal of the Egyptian embassy, accusing it of conspiring in Lumumba's escape, and Nasser at once ordered his ambassador, Morad Ghaleb, and the entire embassy staff to leave the country, and suspended diplomatic relations. At the same time, Nasser denounced Belgium's role in the Congo and broke relations there too, freezing Belgian assets in Egypt.

We had learned that Nkrumah, bypassing the UN command, had instructed his contingent to provide protection to Lumumba if he sought their assistance. Dayal had his political adviser Gustavo Duran and his legal adviser Bill Cox prepare guidelines for the UN troops regarding their response if the Kasavubu-Mobutu regime sought help in arresting Lumumba or if Lumumba and those colleagues of his who had escaped with him sought our protection. The advisers based their proposed guidelines on instructions received from Hammarskjöld a few weeks earlier when a fight had broken out among ANC elements in Stanleyville and Gizenga had sought UN protection. In a personal cable Hammar-skjöld had instructed Dayal that for the time being we had to 'give protection to Gizenga, even while in UN precincts. But it must be understood that he could choose either to rely on our protection and refrain from any tricks (i.e. political activity), or continue with his tricks and forgo all protection.'

In the meantime, good and loyal troops that they were, the Ghanaians reported to headquarters their intention of providing Lumumba with protection if so requested. Dayal had the following instructions sent to them by the force staff: 'Lumumba was under UN guard only while at his residence [when in Leopoldville] and cannot be allowed UN cover or protection in pursuit of his aims, and ONUC must be entirely disassociated from his activities. Different rules could apply if individual lives were in danger, and in specific circumstances, and protection could be given solely as a step to restoring peace.' This formula had Hammarskjöld's approval. Dayal had reasoned that this approach would leave the door open for protection in case Lumumba's life was known to be under threat, but it would disassociate ONUC from his political activities. We thus hoped to keep clear of any charge of improper interference in the Congo's internal affairs while keeping in reserve the possibility of intervention for the express purpose of preventing danger to Lumumba's life.

Mobutu had alerted his troops in the eastern provinces to look out for Lumumba. Captain Pongo turned up at the Royal asking for an aircraft and when he was refused left in a huff. He obtained an Air Congo aircraft and after aimlessly flying around the country returned to Leopoldville. Every day there were rumours that Lumumba had been seen somewhere, but there was no definite sighting. The entire intelligence network of Western embassies and Belgian-owned companies' personnel and communications had joined in the hunt; some of the Western envoys had communicated Kasavubu's false charge of ONUC's complicity in helping Lumumba to escape to New York where the rumour multiplied throughout the UN corridors. At one time it was rumoured that Lumumba had reached the Ghana Brigade and was under its protection, and there was talk of his having left for Accra or Conakry.

The chase continued, causing great suspense. Then, on 2 December, the Ghana Brigade reported by a flash message to headquarters that Lumumba had been arrested by Congolese soldiers about 5 miles north of Mweka, near Port Francqui, from where he was being taken to Luluabourg en route to Leopoldville. The story of his escape was finally pieced together, but some questions remained unanswered. He had left his house by car during a rainstorm on the night of 27 November, but we still do not know who provided the car. It could have belonged to a Congolese supporter, or it may have been from an embassy and thus did not arouse the suspicions of the UN guard. Who had come to fetch Lumumba? Was it a friendly diplomat or was it one of his colleagues later reported to be with him during his journey to Kasai? Once he left his house, either in the darkened back seat of the car or in the boot, it became relatively easy to construct his itinerary.

He was joined at some point by Kashamura, Okito and Mpolo, but this could either have been at the start of the journey or somewhere on the road. They then went on for some hours, and it seemed that during daylight while passing through a village or stopping for food or gas he was recognised and hailed, the local population having no idea that he was actually on the run. Responding to his reception, Lumumba accepted hospitality and addressed the people, declaring that he would oust the illegal regime in Leopoldville and return his government to power. Thereafter, instead of a clandestine escape, Lumumba's movements became a triumphant journey through the countryside. He was a political animal whose political activities had been severely restricted and of course meeting crowds, however small, and making speeches must have acted like a heady wine—it was something he could not resist. The news of his journey travelled fast, and it was not long before it reached his pursuers who were quickly able to arrest him.

At the Royal, while we awaited Lumumba's return to Leopoldville, we wondered if he would be alive or dead and if alive in what physical state. The diplomats at the embassies who sympathised with him argued that he was, after all, the Prime Minister; he had been in distress since the coup in September and once he was out in the open with the people he had to do what he did. They maintained that his arrest by Kasavubu and Mobutu had been illegal and therefore his captors would not dare to maltreat him because of the grave consequences. I thought such a view naive because of the behaviour pattern of the Congolese which had so clearly emerged. The ANC, the police and for that matter the population so easily resorted to violence; Lumumba had been manhandled repeatedly by the ANC in the past and saved only by UN intervention. Surely he could have predicted what would happen to him if he were arrested. When he finally reached Leopoldville, we were relieved to learn that he was alive, although he had been beaten.

The journalists who came to question us about the UN attitude on Lumumba told us of his journey from N'Djili airport to Mobutu's camp: he had been carried in the back of an open truck with his hands tied behind his back, and the soldiers had turned him about violently to exhibit him to the crowds as they drove through the city, pulling his hair and hitting him. This was part of their ritual of treating prisoners, with which we had become familiar in the Congo. On reaching Mobutu's headquarters in Binza he was taken out of the truck, shoved violently into Mobutu's presence and set upon by soldiers of the Baluba tribe. Cut and badly bruised, he was once again put into the truck and driven away. That evening Brazzaville radio reported that he had been removed in a small military convoy to Camp Hardy at Thysville, which was far enough away to keep him from his supporters in Leopoldville; our liaison staff, along with the ANC, confirmed that this report was true.

The press informed us of Mobutu's comments on Lumumba's future. He had indicated that the deposed Prime Minister would be brought to trial for inciting the army to rebellion and other crimes and that it was 'up to the judiciary' to decide on his fate. There was already an arrest warrant, signed by Kasavubu, charging that Lumumba had misused his powers as head of government by persecuting political opponents and subjecting them to atrocities.

While this cruel drama was unfolding, Mobutu told the press that the ANC platoon which had arrested Lumumba was attacked by Ghanaian troops, whom his own troops had repulsed. He also claimed that he had prevented Lumumba from being shot by the ANC. Earlier that day Dayal had received a letter from Kasavubu charging that Ghanaian troops had freed Lumumba at Port Francqui and threatening to break off relations with the UN. A couple of days earlier, when there had been no news of his whereabouts, it was alleged that Lumumba had sought Ghanaian protection during his journey, but without success. There was no end to such stories. The fact was that the Ghanaians had not seen him at any time during this episode—indeed, until after his arrest. In obedience to the ONUC order, they had not interfered. Thus the stories were a fabrication by someone who wished to widen the chasm between the UN and Kasavubu-Mobutu.

We were mobbed at the Royal. All the diplomats at once wished to talk to or see Dayal. ONUC contingent commanders and national liaison officers wanted to know from me the response of the Congolese military command. The Congolese, representing different views, came in droves. One thing became very clear to me on the morning of 3 December: Lumumba's arrest had brought about an historic change in the Congo and consequently in the role of the UN. Furthermore, because of the wide divergence of views among the UN member states, including troop-contributing countries, there would be large-scale withdrawals of contingents and of financial support for ONUC. In fact, there would be immediate problems with countries supporting Lumumba which would adversely affect UN military operations.

The majority of the Afro-Asians urged Dayal to free Lumumba, or at least to station UN personnel where he was held to ensure that he was treated humanely. Some of the francophone African countries that had already given their support to the Kasavubu regime and sympathised with

Tshombe shared the view expressed by the Western embassies that the UN should not interfere. The military staff from those embassies did not mince words with me on what they expected from the UN, whereas the commanders and the national liaison officers of the UN command expressed concern for Lumumba's safety. Our senior military officers, with the exception of a very few who sympathised with the Belgian and Western view, said that ONUC was responsible for the safety of the Congolese leadership, including Lumumba, and that they therefore hoped our political superiors (i.e. the Secretary-General and his Special Representative in the Congo) would not hesitate to act accordingly. None of them suggested the use of force, but they felt that ONUC should do for Lumumba what it had done for others who had been arrested.

The news of Lumumba's arrest, ill-treatment by the ANC and incarceration in Thysville caused a storm at the UN in New York. In a cable to Dayal, Hammarskjöld said, 'Emotional tensions here regarding the Lumumba case are considerable, and if things run wild or summary justice is executed, the consequences may be very bad both for the Organization and its operation. We are in the middle of an extraordinarily complicated and indeed politically dangerous situation.'[1] In a message to Kasavubu, he said that a great number of delegates had approached him and expressed their deep concern at the action taken against Lumumba outside the framework of due process of law. He appealed to Kasavubu's wisdom and fair-mindedness and assured him that he was not expressing a view or interfering in an internal problem of the Congo.

The Soviet Union issued a statement asserting that Hammarskjöld and the UN command were 'directly responsible' for Lumumba's safety, and reiterating the Soviet view that Lumumba was the head of the Congo's legitimate government. They recalled their objections to the seating of the 'one-sided delegation led by Kasavubu', condemned Mobutu's regime, and accused the 'Belgian aggressors and their NATO allies' and the UN command of complicity.

The Indian Defence Minister, Krishna Menon, had hurried to New York on learning of Lumumba's arrest and at a meeting of the Afro-Asian group stated that he wanted the entire group to meet Hammarskjöld to urge him to act on behalf of Lumumba. Eventually a delegation consisting of Cameroon Foreign Minister Joseph Oweno, C.S. Jha of India and Henry Ford Cooper of Liberia called on Hammarskjöld, conveying the unanimous support of the Afro-Asian group for his earlier démarche to Kasavubu. The delegation wanted these messages urgently despatched to Kasavubu—who had left the capital on the same day as Lumumba was taken to Thysville. Dayal sent them by hand via his senior political adviser, Gustavo Duran, who found Kasavubu in the lower Congo. Duran was received coldly and told that a written reply would be sent. In the reply, received a few days later, Kasavubu asked why there had been so much solicitude for Lumumba, who was guilty of crimes against the state and the people, including genocide. Why was the UN not doing anything about Stanleyville? Then he upbraided the Afro-Asian states for showing such concern for Lumumba while they had a poor record for their own treatment of political opponents. It became clear to us that Kasavubu had no intention of doing anything for Lumumba.

Meanwhile, fires still burned in other parts of the Congo. Moroccan troops had to fight the Balubas in Luena to prevent their ransacking the town for food. Other Balubas attacked Swedes and Nigerians in Kabalo and lost nineteen men in the process. In Oriental province Mobutu had announced that his troops had surrounded the Stanleyville gendarmerie; it seemed that he had learned to use propaganda to his best advantage even when the truth was different. In fact, pro-Lumumba forces had invaded Equateur province and were trouncing Mobutu's troops. Our forces, small in number, succeeded in limiting the fighting. There was unrest on the Kasai-Leopoldville border, in the area where Lumumba had been arrested. Although UN troops were thin on the ground, they were patrolling actively to ease tensions.

On 5 December a former secretary to Lumumba, Bernard Salamu, announced the secession of Oriental province from the centre and declared himself the Commissioner of the Eastern District, Oriental province, and parts of adjoining provinces which were pro-Lumumba. He also appointed a former clerk, J.F. Manziala, to be the Provincial President and a leftist rabble-rouser, Jean Gengis, as burgomaster of Stanleyville. Salamu, who was known to have on been visits to the Soviet Union, China and Czechoslovakia, added to the concern of Western powers at renewed Communist penetration in the Congo. The West hoped these fears would be eliminated with the removal of Lumumba from power and of the East European embassies from the country. Two days later Kasavubu placed the rebellious province under martial law, and Mobutu ordered another offensive, which followed the usual pattern, causing more harm to the population of the border villages than to any pro-Lumumba soldiers. Vigorous action by the UN troops was undertaken to contain rival troops and minimise the damage.

In New York, on 5 December, Hammarskjold released Dayal's report on the arrest of Lumumba. Included in this was what our troops in Thysville had reported on Lumumba's condition on the basis of information from the ANC. The Moroccans had reported that Lumumba was in detention at Camp Hardy and was suffering from serious injuries received before his arrival. His head had been shaven, his hands were tied and he was being kept in an unhygienic cell. Dayal had protested to Bomboko against this ill-treatment and appealed for humane treatment and for the due process of law.

The Soviet Union called for Lumumba to be released and for the disarming of his captors, Mobutu's troops, by the UN Force. They also proposed that the General Assembly and the Security Council discuss the restoration of the legitimate government and parliament of the Congo, the creation of a special commission of representatives from the African states to determine where Mobutu had obtained arms and money to equip and maintain his forces, and the evacuation of all Belgian military and executive personnel. The Soviets alleged that American 'imperialists' had helped the Belgians to return to the Congo and invited the French and the Portuguese to join them, and blamed the United States for the continuing unrest and 'for open flagrant interference in the internal affairs of the Congo.' They further alleged that the US embassy in Leopoldville was directing Congolese affairs. The Soviets did not overlook the UN in their condemnation, and repeated that Hammarskjold and Mobutu were both 'lackeys of imperialism'.

At the meeting of the Congo Advisory Committee that day, its members discussed delivering an ultimatum to Kasavubu to come to terms with the UN or run the risk of the UN withdrawing its troops and economic assistance, but this posed some fearful questions. If ONUC were to withdraw, chaos in the country would result and furthermore Hammarskjöld might find it difficult to persuade everyone to comply. If Ghana, Guinea and Egypt placed their contingents at the disposal of the followers of Lumumba to defeat Kasavubu and other political rivals, the UN would have to cope with a far more serious crisis. Faced with this dilemma, the committee agreed to continue consideration of the tough choices before it on the ground.

In the face of Soviet pressure for an early meeting of the Security Council, other members agreed with the United States that more time was needed for consultations. Because of its concern at the reports of Lumumba being ill-treated, the United States made a personal appeal to Kasavubu and Mobutu through its ambassador in the Congo, Clare H. Timberlake, to give Lumumba humane treatment and a fair trial. He also asked for Lumumba to be allowed visits from a physician of the Red Cross. In a statement to the press Mobutu denied cruelty to Lumumba and the allegation in Dayal's report that he was suffering from serious head injuries. He said that Belgian doctors had examined him and pronounced him to be in a satisfactory condition. He conceded that Lumumba had a sprained wrist and a swollen eye from the beatings he had been given by his captors

The Security Council took up the Congo debate with V. A. Zorin, the Permanent Soviet Representative, as the Council President, despite an attempt by the US delegate, Ambassador James J. Wadsworth, to prevent it on the grounds that Zorin had 'participated actively in Soviet efforts to undermine UN actions in the Congo'. This proved to be a diversion which gained the United States two hours of procedural wrangling and time to make some propaganda gains to match Soviet attempts to blame it for the crisis.

While world attention was focused on this debate, Hammarskjöld was informed by Yugoslavia's chief delegate, Dobrivoje Vidić, of the decision of his government to withdraw its troops from ONUC. Vidić said that his country 'does not wish to bear or share the responsibility for what is taking place in the Congo'. Ceylon and Egypt announced similar decisions, and the talk in the corridors was that Indonesia and Ghana would soon follow.

Back in Leopoldville, what I had feared was now upon us. The departure of the Yugoslavs reduced our air crew by twenty-one men: this, while not impairing our operational ability, was of consequence because they were the only East European and Socialist contingent in the Force. The departure of the Ceylon contingent equally did not affect the Force other than by manifesting that country's disapproval of our handling of the Force. On the other hand, the withdrawal of the Egyptian contingent would provide us with some gains as well as some losses. Although it was ably led by Colonel Shazli, the constant interference in its functioning by the Egyptian ambassador in the Congo had proved a headache. Therefore, the first reaction in ONUC on that particular score was relief.

But we had lost a battalion in Equateur, which had become the area of manoeuvring between the followers of Mobutu and Lumumba, and we needed all the troops that we could keep there. Furthermore, their departure would free Nasser to increase his support for the Stanleyville regime and thus add to our problems. Like Egypt, Indonesia had sent a fine battalion, but while the performance of the Egyptians had been marred by the interference of their embassy, the Indonesians earned praise from everyone.

The redeployment of the Force had become my major preoccupation. I made several flying visits to the provincial capitals to talk to our political officers and military commanders and to view critical areas. I took Mobutu along on one of these visits to the former Belgian bases of Kitona and Banana at the mouth of the Congo river. Although our relations had become strained since the Ghana embassy incident, we had met frequently on business and at social events and kept up a correct and polite relationship. Mobutu had discussed the possibility of parachute training at Kitona for his élite battalion and Kettani had recommended this to me; he also agreed when I suggested it might be useful to show Kitona to Mobutu. Mobutu and I were together for the whole day, with the army interpreters. His wife had come along too and when she felt sick on the flight he showed a touching concern for her comfort. He shyly informed me that she was expecting another child.

Mobutu was, as usual, open and frank, and spoke of his desire to learn to be a good soldier. He was caught, unwillingly, in the Congolese political web. He had been loyal to Lumumba and helped him out of his earlier mishaps, but Lumumba had subsequently gone too far; he was not a conciliator and what had happened to him was his own doing. At his own level Mobutu had done all he could to treat Lumumba well, but his soldiers had not forgotten the consequences of the invasion of the eastern Kasai and attempts to enter Katanga. The state had charged him with crimes and due process of law would be followed in dealing with him.

When I asked if he intended to assume full power at the end of the year, he said he did not. He insisted that it was not his intention to play any political role other than what was absolutely essential; he hoped the Congo would cope with its political problems so that he could devote his time and the efforts of the army to its professional training. In an implied reference to continuing UN criticism of his role and of the behaviour of the ANC, he explained that he was doing his best with the resources available. He had sought the UN's help, which had been refused. I explained to him the complexities of UN politics, something I was sure he had heard a lot about from Kettani. A duly-elected government, soon after its independence, had asked for and received the UN's assistance. Then political problems in the country led to a coup, while the UN, which had responsibilities for maintaining law and order, was present. In fact, those who carried out the coup were themselves under UN protection at the time. The UN did not give the coup authority or legitimacy and therefore could render no assistance. It was not until Kasavubu was recognised as the legitimate representative of the Congo that the UN was able to act, collaborating with him and no one else. Mobutu did not comment, but his disappointment was obvious.

On 8 December Ahmed, the CAO, and Madan, the Chief Logistics Officer, reported that Otraco, the Belgian company handling ONUC's road-rail-river transportation, had refused to ship supplies for our troops in Equateur and Oriental provinces. When asked to explain their refusal, they said they were acting under instructions from the Congolese security department. The transport company was a semi-state monopoly, but still controlled by the Belgians. When the Congolese authorities were contacted by Linner's staff, they explained that Otraco's scarce resources were needed primarily for civilian purposes—an explanation at odds with the fact that it was the UN civil assistance programme which was meeting the needs of the population. Clearly, the restriction on the UN supplies was intended to regulate our ability to supply the dissident province controlled by Gizenga, as well as to prevent UN troops from interfering with the

ANC's operations against pro-Lumumba forces. Faced with our strong protests, the Congolese lifted the restrictions a few days later, having caused our troops and the civil population in the northern and the eastern provinces considerable inconvenience.

In the United States, meanwhile, John F. Kennedy, Senator for Massachusetts, had won the presidential election. His youngest brother Edward Kennedy was on a tour of African states, including the Congo, on which he was to report to the President-elect, and about the same time three Democratic senators, Frank Church of Idaho, Frank E. Moss of Utah and Gale W. McGhee of Wyoming, all members of the Senate Foreign Relations Committee, were visiting the Congo. This provided the UN with an opportunity to show off its remarkable achievements in face of the criticism from the regimes in Leopoldville, Bakwanga and Elisabethville and their Belgian and other Western sympathisers. It was encouraging to know that the senators were willing to affirm American support for the UN. Senator Church said in a press statement that the UN was the proper agency to cope with the Congolese problem at that time, and Edward Kennedy expressed similar views in his meetings with Dayal and senior ONUC staff. We therefore had reason to expect increased American support once the Kennedy administration was installed.

As the Security Council continued its debate on the Congo, the Congolese regime in Leopoldville accused ONUC, led as it was by Asians and Africans, of showing a bias towards Lumumba. Reporting on this from Leopoldville in the *New York Times*, Paul Hoffman wrote: 'The levers of command at the United Nations Headquarters are in the hands of Africans and Asians. The special representative of Secretary-General Dag Hammarskjöld, Ambassador Rajeshwar Dayal, is an Indian. Also an Indian is Hammarskjöld's and Dayal's military adviser, Brigadier Indarjit Rikhye, the most important figure in the international force's staff.' Although the report did not mention the Africans, they were Kettani of Morocco, the Deputy Force Commander, and Iyassou of Ethiopia, the Chief of Staff. The two most influential members of the civil team were Mahmood Khiari of Tunisia and Robert Gardiner of Ghana.

The Belgians, angered by Dayal's report on the behaviour of Belgian nationals in the Congo and Hammarskjöld's demand for their removal, were uninhibited in their protests against UN leadership. The Western powers did all they could to persuade the UN to favour the Kasavubu-Mobutu regime. At the same time, the Soviet Union and several Afro-Asian governments accused the UN of colluding with Lumumba's enemies, which caused those of us at the Royal considerable concern. More African states announced the withdrawal of their troops from the UN force, Guinea and Morocco being the latest. The departure of the Moroccans would be a serious loss; next to the Ethiopians they had the largest number of troops and, along with their training team, they had retained their influence with the ANC. Kettani, their wise and able general, was almost revered by the Congolese officers and his counsel to us at the Royal was invaluable.

In his reply to comments on the UN's role in the Congo, Hammarskjöld pointed out that any action by the Force to liberate Lumumba or disarm the ANC under Mobutu would mean overriding the authority of the President, whereas the UN was required to cooperate with the Congolese authorities. While political persuasion could be employed, the use of force was something entirely different, inasmuch as the Security Council and the Secretary-General were bound by the Charter provisions, which preclude any interference in the internal affairs of states. He emphasised that the UN operation could not continue if it was constantly subjected to criticism and suspicion, inside and outside the Congo, and enfeebled by withdrawals and by lack of financial and material support. He said that many opinions had been expressed on the role of the UN. The Council and the Assembly could share responsibility for the interpretation of resolutions. He pointed out that the Council had never invoked Articles 41 and 42 of the Charter which provided enforcement measures. The Council, if it so desired, could define the role of the UN troops. The Council considered three draft resolutions but was unable to agree. The Congo debate in the General Assembly was to be resumed on 16 December.

On 13 December, the College of Commissioners, accompanied by some ANC soldiers, attempted to occupy Kitona by force with the intention of seizing arms stored there to use in their operations against pro-Lumumba forces in Oriental. Our small garrison took a tough stand and refused to hand over the keys to the armoury. On receiving our report on the incident, Hammarskjöld lodged a strong protest with Kasavubu and eventually the Commissioners were persuaded to withdraw. They were incapable of administering the country in a meaningful way and were often used by their advisers to undertake similarly dramatic roles which gave them a sense of importance, but had the effect of heightening their frustrations with the UN. The attempt to seize weapons from Kitona was related to reports from Stanleyville that outside aid, including arms, was beginning to flow to the Lumumba group; UN observers at the airport in Stanleyville had indeed reported their suspicion that arms were being brought in aboard Soviet aircraft. We ordered greater vigilance on traffic into airports in the province.

Lumumba's forces had by now gained control of eastern Equateur and Kivu in addition to Oriental and were gradually working towards North Katanga. The Nigerians had replaced the Irish in Kivu and established good relations with the local ANC. The UN force was short of medical personnel. Most of the contingents could not provide more than normal medical cover for a unit, consisting of a medical officer with orderlies, whereas our units, which were widely scattered, needed much more. I had tried to locate a physician, a surgeon, an anaesthetist, a dentist and nurses at each battalion headquarters to staff a small hospital; serious casualties and the sick were to be evacuated by air to the Indian general hospital in Leopoldville and its detachments at Coquilhatville and Luluabourg. Brigade or regiment-size contingents had brought such medical units, but most of the other contingents were battalions or units of 3-400 men or less, and their countries did not have the resources to spare doctors for duty in the Congo. When the care of the Baluba refugees in South Kasai was added to the Indian hospital's responsibilities, it became urgent to obtain at least one more unit. Austria responded, and ONUC decided to locate it in Bukavu. Our troops there were the farthest from the capital, and there was a severe shortage of local doctors since most of the Europeans had left when Lumumbists took over control of the area.

The advance party of the hospital under Colonel Foltin arrived at Bukavu on 8 December. The chief of the ONUC civilian mission, Robert Miller, immediately informed the provincial civil authorities and the commander of the ANC, Commandant Singha, and expressed his hope that the hospital would also contribute to the local medical needs. The main body of the Austrian unit and its stores arrived on the night of December 14/15, but the next evening, while the stores were still being unloaded, a truckload of ANC arrived and took up positions in the street. The Congolese sergeant in charge expressed the belief that the Austrians were Belgian paracommandos in disguise. On learning of this development, the Nigerian commander, Lieutenant-Colonel Aguiyi-Ironsi,[2] immediately went to the Austrian camp. Very soon, provincial President Miruhu, who had been constitutionally elected and was a Lumumbist, arrived too, declared that he had had no previous knowledge of the arrival of the Austrian hospital staff, and supported the contention of the gendarmes. Ironsi, by now joined by Miller, argued with the Congolese, but to no effect. Unfortunately, Commandant Singha, whom Miller believed to be reasonable, was attending a conference of ANC commanders in Leopoldville, which was indicative of the uncertain loyalties of the Congolese military officers.[3] As discussions with the Congolese were getting nowhere, the ANC decided to take the Austrians to their prison. To avoid what would certainly have turned into a fight, Ironsi and Miller reluctantly let this happen while they continued to argue with Miruhu and the ANC.

An hour later, the Congolese released the Austrians, but they were then stopped by another group of Congolese soldiers who insisted on taking them back to the prison. Because of the ever-present danger of indiscriminate firing, Ironsi again reluctantly agreed to allow this to happen, but this time he sent a platoon of Nigerian soldiers to accompany them to ensure that they were not maltreated. By now Ironsi and Miller had come to the conclusion that force would have to be used to release the Austrians, but in Leopoldville we were most anxious for it to be avoided on this occasion. The Austrians were a Red Cross medical unit, and obviously the ANC in Bukavu, as elsewhere in the Congo, were unaware of the status of Red Cross personnel who wore uniforms although they were unarmed and enjoyed certain privileges and immunities. The UN simply could not allow any casualties to be inflicted on the Austrians, and if a fight could not be avoided, this was something we would have to accept. After discussions with Dayal and our legal and political advisers, I told the military operations staff to approve the line of action being taken by Ironsi and Miller and to caution them to continue doing their utmost to obtain the release of the Austrians without using force.

Negotiations continued during the night and by morning Miruhu was ready to release the Austrians, but the ANC refused unless they received orders from the ANC general. None of us, and least of all the ANC, knew who this general was—the absence of Singha at this critical moment was a grave handicap for the ONUC officers in Bukavu. With his rifle companies in the interior of the province, Ironsi only had his battalion headquarters and the headquarters company in Bukavu. While the negotiations were going on, he ordered a reorganisation of his troops to make up *an ad* hoc rifle company and ordered his infantry company at Goma to move to Bukavu by road. Meanwhile, ANC reinforcements, including heavy machine-guns, had reached the gendarmes at the prison.

At 11.30 in the morning, after exhausting all possibilities of negotiating the release of the Austrians, Ironsi ordered the Nigerians to seize the prison with the express directive that they should not open fire unless fired upon. When the Nigerians reached the prison the ANC fired their machine-guns, at which point fire was returned by the Nigerians. Both sides took cover, and firing by both sides continued intermittently. At 1 p.m. President Miruhu offered to parley provided the Nigerians withdrew from the prison. Ironsi rightly rejected this and continued with his assault. At 4.15 the ANC hoisted a white flag and called for a ceasefire. President Miruhu was allowed to go inside the prison to see the ANC commander, who turned out be a Colonel Miruhu, and arranged for the withdrawal of all Congolese soldiers and police from the prison and the release of the Austrians.

That this came about without any of them being injured was mainly due to the presence of the Nigerians sent by Ironsi to look after them while in prison. One Nigerian soldier was killed and a British officer serving with the Nigerians and a non-commissioned officer were severely wounded.

Ten ANC men were killed and more than forty wounded. The Austrian government decided to bring its hospital unit home for refitting and reorganisation, and therefore the men were flown to Leopoldville en route to Vienna.

After allowing time for cooling-down, Ironsi visited the ANC in their camp and admonished them for provoking the fight. Soon relations were back to normal, and the Nigerians were able to establish joint patrols with the ANC in the city and in the countryside.

While we in the Royal had our attention focused on the events in Bukavu, the General Assembly had resumed its discussion of the crisis on 16 December. We were uncertain what would be the outcome of the Assembly debate after the Security Council had failed to reach agreement, but we realised that this was the only remaining immediate recourse. The Assembly had two draft resolutions before it. The first—moved by Ceylon, Ghana, India, Indonesia, Iraq, Morocco, Egypt and Yugoslavia — called for the UN to implement its mandate fully to prevent a breach of peace and security; to restore and maintain law and order and the inviolability of persons; to take urgent measures to assist the Congolese people in meeting their pressing economic needs; to seek the immediate release of all political prisoners in detention, particularly members of the Congolese central government and of the parliament; to convene parliament; and to prevent armed units and personnel from interference in the political life of the country and from obtaining assistance from abroad. It also called for the Belgian government to withdraw its military and quasi-military personnel, advisers and technicians immediately, and for the setting up of a standing delegation of the Assembly to function in co-operation with the Special Representative of the Secretary-General in the Congo; and finally, it insisted that all economic and technical aid to the Congo by member states should be channelled through the UN. The sponsors argued that ONUC's mandate was adequate but that it had to be implemented more forcefully.[4]

The second draft resolution was proposed by Britain and the United States. It requested the Secretary-General to continue to discharge his mandate and make vigorous efforts to ensure that no foreign military or paramilitary personnel were introduced in violation of earlier resolutions of the Council and the Assembly; in due regard to the Council's resolution of 9 August 1960, especially its paragraphs 4-5, to do everything possible to assist the Congolese head of state to establish conditions in which the parliament could meet and function in security and freedom from outside interference; and to continue his efforts to ensure respect for civil and human rights for all persons. The draft also called on all states to refrain from direct and indirect assistance for military purposes during the temporary period of UN involvement except when so requested by the

UN; expressed the hope that no measures contrary to the recognised rules of law and order would be taken against any persons imprisoned anywhere in the Congo, and that the International Committee of the Red Cross would be allowed to examine them and obtain necessary assurances for their safety; and that the forthcoming visit of the Conciliation Commission would help to resolve internal conflicts by peaceful means and preserve the unity of the Congo. Finally, it requested all Congolese to give practical co-operation to the UN, and called on all states to co-operate in giving effect to the provisions.[5]

The two sponsors of this draft resolution said that their recommendations included everything that was in the eight-nation draft, though excluding parts related to the role of the UN. In their view, the other draft exceeded the limits and competence of the UN and the decisions of the Council, constituted interference in the internal affairs of the Congo, and violated the sovereignty of a member state; it also imposed responsibilities that were unconstitutional and impractical on the Secretary-General as well as on the contingents of the UN Force. These troops could not be used for enforcement purpose or to interfere in the state's internal affairs. The sponsors argued that the UN could not prevent the Congo from employing Belgians and that in any case their withdrawal would lead to chaos. However, the eight sponsors of the first draft rejected the British and American draft because it maintained the *status quo* in the shape of the Kasavubu-Mobutu regime, which had delayed the visit of the Conciliation Commission, and was opposed to the reconvening of the parliament.

The Soviet Union and several other states maintained that the UN operation had failed, and urged that the moral and physical force of the UN should be on the side of the legitimate government of the Congo, which was that of Lumumba. They called for the withdrawal of the Belgians, the release of Lumumba and other politicians arrested with him, and the disarming of all private armies, particularly what they termed the 'armed gang' led by Mobutu. They supported the eight-nation draft resolution, even though it was not sufficiently far-reaching to carry out the tasks they had envisaged.

In his remarks Hammarskjöld doubted the usefulness of a wider mandate, although it would facilitate the task of the UN representatives responsible if their hands were strengthened. He asked the Assembly to help world opinion by expressing its support for a return to constitutionality and national reconciliation. As to unilateral technical assistance, this could be avoided if the UN received adequate financial support. Besides, any civilian assistance, on however small a scale, could not be carried out without UN security. He referred to the deep division among the member-states on the Congo issue and asked that the dangerous influence of such a split on the efforts of the Organization should not be ignored.

Neither of the draft resolutions was adopted, but at the suggestion of Austria the item was retained on the Assembly's agenda. In face of the lack of action, first by the Council and then by the Assembly, Hammarskjöld took the diplomatic route of drawing to the attention of the Assembly President, Frederick Boland, that although no definitive resolution had been adopted, the members had shown concern over the relationship between the UN and the Congolese authorities. The discussion had shown widespread and strong opinion that the convening of the parliament and a return to democratic practices were matters of urgency, that due process of law should apply, and that member-states should refrain from providing military assistance to the Congolese. He added that the developing civil war in the Congo would have its effect on the presence of the UN force. The time had come for the President of the Assembly to use his influence for a peaceful solution to the problem and to make an unequivocal declaration against interference with the UN force in the performance of its task.

The discussions at the UN about the Congolese army and related security issues caused much consternation in the Kasavubu-Mobutu camp. They protested loudly against critical statements and declared that any attempt by ONUC to disarm the ANC would be resisted by force. Kasavubu began to cast around for outside help and Mobutu alerted his troops, thus increasing tensions in Leopoldville and in other areas controlled by their regime.

On Christmas Day, sixty Stanleyville ANC troops arrived in Bukavu and managed to seize control of the garrison. They arrested provincial President Miruhu and Commandant Singha and removed them to Stanleyville. The garrison, who were only nominally loyal to Mobutu, put up little resistance, and the local population displayed no reaction. On learning of the arrival of pro-Lumumba troops, Ironsi visited the ANC camp and was told that UN help was not required.

A strange drama with a comic touch was being enacted at Bukavu. Shortly after the removal of Miruhu and Singha by the Stanleyville ANC, about 100 ANC soldiers were flown from Leopoldville to Usumbura in Ruanda-Urundi, a UN trust territory, and then transported by the Belgian authorities there to the bridge on the Congolese border, by which they entered Bukavu on 1 January 1961. After dismounting from their vehicles, they proceeded on foot towards Camp Siso in Bukavu, flying a white flag; they claimed that their intention was not to use force, but to unify the army. However, the Kivu army opened heavy fire and most of the visitors were captured, eight taking refuge in the UN camp. Because of a fear that Belgian para-commandos in Ruanda-Urundi might attack, the border became very tense. Eight Belgian soldiers, who had apparently strayed across the border, were taken into custody and removed to Stanleyville, where they were eventually released through UN intervention.

The Secretary-General had requested the Belgian government not to allow transit to the ANC through the trust territory and was given its assurance to that effect. However, the trust authorities did not comply with this commitment. After the ANC had crossed into Bukavu, the Secretary-General protested to Belgium for giving the ANC transit rights and called for immediate and effective action to prevent direct or indirect assistance for military action by the Congolese troops. At Leopoldville we were astounded by the Belgians' blatant violation of international borders and direct military intervention. Obviously, they had learned nothing from their earlier intervention in the Congo. In my briefing of the press that day, I said that Belgian co-operation with the Congolese troops, in attempts to invade Kivu from Ruanda-Urundi, was tantamount to aggression against the Congo and was in violation of the UN resolutions prohibiting unilateral military aid.

The Belgian representative at the UN defended the action of the Belgian trust authorities and assured us that no further transit would be authorised. The Soviet mission at the UN requested a meeting of the Security Council to consider threats to peace and a serious violation of the international status of the trust territory. A draft resolution by Ceylon, Liberia and Egypt calling on Belgium to cease action against the Congo and to withdraw its military and paramilitary personnel from the Congo and condemning it for violating the trust territory failed to gain sufficient votes and was not adopted.

Meanwhile Kasavubu complained to the Secretary-General that UN troops had been passive when provincial President Miruhu and Commandant Singha were arrested at Bukavu, and that an Egyptian aircraft had landed at Lisala without clearance. He emphasized that ONUC had not ensured co-ordination with the Congolese authorities or shown impartiality, and therefore requested the recall of Ambassador Dayal. As for the first accusation, when the Stanleyville ANC arrived at Bukavu, Colonel Ironsi had visited the local authorities while they were parleying and was told that no help was required. As for the Egyptian plane, one that had been on a flight to Equateur carrying welfare goods for the soldiers had made a forced landing at Lisala because of mechanical trouble. The UN had authorised another flight with spare parts and mechanics to repair or salvage the plane and fly welfare goods on the second one. Egypt had not given the UN advance warning of the flight and thus the Congolese were not informed. Lastly, Hammarskjöld told Kasavubu that Dayal was not accredited as a diplomat, and in view of the status of the Secretary-General and his representative in the Congo it was impossible to accede to the demand for his recall. But from then on the campaign to recall Dayal was in full swing.

The inter-tribal clashes in Kasai that had ravaged the province led to a mass migration of the population to safer zones. Not only did economic life come to a standstill, but the effect soon became visible in the form of a famine. In early December, reports indicated that some 200 people were dying every day of starvation. The victims were chiefly Balubas who had escaped to the east or south of Kasai province. Dayal, with the assistance of Linner, the UN and non-government agencies, had organized a large-scale emergency relief programme, but several thousand of the refugees died before the UN effort could begin. However, about a quarter of a million were saved. Activities in Bakwanga were slow to start due to mistrust, but as confidence in the UN increased, a full-scale operation developed.

The first UN peacekeeping force in Sinai and the Gaza strip had not been called on to assist refugees except in a limited way, because UNRWA had been established since the start of the Arab-Israeli conflict. On the other hand, ONUC had to play a major role, with the Force headquarters working intimately with the UN administration and with civilian operations. While the logistics, medical and air transport services of the Force had the burden of sharing organisational responsibility, the Ghana brigade, commanded by Brigadier Joseph Michel, and ONUC support service units were responsible for the operational aspects of the emergency assistance programme. The new Austrian medical unit joined a detachment of the Indian hospital that had earlier been sent to South Kasai and given valuable service. Military trucks joined civilian transport, distribution centres were taken over, and Ghanaian soldiers guarded the convoys of road and railway wagons. The emergency effort was no less heroic than peacekeeping, an experience that welded the ONUC civilian and military arms into a formidable team to render humanitarian service.

The new year showed that the pro-Lumumba forces were gaining strength. Kashamura, formerly Minister of Information in Lumumba's cabinet, had taken over the leadership of Kivu province, and Pierre Mulele, Gizenga's representative, opened an office in Cairo. The UN Conciliation Commission had arrived in the Congo and started its meetings. Its colourful and controversial chairman, Jaja Wachuku, the Nigerian Minister of Education, had his own ideas about ONUC's relationship with the Commission. He believed that ONUC should give priority to the Commission's needs before its other responsibilities; he wanted the best offices and the best cars and Field Service personnel to attend to them. He also wanted a large team of secretaries. Such ideas inevitably placed the Commission leader on a collision course with ONUC. The latter took good care of the Commission, but this was not deemed to be enough by Wachuku, who soon joined Dayal's detractors.

A conference of Independent African heads of state was held in Casablanca on 3-7 January 1961 at the invitation of the King of Morocco, to consider the situation in the Congo. Besides Morocco, the participants were Guinea, Mali, Algeria, Ghana and Libya; and a representative of the Prime Minister of Ceylon was also present. The Conference made a number of decisions. These were: to withdraw its troops from ONUC; to reaffirm its recognition of Lumumba's government; to maintain that the only justification for the UN's presence in the Congo was to respond to the requests of the legitimate Congolese government which had invited it in the first place; to implement the decisions of the Security Council on the situation in the Congo; to safeguard the Congo's independence and integrity; to disarm and disband Mobutu's lawless bands; to release from prison all members of the legitimate government and parliament; to reconvene parliament; to eliminate all Belgian and other foreign military or paramilitary personnel serving in the Congo; and to prevent the Belgians from using the trust territory of Ruanda-Urundi as a base for aggression against the Congolese. The Conference concluded that if the purposes and principles justifying ONUC's presence were not realised and respected, then the states represented at the conference reserved the right to take appropriate action.

The new year brought a most welcome visit from Hammarskjöld, who stopped at Leopoldville for two days on his way to South Africa and conferred with the senior staff at the Royal for a briefing and discussion. He looked confident and well. The main issues he had to deal with during his visit were how to persuade Kasavubu to comply with his assurances given in New York to cooperate with ONUC; how to hold Mobutu in check, especially with the weakening of ONUC after some of the contingents had withdrawn; and how the Conciliation Commission could be persuaded to use its influence in helping to resolve the conflicting political dilemmas.

The next morning Hammarskjöld met Kasavubu, who only complained that ONUC had failed to comply with his requests for action in Stanleyville and Kivu. Later the Secretary-General met the government headed by Joseph Ileo which had emerged by this time with Kasavubu's backing. He again raised questions relating to Congolese cooperation with ONUC, but Ileo and his colleagues followed Kasavubu's example. The meeting proved fruitless. Among Hammarskjöld's personal callers was Wachuku, who 'interpreted his role not as a conciliator of Congolese differences but as an inquisitor of the Secretary-General's and ONUC's supposed inadequacies'. When the Secretary-General left for Pretoria, he had made little progress in overcoming the UN's problems in the Congo, but he reinvigorated the staff with his enthusiasm and the example he set of determination to serve the Congo within the framework of international law.

The situation in the provinces was getting worse. With the withdrawals, the UN Force was gradually weakening and it came under increasing pressure from the European embassies, which expected it to give priority to the protection of their nationals and property. The Congolese were calling for assistance against their rivals, whereas ONUC had to continue to provide security in each of the splintered areas to prevent civil war so that the economy as well as normal life could be kept going. With more than six months of experience in the country, the unit commanders were unwilling to send out small patrols or establish small posts, or to deploy units smaller than a company in strength. I supported those views. In spite of the limitations on ONUC and the disturbed conditions in the provinces, the latter were receiving an influx of Belgian women and children from the capital. If disaster struck, they would be the first to demand ONUC protection, and it seemed odd to the UN troops that a minority should demand security at the cost of denying it to the majority, the Congolese, whose security was ONUC's main concern. What the members of the UN force especially objected to was that Western states were prepared to attack the conduct of ONUC operations and the behaviour of its contingents. The media lambasted the UN force without respite, and yet the Western embassies demanded UN protection as if the force had only been hired to act as their guards.

The UN force did its utmost to protect lives and all property, including those of the Europeans. Yet complaints continued to be made to us at the Royal and to the Secretary-General in New York and in public statements that the UN force was passive and its staff were indifferent to their needs. The Western states, all with a history of colonialism, could not differentiate between the conduct of colonial troops in the suppression of lawless dissent and the more humane approach adopted by the UN in dealing with violence.

The fate of the Europeans in Oriental became a matter of serious concern. Dayal sent Duran, and McKeown sent Iyassou, to deal with Gizenga and Lundula and prevent excesses. Mobutu's troops, ferried across the Congo river, were at the border between Equateur and Oriental provinces and there had been clashes. The border between Kivu and Ruanda-Urundi remained restless. Then we received news on 9 January that a Stanleyville ANC unit of about 1,500 had reached North Katanga in trucks and that fighting had broken out. Except for minor infringements, the neutral zone negotiated by me with Tshombe on 17 October 1960 had held up till then, but it all came apart as pro-Lumumba troops captured Manono.

ONUC had taken on responsibility for the security of the tin mines and transportation system by sending a Nigerian unit to Manono. This unit now came under attack from Lundula's ANC, and the Nigerian Brigade Commander, Brigadier Ward, called for reinforcement from the nearby

Moroccans. But the Stanleyville force fought with determination, and ONUC had to abandon Manono and the airport. There was also an exchange of fire between them at Albertville, but here Ward managed to obtain a ceasefire. He reported that he did not have enough troops to carry out his task and that ONUC might have to abandon the area to be pacified by Tshombe.

At Stanleyville, Iyassou succeeded in persuading the Congolese leaders to reduce their pressure on UN troops in North Katanga. Similarly, Ironsi eased tensions in Kivu. However, Tshombe, taking advantage of ONUC's weakness in numbers, started to move his gendarmerie back into the area 'to restore order and reopen the railway'. His pacification efforts, led by white mercenaries, followed the traditional Belgian pattern of indiscriminate shooting, burning of villages, and pillage and rape by the troops. Tshombe rebuffed our protests with accusations that the UN had allowed the Stanleyville ANC to enter Katanga.

On 11 January, Katanga added an aerial dimension to the fighting. Two converted commercial aircraft bombed Manono, and the Katanga authorities admitted that a Belgian pilot, formerly of the Force Publique, had been killed by fire from the pro-Lumumba force. On 30 January Katangese planes attacked the UN's garrison headquarters in Manono. The attack was not aimed at the UN, but it indicated how daring the Katanga forces had become. Tshombe now had a 'foreign legion' of 2-300 white 'volunteers'. These mercenary soldier-adventurers were reported to be arriving daily from different countries *inter alia*, Belgium, the United States, Britain, France, Germany, Poland, Israel, South Africa and Rhodesia. Their monthly pay was reported to be between $400 and $480.[6]

In order to stem the pro-Lumumba troop gains in Equateur, Mobutu had flown about eighty ANC troops to Lisala. McKeown had ordered three UN companies to be deployed along the major routes on the border between Equateur and Oriental provinces. However, the withdrawal of African contingents had begun to hurt ONUC and was reducing available troops to a level which could have made our force ineffective. We were seriously considering withdrawing the Nigerians from Manono, but after Iyassou's successful negotiations at Stanleyville, pressures on our force in North Katanga were reduced.

ONUC had established effective liaison with the four Congolese splinter groups. In approximate terms, Mobutu's ANC numbered 15,000, the pro-Lumumba force 7,000, Kalonji's army 1,000, and Tshombe's force in Katanga 5,000. The size of ONUC would be reduced from 19,000 to 13,000 when the 'Casablanca' group of more radical African states withdrew their contingents. Troops from Guinea and Egypt had already departed, while contingents of 3,132 Moroccans and 1,149 Indonesians were awaiting final orders to withdraw. To do its job properly, ONUC would need replacements.

Hammarskjöld had discussed with me the possibility of asking India for a contingent of one or two battalions, but I said that India had serious reservations about sending combat troops to the Congo. Not only had the Indian Prime Minister told me that if Indian troops were needed he would only agree to provide service troops, but a senior Indian delegate to the General Assembly session had explained to me the reason for India's caution in sending its combat units to the Congo: because there were many Indian expatriates in Africa, 'We cannot risk being placed in a situation where Indian bayonets point at black African chests'. But we were at our wits' end in the search for acceptable troops to replace the departing contingents, and therefore, in spite of the Indian reservations, Hammarskjöld decided to go ahead and request Nehru for a battalion or two for the Congo.

The fate of Lumumba and other political prisoners held by factional leaders continued to be of great concern to us in Leopoldville, as we tried hard to keep abreast of events. We had learned that Lumumba was being cared for by Congolese soldiers and that his injuries were being attended to by a Belgian doctor. He was being kept in a small prison cell, but the many soldiers who visited him reported that his food was adequate. We also heard that at Christmas the officers invited him to join them in their mess for dinner and that he was gaining a measure of popularity in the camp. As Dayal later wrote, 'Lumumba behind prison bars had been no less potent a force than Lumumba in freedom. There was no prison in Kasavubu's Congo secure enough to contain him.'[7]

Soon after the New Year, ANC troops at Camp Hardy in Thysville mutinied over pay and privileges. They beat up their officers and raped the officers' wives—even Colonel Bobozo and his wife were not spared. The soldiers unlocked Lumumba's prison door, but he suspected a trick and would not come out. Shocked by the mutiny of what they had thought was their most loyal garrison, Kasavubu, Mobutu and Bomboko rushed to Thysville to regain control. They had to accede to exorbitant demands from the soldiers before they could restore some semblance of order.

The three leaders met Lumumba and offered him a cabinet position in the Ileo government, but he saw the offer as a political bribe and refused. The leaders were concerned that he should be kept in safe custody, but after the Thysville meeting they had to move him elsewhere. Their first choice was a prison in Boma in the Lower Congo area, but the provincial minister there would not accept responsibility, fearing that Lumumba's presence would disturb the people in the region. There were two other possibilities, Bakwanga and Elisabethville. The Belgian advisers favoured Bakwanga because it was remote and had only an insignificant Belgian presence. However, the Congolese leaders decided on the Katanga alternative with the expectation that Tshombe would be more responsive in developing mutual relations between the central government and Katanga.

Lumumba and two colleagues, Okito and Mpolo were first flown in a small plane to Moanda where they were transferred to an Air Congo DC-4 for the flight to Elisabethville. Tshombe had agreed on 15 January to accept the prisoners, but the arrival of the aircraft carrying them two days later was unexpected. Munungo reached the airport first and arranged for the prisoners to be kept in an unoccupied house. Then after Tshombe had had a meeting with his cabinet, it was decided that the prisoners should be sent to Munungo's brother, the Chief of Bayeka. Events thereafter remain obscure.

There are a number of versions of the murder of Lumumba that became known to us at the Royal shortly after the event. First there was Munungo's version that his prisoner escaped and was killed after being re-captured; the second version was that he was killed in cold blood by Munungo either single-handed or with the assistance of other Katangese; the third was Tshombe's account that the prisoners were already dying when they reached Elisabethville; and the fourth, believed by many Africans, was that they were executed by Europeans. However, the tentative conclusion of a UN Inquiry Commission that the killings occurred on the night the prisoners arrived, probably in the presence of Tshombe, Munungo and Jean-Baptiste Kibiwe, Katanga's Minister of Finance, was probably closest to the mark. The Commission added that it had probably been Colonel Huyghe assisted by Captain Gat (both were Belgians) who committed the actual deed. Many other versions and accounts of this ghastly act have emerged and been published.[8]

Not being aware of the fate of Lumumba, Okito and Mpolo on 17 January, Dayal had spoken to Bomboko, asking him to intervene to ensure that the prisoners would be humanely treated. He had sent a message to the ONUC representative in Elisabethville to obtain all relevant information and remind the Katangese of their responsibilities, while I had instructions sent to the Katanga area command to keep a watch over the fate of Lumumba and his colleagues. On receiving Dayal's report on the transfer of the prisoners to Katanga, the Secretary-General, too, was busy making all possible contacts to call for humane treatment and the due process of law.

The fact was that keeping Lumumba near Leopoldville posed such a serious threat to Kasavubu and Mobutu that they had first tried to send him to Kalonji, the Baluba leader and his worst enemy, and then settled for Katanga where he was especially hated by the local leaders. I had feared that sending him there was like putting him in a lion's cage and that his death could occur at any moment. Thus ONUC had to be ready to deal with the consequences, i.e. demonstrations and rioting in towns and cities, lawlessness in the country and an increase in the scale of the civil war. There would be immediate retaliation. Lumumbists would seek revenge and try to kill prisoners held by them. Without losing any time in consultation with Dayal, I worked out a plan, which we discussed with McKeown, and after we had gone over the details he left to issue orders to his subordinate commands. Threatened by the withdrawal of additional Casablanca Conference states, we still had their troops with us and could count on their loyalty and co-operation in the face of the impending crisis linked to the future of Lumumba's forces.

Egypt was the first to ask the Secretary-General to arrange for the return of its contingent. Its departure was delayed because of the complications caused by the Egyptian plane mentioned earlier arriving at Lisala without having been cleared. Once it was established that the plane's cargo included no weapons or military equipment, the Congolese allowed it to leave. The Egyptian troops were quickly replaced by a Malayan unit from Lisala and Gamena.

McKeown had by now settled into his command, and Dayal and he had established a comfortable working relationship. The time had come for me to leave for New York. An insect bite on my shoulder blade caused an infection and high fever, and I was in bed for three days, which left me feeling weak. According to the doctors I was showing the symptoms of malaria and was therefore advised to rest for a week or two. De Angeles of Administration suggested that instead of resting in Leopoldville, which was not the best place for that purpose, I should fly to Naples and from there take an Italian ship to New York. It would take me a week in all to complete the journey, and by then I should be rested and well able to return to work. The idea appealed to me, and with the approval of New York, I left Leopoldville on 8 February for Naples and took the *Cristoforo Colombo*, a lovely new passenger ship. On 13 February we were in the middle of one of the worst winter Atlantic crossings. The voyage was neither comfortable nor healthy, as I could not retain any food and eventually gave up eating. One afternoon I was asked by the ship's captain to come up to the bridge. He had invited me there before to look at the charts, but this time he handed me a telex with an announcement by the Katanga authorities that Lumumba and his two associates had been killed while attempting to escape.

I had always feared that this would be Lumumba's fate, but now I was in despair at being in the wrong place at this time: I should have been in New York, not in the middle of the Atlantic, and cursed my choice of a luxury cruise—which had turned out to be a horrible experience—instead of taking a plane. When the ship docked in New York harbour two days later, I was greeted by the UN travel officer; his first words were,

'We had better get you to the UN quickly—the SG has been looking for you.' The moment I reached the Secretariat, I was sent up in the Secretary-General's reserved elevator to the 38th floor and went in to see Bunche. His first words were, 'Where were you? We were looking for you. You had better tell Andy (Cordier) that you are here. The SG wants to see you.'

By now I was getting nervous. Cordier greeted me with his usual smile and a short laugh and said, 'Well, you are here now. Dag wants to see you. There will be a meeting at six-thirty this evening. We will meet then.' At the meeting Hammarskjöld greeted me somewhat coolly, and during the discussion he avoided looking at me. I knew he was upset because I had not been available when the news of Lumumba's death reached him. There was plenty for his military adviser to do and I had chosen comfort in preference to duty. There was no point in explaining. Luckily, in a couple of days everything was normal and together we plunged in to deal with the new challenges that followed Lumumba's murder.

NOTES

1. *New York Times*, 10 December 1960.
2. In 1966, as general officer commanding the Nigerian army, (Ironsi briefly became head of government before being assassinated in a further coup later that year.
3. Singha and the ANC troops in Kivu were under the command of General Lundula, who had joined the pro-Lumumbist Gizenga regime in the eastern provinces. Thus Singha's acceptance of Mobutu's invitation to participate in a conference in Leopoldville to help consolidate his power was indicative of changing loyalties.
4. UN Document, A/L. 331. Add. 1.
5. UN Document, A/L. 332.
6. Associated Press, 30 January 1961.
7. Rajeshwar Dayal, *Mission for Hammarskjöld: The Congo Crisis* (Princeton University Press, 1975), p. 190.
8. The most credible one in my view is in a book by G. Heinz and R. Donnay, *Lumumba: The Last Fifty Days*. Urquhart (in *Hammaraskjöld*, p. 505) and Dayal (in *Mission for Hammarskjöld*, p. 190) are of the same opinion.

9

CIVIL WAR SPREADS

Hammarskjöld circulated Munungo's statement[1] on the death of Lumumba to the Security Council on the day it was issued. Fears and doubts were over and an uproar began.[2] Having returned to the Congo Club in New York, I too was caught up with the sudden twists and turns of the storm which now raged about the person of Hammarskjöld and which was fanned through the UN corridors to the Security Council. Munungo's account of the tragedy caused universal disgust with the conduct of the Katangese, and revulsion at the brutal killing of Lumumba. Hammarskjöld was greatly pained by its cruelty and violence and the realisation that such acts could be perpetrated in current politics.

His personal feelings about the dead man had changed significantly. When Lumumba first came to the UN at the end of July, Hammarskjöld had welcomed him warmly and tried enthusiastically, in spite of his temperamental behaviour, to help him and his fledgling state, but subsequent events, notably the developments over Katanga, had greatly soured their relations. Hammarskjöld shared the view that Lumumba was unstable, had dictatorial inclinations and could therefore be easily exploited. With his firm belief in the rule of law, he could not be pleased with the unconstitutional way Lumumba was removed from power, but notwithstanding his tact it was evident that he was relieved at no longer having to deal with the man. This did not prevent him from ceaselessly pressing the Congolese to comply with due process of law in dealing with the deposed Prime Minister and to assure him humane treatment. He was thus repelled and shocked at the murder, not only as something inhumane but also as an insane act which would result in grave consequences for the Congo, the UN operations and himself.

On 13 February, Hammarskjöld officially informed the Security

Council of Lumumba's death and called for a full investigation.[3] He said that he had already sent General Iyassou, ONUC's Chief of Staff, to Katanga with international security experts, but Tshombe had not yet received them. Iyassou had instructions to remain there and continue his inquiry. In the Security Council, Zorin charged Hammarskjöld with the immediate responsibility for Lumumba's fate, asserting that the proposal for an investigation appeared 'hypocritical' and that the Soviet Union had not 'the slightest confidence in the Secretary-General or in his staff'.[4]

The next day the Soviet government issued a statement through Tass, and an English version was immediately distributed by AP.[5] It repeated its accusations against the role of Belgium, the UN and in particular its Secretary-General, as well as Tshombe and Mobutu. The statement demanded that the UN should condemn Belgium and apply sanctions; that Tshombe and Mobutu be arrested, their military units disarmed and Belgian troops and other personnel removed from the Congo; that the so-called 'UN troops' be called off within a month and all foreign troops withdrawn to enable the Congolese to settle their own internal affairs; and that Hammarskjöld be dismissed from the Secretary-Generalship as an accomplice and organiser of the murder of the Congolese Republic's leading statesman—for its part the Soviet Union would not maintain any relations with him or even recognise him as an official of the UN.[6] It further stated that the Soviet Union would render all assistance to the legitimate government of the Congo led by Acting Prime Minister Antoine Gizenga, the pro-Lumumbist leader of Oriental province, and called on all states to give their support. On 15 February, the Soviets circulated a draft resolution to the Security Council covering these points.

The debate in the Council was acrimonious and charged with emotion. Adlai Stevenson, a brilliant liberal Democrat from Illinois and twice a presidential candidate, was President Kennedy's ambassador to the UN and in his first major statement on behalf of the new administration he supported the UN and defended Hammarskjöld. The Kennedy administration had few illusions about the Soviet Union's intentions in the Congo, but had hoped to reach a measure of agreement to enable the UN to cope with this conflict. Zorin's statements and the communiqué issued through Tass had made clear the Soviet support for the Stanleyville regime led by Gizenga. Thus the Soviet Union did not intend to support the UN's efforts at conciliation. Stevenson accused the Soviet Union of waging a 'virtual war on the United Nations'. In outlining the United States' approach, he said that all foreign intervention should cease; that the ANC and all other Congolese forces should be quarantined from the civil war and political life; that all political prisoners should be released so that they could participate in the country's political life once law and order was restored; that it would support the Secretary-General's recently instigated investigation into the killing of Lumumba; and that it would promote the reconciliation of political parties in a full return to the Congo's constitutional process.

It was clear that once Lumumba had been transferred from Thysville to Katanga, his fate lay in the hands of people who were his worst enemies, raising great concern and alarm among his sympathisers and those who believed in the due process of law. Not only were important leaders of developing countries like Nasser, Nkrumah, Sekou Touré and Sukarno critical of the UN's handling of this episode but so was Nehru, who spoke of the UN's passivity in the face of what was happening. Nehru urged Hammarskjöld to try to persuade the Western powers to agree to some 'minimum common policy' in the Congo.[7] Hammarskjöld discussed this letter with me personally because Nehru had also said that the UN's passive attitude would make it difficult for India to provide troops to make up the numbers lost through withdrawals.

Encouraged by the Kennedy administration's attitude to try to isolate the Congo from East-West rivalries, Hammarskjöld discussed Nehru's idea with Stevenson and asked for Kennedy's support to obtain more troops for the UN in the Congo, particularly emphasising the need to approach Nehru. Hammarskjöld also urged that the administration approach the Soviets to deal with their differences: it seemed at that time that they might well respond to an initiative to arrive at some understanding with the United States. The murder of Lumumba had made this practically impossible, but the Kennedy administration did urge Nehru to provide additional troops and assured him of a generous and speedy air and sea lift for Indian troops.

Stevenson's address was interrupted at about noon by a disturbance in the visitors' section of the Security Council chamber. A group of black Americans had burst into the chamber shouting 'Viva Lumumba!' and 'Down with the murderers of Lumumba!' As the UN security guards moved to drive them out, the intruders fought back, injuring a number of the guards, and some visitors as well. The demonstrators were later identified as members of certain movements of black people supporting the African struggles for freedom. Their demonstration was directed against Hammarskjöld and Stevenson. Hammarskjöld had sat through the incident but was later persuaded by his American aide, Donald Thomas, to leave the chamber. Meanwhile Sir Patrick Dean, the leader of the British delegation and current Council President, suspended the meeting until the chamber was cleared of all visitors. While the demonstration caused Hammarskjöld great concern, he was especially disturbed to learn that there was a group of Africans in the UN, including some diplomats, who actually felt personal hatred towards him because of Lumumba's death.

His security, which had hitherto been somewhat casual, had now to be stepped up.

I was mostly at my desk during these hectic days and kept a spare shirt, underclothes and toilet kit in my desk. My staff, consisting of Bowitz, Cavalcanti and a Canadian air force officer, were being overworked in the effort virtually to run an operations room. I needed extra staff and with Hammarskjöld's approval solicited help from among the troop-contributing countries: Colonel Alemu came from Ethiopia and others from Ghana, Indonesia, Malaya and Nigeria. Our immediate problem was to plan a redeployment of the remaining troops once the signatories to the Casablanca declaration had withdrawn their contingents. Our second major problem was to cope with the increase in tension caused by the statements of many delegates at the UN and their governments at home calling for curbs on the ANC and requesting that the UN undertake their training and reorganisation. I had kept this question under review to enable us to set the machinery in motion at short notice to assist the Congolese forces.

Hammarskjöld was busier than ever preparing his recommendations for future action by ONUC and defending his personal position against Soviet and African attacks. Our Congo Club meetings were brief but frequent, and Hammarskjöld also consulted with key delegates. As to his own position, his mind was made up: he intended to put up a tough defence and the support of many delegates and of us as his advisers added to his resolve.

Thus, while Hammarskjöld was dealing mainly with the Council's affairs, the rest of us were occupied with the day-to-day operations in the Congo. Leopoldville feared a chain-reaction to the news of Lumumba's death and to the subsequent developments at the UN. Mobutu and his troops were tense and we kept ONUC on high alert with orders to deal firmly with any lawlessness on the part of the Congolese troops or civilians. There was a fight between Lumumba's Batetela tribesmen and Kasavubu's Bakongo group resulting in some being wounded and the pro-Lumumba troops in Kivu arrested twenty-five Europeans, including missionaries, whom ONUC had to rescue and assist in their evacuation. Two Europeans were killed in Luluabourg by a Congolese civilian for making slighting remarks about Lumumba. The garrison there, which was nominally loyal to Mobutu, was in fact more sympathetic to the provincial government which was pro-Lumumba. Stanleyville was a dead city with all activity having come to a halt. Lastly, Tshombe announced that he would not permit an inquiry into Lumumba's death. However, it was at the Security Council that the most important drama was unfolding. The future of the UN and Hammarskjöld was at stake.

In his well-prepared statement, Hammarskjöld summarised the actions taken by ONUC and by himself from the start of the operations and their efforts to assure that Lumumba be treated in accordance with due process of law. In answering charges against ONUC and his failure to act in defence of Lumumba against Mobutu's ANC and other anti-Lumumba factions, he said, 'If those who have established the mandate and those who have decided on the means by which the mandate should be fulfilled attack the representatives of the Organization because they have not exceeded the mandate, thus established, or acted against it, and because they have not used means which were never put at their disposal, then it seems to me to be fair to point out that it is not the Secretary-General who has determined the mandate, nor is it the Secretariat which has decided on what means they should dispose of for its fulfillment.'[8]

Hammarskjöld then dwelt on Zorin's personal attack, the Soviet government's communiqué and its draft resolution before the Council. In a firm, confident voice he recalled the events the previous October when Khrushchev had called for his resignation and the appointment of a troika to replace the office of Secretary-General. He said that his reasons for refusing to comply with the Soviet demand that he resign were the same now as in October. It was true that at the time of the Suez crisis in 1956 he had said that a withdrawal of confidence in the Secretary-General by one of the permanent members of the Security Council was reason enough for him to resign. But in this case, 'the Soviet Union, while refusing its confidence to the Secretary-General, has at the same time taken a stand which makes it absolutely clear that were the present Secretary-General to resign, no new Secretary-General could be appointed, and the world would have to bow to the wish of the Soviet Union to have this Organization on its executive side run by a triumvirate which could not function and which most definitely would not provide the instrument for all the uncommitted countries of which they are in need.'[9] He reiterated what he had said in October: 'Whatever the members of this Organization may decide on the subject will naturally be my law.'

Hammarskjöld then turned to the situation in the Congo and suggested various steps. There should be an international investigation of the circumstance surrounding the assassination of Lumumba and his colleagues; they should re-issue instructions first given in September 1960 that all civilians be protected against attacks from armed units, whatever the authority under which those units might be acting; the UN should use all means short of force—negotiation, the establishment of neutralised zones, ceasefire arrangements and so on—to forestall clashes between armed units; and the ANC should be withdrawn from political life and reorganised so that it could carry out its normal functions in the service of its government. He renewed his appeal of 8 October for the Council's moral support in applying his earlier recommendation that Belgium and Tshombe should together eliminate the Belgian political factor in the Congo.

In his first three weeks in office the young President of the United States made efforts 'to talk softly to the Communists.'[10] But the Soviet attack on the UN and on Hammarskjöld and its threat of unilateral action brought about a sudden change in the administration's attitudes. At first Stevenson took a firm position in the Security Council in support of the UN and its Secretary-General and later, at a news conference in Washington on 15 February, Kennedy declared his intention to work through the UN, if possible, in the Congo and urged the Soviet Union and others to do the same. But he insisted that it would be the 'duty' of the United States 'to defend the UN by opposing any attempt by any government to intervene unilaterally'.[11]

A meaningful unilateral military intervention in the Congo would require a large military force with enormous troop and cargo airlifts and sea capability. ONUC had received airlift support from the US Military Air Transport Service, using about fifty C-124s; this had been spread over a period of time, but it included intense periods when 9,000 troops had been flown in within a space of two weeks. To move an infantry division, hundreds of large transport aircraft, C-124s and C-130s, would be needed, and even the vast resources of the United States would not have the capability to mount such an operation. In addition to the airlift, all heavy equipment would need to be transported by sea. Thus, a unilateral intervention was likely to be covert, as had already happened with several member-states in the Congo or small-scale overt assistance, such as the air transport the Soviets had sent to Lumumba for the ANC's attempt to invade Katanga.

Other than by air and sea, military intervention was possible from or through adjoining countries. Congo-Brazzaville, a supporter of Kasavubu and friend of Tshombe, had already established a pattern of assistance across the Congo river that was politically valuable but militarily small. In spite of pressures from Nasser, the Sudan had complied with the UN resolutions. Ruanda-Urundi was controlled by Belgium and remained available to the latter's favourites as had been seen a few weeks earlier when Mobutu's troops had passed through it. The land and lake routes across Tanganyika were effectively closed, and were in fact available to the UN. British-ruled Northern Rhodesia (now Zambia) openly sided with Tshombe, and although there had been no occasion to test Portuguese-ruled Angola it could not be relied upon to co-operate with the UN.

In working out the reorganisation of the UN Force in consultations with Hammarskjöld and Bunche, I arrived at its priorities based on anticipated operational requirements. Besides Leopoldville, each of the provincial capitals needed troops for the security of political leaders, vulnerable points and UN installations, and a reserve to assist in the maintenance of law and order.

The problem of coping with refugees in Equateur had eased, but troops were now required to deal with fighting between Mobutu's troops in Equateur and the Stanleyville forces. There were many European-owned plantations in Oriental that needed assistance, and this called for additional troops. As in Oriental, troops were also needed in Bukavu. Nothing less than a brigade could maintain the neutral zone in North Katanga with a garrison in Kalonji's Bakawanga area, and as long as the UN was responsible for the former Belgian military bases, security and maintenance personnel were required for Kamina, Kitona and Banana.

ONUC's military and civilian operation throughout the vastness of the Congo relied on the existing network of communications, which had to be kept safe and working. Besides the security of major airports and many smaller airfields throughout the country, ONUC relied on surface communications for heavier cargo. The major port of entry was Matadi, about 100 miles inland from the Atlantic, on the Congo river. Banana, at the mouth of the river, was more vulnerable than Matadi. Thysville, the second-most important ANC garrison after Leopoldville, was nearby. Port Francqui, at the junction of the river and the railway running from there through Kasai to Katanga, was the next key-point. Further east along the river, the transport system terminated at Kindu from where the railway ran south through Bukavu and then joined with the Kasai and Katanga systems. All of this had to be protected. The task of keeping the railways moving through the interior would continue to the responsibility of the UN troops in the provinces.

I realised that McKeown needed more than the UN was able to obtain. In working out troop requirements, I had to be mindful of the expected withdrawals and the difficulty of replacing them. I chose the lowest possible figures, for it was easier to add than to reduce troop availability. Thus my estimated infantry requirements were twenty-five battalions with a minimum strength of 15,000, with another 3,000 service troops to support the Force. With the expected withdrawals, ONUC's infantry strength would be lowered to about 11,000; therefore an addition of between 4,000 and 6,000 troops (depending on the size of the units, which varied between countries) would be required to carry out no more than the essential tasks. But if the Security Council decided that ONUC should establish a measure of control over the ANC, there would have to be adequate reserves available, i.e. another three battalions to be kept in Leopoldville and Kamina for a quick response. This made a total of 16,500 men, plus some 3,000 support troops.

As to the support services, I was reasonably confident that they would continue to be available because their contributing countries with the exception of Yugoslavia were not among those that had announced their withdrawal from the UN Force. Our airlift capacity was barely sufficient to support the troops in the field; however, we had been working to improve the maintenance of the aircraft.

Dayal reported from the Congo that a group of Lumumbists in the Kasavubu government's custody had been transferred to Bakwanga and then killed by Kalonjists. The transferring of prisoners had become a matter of great concern to the UN because, like Lumumba and his colleagues, the prisoners were all being killed. It was later confirmed that the victims in this case were Jacques Lumbala, a Secretary of State in Lumumba's cabinet; Jean-Pierre Finant, former President of Oriental province; Major Jacques Fataki, formerly commander of the gendarmerie in Stanleyville, and four others. There seemed to be no limits to what Kasavubu and other Congolese leaders would do to rid themselves of opposition. As we feared, news of these murders touched off large-scale tribal fighting in Kasai, which the UN Force had previously managed to quieten down.

There was now dissension in the Lumumbists ranks. After Lumumba's death, Anicet Kashamura, former Minister of Information, and Christophe Gbenye, former Minister of the Interior, who were residing in Bukavu, became rivals for power. Kashamura tried to arrange the arrest of Gbenye, who asked for and was given UN protection. Subsequently Kashamura was arrested by Gizenga's forces but released by a military police unit loyal to him, and he then sought UN protection too. In the mean time McKeown met Mobutu at Bumba on the western border of Oriental, centre of the rival ANC movements, in an attempt to negotiate a neutral zone. He had planned to hold a similar meeting with Lundula if Mobutu should indicate that he was willing to end the fighting in that area. There had already been several contacts between Mobutu and Lundula. Mobutu's troops did not have either strength of numbers or the will to fight, despite Western press reports that the ANC was 'poised for a major offensive'. His forces there consisted of one or two infantry companies and scattered platoons; Lundula had rather more, but to talk of a battle between these troops as 'a major offensive' was clearly either a journalistic exaggeration or an armchair military pronouncement. In any event, ONUC had been actively engaged in preventing an escalation of fighting between Mobutu's and Lundula's troops; if McKeown could formalise the arrangement into a ceasefire it would ease ONUC's burden, and I therefore urged Hammarskjöld and Bunche that Dayal and McKeown should continue their efforts to obtain a ceasefire in the north.

Since my return to New York, besides the military situation between Equateur and Oriental provinces, other disturbing incidents had occurred. In Kivu, some Nigerian troops became involved in a brawl in a local bar at Kindu, and as the result the ANC attacked the barracks which the Nigerians were occupying on the evening of 3 February. To avoid a fight, the Nigerians abandoned the barracks and concentrated in the area of their headquarters. They were pursued by the ANC, and in the ensuing fight forty-five Congolese soldiers were killed. Four Nigerians were missing, of whom two returned alive. Of the remaining two, the body of only one was later found. The Congolese stole all the Nigerians' possessions. Brigadier Otu, on a visit to Stanleyville to calm tensions there, was flown on to Bukavu where he picked up Ironsi, the Nigerian commander. They were to land at Kindu, and a Nigerian officer, Lieutenant Ezengbana, with a small detachment was sent to secure the airport. The detachment was ambushed by the ANC: Ezengbana was killed and four Nigerians were reported missing. Otu and Ironsi were only able to land on 5 February. They were joined by Lundula, who had been flown in by ONUC, but attempts at reconciliation failed and ONUC decided to replace the Nigerians with Malayan troops.

Because they feared attacks by the ANC after Lumumba's death the European community in the Maniema district of Kivu asked for assistance in their evacuation. The local authorities and the ANC commander had to sign the *laissez-passer*, which proved time-consuming, and several special UN flights had to be arranged to obtain clearance from Stanleyville since the local officials often refused to sign.

On 12 February, Dayal in his report to the Secretary-General[12] described a situation in Katanga so serious that it approximated to civil war, with evidence that similar developments were impending in other parts of the Congo. He said that the authorities in Katanga had been engaged for some months past in building up their forces; they had purchased planes capable of small raids, and obtained arms and ammunition as well as military trucks and vehicles. As a result of internal and external recruiting campaigns, they had at their disposal a well-equipped force of about 5,000 men, strengthened by non-Congolese officers and non-commissioned officers, estimated to be some 400 strong.

The report continued: 'In recent weeks, and in particular on 11 February 1961, Mr Tshombe has made statements in which he has referred to the United Nations as the greatest enemy. These threats have been accompanied by demands for the withdrawal of the United Nations Moroccan troops stationed in Katanga.' In referring to the violation of the UN's neutral zone in North Katanga by Tshombe's forces, Dayal noted that the Stanleyville ANC had penetrated positions held by the Katanga gendarmerie. The UN had not accepted this as an abrogation of the neutral zone and continued with its efforts at pacification, but in spite of this Katanga had embarked on a military offensive against North Katanga. On 11 February, 3-400 Katanga gendarmes under the command of Colonel Crèvecoeur had attacked Mukulakulu; the number of casualties was not known although the village was burned out. Thereafter the gendarmes in sixty trucks continued towards Luena, burning and plundering villages along the route. Another column of 300 gendarmes was reported to be on the move from Kabongo-Dianda to the same area. Some 2,000 gendarmes were reported to be in the Lubudi-Bukama area, and the Katangese had declared an area 10 km. deep on either side of the railway to be a military zone under the occupation of their gendarmerie. The majority of the Balubas in the area were forced to flee into the bush. A statement issued by Tshombe defending his actions was included as an annex to the report.

In a further report on 20 February,[13] Dayal informed the Secretary-General that Iyassou, who was in Elisabethville to inquire into the death of Lumumba, had confirmed that fighting had extended northwards beyond the railway. The Katangese were following their traditional method of warfare: after burning Mukulakulu and causing the population to flee, a force of about 300 in sixty trucks officered by Belgians occupied Luena, from which the population had fled. An area of 10 km. on either side of the railway between Lubudi and Luena was then evacuated and the villages were burned. Thereafter the Katangese started to repair the railway track that had been cut by the Baluba fighters.

The Katanga gendarmes had occupied Bukama with 600 troops. Another 200 gendarmes, supplemented by 500 armed civilians, advanced from Bukama to Kabongo-Dianda. Bukama was empty when the Katangese occupied it. However, armed Balubas returned and during the ensuing fight the Luena waterworks was damaged depriving the town of water and power. Meanwhile, the Katangese were repairing the tracks running towards Manono, which was the next objective. The Balubas, after their earlier defeats, were gathering their forces and had started to attack in small numbers. Dayal concluded his report: 'It is thus clear that the offensive launched by Mr Tshombe on 11 February is aimed not merely at opening up the Lubudi-Luena railway, as he had declared, but the subjugation of the entire region populated by the Baluba tribe, by the use of overwhelming force, including the burning of villages and the elimination of all opposition and resistance and the terrorisation of the population.'

In a letter to the Secretary-General on 18 February, Nkrumah recommended that the UN Force in the Congo be replaced by an all-African command; he offered to come to the UN to expound his views. He said that at the beginning he had advised that the UN operations in the Congo should be in two phases: the first military and then, after the restoration of law and order, a political phase for conciliation. The general flow of arms and equipment into the Congo was creating the kind of conditions that could lead to civil war of the Spanish type, with grave consequences throughout the world. All Belgian personnel had to be expelled from the Congo. The situation was so serious that in his view the Security Council mandate of non-interference in the internal affairs of the Congo was no longer tenable.

His plan envisaged the following elements:

1. an African command under the UN should replace the present international command;
2. all Congolese armed units should be disarmed, involving their return to their barracks and the surrender of their weapons, which would be kept in UN custody;
3. Congolese troops would be reorganised and trained;
4. any troops belonging to the ANC or to different factions who did not cooperate should be disarmed by force;
5. all non-African personnel serving with the Congolese forces should be expelled;
6. once the military situation was brought under control, political prisoners should be released by the new UN command and that command should convene parliament under its auspices; and
7. all foreign diplomatic missions and representatives should leave the Congo for the time being in order to give the new UN command a fair chance and to eliminate the Cold War in the Congo.

Considering that Nkrumah's own army was British-led, as were the Nigerians, and that the French-speaking African countries had French staff officers and advisers, I wondered aloud at the staff meeting with Hammarskjöld that day how an all-African UN command could take to the field so quickly. I was not alone in thinking the proposals impractical, setting aside the political considerations involved. Hammarskjöld told me that on my next visit to the Congo I should stop in Accra and see Nkrumah to discuss what was involved in organising an African UN military operation in the Congo. Meanwhile, Nkrumah could well come to New York, but it would be better for me to meet him and his military advisers in Accra.

Nkrumah's letter and a report received from the Congo Conciliation Commission were discussed by the Congo Advisory Committee that day. The former met with a lack of enthusiasm on the part of the delegates and in fact was barely discussed. However, at this critical stage of the deliberations, the Commission was putting forward its conclusions in advance in the Security Council instead of submitting them formally to the General Assembly. These were important and timely:

1. The *Loi fondamentale* should be upheld until it was amended or replaced by another constitution.
2. The newly-formed provisional government of Prime Minister Ileo should be broadened, as he was already attempting to do, to include nominees of all

important political groups.
3. All military operations in Katanga and those about to be launched elsewhere should be halted, and attempts to seek military solutions to political problems checked, particularly to avert foreign interference.
4. With the assistance of the UN, the ANC should be insulated from politics reorganised and retrained, with the UN guaranteeing law and order and the Congo's territorial integrity.
5. A meeting of the political leaders should be convened in a neutral place, with the Congo retaining a unitary system of government but with greater decentralisation.
6. Political prisoners should be released and a general amnesty announced.
7. On completion of the above steps, parliament should be convened to discuss the structure of a government of national reconciliation and the implementation of the constitutional process.
8. Effective measures should be taken urgently by the UN to implement the General Assembly and Security Council resolutions calling on member-states to refrain from sending military assistance and from interfering in the international affairs of the Congo.

Hammarskjöld and his advisers were involved in intense negotiations in a draft resolution for the Security Council which would meet his own criteria, be acceptable to the Soviets, and enjoy the support of the members of the Security Council. The draft being put together by Correa of Ceylon, Barnes of Liberia and Loutfi of Egypt included Hammarskjöld's suggestions. Several representatives of Security Council members and of troop-contributing states called on me to find out my views on how ONUC could deal with the worsening civil war. Hammarskjöld had told the Council that the UN Force already had orders to deal more firmly with a number of situations. Fearing the disarming of their respective armies, the Congolese leaders were in a frenzy and had put their troops on alert, thus creating specific conditions that the UN Force had to cope with without waiting for a clear and firm mandate from the Council. I told my visitors that given the size of the Force, as it was before withdrawals started, as well as a stronger mandate, ONUC would be capable of carrying out its tasks. Furthermore, once the Congolese political leaders and their armies became aware that the UN intended to maintain a strong force and give it unyielding support, the wind would be taken out of their sails, and the chances of clashes and casualties to our troops minimised. I urged all who came to see me and many others whom I ran into in the corridors to give us a strong mandate.

On Saturday, 20 February, the sponsors of the draft resolution and the secretariat had intensified their consultations and, in a resumed session, the Council took up consideration of the draft. By early the next morning, it had adopted the resolution[14] by nine votes to zero, with France and the Soviet Union abstaining. The resolution was in two parts, dealing respectively with security and political questions. In the first part the Council

1. urged the UN to take appropriate measures to prevent the occurrence of civil war in the Congo, including arrangements for ceasefires, the halting of military operations, the prevention of clashes, and the use of force, if necessary, as a last resort;
2. urged the UN to arrange withdrawal and evacuation of all Belgian and other foreign military and paramilitary personnel and political advisers not under the UN command, and mercenaries;
3. called on member states to take steps to prevent the departure of such personnel from their territory, and to deny transit and other facilities;
4. established an impartial investigation into Lumumba's murder and demanded that the perpetrators of the crime be punished; and
5. reaffirmed its previous resolutions.[15]

The second part

1. urged the convening of parliament and adequate security measures in that connection;
2. further urged that the Congolese armed units and personnel be reorganised and brought under discipline and control to eliminate any possibility of their interfering in the political life of the Congo;
3. called on states for their co-operation in the implementation of the resolution.

Before the meeting ended, Hammarskjöld asked member states to strengthen the Force in the Congo with 'further generous contributions', because inevitably the resolution would add to its duties.

While Hammarskjöld and his staff were pleased with the resolution, and a *New York Times* editorial on 22 February exulted over 'a new defeat for the Soviet Union', the Congolese leaders reacted angrily and denounced it. Tshombe ordered general mobilisation and said that the UN resolution was 'a veritable declaration of war on Katanga and on the whole of the former Belgian Congo'. He announced that he had invited Gizenga from Stanleyville and Kashamura from Kivu to meet him in Geneva for talks, to which he had also invited Kasavubu and Kalonji. None of us could imagine such a meeting taking place under Tshombe's auspices. In Leopoldville, not to be outdone by Tshombe, Ileo warned on 22 February that the Congolese government would use force if necessary to prevent the implementation of the resolution. In a cable to Hammarskjöld, Kasavubu rejected the resolution on the grounds that it violated Congolese sovereignty.[16]

Hammarskjöld had called a meeting of the Congo Advisory Committee for that same evening and asked me to give a military analysis of the situation in the Congo and of ONUC's troop requirements if it were to undertake the Council's new mandate. I sat down with my staff and prepared a written statement which I then went over with Hammarskjöld to ensure that it reflected his political objectives. I also had two documents prepared for distribution at the start of the meeting—one showing troop strength and deployment before withdrawals and the second showing redeployment after some withdrawals had taken place. Immediately after calling the meeting to order, Hammarskjöld gave me the floor. I had addressed the Committee before, but now that I was back in New York this was the beginning of my giving frequent briefings on the military situation.

I started by reiterating the tasks given to the UN Command by the Council resolution adopted that morning. The first was to take immediately all appropriate measures to prevent a civil war. These would involve the halting of all military operations, the prevention of clashes, arrangements for ceasefires, and the establishment of neutral zones.[17] The second was to arrange the withdrawal and evacuation of all Belgian and other foreign military, paramilitary, and mercenary personnel in the Congo. And the third was to block all ingress of military personnel and material into the Congo from outside.[18] In drawing the Committee's attention to the two documents showing strength and deployment, I said that the deployment in progress was being seriously hampered by the shortage of air transport and was therefore incomplete.

There were two available alternative ways to implement the mandate. The first was along the lines already developed by ONUC in which force was used only in self-defence and as a last resort when all other means had failed. The second choice was to resort to military initiative, and for this a minimum of 40,000 troops would be needed. In military parlance it would mean a corps consisting of two infantry divisions with supporting arms including tanks and artillery. A strong air component would be necessary for such a force: this would include a large air transport unit as well as aircraft for air reconnaissance and possibly fighter-bombers. However, as such a method of achieving our tasks was not envisaged, I turned to the assessment of our tasks on the assumption that the use of the Force could be avoided in our operations in the Congo except in self-defence. I presumed that all further UN military action would follow political negotiation and mediation, as the earlier statements of many of the members of the committee had envisaged.

I dealt first with the requirement of troops in Leopoldville. The Committee already knew of the situation in the city where a number of arbitrary arrests were being carried out, seriously disturbing law and order. Adjacent to the city was the country's largest airport, N'Djili, which was also the main base for the air operations and therefore had to be suitably guarded. A minimum of three battalions were needed for the security of Leopoldville, with a fourth battalion as a reserve.

Elsewhere in Leopoldville province there were five other important or vulnerable places: Matadi, the main river port for oceangoing liners; Thysville, with its large ANC garrison, including an armoured unit, which was known to have an effect on the law and order situation generally; the former Belgian base of Kitona, with its large stores of arms and ammunition, possession of which by the ANC would greatly strengthen that force; and lastly, Banningville and Kikwit, both at the centre of large plantation areas. The security of these areas called for at least two battalions.

In Equateur province, the presence of an infantry battalion in Coquilhatville, its capital, was essential because of a large ANC garrison there; some troops were also required in the northern part of this province to take care of Gemena. In Oriental province there had to be at least two battalions in Stanleyville and another for deployment in the rest of the province. Since Stanleyville was the centre of the pro-Lumumbist movement and had elements of the ANC who were loyal to Lumumba, it had become an important military centre. It was rumoured that Mobutu was planning to attack the Stanleyville ANC with his Leopoldville ANC, and had concentrated his troops in the Lisala-Bumba area. The main means of moving troops in this area remained the river, an approach that was the shortest to Stanleyville, but from Bumba two main road approaches were also available, and there were third and fourth road approaches in South Equateur at Djolu and Ikela respectively. To prevent an armed conflict between Mobutu and Lundula it was necessary to place one or preferably two battalions of UN troops along these approaches. In the province of Kivu, there were three vulnerable areas—Bukavu, Goma and Kindu—which required two UN infantry battalions. The behaviour of the ANC in this area was lawless, and atrocities by them against Congolese and non-Congolese alike had to be prevented.

Katanga, with its gendarmerie led by foreigners, presented our greatest difficulty. The armed conflict between Tshombe's troops and the Balubakat, temporarily halted with the establishment of UN neutral zones, had begun again with full intensity, and now the withdrawal of contingents from the UN Force would seriously hamper our ability to maintain the neutral zones. The ex-Belgian base of Kamina was another heavy UN commitment. Katanga required a minimum of two infantry brigades, each of three battalions.

In the province of Kasai, tribal war, which had been halted through UN efforts, had broken out again following the recent political murders. Kalonji's private army continued to be a threat to law and order in South Kasai. The presence of pro-Lundula troops at Kindu and the reported advance by some of their elements up to Lodja were other important factors. A minimum of four battalions were needed for this province. Hence the need for a minimum of twenty-three and preferably twenty-four battalions to carry out the command's first task as required by the recent Security Council resolution.

ONUC did not lack the experience to do its tasks, such as arranging ceasefires and neutral zones. However, there were no set methods for them, and so the means had to be adopted according to the situations that presented themselves. For instance, when ONUC arranged the withdrawal of Lumumba's ANC from Bakwanga in August so as to prevent Kalonji's Balubas from entering South Kasai, a neutral zone was established between Katanga and Kasai. When this was abrogated by Kalonji and it became necessary to protect the Balubas returning to their homes in South Kasai, a ceasefire zone was established from Bakwanga to Mwene Ditu on the Elisabethville-Luluabourg railway to prevent fighting between Kalonji's private army and Lulua tribes.

And again when fighting broke out in October, new ceasefire lines were arranged and a neutral zone was established in the Mwene Ditu area. In Katanga, similar neutral zones covered nearly one-third of the whole province, in which all rival forces and armed bands were neutralised, and the UN command had one under negotiation between Ruanda-Urundi and Kivu. Two other such zones, between Kivu and Katanga and Kivu and Kasai respectively, were also under discussion. For the last few days McKeown had been actively engaged in arranging a ceasefire and establishing a neutral zone between the Mobutu ANC and the Lundula ANC. However, ONUC was unable to man these neutral zones fully because of the lack of troops.

There was no set pattern for arriving at these arrangements. We might start negotiations at any level, from the lowest to the highest, where contact could be established. ONUC civilian representatives assisted the military command right from the start of these arrangements, indicating the importance of providing political and legal advice. When a reasonable stage in negotiations was reached, they would be taken over by the UN command, which usually dispatched a high-ranking military officer accompanied by a UN legal adviser and any other expert whose help might be useful.

The ONUC military staff included a liaison section, then headed by Brigadier Otu of Ghana who had a number of officers available to him with a mastery of both French and English. We had been attempting for several months to increase this establishment to provide bilingual military observers for various tasks, including the duties relating to the establishment of neutral zones and ceasefires. Our new commitments required about forty additional officers and the UN had to appeal for contributions to assist us in this.

The second task allotted to the UN command by the new resolution was to arrange the withdrawal and evacuation from the Congo of all Belgian and other foreign military, paramilitary and mercenary personnel. For this their numbers would have to be assessed, and their evacuation supervised. The foreign elements would be replaced by UN military advisers and military technicians—here again, there was a need for additional personnel.

The UN command's third and last task was to prevent the entry into the Congo of military personnel and matériel for which it had not itself been the channel. Thus major airports, the seaport of Matadi, river ports, railway lines and roads would all have to be controlled. I had already mentioned the number of troops needed for Matadi and the security of airfields had been considered in my previous assessment; however, infiltration into the Congo from neighbouring territories had not been catered for and thus once again additional troops would be needed. For all the above, the requirement would be a minimum of twenty-five battalions. Since we only expected to be left with sixteen battalions after the planned withdrawals, it was clear that without at least nine additional battalions the UN command would not be able to carry out its new tasks satisfactorily.

I concluded my report with a few words about the UN's air transport in the Congo. It had met with many difficulties from the beginning and every effort was made to improve matters. We had even gone to the length of obtaining a large civilian charter to provide the requisite number of aircraft. A civilian charter had many drawbacks, and it was therefore necessary to enlarge our air transport unit and reorganise it so as to make it more functional. The UN hoped that generous contributions would continue to be made in personnel to achieve the desired efficiency so necessary for the smooth functioning of its command in the Congo.

During the next two weeks the civil war intensified, and at the same time the UN encountered opposition from nearly all the factionalised ANC because of the possibility of their being disarmed. Mobutu reinforced his ANC in Equateur to an estimated 1,500 troops mainly concentrated between Bumba and Lisala. Because of the developing civil war, the UN command intensified its efforts to negotiate a neutral zone. McKeown met Mobutu in Equateur province and made a similar approach to Lundula at Stanleyville. The rival ANC commanders gave assurances that they would remain on the defensive to prevent infiltration into the areas they respectively controlled. They also agreed that the UN should negotiate to promote discussions at the senior staff officer level in the ANC.

In its attempts to avoid an armed conflict and thus stem the tide of the civil war, the UN command as a first step appealed to Kasavubu,

Gizenga, Kalonji and Tshombe to freeze all troop movements. Gizenga did not reply, but the other three refused to co-operate with the UN. In fact, public declarations against the UN by Kasavubu and Ileo led to the local ANC garrison in Leopoldville assaulting and detaining UN personnel and subjecting them to brutal treatment.

Since the middle of February the UN command had been receiving reports that some ANC elements from Stanleyville had infiltrated into North Kasai up to the Sunkuru river. A UN patrol was dispatched there to prevent any further advance, but the Leopoldville authorities reacted to this new threat by rushing in reinforcements for the same purpose. The estimated strength of ANC under the orders of Leopoldville in Kasai was 2,000-3,000 men, mainly located at Luluabourg.

On the night of 23 February, some 200 Stanleyville ANC troops arrived at the outskirts of Luluabourg. Colonel Ndjoko, commander of the ANC garrison, sought and was granted UN protection. The UN troops attempted to persuade the intruders to withdraw peacefully but without success. They then warned the rival ANC that they might be obliged to use force as a last resort to prevent an armed conflict. The intruders made no attempt to move into the town, but they relieved the local ANC guard at the airport—which, however, continued to function as usual; they were welcomed by the local Lulua population, and the provincial government, whose 'President' Mukenge was in Brussels, appeared to accept the situation and readily cooperated with them. There were many palavers between the rival ANC groups. Some of the local ANC officers were arrested by their men, and the situation became highly dangerous, but after considerable persuasion the UN officials succeeded in reaching an agreement that the rival ANC groups would deposit their arms in UN custody.

On 27 February the Stanleyville ANC detachment withdrew from Luluabourg to return to Oriental province, leaving behind its commanding officer and adjutant under UN protection. It was reported that the Stanleyville authorities had sent this detachment to capture Colonel Ndjoko and bring him back with them, but when they failed to carry out their mission they decided to return. It was also confirmed that ANC's 3rd paracommando battalion, numbering 3-400, which had been rushed from Leopoldville, was still at Lusambo in Kasai and had apparently been by-passed by the Stanleyville ANC detachment. Because of the departure of the Stanleyville ANC and indiscipline among local ANC, UN troops were unable to arrange the storage of ANC weapons in UN custody.

On 24 February it was reported from Lisala that the civilian population had risen against Mobutu's troops. Road-blocks were erected and there were reports of many people being injured. The operation of Lisala airport was hampered and regular Air Congo flights had to be diverted. The Congolese authorities had no clear view of what was going on in Equateur. The ANC remained idle and with inadequate logistical support. Following their usual practice, they pillaged the town, causing disturbance and injuries.

By 28 February the towns of Ikela and Boende were captured by a force of the Stanleyville ANC, estimated at about two battalions, and Mobutu's troops there were disarmed without a shot being fired. The capital of Equateur now lay wide open with its local garrison small and demoralised. In addition no one knew where Mobutu was; it was rumoured that he was in Gemena or Banningville, but the local populations of Gemena and Lisala were hostile to him and there were reports that Belgian nationals were fleeing from Lisala to Coquilhatville. Some Congolese officials who had asked for UN protection including Robert Yango, a former provincial minister, were being looked after and a UN aircraft was flying emergency supplies to Lisala, which was guarded by the Malayan contingent. The main armed groups on each side had not made contact. McKeown had gone to Stanleyville to negotiate with Lundula for a neutral zone.

On 28 February one company each of ANC and gendarmerie were sent from Coquilhatville by truck to Ingende. As these trucks moved through Coquilhatville they shouted '*Vive Lumumba!*', which was echoed by bystanders. According to the local authorities at Coquilhatville, ANC troops at Boende surrendered to the intruders.

In March the situation in Lisala, where Mobutu's troops were reported to be continuing their depredations, continued to be tense. Some Europeans, including a Swedish Red Cross doctor, were severely beaten. The airport was now unsafe for UN planes. The situation in Gemena was also reported to be disturbed.

In Stanleyville, the authorities had ordered the Western consuls to leave within six days and five journalists—three Czechs, one Pole and one from the Soviet Union—were asked to leave on 28 February for Usumbura. However, the town of Stanleyville seemed calm. Kashamura[19] was said to have arrived there and to have resumed his official functions. The civilian population feared the arrival of new troops from Leopoldville, and ONUC had undertaken to prevent any reinforcement of the garrison which could precipitate another crisis.

The situation in Luluabourg remained very tense owing to the hostility of the population towards the local ANC; the UN, however, had agreed to associate the ANC with its own patrols in the city. The civilian population in Luluabourg was reported to be pro-Stanleyville, while the local ANC was pro-Leopoldville but leaderless.

The 3-400 ANC para-commandos were still idle in Lusambo, where the UN forces were in complete control of both the city and the airfield.

Rumours about the Stanleyville ANC advance against Port Francqui and even into Leopoldville province had caused panic in the capital, but the rumours were not confirmed. By the end of the month the situation had worsened in Luluabourg, with the local ANC becoming involved in disturbances with the civilian population, resulting in one ANC soldier dead, three wounded, and forty-four civilians killed. The local ANC gendarmerie remained leaderless. The ANC had established their road-blocks in the vicinity but had stuck to their assurances of keeping armed troops out of the city.

Mukenge, the 'President' of Kasai, had returned from Brussels and was welcomed by the ANC and the population. He made a speech to calm the people and declared his intention of opposing any military intrusion from Luluabourg.

In Katanga, Tshombe's gendarmerie had one column advancing on Bukama, which it captured on 14 February, but it then ran into serious opposition from the Balubakat. A second column was directed on Manono, moving along the Kishiale-Piana road. En route it burnt villages and killed several Balubakat members.

It was only to be expected that the Congolese factional leaders would reject the Security Council resolution. Joseph Ileo, head of the government recently appointed by Kasavubu to replace the College of Commissioners, was the first to do so. He gave his first press conference on the day of the resolution and, before denouncing it, declared plans to include pro-Lumumba and Balubakat political leaders in the new cabinet. His words were: 'If (the UN) mean to disarm our army, that will be a declaration of war. . . . I have talked to leaders of the army, and we are ready to defend ourselves.'

I was certain there would be trouble in Leopoldville, and it came four days later. On the evening of 26 February, a female employee of the UN was reported to have been raped by Congolese soldiers while her escort, a UN military officer, was held at gunpoint with his face pushed into the ground. Four Canadians—two officers and two enlisted men—were badly beaten the next morning. Congolese soldiers at road-blocks stopped UN vehicles, and searched, manhandled and threatened UN personnel.

The UN command contacted the ANC commandos and warned that such harassments by their soldiers would be resisted by force. This upset the Congolese even more and Kasavubu accused the UN mission of 'treason' and complicity with 'rebel soldiers' who were supposedly advancing on Leopoldville from Stanleyville. In a broadcast, he appealed to the nation to mobilise all its energies against the double threat of UN tutelage and 'rebel' advances.

There were limits to the UN command's patience with the hopeless Congolese leadership and the ANC rabble. In dealing with the inexperienced and disorganised Congolese in the past, the UN Force had based its military response on passivity. But the situation in Leopoldville had now gone beyond the limits of acceptability, because it threatened the security of UN operations. In my discussion with Hammarskjöld that evening, I took the line that from this time on the Congolese must be checked, the dignity of UN personnel protected and the UN operation made secure. There was unanimous support for this position, and Hammarskjöld authorised the dispatch of a warning to Kasavubu and other Congolese factional leaders that the UN would acquire the military strength to halt the strife in the Congo; further interference with the UN would not be tolerated. The Congolese were reminded that the Security Council had authorised the UN to use force, if necessary, to prevent civil war.

In its fear of how the UN would implement the Council's resolution, the Congo's central government sought an alliance with Kalonji of South Kasai and Tshombe of Katanga. It also invited Gizenga and Lundula, but these did not respond. In a ceremony, from which the Belgian advisers were asked to withdraw, the pact to pool forces to defend the Congo and to resolve their problems without outside interference was signed in Elisabethville on 28 February by Kalonji, Tshombe and Ileo.

My military staff, the Field Service and I were busy organising the deployment of our troops in anticipation of the Indonesians and Moroccans leaving. Our only encouraging note was that India was seriously considering sending a new contingent. Based on information received from their contingent already serving in the Congo and my discussions with Colonel Jai Dalvi, Military Adviser to India's permanent mission at the UN, the Defence Ministry in New Delhi had many questions. Hammarskjöld had asked for a battalion or two, whereas India had followed a consistent policy, based on military considerations, of sending abroad a self-supporting contingent. When a battalion was asked for from UNEF, a battalion group was sent including support services to enable the unit to operate independently for a short time. The military situation in the Congo was chaotic, support services were barely adequate and very little was available locally. India wanted to ensure that its infantry units and support services would be large enough and of the right composition to enable them to cope with the situation. The Indian government decided to send a high-level team to New York and then to the Congo to examine the factors that would finally determine the composition of their additional contribution. Happily the team included Harish Sarin, a respected senior Defence Ministry official; Lieutenant-General M.S. Wadlia, Chief of the General Staff, who was also my former divisional commander and the colonel of my regiment; and Brigadier Sartaj Singh, the next Indian contingent commander.

The francophone African community had also been active in

helping to resolve its internal conflicts. The President of the Malagasy Republic, Philibert Tsiranana, agreed to host a meeting of the Congolese leaders at Tananarive starting on 5 March. Gizenga agreed to attend as well as Kasavubu, Tshombe and Kalonji. Kasavubu and his team departed for the meeting ahead or time, leaving Delvaux as Acting Prime Minister.

While our attention was focused on the Tananarive conference and the future size of ONUC, bad news came from the lower Congo. A UN civilian administrator at Kitona and a NCO had been arrested and disarmed. Also on 3 March a UN civilian radio operator had arrived at Moanda near Banana and been arrested by the ANC for not being in possession of a UN identification document. Released to have dinner, he returned to the airport with the commander of the Sudanese contingent, escorted by a Sudanese guard. When ANC soldiers halted them the Sudanese fired warning shots over their heads, causing them to drop their arms and flee. Two of the ANC men surrendered. After the Sudanese commander's departure, his escort tried to return the two to their camp at Banana, but they were fired upon and in the ensuing fight a Congolese was killed. Later the Congolese opened fire on the UN camp and the Sudanese decided to withdraw to Kitona.

This incident led the ANC to cut off the Sudanese in Matadi. On 4 March, fighting broke out when a guard from the Sudanese battalion in Matadi was placed on the house containing the Canadian signals office serving the UN in the port. This guard had been requested two or three days earlier because of the tension in the town and the incident in Banana. The posting of the guard alarmed the ANC, who pointed out that the Canadian house had never been guarded before; it was right by the perimeter of the ANC camp, and thus they suspected the UN of having aggressive intentions. Some thirty minutes after the arrival of the Sudanese at the Canadian house, an exchange of fire started - it could not be established who fired first. Captain Gérard Bélanger, commander of the Canadian signals detachment, went out to order a ceasefire and disappeared.

The ANC were shooting at the house with rifles and 37 mm. guns. More than fifteen 37 mm. armour-piercing rounds were fired, seriously damaging the house and the signals equipment. At about this time the signals detachment went off the air. One Sudanese soldier was killed in the engagement by a 37 mm. shot. After about forty-five minutes, the firing ceased when the UN troops hung a white piece of cloth from a window.

There was a second shooting engagement in the evening when the ANC fired mortars, rifles and machine-guns. The UN troops were only armed with rifles and light machine-guns. The Sudanese were engaged at two locations in the town, the hotel and the cinema. A UN Indian medical team of two doctors and four nursing orderlies was despatched to Matadi from Leopoldville that afternoon. Earlier three C-119 aircraft left Leopoldville for Kitona to airlift the Indonesian company to Matadi. The Moroccans at Kamina were alerted. A third engagement took place the next morning.

Dayal and McKeown then persuaded the Congolese government to send its Acting Prime Minister Delvaux[20] and the ANC Chief of Staff Colonel Albert Kiemba, accompanied by the ONUC operations officer Major Clem Bouffard, on a UN aircraft to arrange a ceasefire. At noon on 5 March, while the negotiations were going on at Matadi, a fourth engagement started. The meeting to halt the fighting was adjourned, but when the shooting stopped thirty minutes later it resumed. No conclusion was reached as to who had been responsible for breaking the ceasefire in this engagement.

Delvaux told Bouffard that 'the Sudanese must leave Matadi, and as an interim measure they must be concentrated in one central location.' The Sudanese commander declined to accept this since in his view no suitable accommodation was available for his men. Delvaux then promised to make the necessary arrangements for accommodation and for a special train to leave immediately for Leopoldville with the Sudanese troops. A little later, Delvaux said to Bouffard: 'A train will leave immediately for Leopoldville and the Sudanese should board this train. If the Sudanese company commander does not accept this solution, I will order reinforcements into Matadi and a full-scale attack will be launched on the Sudanese which will result in their complete destruction.'[21]

Bouffard noted that the total strength of the ANC in the Lower Congo was 1,068, distributed as follows: 600 in Matadi, 300 in Boma, 50 in Banana, and the remainder at various small posts. In addition, there was a large garrison at Thysville. Bouffard argued that Matadi was vital to the UN for the rotation of personnel and incoming supplies, and for that reason could not be abandoned. Delvaux replied that he realised this fact but would not allow the Sudanese to remain at Matadi, adding that the UN troops who replaced the Sudanese would have to be acceptable to the Congolese authorities; this would be the subject of a meeting that he hoped to have with the UN authorities in Leopoldville on 6 March. Delvaux agreed to ensure the security of UN equipment and stores in Matadi until new UN troops arrived.

Bouffard, accompanied by Colonel Kiemba, returned to Leopoldville with eight Canadian soldiers and four Sudanese who had been taken prisoner by the ANC. Three of the Canadian soldiers were slightly wounded but two of the Sudanese were in a serious condition. Delvaux remained in Matadi making arrangements for the departure of the train which was to take the Sudanese troops to Leopoldville. Of the Sudanese one had been killed during the engagement at Matadi, and seven were reported missing and believed to be in the custody of the ANC. Delvaux promised that these seven would be on the train to Leopoldville.

Bouffard reported that he had not accepted Delvaux' ultimatum and had insisted that the presence of UN troops in Matadi was essential. Hammarskjöld, Bunche and I learned in a telex conversation[22] with McKeown that the situation appeared as follows:

1. The withdrawal of the Sudanese must, from the Leopoldville point of view, be regarded as irreversible because they had already agreed to it and the Congolese had made it clear that they would not reopen Matadi before the Sudanese had departed.
2. The Sudanese concession had been the result of an effective threat by the Acting Prime Minister to use superior force.
3. The same was true of the imposed conditions that it was for the Congo authorities to approve of our way of deploying troops and choosing their nationalities.

Hammarskjöld asked McKeown, 'Would you in the circumstances and given the development of the incident regard Delvaux's stand as a threat of aggression for enforcement of their will against UN principles?' He added: 'If our people in Matadi did not protest on this issue, which is vital, they at least did not commit themselves to an acceptance which bars us from the most vigorous political initiative in order to break up this intolerable stand. In my view we cannot accept to send troops back on the basis of the stand taken by Mr Delvaux. On the other hand, we must send troops back. It is therefore absolutely essential to break up by negotiation the state of affairs created by the acquiescence (in) Mr Delvaux's position. I most sincerely hope that nothing was said or done which would tend to block the road for us in this respect.'

McKeown answered:

1. Unfortunate decision of the Sudanese was irreversible before any action could be taken by me. The Sudanese reaction was the result of an overwhelming demonstration by ANC in numbers and material supported by the threats of the Acting Prime Minister who was obviously influenced by the superiority shown by the ANC.
2. We do not propose to concede that the Congolese authorities should dictate to us the nationality of troops to be employed in any particular situation.
3. I do not regard Mr Delvaux's stand as a threat of aggression for enforcement of their will against UN principles. In this case I feel the stand was rather anti-Sudanese because of the incidents leading up to the major outbreak.

McKeown then informed the Secretary-General that the remaining Moroccans, numbering about 1,000, were being flown the next day from

Katanga to Kitona since he intended to arrange the introduction of fresh UN troops at Matadi as quickly as possible.

The Secretary-General then said, 'I think this clarifies your stand. Naturally you are aware of the fact that not only is it impossible for us to permit a stranglehold in Matadi, but it is also impossible to make any concession regarding principle that UN Command alone decides on way of disposing and using troops.'

The telex conversation closed with McKeown reporting that the Congolese authorities had agreed that neither side would make any military moves in the lower Congo. The Congolese forced the Sudanese battalion to leave Matadi by train at 7 p.m.

On 6 March, the US Ambassador Clare Timberlake, concerned at the loss of Matadi and the forced evacuation of the UN's Sudanese troops from the port, called on his own initiative for US naval units, which were on a flag-showing mission along the west coast of Africa, to prepare to assist the UN. It was a sympathetic act but overlooked the reality that such assistance required prior approval from the Security Council; and because this was most unlikely to be granted, the move of these naval ships only added to the existing tensions.

ONUC had to regain control of its only access to the Atlantic, and thus had to secure Banana and Matadi, but the Congolese refused. Dayal and McKeown pressed their negotiations, including visits to Bomboko at the hospital where he was recovering from surgery, but he insisted that there should first be an impartial inquiry into the fighting at the two port cities. He accused the Sudanese troops of having opened fire first in the recent engagement.

The Congolese were also demanding control of the N'Djili air base near Leopoldville, apparently with the intention of controlling UN troop movements. ONUC had flown a Moroccan battalion from Kamina to N'Djili once the critical situation at Matadi became known, and rotation of Tunisians was also planned for this time. Thus ONUC refused to give up or share control of N'Djili, and our flights continued without interference. However, the Congolese were in an excited state at the imminent arrival of Indian troops, whom they declared they did not want in the Congo. This was why they were anxious at least to share control of N'Djili as well as other airports.

On 9 March, Hammarskjöld discussed the Banana-Matadi situation with the Congo Advisory Committee and I briefed its members. Dayal reported that the UN's withdrawal from the ports was a 'serious blow' to our operations since it deprived the UN force of its 'lifeline to the sea'. The Congolese authorities had demanded that no UN troopships should enter Matadi (pilots were forbidden to take such vessels up the river), that UN air traffic should be controlled by them, and that there should be joint control over all airfields. At the conclusion of the Advisory Committee's meeting, Hammarskjöld endorsed Dayal's recommendations and rejected the Congolese demands. Dayal had recommended that Matadi, being vital to ONUC logistics installations, must be held by the UN troops, and that control of airports, shipping and other transportation must also be retained by the UN. In view of this, ONUC should only rely on the Congolese for the security of installations, but it had to retain its own control in every case.

Dayal also reported that McKeown had offered to establish joint patrols in Leopoldville without an agreement, but that the Congolese had used physical and psychological pressure to force the Sudanese to withdraw their troops from Matadi; during the negotiations, they opened fire with artillery to convince the Sudanese commander, Captain S.A. Hafiz, of their overwhelming military superiority. It was a humiliating experience for the Sudanese who had a good military record. In mid-March the missing Sudanese soldiers were returned by the ANC. Kitona was secure in the hands of the Indonesian battalion, which had been moved there for repatriation aboard USNS *Eltinge*—now waiting in the mouth of the Congo river. Banana and Matadi were still held by the ANC—and their use was denied to the UN.

Two other major events were taking place at about the same time. The meeting in Madagascar of the Congolese leaders (without Gizenga, the pro-Lumumba leader of Oriental province) reached a tacit agreement to scrap the formula of a central government and to recognise the existing states. They shared a fear of the UN and discussed ways of dispensing with its forces in the Congo.

The other event, a significant one, was the departure of Dayal from Leopoldville for 'consultations' in New York; whereupon Mekki Abbas, an able Sudanese administrator who was head of the Economic Commission for Africa (ECA), was appointed as his temporary replacement. In New York Hammarskjöld was beleaguered by the unyielding opposition of the Soviets, who had the support of several African states; only the United States among the Western countries backed him fully. But at the urging of Ambassador Timberlake, and as the result of lobbying by Katanga and Belgian and other Western economic interests, Kennedy, Stevenson and others in the new administration had become convinced of the need for change in the ONUC leadership. Once the Congolese realised that they could not stop the entry of the Indian troops, they panicked as they contemplated the possibility of a powerful Indian military presence, the strongest single national contingent, in the hands of the Indian head of the UN operation who had made no secret of his views on the abilities of the current Congolese leadership. Hammarskjöld resisted demands for the recall of Dayal but agreed to recall him temporarily with the expectation that opposition to his presence would subside and he could return.

Mekki Abbas started by seeking to negotiate the return of the UN troops to Banana and Matadi, but made little progress. Several tons of cargo for ONUC had arrived by sea and the ship had to be unloaded. The Congolese agreed to allow the UN civilian staff to handle the stores, but insisted that they should be kept under the custody of the ANC.

In the Congo Club there were two changes in the position of Adviser for Civilian Operations. First, Macfarquhar was promoted and transferred to the Office of Personnel, to be replaced by Godfrey Amachree, former Solicitor-General of Nigeria; then after some months Amachree was promoted as Under-Secretary for Trusteeship Affairs and replaced by Francis Nwokedi, a senior Nigerian official. Hammarskjöld invited him to join the Ghanaian administrator Robert Gardiner, who was in charge of Congolese civil service training, to negotiate with Kasavubu's regime the reorganisation and training of the ANC. In anticipation of such a move by the UN, Kasavubu wrote to Hammarskjöld on 6 March expressing the view that the reorganisation of the ANC should be basic for the maintenance of the country's unity. He blamed responsible UN officials for talking of disarming the ANC; this had induced that force, with its already weak discipline, to increase acts of hostility towards the UN. He claimed that these acts were contrary to the orders of the Congolese authorities and their efforts to calm feelings, and added that the arrival of Lumumbist forces at Luluabourg, at a time when UN leaders were restraining Mobutu's ANC from taking offensive action, outraged the Congolese. He predicted that after the incidents at Moanda, Matadi and Boma there would be further outbreaks in other parts. Kasavubu contended that Mobutu had fourteen Belgian officers under command and not 100 as claimed by the Secretary-General's representative in Leopoldville; their departure, he said, would solve nothing, and he then contradicted himself by stating that if their departure were not accompanied by steps to bring the army under control and discipline, it would further disturb the ANC and increase the risks facing the country.

Kasavubu concluded that measures based on the provisional report of the Congo Conciliation Commission should be taken, and in this connection he made five proposals. First, the ANC should remain under the President's command as he was the best person to insulate it from politics and could at the same time ensure that the country was not deprived of its army, which was a vital element in its sovereignty. This alone would ensure reorganisation and avoid flights into the bush and prolonged guerrilla warfare. Secondly, the reorganisation must embrace the entire country. He agreed to start the operation with Mobutu in command without waiting to start it with other armies; however, an agreement should first be reached between the military leaders in Stanleyville, Bakwanga and Elisabethville. Thirdly, a National Defence Council should be set up under the President, to include the Congolese military leaders and representatives of the UN Force and presided over by a high-ranking neutral officer responsible only to him. The Council would draw up a detailed programme of training and reorganisation. And finally, the Congolese government retained the right to accept or refuse the technicians proposed by the National Defence Council and recruited through the UN. It thus intended to safeguard the army's neutrality.

Kasavubu's recommendations were generally sound, but they contained contradictions. There were certain basic factors on which the Security Council resolution had to be implemented, i.e. the nomination of UN representatives to meet Kasavubu and those responsible for the other ANC elements and the armed bands; and the selection of a high-ranking neutral officer as military adviser to the President. This officer would be the best person to head the National Defence Council, or any similar organ agreed upon, to select military advisers and instructors for the Ministry of Defence, the General Staff, schools of instruction, formations and units, and staff to take care of personnel matters like pay, rations and social services.

In New York, I was not alone in being convinced that if the ANC could return to their barracks at an early stage and be insulated from the country's political life and reorganisation, this would be of great assistance in curing the present ills of the Congo. Nwokedi was soon sent to join Gardiner in the pursuit of a negotiated agreement on the future of the ANC with the Congolese leaders.

In the light of Kasavubu's accusation that the UN troops had allowed the Stanleyville ANC to overrun North Kasai, while preventing Mobutu from launching his 'offensive', a full report on developments was needed. ONUC's reports were put together by my staff and myself, and a clearer picture emerged which showed beyond doubt the important role played by our troops in curbing the civil war.

North-east Kasai was mainly inhabited by the Batetala tribe, and since Lumumba had been a Batetala himself, this area was not effectively controlled by the provincial government, which was loyal to the central government in Leopoldville. During early February, reports had been received of Stanleyville ANC elements having been seen at Kole, Lomela, Katako-Kombe and Lodnja. ANC detachments in the Luluabourg garrison had been withdrawn below across the line of the Sankuru river. Then the Stanleyville ANC arrived in the suburbs of Luluabourg, which was a complete surprise—possibly because they had avoided the main roads and thus escaped detection.

Colonel J.A.L Ankrah,[22] commander of the Ghana brigade, intervened and informed the commanders of the various factions that he would not permit an armed clash under any circumstances and to ensure this he sent strong patrols to the local military camp. He also obtained the release of the two Stanleyville officers, who were imprisoned at the Ecole Centrale. The next morning he visited the airport and cleared the area of soldiers of both factions. Later a conference of all parties was held at the Ghana brigade headquarters; which was also attended by Majors Azim and Linde from ONUC headquarters in Leopoldville, who had arrived the day before to investigate the situation. Ankrah explained at the outset that an enduring peace in Luluabourg could only be achieved if the various contending factions handed in their arms to the UN, which could then ensure that no armed troops were allowed to enter Luluabourg, either by air or by road, and enable the local ANC to carry out normal training under its security shield. It was then agreed that the arms of the local ANC and gendarmerie battalions and of the Ecole Centrale would be deposited in their respective magazines, and those of the Stanleyville ANC in the *Ecole Centrale* magazine. These magazines would then be locked and the keys handed over to the UN, which would also arrange to guard the buildings. However, the Stanleyville soldiers appeared to have received word in advance and they vanished that afternoon as mysteriously as they had arrived. Since disarming depended on mutual and simultaneous action by all parties, the disappearance of the Stanleyville ANC knocked the bottom out of the plan and it could not be put into effect.

February 27 passed off quietly at Luluabourg: UN troops established a road-block outside the military camp to prevent armed soldiers from going into the town. Attempts were made to contact the Stanleyville ANC but without success. An abandoned ten-ton truck was discovered near the airport, containing stores, food, some ammunition and Nigerian army uniforms; obviously it had been stolen from Kindu earlier in the month. The next day, a large crowd of civilians gathered outside the UN headquarters at Luluabourg and demanded the release of Commandant Mulamba, the commander of the gendarmerie battalion, who had been arrested by the ANC when he appeared sympathetic to the Stanleyville ANC. After considerable argument, during which the UN agreed to restore the ANC element at the airport, he was finally released. It was also agreed that the town should be patrolled jointly by the UN and the ANC, and that no armed soldier would be permitted to enter the town. Mulamba's release caused scenes of wild enthusiasm among the civilians who considered it a victory over the ANC. However, the civilians were unable to contain their enthusiasm, and attacked unarmed ANC soldiers in the town, killing four and wounding eight. When they heard of this, the ANC went completely out of control and invaded the town fully armed. Within an hour, they had killed thirty-eight civilians and wounded thirty.

UN troops moved in quickly, but by the time they were able to round up the ANC and send them back to their camp, the damage was done. However, there were no further incidents. A pall of gloom and an uneasy calm returned to the city of Luluabourg. When the doctors examined the wounded soldiers, most were found to be in various stages of drunkenness —which once again proved, if proof were needed, that beer and soldiers do not mix well together.

On 13 March, the ANC in Kivu went on the rampage: their victims were white businessmen, missionaries and nuns. Four nuns were beaten and stripped and an American girl missionary was raped. The Europeans were spread over a large area with poor communications, and at UN headquarters their situation was viewed with concern. It was not the UN's primary task to guard isolated farms, businesses in smaller towns or Christian missions in the bush, nor did it have the resources to do so. These Europeans did not heed the warnings given them by UN officers in the field, but they were the first to blame the UN for their lack of security. Our reports showed that there were some 300 Europeans needing to be evacuated, but in New York Belgium alleged that 2,000 Europeans had fled from Kasai, and accused the UN of responsibility for the disorders. Whatever the rights and wrongs, we had ascertained that some 300 Europeans in the Kindu area needed immediate assistance, and UN troops were despatched to help. Similar misconduct by the ANC in Kasai required the evacuation of 130 Europeans from Lodja to Luluabourg in UN aircraft. There was fighting between Kalonji's supporters and the ANC in the border towns, and the UN's Liberian and Ghanaian troops were ordered to intervene.

The UN command had secured Leopoldville and N'Djili airport in time for Kasavubu's return from Madagascar and the arrival of the Indian troops. A parade and other public ceremonies were held for Kasavubu, and several thousand Congolese were in the streets. Thanks to the vigilance of the UN troops and the police the day passed peacefully.

The Congolese remained adamant in their refusal to let UN troops return to Matadi in spite of Abbas' efforts to persuade Kasavubu. Ileo too refused the UN's request to reinforce its existing 500-man Indonesian garrison in Kitona. Kitona was low on fuel, and would eventually have to be resupplied by air. Meanwhile, the arrival of the Indian troops helped to rebuild the UN's strength.

In Katanga, Tshombe had indicated his plans to regain control of the northern part of the province. The British mercenary, Captain Brown, had reappeared in Elisabethville, and a number of South African volunteers had been arriving at the airport. Meanwhile, Belgians were leaving: Colonel Tranquier from Elisabethville and all but one officer and a NCO from Kamina.

On March 9 Colonel Crèvecoeur met the UN Nigerian commander in Albertville, and communicated the following information. First, Katanga intended to open the Albertville-Kabalo railway; secondly, the gendarmerie intended to occupy Manono and to avoid fighting would drop leaflets from the air to warn the population; thirdly, Tshombe was willing to be reconciled with the Baluba leader Muamba but not with Sendwe, the leader of the Balubakat; and, fourthly, Katanga did not wish to interfere if his (Crèvecoeur's) orders were conveyed by UN representatives to the UN operations. Sendwe, the president of 'Lualaba' province, rejected these demands and stated categorically that the Balubakat Jeunesse had orders to fight all intruders except the UN troops.

The UN command's attempts to prevent a civil war in Equateur and along its border with Oriental led—as we expected—to friction with Congolese troops. Towards the end of February the ANC beat up civilians at Lisala and the UN attempted to move troops there by air, but they were not permitted to land. Later the plane landed at Gemena, where the Malayan troops gave shelter to the air crew. Their camp was surrounded by the ANC during the night. The UN command arranged for an ANC officer to be flown to Gemena and this resolved the problem.

During the first week of March the remaining UN Indonesian troops were moved from Coquilhatville to Leopoldville for return to their own country. An Ethiopian battalion was moved from Kabalo to Coquilhatville to replace them. On 15 March, Mobutu appeared in the town, and relations between the UN troops and the ANC were resolved in Equateur.

Lumumba's murder had caused fighting to spread throughout the Congo, including Katanga, and on 21 February the Security Council strengthened the UN mandate. The UN had been weakened by troop withdrawals from countries sympathetic to Lumumba, and it found itself opposed by every factional leader. The civil war was stretching its resources to the limit, but the men and women of the UN command, realising that their ability to curb the violence provided the single, fragile barrier between chaos and a return to some sort of sanity, strove hard and relentlessly to cope with the conflict. The arrival of the Indian brigade was timely and enabled ONUC to manage better. For the time being, apart from one battalion and all heavy vehicles, it was located in Leopoldville for deployment.

It was clear to Hammarskjöld, as it was to everyone else dealing with the Congo, that the key to the imbroglio was to promote reconciliation and seek an end to the secession of Katanga. From here on we turned all our efforts to dealing with this all-important problem.

NOTES

1. S/4688 and Add. 1, 2, 12 February 1961. Report to Secretary-General from his Special Representative in the Congo concerning Mr Patrice Lumumba.
2. Brian Urquhart, *Hammarskjöld* (New York: Harper and Row, 1984).
3. UN, Security Council Official Records, 933rd meering, SG/1006, 13 February 1961.
4. UN document S/4704, Letter of 14 February 1961, from the Soviet Permanent Representative.
5. *New York Times*, 15 February 1961.
6. The Soviet Mission returned a note from Hammarskjöld on 23 February. However, it continued to deal with the Secretariat
7. Also referred to by Brian Urquhart, op. cit., p. 503.
8. UN SCOR, 935th meeting, SG/1008 15 February 1961.
9. Ibid.
10. *New York Times*, 16 February 1961, James Reston.
11. *New York Times*, 16 February 1961.
12. UN Document, S/4691 of 12 February 1961.
13. UN Security Council document. S/4691, Add 2, Report on recent Development in Northern Katanga from Special Representative of Secretary-General, 12 February 1961.
14. UN Security Council Doc. S/4741 and Corr. 1 of 21 February 1961.
15. UN Security Council Docs: S/4405, 22 July 1960; S/4424, 9 August 1960; and S/4525, 17 September 1960.
16. UN Security Council Doc. S/4743, 22 February 1961.
17. For the first time in UN history, the Security Council was authorised to use force beyond the strict need for self-defence to prevent civil war.
18. From its inception, ONUC was concerned with the prevention of civil war and armed clashes. The new resolution had reinforced an existing mission. ONUC did not have sufficient troops to cope with the possibility of the outbreak of a major civil war, which was imminent. In fact, the threat of a withdrawal of troops by the troop-contributing countries who were signatories to the Casablanca declaration posed a serious threat to the ability of ONUC to continue with its operations without adding to the threat of civil war.
19. Ileo was with Kasavubu at Tananarive.
20. UN Archives, unpublished report by Major Clem Bouffard to ONUC headquarters.
21. From an unpublished report of telex conversation between UN Secretary-General and Commander, ONUC.
22. Col. Ankrah was later Ghana's head of state.

10

ATTEMPTS AT CONCILIATION

The surging civil war in the Congo, the imminent departure of the Indonesians and Moroccans from ONUC and the lack of progress in the talks between the Congolese political leaders were the major concerns of Hammarskjöld and his advisers. The period following the announcement of Lumumba's murder was extremely tense and fraught with much more complicated problems than we had faced in the early days of the Congo operations.

At the end of March, I had a rare quiet evening and sat in my office till quite late, thinking over the events of the past six weeks. At meetings of the Congo Club, we dealt primarily with day-to-day problems; we were like a fire brigade, and thus I felt it was time to evaluate the military situation and make my recommendations to Hammarskjöld for managing our operations better in future than we had done up till now. When we next met, on 27 March, I took up with him the consideration of a short paper I had prepared and distributed in advance to my associates. I said that the UN Force had recently suffered reverses, which had had a negative effect on the political situation and consequently on law and order in the Congo. I intended to suggest a means of welding our force into a satisfactory instrument to further the UN's aims in the Congo.

The Congolese leaders were far from being reconciled. The struggle for dominance between Tshombe and Kasavubu continued, and Gizenga maintained a tenuous hold over the eastern provinces. In the present context, therefore, political leaders were not inclined to give up control of their armed units. However, it should have been possible to arrange at least a partial withdrawal of Belgian personnel from strategic areas, but their replacement through the UN posed many problems that were yet to

220

be resolved. Thus, looking at the political trends, there did not seem to be any immediate prospect of a reduction in tension and the likelihood of disturbances.

The law and order situation had become worse in Leopoldville province, and incidents involving foreign nationals and the Congolese continued in the eastern provinces, particularly in Kivu where the political leaders appeared to have no influence whatever over their security forces. In Katanga Tshombe's gendarmerie were poised for an offensive against the Balubakat, which would result in a chain-reaction affecting other areas.

The best weapon available to the UN force in the Congo was its mere presence; this implied the moral strength that lay behind it, as well as the backing of the international community. Differences in the policies of the contributing countries towards the Congo and the effects of the Cold War blunted international backing for the force, but it continued to operate, relying on what remained of that moral force. That was up till 21 November 1960, the date of the planned attack on UN troops at the Ghana embassy. On that day its moral force was considerably weakened. And the series of incidents since then—the attack on the Nigerians and Moroccans at Manono; the attack on the Moroccans at Luena and Tshombe's attitude towards them; the attempt to take Kitona; the incidents at Banana and Matadi—all showed that the Congolese had no respect for the international community or any regard for the moral force underlying the UN. They had noted that whenever they attacked the UN force it withdrew, and in their eyes such a body could not be deserving of respect. They had now virtually neutralised the Force, which had been sent to the Congo to prevent the involvement of the Congolese armed forces in factional politics and to uphold law and order. It was clear from this development that the UN force was no longer fully serving its original purpose, except that in a way its presence filled a vacuum relative to the Cold War. This purpose alone could not justify the present level of expenditure and involvement. If ONUC was truly to be an instrument of the UN, it had to be reorganised and revitalised.

The Force was organised to exercise authority through peaceful means; it was only allowed to resort to arms in self-defence and that only when every other means had failed. During the early days, members of the Force, trained to fight, found it difficult to adjust to this approach, for they were under constant threat to their own safety, and even their lives. However, over a period of time they were educated in the 'UN approach'. The changed situation after 21 February 1961 made it necessary for the Force to act as an army, which meant re-educating it to use military means under certain permissible circumstances. This, together with a new direction from their respective governments, would be the only way to give the members of the Force a true perspective on their future role in the

Congo. But re-education might be somewhat difficult, and for this reason it would be more convenient to start repatriating troops who had completed their service with ONUC and replacing them as soon as possible. Since a major portion of the Force was due for rotation, I suggested that we ought to pursue this process and complete it as soon as possible.

To achieve parity with the other armed units in the Congo, the strength of the UN Force should have been about 20,000.[1] After the Security Council resolution of 21 February, ideally a further 5,000 should have been added to enable the extra responsibilities to be met. But withdrawals had cut the combat strength of the force to about 18,000, which was less than the minimum number needed. Taking the factors already mentioned and the reduced numbers together, the consequences were inevitable. While we had fully realised the need to reinforce, experience had proved that recently offered contributions did not become available immediately, and when they did, their movement to the Congo was slow. In fact, the present rate of build-up had taken the psychological sting out of our decision to reinforce, and at the same time it had built up resistance which we were unable to counter.

The Congolese armed units were also equipped with superior weapons. While not subscribing to an arms race, I did recommend parity. The Congolese had always possessed these weapons, and there had been no increase in the quality of their arms, although there had been an increase in quantity. Since they no longer respected the UN Force, as we have seen, and since there had been repeated attacks against elements of the Force with disastrous results, it was absolutely essential that the UN troops should be given adequate weapons so that they could at least defend themselves. This ability would not only prevent disasters in future but would stop the Congolese from launching further attacks on the UN. I therefore recommended that all infantry units must include infantry-type heavy weapons. We should also arrange for heavy mortars or artillery in small quantities, and finally the inclusion of an armoured squadron unit should be seriously considered. From now on, only a force with an adequate deterrent power would restore its position and ability to be a suitable instrument for the UN in the Congo.

Our staff establishment in the UN command had always been weak because suitably trained staff officers were not available, but I had already taken steps to improve this situation. I was also not satisfied with the present practice of command and control of contingents; the UN command must exercise its authority without hindrance, and contingent commanders must not be allowed to seek instructions from their governments through their embassies or directly by radio. Perhaps the best way to achieve this objective would be to circulate draft rules for ONUC to contributing countries and raise this matter in discussion with the Advisory Committee. The rules should thereafter be immediately published so that the Force commander could circulate them for compliance by contingents.

There was no need for me to overemphasise the adverse effect of recent events on the morale of the Force. Our achievement in UNEF had given us an excellent name in the eyes of the world and produced valuable ideas concerning the use of an international force to ensure future peace. I believed that the way ONUC was being shaped at present was not conducive to our organisation keeping its reputation. For the maintenance of good morale in an army, personal comforts could only have a secondary place; the most important factors were that the men should be well trained and well led, be equipped with the best available weapons, and be called on to fight for a recognisable cause. Many of these ingredients of good morale were lacking in the Force and therefore needed to be rectified without further delay.

My final proposal was that the Secretary-General should send a personal message to the Force containing a simple appraisal of the present trend of events and a word of encouragement to the men.

In view of the many incidents between the ANC and the UN troops and the need to establish a better relationship with the ANC before its training could begin, I felt that the agreement with the Congolese government on the status of the Force should be formalised. An interim agreement, based on the experience of UNEF, had been negotiated with the government and initiated by Bomboko, but then Lumumba had been overthrown. Only after Kasavubu's authority was reaffirmed by the General Assembly was it possible to reopen the question. Negotiations for the training of the ANC also offered a good opportunity to formalise the status agreement, and accordingly Hammarskjöld instructed Nwokedi and Gardiner to include this matter in their discussions with Kasavubu and his cabinet on the implementation of the Security Council resolution of 21 February.

In the Congo on 11 April, following a discussion in the Council of Ministers, Ileo and Bomboko presented a memorandum setting out the formal position of the Congolese authorities on all the major points at issue and the suggestions previously discussed. The memorandum contained the following points:

1. The Congolese authorities intended to collaborate fully for the success of the UN operation, but on condition that the sovereignty of the 'Government of the Republic' was respected.
2. Any open acceptance of paragraphs A-2 and B-2 of the Council resolution was resisted, on the grounds that they represented a 'characteristic intrusion'

by the UN into the exercise of sovereign rights.
3.   The proposals made by Kasavubu on March 6 were to be used as a basis for
     negotiations on the reorganisation of the ANC, although this did not
     preclude discussion of the withdrawal of foreign military personnel—
     however, there was objection to giving priority to withdrawal over the whole
     problem of reorganisation.
4.   The UN proposals for a Joint Commission to analyse all posts held by
     foreigners were rejected on the grounds that this would mean the Congolese
     authorities delegating a part of their sovereign rights (this represented a
     hardening of their position on the question of political advisers).
5.   They were receptive to the idea of establishing a Congolese Public Service
     Commission, but with UN assistance only and not with UN participation—
     they accepted the assistance of the UN in external recruitment but without
     giving it a 'monopoly'.

In addition, Bomboko put forward a new proposal which he believed
would be acceptable to his colleagues and to Kasavubu. This was that 'the
central Congolese authorities accept the Security Council resolution of 21
February 1961, paragraphs A-2 and B-2, on the understanding that the UN
will assist the President of the Republic in withdrawing and evacuating all
foreign military and paramilitary personnel, mercenaries and political
advisers not engaged on the authority of the head of state; and that the
President will appoint a committee to review other cases engaged on this
authority.'

The UN stand on the first, fourth and fifth points of the memorandum
was immediately made clear by Nwokedi and Gardiner. On the second
point it was explained that A-2 and B-2 did not infringe the sovereign rights
of the Congo any more than it did those of other members. On the third,
Nwokedi and Gardiner continued to press for a joint examination at the
military level in the light of Kasavubu's proposals and based on the
following principles: a training programme with UN assistance; replacement of foreign personnel to the necessary extent with personnel recruited
by the UN and approved by the Congolese authorities; decision on the
date for withdrawal; and unification of the armed forces under a national
defence organisation responsible to the head of state. On this procedure,
our people felt they were reasonably close to agreement. On Bomboko's
proposal, Nwokedi and Gardiner were seeking further clarification because the formula he had used gave the impression that implementing the
resolution was not mandatory and because there were no suitable
personnel in Leopoldville and other areas where the civil service and
armed forces were actually, as well as constitutionally, under the control
of President Kasavubu. Such a situation was obviously unacceptable.

On 12 April, following further discussions, the text of a draft
agreement along the lines of their memorandum was presented by the

Congolese ministers to the Secretariat delegation. But in view of its second paragraph, it could only be accepted if specific approval were given by the Security Council.

Because of the critical situation, the UN command in North Katanga further reinforced its troops in Kabalo consisting of one Ethiopian and two Malayan companies. At the same time, UN officers in Elisabethville again approached Tshombe, drawing his attention to the fact that his present offensive was in violation of the Security Council Resolution of 21 February 1961, and appealing to him to stop the advance and make no further movements.

On April 7 a Katangese aircraft landed at Kabalo airfield and disembarked twenty-eight Europeans with automatic weapons; it then took off again. Their identities were checked and they were found to be mercenaries in the service of Katanga. They were disarmed, kept under protective custody and later flown to Kamina for interrogation. Six other Katanga aircraft tried to land at Kabalo but did not succeed because UN troops had by then closed the airfield. At the same time about 150 Katangese gendarmerie arrived at Kabalo by river and tried to approach the airfield, but were driven off by the UN's Ethiopians. The gendarmerie then moved to the railway station and on the way opened fire on some Balubas from their boat, causing casualties. McKeown gave orders for the gendarmerie to be immediately ejected from the town of Kabalo, including the railway station and the airfield; he also ordered every effort to be made to disarm them. It fell to the Ethiopians to call on the gendarmerie to leave Kabalo; they withdrew but then took up positions by a bridge 6 miles outside the town. An Ethiopian platoon was sent to the bridge to investigate and was ambushed by the gendarmerie; an Ethiopian officer and a soldier were wounded and another soldier was reported missing. The next day, 8 April, some 300 gendarmerie were said to be preparing to move to Kabalo from the town of Kitule, 20 miles to the north, but their advance was stopped by a UN force 2-3 miles from Kabalo.

The airport at Elisabethville remained under the control of UN troops, but after the incidents in North Katanga, the gendarmerie barred all approaches to the airport and indicated that they might try to seize it. On 5 April McKeown ordered two Irish companies from Kamina to Elisabethville, and the same morning Tshombe, contrary to his previous verbal agreement with McKeown, called the crowds together for violent demonstrations against the UN at different places such as the airport, UN headquarters and the Swedish and Indian camps. Electricity and water supplies were cut off at the headquarters, the two camps and several houses occupied by UN personnel, seven of whom were arrested and detained for several hours. The windows of UN cars were smashed. Several Belgians, men and women alike, participated in these anti-UN

demonstrations. McKeown met Tshombe and got him to agree to stop all
such demonstrations, but this promise had little effect on crowds who had
already been incited.

On 6 April two Swedish detachments at Sakania and Dilolo were
threatened by superior Katangese forces and ordered by their commanders to pull back to Elisabethville; a week later the UN troops in Elisabethville were still confined to their quarters. Water and electricity supplies
had been restored, but many shops and restaurants were still closed to UN
personnel and UN vehicles which had been confiscated by the local police
during the disturbances had not yet been returned.

At the end of March and in the early weeks of April, Katanga was
the main focus of military activity. After occupying Manono, the Katanga
gendarmerie closed the airports there and at Albertville to UN troops. In
order to prevent further moves by the gendarmerie in North Katanga
which could lead to clashes with the Stanleyville ANC still in that area and
with the Balubakat Jeunesse, the UN command decided immediately to
reinforce key areas. Early in April the Ethiopian battalion at Kabalo was
further reinforced. One Indian battalion was flown from Leopoldville to
Kamina to strengthen our positions in North Katanga, a Malayan detachment of 190 was dispatched from Kasongo to Kongolo where previously
we had had no troops, and a Nigerian company was sent from Bukavu to
Albertville to increase the strength there to over 300.

Fearing that Indian reinforcements might be sent to Elisabethville,
sixty gendarmes appeared at Elisabethville airport early in the morning of
2 April and started to place obstacles such as oil drums across the runway.
The UN Swedish contingent deployed two companies immediately and
took into custody a Katanga gendarmerie detachment of twenty-five men
with a Belgian officer. The Katangese authorities were approached to
order the removal of their troops and the obstacles, and this was done by
4.30 a.m. The gendarmes in UN custody were released.

On 10 April, at a meeting of his staff, I told Hammarskjöld of the
military situation in North Katanga. At Kabalo the Ethiopians were in
control of the airfield, the railway station and the rest of the town. A
gendarmerie company that had come via the river had been cut off, was
unable to withdraw south and was short of supplies. The 300 gendarmes
who had attempted to move on Kabalo from Kitule were still only a short
distance to the north of Kabalo, although there had been some reports
that they were seen boarding a train, destination unknown. There were
also indications that Katanga might fly two battalions to Kongolo to
reinforce their position at Kabalo.

In New York we were not clear about our numerical strength in
Kabalo. As well as the original 400 Ethiopians, an additional company of
Ethiopians and 400 Malayans should by now have arrived there. This

should take care of Kabalo for the time being, and enable our troops to prevent Katangese reinforcements from landing at the airfield. If Katanga decided to fly reinforcements to Kongolo, the situation there would be impossible, for as far as we knew there were only about ninety Malayans or Nigerians there. It was clear that Kongolo had to be reinforced immediately and the airfield held. It was likely that elements of 300 gendarmes held up north of Kabalo were returning to Kongolo in order to seize the airfield and so enable a fly-in of Katangese reinforcements.

I estimated that Albertville should have about 350 Nigerians, but apparently the Katanga gendarmerie were in a superior position as they were in control of the airport and had closed it to all UN traffic. A similar situation existed at Manono where our garrison of 400 had been neutralised by Katanga gendarmes and the airport was in their control.

While we controlled the Elisabethville airport, it was still possible for Katanga to use other airports in South Katanga or even Manono or Albertville to move in their reinforcements. While we could not prevent reinforcements from actually being despatched to North Katanga, we were able to exert some control when it came to their getting through to their destination.

Thus, with our two battalions in Elisabethville tied down to that city, the battalion at Kamina tied down at the base there, and our garrisons in Manono and Albertville neutralised by the Katanga gendarmerie, the initiative was with the Katangese: if they had two or three battalions available, they could reinforce Kabalo-Kongolo with a view to arriving at a military decision favourable to them. Militarily we were weaker, and what we had gained so far was through bluff rather than by force. The Belgian military advisers were capable of finding this out, and it was therefore necessary for us to do all we could to improve our situation.

For operations against Katanga, our troops in Stanleyville and Leopoldville should have been able, at least indirectly, to support our actions. Also, we could afford to reduce our strength there, particularly in Stanleyville. Reduction would have a certain effect on those leading Tshombe's army because they would correctly assume that more UN troops were being made available for Katanga . I therefore suggested that an Ethiopian battalion from Oriental should be sent to North Katanga. Further reinforcements could also be considered.

In North Katanga, for the first time, the UN Force was involved in a major civil war situation, to an extent which was perhaps not yet fully realised. We were, in effect, opposing Tshombe's gendarmerie in strength, and this was more in the nature of a military operation than one strictly for maintaining law and order. The casualties from the incident at Kabalo indicated the seriousness of the operations: Katanga had suffered 50-60 killed and fifteen wounded, and the UN two killed, and one officer and six soldiers wounded. I suggested that we should ask Abbas to give us a report on the situation in Katanga for immediate publication. We had to give this full publicity since there would be a very strong reaction, and this might have some influence on Tshombe and others. I recommended that either McKeown or Iyassou should take personnal command of the operations in Katanga as this would give it both the necessary importance and the necessary coordination which was so necessary in an operation of this kind.

In another discussion with Hammarskjold, Bunche, Cordier and Vaughan, I said it was necessary to take stock of the logistical situation of the UN Force in the Congo; it had already reached a critical stage and would thereby have a decisive effect upon our future operations. In order to make our financial and manpower commitment as economical as possible, assist in the development of the Congolese economy and help to restore its essential services, we built up a logistical system based primarily on the means available in the country, which were almost entirely controlled from Brussels.

As has already been mentioned, there was only one port of entry into the Congo from the sea, Matadi, and this had been closed to us. For several months the Belgian company Otraco, which controlled all surface transportation in the country, had had instructions not to carry any UN war material, vehicles or troops. We were therefore denied a port of entry, and as long as this continued, we had no option but to bring material in by air. On the other hand, once we had these supplies, nothing - food, which would be open to examination by the Congolese authorities - could move in the Congo. A similar situation existed in Katanga where all surface transportation had been closed to us. The problem, therefore, was that there were no surface means of transport to reach the Congo from the outside or to move within the country. We were faced with arranging an external airlift for our total requirements and further redistributing them within the Congo by air transport. The latter was dependent on fuel brought up through a pipeline from Matadi to Leopoldville. This too was controlled by Belgians and could be shut off anywhere by the ANC at Matadi or Thysville or in Leopoldville. Somehow this had escaped their notice.

The average tonnage per day for the Force was about 120 tons and would require twenty air sorties. The nearest reliable port—even though it was a considerable distance away—was Lagos, provided the Nigerian government agreed to our using it. A fleet of 50-60 aircraft would be needed to provide the airlift. It was obvious that such an airlift could only be undertaken in an emergency for a limited time: we could not base our planning on this, and the issue of Matadi remained absolutely vital to the UN operations.

The internal redistribution of supplies, after airlifting from Lagos, to the main centres within the Congo would not add to our internal airlift responsibilities. However, our present aircraft, including charters, would be fully committed for delivering supplies within the Congo and taking care of limited operational moves. We had about two weeks' supplies left in the Congo, and there were deficiencies in certain items. After two weeks we would have to place the force on reduced rations, which was obviously undesirable and had to be avoided if possible. Thus it was necessary to make alternative arrangements and establish a supply-line to bring in emergency supplies by air. I had advised Field Service to go ahead and place an order for emergency rations for fourteen days for the whole Force. General purpose rations amounting to half the total requirement should be in the Congo within a fortnight. Pork-free or beef-free rations, which had to be specially prepared, should also be available within two weeks for air shipment from the United States.

With Hammarskjöld's approval, I had advised Field Service that Pointe Noire in Congo-Brazzaville was out of the question as a port of entry. I was also doubtful of the advisability of using Luanda in Angola; perhaps it could be used for a few initial shipments to ensure continuity of supply, but for any longer period Lagos was the nearest port that we could hope to use with any degree of satisfaction. I had suggested to Field Service that all ships except those that were about to enter Matadi and could be diverted to Luanda should be diverted to Lagos. For Field Service it was a tremendous problem, because sometimes up to thirty ships at a time were on the move from different parts of the world to the port of supply for the UN Force in the Congo. It would, therefore, take some time to arrange, which could result in the Force being dependent for a longer period on emergency rations. Needless to say, the cost would rise astronomically.

With the latest report from Coquilhatville on the closing of the river to shipping, I had little doubt about the intentions of those who were against the UN effort in the Congo. The grand design had unfolded itself fully. Matadi was closed. We could not use surface transport. Coquilhatville was closed. Thus, in the area controlled by Kasavubu, we were only free to use N'Djili airport, which again was dependent on a small oil pipeline that could be cut off at any minute and thus bottle us up completely. In Katanga we were already bottled up and had to depend entirely on air supply, which itself was dependent on fuel flown from Leopoldville.

I therefore submitted that those who had entrusted the UN with its enormous task in the Congo should face up to the consequent responsibilities and be asked to remedy a state of affairs that placed the Force in such serious jeopardy. Meanwhile, to simplify immediate supply to the

Force, we should find the means to use what was already in Matadi.

As Abbas had pointed out, our freedom of movement in Congolese territory was decreasing rapidly. This situation had to be reversed to give us full freedom. Since a number of airports were closed to us, we were unable to reinforce even if we had had additional troops; for instance, we wanted to reinforce Coquilhatville, Manono and Albertville, but could not. I suggested that this too should be brought to the notice of those who expected us to perform the impossible. We were reaching a point where it was getting increasingly difficult to continue without more active support from the key member-states.

Abbas's efforts to arrange the return of UN troops to Matadi and, failing that, of Nigerian police as an interim step met with little success. When he pressed for a reply, Kasavubu and Bomboko did not reject the idea of using Nigerian police, but raised several questions on the proposed phases for the entry of UN personnel. Because the situation in Katanga was a matter of concern to the Congolese leaders, it gave us a good opportunity to take up with them the question of freedom of movement and the status of the Force agreement. The UN needed endorsement to operate in Katanga, just as it did to move freely anywhere in the Congo to carry out its tasks, but there was no discernible progress. I had little doubt that the Congolese leaders and those who supported them, namely Belgian and other foreign advisers, were using their best efforts to throttle the UN operation. This only made me more determined to overcome the obstruction and rapidly find ways to reopen supply lines.

Since use of the port of Matadi had been denied to the UN on 10 March 1961, no UN supplies had entered there. Fortunately, the UN Force had a total of forty-five days' reserve rations, and all new troops coming into the Congo were immediately instructed to bring with them thirty days' rations. Also, it had been possible to send to the UN depots in Leopoldville some of the supplies which had arrived in Matadi and been cleared by the UN before the closure. However, it was necessary in one way or another to open a channel through which the UN Force could be regularly supplied. At present there were about 800 tons of supplies in Matadi, but regular supply ships to that port were now being diverted elsewhere. Some supplies, though not a large quantity, had been landed at Luanda; but it was a fact that 120 tons of frozen food had been sent to Antwerp, where we had refrigeration space, and some of it had been withheld from shipment.

ONUC had estimated at the beginning of April that essential food requirements could be assured up to the end of that month by means of adjustments and substitutions. This estimate included procurement from local and regional areas and some supplies which could be imported into Katanga from Northern Rhodesia through Kenya. However, a few items such as lamb and fish and tomatoes, condiments and pickles were already in critically short supply, and the restriction that Tshombe had imposed on the UN's purchasing fresh food in Katanga had also aggravated the situation. It was imperative to get the flow of supplies for the UN Force moving again very soon. It was estimated that 2,300 tons of supplies were needed monthly and this was without fuel for aircraft. The UN air force in the Congo needed about 2,000 tons of fuel each month for internal use alone—this did not include rotation or troop movements to and from the Congo undertaken by USAF, RCAF and RAF airlifts. In other words, it would be necessary to supply approximately 80 tons a day on average to the UN Force in the Congo, excluding aviation fuel.

At the UN we had been studying for some time the various possibilities for supplying ONUC through routes other than Matadi, and I presented these to Hammarskjöld and his advisers. The first was the airlift from Lagos to Leopoldville, which would require many heavy aircraft and be extremely costly. Furthermore, even if we got the supplies to Leopoldville, it would still be necessary to airlift them to other parts of the Congo: the bulk of ONUC—9,000-10,000 men—were now in the eastern provinces of Katanga, Kivu and Oriental. Then there was the route to Leopoldville from Pointe Noire via Brazzaville, which was shorter than the Lagos route but would be complicated because, even if we got the supplies to Brazzaville, they would have to be ferried across the Congo river and the ferry was not under UN control. The third possible route was from Angola by rail to Katanga, but transit through Angola was unreliable and the railway from the Angolan border to Elisabethville was under Tshombe's control. The route from Rhodesia to Katanga was not practicable, as Rhodesia itself was far from the coast. The route from Dares Salaam in Tanganyika to Tabora was a definite possibility and was being explored. The railway from Dar es Salaam extended as far as Kigoma on the eastern shores of Lake Tanganyika. However, the ferry across the lake was not controlled by the UN and the roads on its western side were probably not capable of serving as a main line of communication. If this route were used, it would probably be by rail from Dar es Salaam to Tabora and then by air to the Congo. Finally there was a route through Kenya and Uganda comprising a railway line from Mombasa to Entebbe and a fairly good road from Entebbe to Goma and on to Kindu. Entebbe also had a good airfield. The flying distance from Mombasa to Entebbe was about 1,000 miles and the road from Entebbe to Goma another 400 miles. There were thus several choices but clearly not all were practicable for various reasons. I had contacted the British permanent mission to the UN to investigate the two most likely routes (all things considered), namely those between Dar es Salaam and the southern part of the Congo and between Mombasa and Entebbe-Kindu.

I also summarised the movement of troops. The whole Moroccan contingent had now been repatriated, with the last group being airlifted out by the USAF on 1 April. The Sudan government had asked for its contingent of about 400 men, now located in Leopoldville, to be repatriated and the USAF agreed to provide the airlift. The movement was expected to start any day. The Indonesian contingent was now concentrated at Kitona and arrangements had been made for its repatriation by 10 March, but the unhappy incident at Matadi prevented it from being carried out. We now hoped to be able to have the Indonesians taken by sea from either Matadi or Lagos in late April. The RAF had airlifted 255 reinforcements for the Malayan contingent in Kivu to Kamina. This was completed on 11 April, and an additional 431 Malayan troops left Malaya on 7 April on board the USNS *Eltinge*.

This ship also took about 650 Indian troops on the same voyage, leaving Bombay on 14 April. The status of the Indian brigade group's transportation otherwise was as follows: 1,769 troops with about 350 tons of equipment and some vehicles had already arrived in Leopoldville by air, and these were later flown to Kamina. Some 2,225 troops with about 635 tons of equipment and some vehicles left Bombay on 1 April bound for Matadi or Lagos, but because of developments in Katanga the ship was diverted to Dar es Salaam, where it arrived on 8 April. From there the troops, equipment and vehicles were airlifted to Kamina where it had been decided to concentrate the whole Indian brigade except for one battalion which would remain in Leopoldville: this airlift began on 13 April in UN aircraft (C-54s). The United States had been requested to airlift about 1,150 men, 300 tons of stores and some vehicles, and this operation was expected to begin shortly. Britain was to contribute to this lift with two Britannia aircraft.

USNS *Blatchford* was expected to depart from Dar es Salaam within a few days for Matadi and there load the Indonesians for repatriation; if there were any difficulties with the Congolese authorities the United States had agreed to airlift the men to Lagos where they would then board the transport ship. Since most of the Indian brigade was going to be deployed in Katanga and since the Malayan contingent was in Kivu, we now considered diverting the *Eltinge* to Mombasa and using this route into the Congo for the Indians and Malayans. If it proved to be practical, we would also send the cargo ship *Sgt. Kimbroke* there; it was carrying the heavy vehicles and stores for both the Malayan and Indian contingents and was scheduled to leave Bombay on 29 April. Consequently, we hoped to have most of the Indian and Malayan contingents deployed with their equipment and vehicles in the first two weeks of May. The Liberian company of 205 men was ready for departure, and would be airlifted out as soon as aircraft were available. The Ceylon government had announced that its contingent, consisting of a reinforced infantry company, would be ready in Colombo at the end of May; it would be transported on board the *Blatchford* on its return trip after completing the repatriation of the Indonesians.

Hammarskjöld remained firmly determined to achieve his twin objectives of removing foreign advisers and mercenaries from Katanga and promoting national reconciliation, and was therefore anxious for Dayal to return to the Congo to pursue these goals. However Kasavubu, encouraged by the British and American ambassadors, Ian Scott and Clare Timberlake, continued to oppose Dayal's return and refused to take responsibility for his security. Kasavubu was engaged in efforts to reach an agreement with Tshombe and Kalonji, but had decided to use force to settle his differences with Gizenga. Along with the Americans and the British, he felt that Dayal's attempts at national reconciliation included Gizenga's pro-Lumumba group, whom they wished to exclude, believing it to be pro-Communist. Scott and Timberlake had made no secret of their view that a government had to be built around Kasavubu.

Timberlake's persistent recommendation that Dayal be replaced had its effect on President Kennedy, who accepted the ambassador's evaluation of Dayal and ordered the State Department and Adlai Stevenson to step up their efforts to this end.[2] On seeing an article in the *New York Times* on 20 March reporting that Hammarskjöld had asked Dayal to stay on in his job for another two or three months, Stevenson came to see him and asked in strong terms for Dayal to be replaced, conveying the fact that this was the wish of Kennedy. This greatly perturbed Hammarskjöld, who told Stevenson that undue pressure by the Western powers made Dayal's replacement even more difficult and would upset Nehru, who held Dayal in high esteem, at a time when the Indians were badly needed to replace troops leaving the force. Meanwhile, the Western press continued its adverse treatment of Dayal.

Since his arrival in New York, Dayal had been busy meeting important delegates at the UN, the press and prominent Americans. He was not short of friends, and had a range of admirers in the American community whom he had cultivated during his earlier years with India's permanent mission to the UN. His efforts resulted in a better understanding and sympathy for his role in the Congo and counteracted the bitter denunciations of Kasavubu and his cohorts, which had received wide publicity with the help of the western ambassadors in Leopoldville. But his detractors remained adamant, and this put Hammarskjöld in a quandary.

Dayal was a brilliant as well as a devoted and loyal UN official. He acted in tune with Hammarskjöld and sought to interpret his policies. He had done no more than what Hammarskjöld had asked him to do, and had done it well. So how could the Secretary-General ask him to leave when all Dayal had done was implement his policies? Hammarskjöld and other senior UN staff who had been associated with him gave no credence to Kasavubu's charge that Dayal was arrogant and a Communist sympathiser. Dayal epitomised the best traditions of the Indian civil service, which independent India had inherited from its former British rulers and continued to nourish, and would never have allowed his own political views to interfere with his responsibilities. It was the policy of the UN to reconcile all factions in the Congo, and Dayal put all his efforts into achieving that goal regardless of what he thought of the Congolese leaders as individuals.

The dilemma before Hammarskjöld was that while on the one hand he was being asked to replace a loyal and capable colleague whom he greatly liked and who had the strong support of Nehru, on the other hand he needed the co-operation of the Congolese leaders to push forward his twin goals and needed American support to achieve these goals. In the event he had to choose the latter. He communicated his predicament to Nehru, who realised the importance of pressing on with the task in hand, and agreed to reappoint Dayal to his previous post as India's ambassador to Pakistan. Dayal was kept informed of these developments and was in Hammarskjöld's confidence throughout the painful process of coming to a decision. He not only took his return to the Indian service well but also with a sense of pride that he had done his job well and won the gratitude and appreciation of many countries and their leaders. His departure was a blow to me because not only did I greatly admire him, but I had also learned from him a great deal about diplomacy. It was now almost ten months since I had started to work with the Secretary-General, and during this time I had come to know many high-level officials. I was convinced that Dayal's departure would deprive the UN of its ablest man in the field and that he would be extremely hard to replace.

I was never busier than at this time in attending to the military situation and providing the operational and logistical backing to ONUC to ease McKeown's difficult task. During the frequent meetings of the Congo Advisory Committee, — I was invariably asked by Hammarskjöld to present the military situation—which was that the UN Force was dealing with several difficult situations simultaneously. Kasavubu was trying to gain ascendancy over the UN in Leopoldville, including N'Djili airport; Kalonji's troops were trying to consolidate their power over eastern Kasai and further expand the area under their control; Tshombe was trying to regain control over North Katanga and end the Baluba 'state' of Lulaba; Lundula's ANC and other elements not entirely loyal to Mobutu were fighting it out in Kivu; the ANC was making attacks on the European community; and, lastly, Lundula had launched military operations to gain control of Equateur, and Mobutu had started his much—publicised offensive to defeat the Stanleyville troops. The UN had to deal with all this while its only seaport was closed and surface transportation was blocked by the divided forces of the host-country.

The departure of troops from countries angry at the UN's failure to protect Lumumba was being offset by the arrival of the Indians, but this could not completely remedy the loss. However, when the third Indian battalion and the brigade's heavy transport reached the Congo after about a month, the operational ability of the UN force should improve considerably.

Repeated incidents involving European mercenaries and Belgian officers of the Katanga gendarmarie had caused 'conflict of interest' problems for Nigeria's British officers. Brigadier Ward, an able and upright brigade commander, had expressed his views to me on UN policy for dealing with North Katanga in a frank conversation during one of my visits. He said that the UN should learn from its experience with the ANC, led by its own untrained officers. The removal of Belgian officers from the Katanga gendarmerie would make this force less efficient than the rest of the ANC, and then our difficulties would be worsened. The Balubakat Jeunesse, because of the failure of its leaders, was out of control and attacked indiscriminately; thus it was better to let the gendarmerie deal with them. Ward's other problem was that the UN's instructions required the apprehending of foreign mercenaries. Since Tshombe had only hired Europeans, Ward and his British officers were in the awkward situation of having to apprehend their own nationals and allies.

I did not accept Ward's recommendations but agreed to take up his views with the Secretary-General and the Nigerian mission to the UN. From the beginning of the ONUC operation, I had been dubious about the presence of British or French officers in our contingents, whereas I was totally opposed to any foreign officers serving with the ANC—a view which by now had the Security Council's backing. However, my views on the national origins of contingents in the UN Force were based on political reality. How, for instance, could Ghana and Nigeria call for the removal of foreign advisers in the ANC when they had their own? My other reason was that while foreign advisers could legitimately be provided from one sovereign state to another, their presence in military operations was an embarrassment to their adopted countries and to the UN. I was impressed by the high quality of the seconded officers from Britain and France but finding them on the ONUC staff when I first came to Leopoldville, calling themselves Ghanaians or Senegalese, took me beyond my ability to play charades. I gradually changed these posts and built up the staff from well-qualified Africans. The UN's problem became acute when a foreign-commanded African unit became involved with Europeans, as in North Katanga. With Hammarskjöld's approval, I recommended to Ghana and Nigeria that they replace their British officers in the field with their own nationals. Since such a change could only be made when the troops were rotated, we had to wait.

The operations in North Katanga by the Katanga gendarmerie and the UN's attempts to prevent civil war and remove mercenaries had in effect developed into a major military confrontation that could no longer be called a law-and-order operation. At Hammarskjöld's request, Abbas and McKeown had sent their recommendations and I gave my own comments to Hammarskjöld, as described below.

In view of Ward's reluctance to be involved in the operations against European-led Katangese and concern that the Nigerian Prime Minister should not be associated with any incidents that might result in casualties, I concluded that it would be inadvisable to use the Nigerian brigade then in North Katanga. Consequently, of the troops available only Malayans and Indians could be used.

The UN were in control of Kabalo, and therefore the relief of the Ethiopians who were due for rotation could be carried out without any difficulty. At Nyunzu there were 450 Malayans and 200 Katangan gendarmes including mercenaries. We were informed that the Malayans were in sufficient strength to hold out but not to operate against mercenaries. The Nigerian force in Albertville consisted of five combat platoons totalling 117 men whereas the gendarmerie was 500 strong. In Manono there were 400 Nigerians and 800 gendarmes. Thus the Nigerians in Albertville were outnumbered five-to-one by the Katanga gendarmerie and in Manono two-to-one. If they were attacked in Albertville they would not be able to hold their own; in Manono they should be able to do so for a limited time. Withdrawing them would not be easy, and if it were done, a large-scale operation would be needed to re-enter the two towns. It was therefore essential that our primary move should be directed towards Albertville which in turn was likely to reduce pressure on the Nigerians there. A possible counter-argument was that the gendarmerie might use the Nigerians as hostages and thus make their situation even more dangerous. I believed that once we were in a position to pose a threat with superior numbers in Albertville, the gendarmerie would be unlikely to stand up against us. As Manono could not be left to its fate for too long, a simultaneous move had to be made in that direction. If ONUC could not move on Albertville and Manono at the same time, they should at least arrange a diversionary move towards Manono to relieve pressure on our garrison there.

ONUC's suggestions about relief and the future deployment of Nigerians and Malayans did not allow for a Force reserve and a review of operations highlighted the importance of creating one. ONUC had been at its most effective recently when it had had the Indian brigade in reserve at Kamina available for deployment. It should arrange priorities and allot troops accordingly.

Abbas and McKeown had indicated their intention of transferring the third Indian battalion from Leopoldville to North Katanga. I agreed that for the intended operations in North Katanga Brigadier K.A.S. Raja should have all three of his battalions, but ONUC had to consider the importance of Leopoldville and the need to maintain adequate strengths there. We could never afford to be complacent in the capital despite improved relations with Kasavubu and his men. Congolese demands for the return of our hangar space in N'Djili in an effort to gain complete control of the airfield could not be ignored. The Matadi issue still remained unresolved. Thus my response to the Abbas-McKeown view was that in returning the third Indian battalion to its parent brigade in Katanga, another unit of about the same size should be brought to Leopoldville.

The best way that we could achieve results was by establishing an overwhelming numerical superiority in the area of our intended operations. If this saved us a fight, it would have proved itself as the best policy. Thus we should suggest to ONUC that it provide or replace garrisons and thereafter create a reserve in key areas which it could employ according to the tasks confronting it. For the reasons already mentioned, Malayans and Indians would be most suited for this purpose. As Ethiopia had already requested that its fourth battalion should remain under the command of its own parent brigade, a good all-round solution would be to replace Malayans by Ethiopians in Kivu province. My suggested relief plan for the garrisons in Kivu was for a company of Ethiopians to replace a similar Nigerian unit at Goma; the Ethiopian battalion, less two companies, to replace the rest of the Nigerian battalion at Bukavu; and two Ethiopian companies to replace 300 Malayans at Kindu. The situation in Kivu had changed somewhat. Tension along the Ruanda-Urundi border had subsided, but the European expatriates continued to need protection, mainly through the stationing of troops in Bukavu and Goma and by patrolling. We had to retain control of Kindu airport and keep the ANC there in a calm state. An Ethiopian battalion reinforced by one or two companies should be able to carry out this task.

In Katanga, the Indian brigade would replace Ethiopians at Kabalo and concentrate troops for the operations which it was hoped would free Nyunzu, Albertville and Manono. The Malayans would concentrate in the area of Kabalo for these operations in conjunction with the Indian brigade and then be diverted to Manono. A Nigerian battalion should be available for duties in either Leopoldville or Kamina. If it replaced the Indian battalion in Leopoldville, the latter could be moved to Kamina, or the Indians could stay in Leopoldville while the Nigerians went to garrison Kamina. Although the latter alternative was easier, it might have been a sounder plan to put Nigerians in Leopoldville and keep all the Indians in Katanga.

As operations in North Katanga were likely to have repercussions elsewhere in that province, our relative position had to be examined. At Elisabethville we had about 1,200 Swedes and Irish against 700 gendarmerie, which was a reasonably satisfactory proportion. However, 100 Irish in Luena were out on their own and it was therefore desirable to withdraw them. At Kamina the gendarmerie had about 500 men and so with a battalion at the base there our position should be fairly secure. Overall, our position in Katanga was superior to that of the gendarmerie which, with a total strength of 6,000, had small detachments all over the province.

Katanga called for our fullest attention, but our redeployment should not affect our basic positions. I suggested the following operational priorities: Leopoldville, Elisabethville, the former Belgian bases, Katanga, Kasai, Stanleyville, Coquilhatville, Kivu. When our operations in North Katanga were concluded, ONUC should redeploy troops after a fresh appreciation of priorities. It should also immediately create another force reserve.

The intended operations in North Katanga should be carried out as speedily as possible, with secrecy up to the stage of the completion of redeployment. Thereafter we should make our intentions public, issue the necessary warnings to the Katanga gendarmerie and provincial authorities, and proceed with military action if our demands were not met. I had reason to believe that once we had completed our preparations, we should find this operation fairly simple to conduct.

The UN efforts to prevent fighting between Mobutu and Lundula's ANC created a situation in which the forces of the two sides were living close to each other but without fighting. After all, they were part of the same army and knew each other. The period of quiet led to fraternisation and serious talks on reconciliation. The local commanders held meetings at Bundoki near the border which led to the Lundula officers agreeing to accept Mobutu as head of the ANC. Mobutu had visited the border a number of times and participated in these meetings and his offer of regular pay and equipment persuaded the Lundula officers to accept him as their chief. How serious this agreement might be could only be judged in the course of time, but certainly it was something the UN wished to encourage. Mobutu also announced that a ceasefire had been ordered along the border between Equateur and Oriental provinces. Gizenga denied the agreement, but this provoked Mobutu in threatening force if Gizenga in fact prevented the accord.

On 17 April, Kasavubu signed an agreement with the UN representatives Gardiner and Nwokedi accepting the Security Council resolution of 21 February, with the understanding that while implementing it the UN would respect the Republic's sovereignty. The Congo recognised the need for the ANC to be reorganised; this task would actually be undertaken by the UN but under Kasavubu's personal authority. Kasavubu also agreed that any civilian, military and paramilitary personnel and political advisers who were not engaged under his authority would have to leave the Congo as soon as possible. In a press statement he said that the talks had dispelled some fears and suspicions, but that he had not agreed to the return of UN troops to Matadi for the time being. He said that he welcomed UN officials who had come as friends, but that the others would be excluded. However, despite the rhetoric, he did allow the UN to send Nigerian police to Matadi and the agreement was a success for the UN in that it implied recognition by Kasavubu and his group of the UN's importance at a time when he and Mobutu's ANC had little control over developments elsewhere in the Congo. Only the UN could rescue them from the present chaos.

During the time when he was negotiating with the UN and the parleying was taking place between the rival ANCs, Kasavubu continued with his pursuit of a meeting of the Congolese leaders and now also wanted to include Gizenga, who was still reluctant to attend. The round-table talks were first scheduled to take place at Elisabethville, but these were postponed several times. He now invited the leaders to Coquilhatville, and they met there on 24 April. This meeting was a continuation of the Tananarive conference where Tshombe had pressed for a confederal solution. Kasavubu's group had considered the matter and concluded that true federation would be preferable to a loosely-knit confederation. They had hoped at this meeting to persuade Tshombe to accept this arrangement.

As well as the Leopoldville lot, the meeting was attended by Kalonji who appeared wearing a remarkable head-dress and a leopard-skin over his business suit; he had recently been crowned king of the Baluba tribe in the Kasai. Sendwe, the Baluba leader from North Katanga, was there as head of the state of Lualaba. Tshombe also attended, but Gizenga stayed away.

Right at the opening of the conference, there was a dispute caused by Tshombe's refusal to take his seat because of the presence of Sendwe. After some wrangling, Tshombe and Sendwe shook hands and the meeting began. All the regions of the Congo were represented except for Kivu and Oriental provinces. Tshombe demanded that Kasavubu should renounce all cooperation with the UN, but after three days of bickering he abruptly left the conference, to be arrested by the ANC at Coquilhatville's airfield. His captors pleaded with him to return to the conference, but he refused and continued to be held at the airfield. The UN took advantage of the presence of Tshombe's Belgian advisers, who were also being held, by removing them from Congolese custody and shipping them back to Belgium. This annoyed Tshombe even more and he refused to eat and would only drink soda-water. He was eventually persuaded to go to the city, but would not rejoin the conference.

At the conference there were denunciations of Tshombe and demands for the disbanding of his army. Some of these statements by the Congolese leaders sounded similar to those they had made against Lumumba. The Katangese leaders in Elisabethville began to adopt a friendly attitude, perhaps more to avoid harm befalling Tshombe than in good faith. Tshombe's ally, President Fulbert Youlou of Congo-Brazzaville, retaliated by closing the traffic across the Congo river from his capital to Leopoldville. However, on 6 May Munungo made an offer of co-operation to the UN in order to save Tshombe, but he affirmed his refusal to place Katanga's gendarmerie and its currency under Congolese control. On 9 May the Congolese Interior Minister, Cyrille Adoula, declared that Tshombe would be held in Leopoldville for six months or until he was brought to trial for treason. A commission would review charges against him, namely that he had fraudulently assumed the powers of a head of state by declaring Katanga independent in violation of the law; that others under his leadership had committed crimes prejudicial to law and order in the state; and that he had printed his own currency, created a secessionist army, hired foreign mercenaries, waged war and dealt directly with foreign powers.

Tshombe's absence did not interrupt the deliberations at Coquilhatville, which took a dramatic turn when Kasavubu challenged Gizenga to a political test of strength at a session of parliament, to which the UN had been quietly pushing the Congolese leaders. At ONUC's suggestion, he reiterated that he would ask the UN to guarantee the safety of all members of parliament. The conference concluded at the end of the month with an agreement which called for a federation, increased the number of provinces from six to twenty-one and, more important, recognised tribal differences.

It was usual for the UN to provide escorts for Congolese leaders when asked to do so and on 26 April, to avoid the many roadblocks set up by the ANC, high Congolese provincial officials on a visit to Port Francqui asked for a UN aircraft and an escort. They also asked to be lodged at the Hôtel des Palmes, which the UN had taken over from the Lower Congo-Katanga railway as billets for its personnel. There was already friction between ONUC and the ANC because the UN had closed the bar in the hotel to the Congolese, and the ANC had been further angered when the railway flag was hung up, reportedly to dry, which they took to be a sign that the Belgians had returned.

Some twenty ANC soldiers called on the visiting officials to ask them why they had sought UN protection and, dissatisfied with their replies, began to arrest and disarm UN Ghanaian soldiers who were going about their normal business. Two British officers in command of the Ghanaian troops were intercepted on the road and arrested, and later three Swedish members of the UN movement control unit, stationed at Port Francqui for reshipment of supplies, were seized as they arrived at the hotel. A request by the UN troops to their brigade headquarters at Luluabourg led to the despatch of more Ghanaian troops by road, but these were held at a road-block and became involved in an exchange of fire. On learning of this fight, the ANC at Port Francqui murdered all the Ghanaians, British and Swedes in their custody. Only two bodies were recovered, the rest having presumably been thrown in the river.

The Ghanaian column withdrew to Luluabourg. When UN officials, with ANC officers from the provincial capital and from Mobutu's headquarters, reached Port Francqui, they learned that the total of UN personnel killed was 120.[3] Two had been wounded. The ANC reportedly lost two men at the road-block.

My colleagues on the 38th Floor could see my agony and fury as the telexes came in from ONUC. According to the first reports, forty-seven of our officers and men had been killed; the final figure came later. I found it hard to believe and asked for confirmation. We had indeed lost 120 men. Was it all the fault of the ANC? No one could convince me of that. None of us in New York was seeking revenge, but we insisted that due process of law be followed by the Congolese, whatever it might mean to them. What calmed me, perhaps more than anything else, was that Ghana wanted to keep the affair quiet.

Hammarskjöld had been looking for a suitable person to appoint as his representative in Katanga, who would have the necessary professional skills—and determination—to implement his plans in face of the numerous difficulties thrown up by Tshombe and his Western supporters. His choice fell on Conor Cruise O'Brien, a member of the Irish Foreign service with UN experience and a reputation as a writer, whom he appreciated as a fellow-intellectual. O'Brien arrived in Katanga at a critical period when the preparations for the implementation of the Security Council Resolution of 21 February 1961 were in full swing. His personality made a deep impression on the UN troops, especially Brigadier Raja and his subordinates.

NOTES

1. This was based on the assumption that although the combined strength of all Congolese forces was now the same as it had been and that it had better weapons than the UN they were none the less poorly led, received little training and their morale was low.

2. Also see Madeleine G. Kalb, *The Congo Cable: The Cold War in Africa, from Eisenhower to Kennedy* (New York: Macmillan, 1982), p. 245.

3. Maj. Gen. H.T. Alexander, *African Tightrope: My Two Years as Nkrumah's Chief of Staff*, London: Pall Mall, 1966, p. 66. UN records show 44 UN personnel killed, a figure I believe to be an under-estimate.

11

ATTEMPTS TO END SECESSION OF KATANGA

Since 22 February, we had worked hard at the UN to support Hammarskjöld's efforts to implement his dual objectives of bringing about national reconciliation and ending Katanga's secession. The parliament had finally met and approved a government which included all the factions. Only Katanga had spurned invitations to participate and Tshombe, on his release and return to Elisabethville, reneged on his promises and reasserted its independence. This did not augur well for the future of Adoula's government, as Katangese intransigence threatened the fragile new unity. Any further delay on the part of the UN in its vigorous pursuit of Congolese reconciliation would lead to more attacks on the Organisation and its Secretary-General for giving in to Western pressures.

Meanwhile, the Indian Independent Infantry Brigade Group, under the command of Brigadier K.A.S. Raja, had taken over from the Nigerians in North Katanga as part of the redeployment plan of the UN Force in the Congo. On 1 May, the Indian Dogra battalion had been flown from Kamina to Kabalo from where it moved by road to Nyunzu and Niemba. The brigade headquarters and ancilliary troops were flown from Leopoldville to Albertville. The Gorkhas were airlifted from Kamina to Manono. This move had been opposed by the Katangese, but they yielded when the UN warned them that any interference in the move of the Gorkhas would require their diversion to Albertville from where, if it became necessary, they would fight their way to Manono. The Jats, the third Indian battalion, remained at Leopoldville as a reserve force. By the end of May the Indian brigade, less the Jats, had completed its deployment in the area.

Katanga Province
Congo, 1960

╀╀╀╀╀ *Railroads*   -------- *Roads*

| 0 | 100 | 200 | 300 km |
| 0 | 50 | 100 | 150 | 200 mi |

The Indian brigade was well aware of the opposition of Kasavubu and others in his central government to their joining ONUC. The conduct of the Indian service troops and staff personnel from the outset of the UN operation was beyond reproach. The Indian contingent commanders, Brigadiers Harminder Singh and (now) Sartaj Singh, had kept a firm yet benevolent control over their personnel and worked hard to establish good relations with other contingents and above all with the Congolese. The French-speaking Indian officers may not have been as fluent as their French-Canadian counterparts, but they were no less effective in their performance and in gaining the goodwill of the ANC officers. This could be said equally of the entire Indian staff at ONUC, and the General Hospital enjoyed a high reputation. However, the policies of the Indian government in support of the UN in implementing UN resolutions as directed by the Secretary-General were counter to the wishes of the Kasavubu regime and had soured relations for all Indians.

There were other factors too that caused the Congolese to mistrust and fear the Indians. A misguided British embassy official in Leopoldville had spread rumours of India's intention to colonise the Congo as a way to solve the problem of its growing population. He had alleged that an Indian plan existed to disarm the ANC and replace the Kasavubu-Mobutu clique with a pro-Lumumba regime. Horror stories of the Indian troops' behaviour in war, e.g. rape, pillage and murder, were spread effectively among people who had often committed those crimes themselves. The presence of Gorkhas from Nepal in the Indian brigade surprisingly received special attention in the English-language press and in the British press especially. It was said in the papers and on the radio that instead of sending its own national troops, India used mercenaries. This distinguished the Gorkhas in the British service, who were the pride of the British forces, as the regular guys from those serving India who were depicted as mercenaries like the ones hired by Tshombe. The media failed to point out that both the British and the Indians recruited Gorkhas from two separate areas of Nepal by treaty. Furthermore, India had its own population of Gorkhas who provided a sizeable, if not a majority, of the Gorkhas in the Indian Army; and Gorkhas in the Indian Army, unlike those in British service, had the same promotion opportunities as native Indians, and some had risen to the rank of general.

In this atmosphere, where a lie repeated often enough became a fact, such misinformation simply had to be dealt with, but efforts were thwarted by the campaign that led to the departure of Dayal and a check on my travel to the Congo. It was first explained to me by Bunche that it was because of Sean McKeown's view that I should not interfere in the command as I had done under Bunche's direction during Von Horn's time, but this issue had been settled after my talk with McKeown; at least

I thought it had. In time, McKeown and I had become good friends, but there always seemed to be a reason why I should not leave New York.

It was only after the second round of fighting in Katanga and the death of Hammarskjöld that I was asked to return to the Congo to find out what had happened and advise on improving operations for the future. During this period I had the frustrating task of reviewing ONUC plans without the benefit of a direct meeting or a radio or telephone conversation with any of the key players in the field. I knew for a fact that the Western embassies did not relish my visits since I was viewed as too close to Dayal, and there was a residual feeling on the part of Mobutu, fuelled by his Belgian advisers and Western supporters, that during the fighting around the Ghana embassy in November 1960 I had intended to put an end to his so-called coup and reinstate Lumumba.

Of all the reasons that kept me out of the Congo during these crucial months the most potent was the fear among the Congolese, shared by their Western supporters, especially the Belgians and British, that I might counsel the Indian commanders to act in a way that was counter to their interests. I believe they realised that I would never act contrary to my instructions and they knew of their total inability to exert undue influence over me. Therefore, I was safer in New York than in Leopoldville. The cost of this bad judgement in keeping me from visiting ONUC turned out to be much higher that even I had anticipated.

In deciding the plans for the deployment of the Indian brigade, in consultation with ONUC, it was evident that it could not be sent to Katanga without an incident and protests by the Western powers. However, we controlled Kamina, and the location of the Indian brigade there would place it strategically for future use. The withdrawal of the Moroccans had exposed our installations at Leopoldville to the numerically stronger ANC. At least a battalion was needed there, but I was opposed to dividing the Indian brigade. Eventually, we agreed to keep the brigade together at Leopoldville because the very suggestion of Indian troops at Kamina frightened Tshombe and his cohorts.

In the spring, as the situation in Katanga deteriorated and we lost troops due to the withdrawal of some of the contingents, I had already proposed that the Indian brigade replace the Nigerians in North Katanga where there was a task for a force of its size. This had been approved by Hammarskjöld and we suggested it to McKeown, who liked the idea. But as the crisis heightened in Elisabethville, I had barely reached my apartment after an usually late day at work when I received a call from Hammarskjöld's office to say that Bunche was with him in his office and that he had dictated a cable to McKeown and wanted to read it to me in case I had any comments. On learning the contents I said that I did not like the cable.

After Bunche had spent a few minutes persuading me to agree, Hammarskjöld came on the line and asked me to come over to his office. The Secretariat was only a few minutes by car from my place and there was hardly any traffic at that hour; I was with Hammarskjöld and Bunche within ten minutes. I was told that shortly after 10 p.m., as Hammarskjöld and Bunche were leaving the 38th floor, a cable arrived from Elisabethville reporting critical developments in the city and the interior. ONUC had called for more troops and in an urgent diplomatic effort by the Secretary-General to ease the situation, Bunche had proposed that the Gorkhas, whom the Katangese feared most, be flown to Kamina in a show of force. Hammarskjöld agreed and a cable was drafted accordingly. He then sought my views.

I disagreed with this approach. During the last week of March only the brigade headquarters and two infantry battalions had reached Leopoldville by air. The third battalion and supporting troops were being moved in three US naval transport vessels from Bombay and were due to reach Dar es Salaam and Mombasa in April. The brigade, or any part of it, could only be operational after all its elements had joined together. The guidelines that we had agreed with India for the use of the brigade permitted the use of separate battalions, but this would only be possible in exceptional circumstances for short periods and in a battalion group, i.e. with its share of supporting arms and services.

My other objection to the draft cable was to the assumption that moving the Gorkhas to Kamina constituted a threat to Katanga. I maintained that the arrival of the Gorkhas and the Indians in the Congo had already led to alarm in Katanga and that many of the actions of Tshombe and his Interior Minister Munungo were hysterical responses to their presence. Yes, the threat to Kamina would be increased by the move, there would follow cries from Katanga to the West for help which would result in their ambassadors streaming to the Secretary-General's office and asking him not to let the Gorkhas—or the Indians for that matter—loose on their favourite Congolese. We already knew enough of the Western response to the use of Indian troops in Katanga, and had accordingly decided that, at least for the time being, we could not use them in South Katanga. I said that once Tshombe and his advisers became aware that the move of the Gorkhas to Kamina was a hollow threat, they would make life even more difficult for the UN troops and civilians in Elisabethville. I therefore advised Hammarskjöld and Bunche that Tshombe should be warned to curb the activities of his mercenary-led troops, otherwise the UN would take suitable action by flying reinforcements to Elisabethville. Everyone knew of the fact that at this time the only available troops were the Indian brigade.

Bunche strongly argued for ordering the Gorkhas to Kamina, but I could not agree in spite of the ultimate argument, which devastates all military advisers, that on political grounds the move should take place. I could see that Hammarskjöld was getting tired of the discussion, so I said that as our instructions in the proposed cable were contrary to the guidelines laid down by India, I doubted if Raja, the brigade commander, could agree. Therefore, the cable should be couched not as an order but in diplomatic language so that McKeown could discuss the move with Raja. On 25 March McKeown took it up with Raja, who did not agree, pointing out that no operational move should be made until his brigade was concentrated and fully operational. But Bunche had set his mind on it. I had done all I could and if my political superiors desired the move I felt confident that Raja, who was adept at handling politicians and civilians in the corridors of Indian power in the South Block of the Secretariat in New Delhi, would take care of his own interests. On 31 March, McKeown ordered the move of the Gorkhas to Kamina, but Raja again demurred, pointing out that he would agree to it if Kamina was to be the base of operations for his brigade. It was so agreed. Just as I had anticipated, there was hardly any wind in this bag, which only added to the UN's difficulties in Elisabethville.

There were two areas where the Indian brigade could be deployed most usefully, i.e. Elisabethville and North Katanga. Since it was not politically feasible to deploy them in Elisabethville, I had begun to consider North Katanga; this became possible in May.

The news from Stanleyville was not encouraging. On his return from the parliamentary session, Gizenga had ostensibly dissolved his government, yet there were disturbing signs. His ministers continued to function and diplomats from countries that recognised his regime remained. Encouraged by these developments, pro-Lumumba elements resumed violence.

In Kasai, Kalonji had given his support to the government of national reconciliation but was opposed by some local leaders, who feared a loss of their independence. Kasai had witnessed spasmodic inter-tribal warfare. Presently the Ghana brigade under the command of the able and likeable Brigadier Joseph E. Michel,[1] had continued to keep law and order following the fine tradition set by the Tunisians before them. The Ghanaians were replaced by the Nigerian brigade under the command of Brigadier Frank Goulson from North Katanga. The Nigerians had barely settled down when fighting broke out between Kalonji's troops and the Luntus, who lived near Lake Makamba. The Luntus, who apparently opposed all other tribes, had run into a platoon of Luluabourg ANC on its way back from border duty and killed the lot. Now the ANC at Luluabourg had joined in the fray, coincidentally fighting the Luntus together with their foes, the Kalonjists. The Nigerians and the Irish infantry group at Mwene-Ditu in South Kasai brought the fighting under control. More fighting broke out in South Kasai between the Kaniokas and Kalonjists. The Irish troops at Mwene-Ditu dealt with this conflagration with the help of the Nigerians, who were also engaged in maintaining law and order in the Port Francqui area and along the border with Stanleyville where pro-Lumumbists had become active. The well-trained Liberian contingent also played an important role in pacification.

By early August, the Indian brigade had established its dominance over the Katanga gendarmerie, and clashes between the two at Niemba and Nyunzu provided a lesson for Katanga not to trifle with the populace in the area. Meanwhile, the situation in the south was worsening. The UN was going ahead with the process of removing white advisers and mercenaries. Dealing with the Belgians had improved with the co-operation of the government in Brussels. Hammarskjöld had approved the use of more stringent measures by ONUC in Elisabethville to remove foreign personnel employed by Katanga; O'Brien managed to have Georges Thyssen, political adviser to Tshombe and a determined opponent of the UN, sent home. With the increase of pressure by the UN and the departure of his Belgian advisers, Tshombe increased his recruitment elsewhere and a number of former French officers who had been involved in the attempted coup against President de Gaulle in Algiers joined him. These men were idealists, ruthless in the pursuit of their anti-Communist goals. They came to Katanga to maintain the last bastion against the so-called Communist-inspired movements for independence. They were of course convinced too of the superiority of the white race, which was under challenge in the Congo.

In his meetings with Tshombe O'Brien tried to persuade him to go to Leopoldville, but Tshombe resorted to his usual habit of promising something one day and reneging on it the next. The pressures of Adoula were building to end the secession of Katanga. In Stanleyville, Gizenga was watching Adoula's actions, and kept his options open by keeping intact the structure of his former regime.

The government of Adoula was persisting in its effort to end Katanga's secession and had turned to the UN for assistance. Hammarskjöld anticipated such a demand by Adoula's government and he was also only too well aware of the mounting pressures on the UN to act more vigorously. Clearly, Adoula's government and the UN were partners in this venture. Hammarskjöld had a number of political and military steps in mind. Due to withdrawals we had lost a large part of our Force, but we would need more troops to match our political gestures with a show of strength to minimise the chances of fighting and casualties in Katanga. The ANC could provide the answer. They needed to be reorganised and trained to bring order instead of the chaos they had created so far; besides, after some improvements, they could replace UN troops in areas which were relatively quiet and under a semblance of control by the central government. We could, as a case in point, turn over to them the former Belgian bases of Kamina, Kitona and Banana. An improved ANC would also facilitate the concentration of our troop strength in Katanga and an eventual phased withdrawal by our troops from the Congo.

In New York we began to consider plans to run down the size of the UN Force. There had been little progress in removing other Europeans once most of the Belgian advisers had departed. The tempo of the campaign against the UN in the local Katanga press and radio had increased, and Hammarskjöld realised that the UN would have to act much more vigorously to achieve its objectives. If the UN pressed ahead to arrest mercenaries and remove them, they were likely to resist by force. The UN therefore had to be prepared for this eventuality, and Hammarskjöld called for appropriate plans to be made. As a first step in the preparation of a showdown in Katanga, the ANC had to be retrained as a matter of urgency. Accordingly, instructions were sent to Linner to take up this question with Adoula. Linner came to New York in mid-August when this and our future plans for Katanga were discussed.

The earlier part of the operations in Katanga had proved demanding. In the south, the UN kept an effective presence and had kept the gendarmerie under restraint. The situation in the north absorbed most of our attention. Based on my recommendation, a Katanga area was established initially with its headquarters at Elisabethville. This was divided into three sectors: North Katanga with headquarters at Albertville, Kamina with headquarters at the military base, and South Katanga at Elisabethville. Each sector dealt with the government at its own level, while collaboration with the UN representative and liaison with Tshombe's government were the responsibility of the area commander.

When Tshombe tried to bring the north under his control and fighting became more intense, the Nigerian brigade was deployed there and the Irish were moved to Kamina. It had become evident to me at this juncture that ONUC should establish a unified command because all operations in Katanga had to be politically directed by the UN representative in Elisabethville, who in turn communicated with Linner and the Secretary-General. I discussed the command structure for Katanga with Hammarskjöld and at length with Bunche. As to the appointment of an area commander, I had found it difficult to come up with one or more suitable names. With McKeown as Force Commander and O'Brien as UN representative it would be unwise to appoint another Irishman as the area commander. The Nigerians only had British officers at senior level. The Moroccans had gone. The Indians had arrived and, although they were well organised for this task, we were keeping them at a distance from

Tshombe. The Ethiopians were the next largest contingent, and by now had two battalions in Katanga. My choice finally fell on the Ethiopian General Iyassou, who had been an able chief of staff and proved his skill in military-diplomatic negotiations.

I felt that there was some resistance among Hammarskjöld's advisers to Iyassou's appointment, but could not put my finger on its cause. My chief operations officer in New York, Alemu of Ethiopia, had mentioned that Emperor Haile Sellassie might not be pleased at the idea of one of his senior officers possibly having to take a position counter to the interests of some Western states. Besides, said Alemu, in an atmosphere rife with racial prejudice there were already enough complaints against the behaviour of the Ethiopian troops. He therefore doubted that Iyassou would be well received by the Europeans in Katanga.

I had become aware of Alemu's views. He had often said more against his Emperor than was good for him and he had only recently been through a traumatic experience in Grand Central subway station at midnight as he waited after the end of his day's work for a train to take him home to Brooklyn. While attending military training courses in the United States he had been exposed to racial discrimination, and had rented a house in Brooklyn to avoid a refusal by apartment owners in Manhattan. While waiting for his train he was approached by young blacks who wanted to strike up a conversation. When Alemu showed be did not welcome their advances, an argument developed leading to a fist fight. A police patrol arrived and arrested the lot, took them to the police station over Alemu's protests that he held a diplomatic passport, and locked them up for the night. He made the one call that he was allowed to make to me at about 3 a.m. With the help of the duty officer at the US mission I was able to have him released before daybreak, but this experience had only made him more bitter. He had proved a good staff officer and gave me wise counsel. Therefore I decided to share with Bunche his concerns regarding Iyassou's appointment to Katanga. However, Iyassou was Hammarskjöld's final choice and he was appointed to head the unified Katanga area command.

Iyassou's arrival in Elisabethville certainly disturbed all quarters. The Ethiopians had performed well in Oriental and in North Katanga, but Iyassou was the first senior black African military officer in a highly sensitive detached position. Shortly after his arrival, he asked to be relieved because he said that he was due for rotation and had to return home for personal reasons. I was certain that, although the reasons he gave were possibly justified, there had to be other reasons for his asking to be relieved so soon after he had accepted the appointment. I could not ignore what Alemu had said. I also suspected that O'Brien did not go along with Iyassou's style, which was deliberate, methodical and cautious, as against his own flamboyance and spontaneity. Raja was left as our only remaining choice, and we were far from certain how his appointment would be received by the Katangese and their supporters.

I had told Bunche that I did not know Raja well because we had never served together. Most of the senior Indian officers knew each other at least by reputation, and thus I had known of Raja as a good staff officer at army headquarters in New Delhi. We recognised that the Indian government had selected him with care to lead the first Indian combat brigade group sent abroad. However, I had to admit that the qualities required for an area commander in Katanga were not entirely the same as for a brigade commander. The big question before us, therefore, was whether Raja would be able to maintain the ability to arrive at his own views on military matters or would allow O'Brien to dominate him. The chain of command was by no means an easy one: Raja was under the command of General McKeown and not O'Brien; he held a parallel position to O'Brien and was certainly not subordinate to him. However, Raja did have to accept O'Brien's political counsel.

After some hesitation, we decided on Raja. Before I could draft the cable for Bunche and then for Hammarskjöld's approval, a cable from O'Brien reached the Secretary-General recommending that Raja be appointed area commander in Iyassou's place. On reading the cable Hammarskjöld responded, 'O'Brien wants Raja. Let us go ahead with his appointment.' We were greatly relieved; we had not been sure how O'Brien would respond to the appointment of an Indian because such an appointment could further exacerbate his relations with Tshombe. On 5 August, the Indian Infantry Brigade Group was split up with its main part remaining in Albertville under the command of Lieutenant-Colonel M.G. Hazari, a fine officer who had served with me in UNEF, while the other part moved to Elisabethville where Raja set up the Katanga area headquarters.

Within a few weeks of the teaming-up of O'Brien and Raja, the UN in Katanga met its worst disaster a situation that led to the death of Hammarskjöld in an air crash. To understand the relationship between Raja and O'Brien, a semi-official letter written by Raja some six years later is relevant. Raja wrote: 'Dr O'Brien was instrumental in getting Brigadier Raja selected as Commander of the unified Katanga Command after being favourably impressed by the achievements of the Indian Brigade Group in North Katanga.' [2]

Under considerable pressure from O'Brien, Tshombe agreed to dismiss about 100 foreign advisers and on Hammarskjöld's request for urgent action the Belgian government too agreed to withdraw 208 of their officers. Among the 304 who remained were included in the core of the cadre of mercenaries, whose countries of origin claimed not to have any control over them. Lt. Col. Bjorn Egge had been selected by me to head the information branch of ONUC headquarters, which was intended to function as an intelligence unit. At this point, he returned to Elisabethville where he had done excellent work in obtaining information about the Katanga gendarmerie and their white cadres. His interrogation of mercenaries caught earlier and held at Kamina proved invaluable. He had updated his list of their names, and it was on the basis of this information that O'Brien had negotiated with Tshombe for the removal of European advisers and mercenaries.

In mid-August Bomboko called for urgent UN assistance to deal with Stanleyville, where Gizenga had returned, and with the continuing crisis in Katanga; but the Adoula government was in danger for other reasons as well. The Afro-Asian group at the UN was also demanding firm action for the implementation of the Security Council resolution of 21 February, but on the other hand the Western media and public sympathised with Tshombe. As August went by without any real progress, pressures on Hammarskjöld increased. Meanwhile, European-led mobile groups of the gendarmerie intensified their campaign of atrocities against the Balubas in North Katanga. There the Indian troops were determinedly restoring the neutral zone which I had negotiated with Tshombe the previous October, and they had pushed the Stanleyville ANC out of the zone, thereby removing a cause for the Katanga gendarmerie to operate in the area. The Indian troops also introduced an escort system for trains, making safe travel and freight movements possible. It was evident to all of us in New York that the best way to neutralise Tshombe's activities in the north was to remove the Europeans from the mobile groups. I felt certain that our attempts to do this would be opposed by force, and therefore I sought clear instructions from Hammarskjöld for the troops in the field; Hammarskjöld realised the risks involved and instructed ONUC that all means short of force should be used to remove the Europeans from the gendarmerie mobile units. This did not preclude the use by our troops of minimum force in self-defence as a last resort. More troops were required to undertake this task and therefore the sending of reinforcements to Katanga from relatively quiet areas of the Congo was approved.

In a courageous move, Adoula flew to Stanleyville to see Gizenga accompanied by Gbenye, Interior Minister and formerly a member of Gizenga's regime. At the meeting they affirmed their unity, and Adoula declared that Gizenga would soon assume his duties as First Vice-Premier, adding (in a reference to Katanga), 'I intend to use all means, and by that I mean force if necessary, to prevent secession.' Gizenga acknowledged Adoula's regime as the legitimate government of the country and he advised diplomats from countries that had recognised his regime to move to Leopoldville. Adoula also obtained an agreement for General Lundula to go there to report to Mobutu for an assignment.

Khiari reported that he had received a letter from Adoula asking for the UN's assistance to resolve the Katanga deadlock. In his reply Hammarskjöld said 'We must at all costs avoid pursuing long discussions, either with the Katangese authorities or with the Belgian authorities. It seems to me, then, that the Adoula government should immediately issue an order, the terms of which should declare as "undesirable" all the non-Congolese officers and mercenaries serving in Katanga forces who have not accepted a contract of obligation from the central government, and demand that they leave the Congolese territory without delay. The government should then inform us of this order in a new letter. . . .' Furthermore, Adoula should ask the UN to assist the Congolese in its implementation. This order would strengthen the hand of the UN, providing an added legal basis to achieve its objectives. On 24 August the Adoula government issued the order[3] and sought the UN's help in its implementation.

On 26 August an Indian battalion was flown from North Katanga to Elisabethville in preparation for introducing stronger measures to remove the mercenaries. Irish and Swedish troops were deployed at Kamina and Jadotville. The Katangese stepped up their harassment of the Baluba refugees in Elisabethville, many of whom left their camp to seek shelter in the UN military camps, thus increasing the difficulties of our troops. O'Brien made another effort to persuade Tshombe to go to Leopoldville in a UN aircraft but met with a refusal. Katanga radio increased its invective against the UN. During the day, UPI and Reuter reports from Elisabethville quoted O'Brien as saying that if Tshombe did not go to see Adoula the UN would place its troops at the disposal of the central government. Concerned at these reports, Hammarskjöld cabled Linner reminding him of his instructions and that he hoped the press stories were propaganda by Katanga. The UPI had also reported this statement by Tshombe: 'We are ready to die rather than negotiate with the central government under a threat that the United Nations military force may be used to end self-proclaimed independence of Katanga Province....' Tshombe had by now placed his army on the alert, and some of his troops under European officers had begun to dig trenches near the airport in Elisabethville. They were apprehended by UN troops and two Belgian officers were expelled.

On August 27 O'Brien and Raja met Khiari and Fabry, Special Counsellor to ONUC, at Kamina. They finalised the plan for actions to be taken in Katanga for the removal of Europeans and mercenaries. The original plan, known as Operation Rumpunch, had been reviewed by me, checked by Bunche and approved by Hammarskjöld. Anticipating strong opposition from Munungo and vitriolic attacks from Katanga radio, the decision from the Kamina meeting was to add three objectives to the original plan, namely the temporary detention of Munungo and occupation of the radio station and the post office which had become a telecommunications centre. The three actions were intended to minimise bloodshed by pre-empting the use of the radio for attacks on the UN and preventing Munungo from getting in touch with his mercenaries. These actions did not have the Secretary-General's approval and were questionable, considering the instructions given to ONUC. The Force commander and his military staff were equally in the dark in regard to the important changes made in Operation Rumpunch.

On their return to Elisabethville, O'Brien and Raja learned that the Katangese suspected action on 29 August, the original day for the launching of the operation, and therefore decided to advance it by one day to achieve surprise. The UN troops were well prepared for the task. The relative strengths of Katangese and UN troops were: in Elisabethville the Katangese had 3,000 and the UN 1,060 troops; in Jadotville-Shinkolobwe the Katangese had 2,000 and another 1,000 at Kolwezi, while the UN had 120 in Jadotville and 1,000 in Kamina; in the Manono area the Katangese had 800 and the UN 400; in North Katanga Tshombe had 400 and the UN 1,200. With good airports and availability of transport aircraft the UN had considerable flexibility for response.

At 5 a.m. on 27 August, the UN troops in Elisabethville and other towns in Katanga moved swiftly to seize the objectives in accordance with the plan. Since the Katangese did not suspect these moves, they were taken completely by surprise and all objectives were achieved without a fight. The Indian Dogras held the post and telegraph office and Radio Katanga; the 35th Irish battalion had sealed off Munungo's residence and surrounded Camp Massart, the gendarmerie's main barracks and headquarters; and the 12th Swedish battalion had sealed the European quarter from the African residential area and placed a reserve in the centre of the city. A total of fifty-three mercenaries were rounded up and sent to Kamina for repatriation. At 8 a.m. Michel Tombelaine, deputy UN representative at Elisabethville, was able to report the action by the UN and the compelling reasons for it on Radio Katanga.

While the UN action in Elisabethville was proceeding, good progress was also being made in North Katanga. Our troops at Nyunzu, Nyemba, Manono and Albertville captured twenty-nine foreign officers and had turned over command of the gendarmerie to Katangese officers.

At 8.30 Raja's troops had accomplished their tasks, and he and O'Brien drove over to see Tshombe and meet his cabinet. Tshombe asked that the operation be ended immediately but was informed that this would only be agreed to if he co-operated fully with the UN in removing the remaining foreign officers and mercenaries. He promised to give his reply by 11 a.m. At the promised hour he sent his reply agreeing to the UN demands, but asked that the siege of Munungo's house, the radio station and the post office be lifted. Within the hour the UN complied with this request, and at 11 a.m. Tshombe declared on the radio his acceptance of the UN demand to remove all foreign personnel; two hours later he announced on the air that he had dismissed all foreign personnel. The UN had opened centres to receive them. A total of 250 out of an estimated 520 were expelled from Katanga. Of the remainder 270 disappeared, many in civilian clothes, which made it difficult to identify them. Some (many of them French) continued to lead their soldiers in the Katanga service.

There was consternation among the Western consulates in Elisabethville, and Paul-Henri Spaak, the Belgian Foreign Minister, sent a strong protest to Hammarskjöld for arresting and expelling their officers and thereby dishonouring them. Hammarskjöld reminded the Belgian minister that the officers had been given sufficient notice and that moreover they had been urged to leave by the Belgian government itself. They had been expelled by order of a sovereign government and the UN had acted on that government's request to assist in implementing this order and in accordance with a Security Council resolution. At Elisabethville, the consuls concerned pressed O'Brien to halt the arrests and gave assurances of co-operation in sending their nationals employed in Katanga out of the country. This move was not liked by Linner, who presumably represented Khiari's views as well, and when we received news of it in New York, it also displeased Hammarskjöld. These consulates had a poor record of support for the UN in Katanga, and the news dampened our hopes for an operation that had started well and promised to be successful.

By 31 August the Belgian, British and French consuls had not come through with their promises. O'Brien reported that the Belgian consul had given asylum to about ninety Belgian nationals employed by Tshombe. Tshombe had also expressed to O'Brien his fear of a coup by Munungo if he went to Leopoldville. Cremer, a Belgian defector, alleged that a group of tough mercenaries had gone into hiding and begun to plot against the UN. Munungo intended to harass the UN and have Tombelaine murdered; he had been the most vocal antagonist of the UN and had carried out a vendetta against a number of its senior officials, starting with Bunche. Dayal and I had received his special attention; during my last visit to Katanga, at Christmas 1960, when I stopped at a drugstore, the Belgian owner took Victor Noble, my security guard, aside and asked my name. When Victor told him, the Belgian warned, 'You better get him out of Katanga because they intend to kill him.' I heard loud snorts from Victor, but he said little until we were back in our car, when he told me what the store owner had said. His own reply, which I had heard as snorts, was Victor's colourful remarks about the Katangese and the Belgians (whom he had understood to be the 'they' referred to by the store owner) and what he would do to them before they met an even worse fate at his hands. It was all very well to frighten the store owner, but the fact remained that such threats were genuine and had to be considered in deciding on the degree of freedom of movement of VIPs and the security they required. Such threats were also being used as part of the psychological war being waged against the UN and a certain determination was required not to fall prey to it. Subsequent events showed that a threat to Tombelaine's life might have influenced O'Brien's decision to deal firmly with Munungo.

The descriptive cable sent by O'Brien conveyed the overheated atmosphere as yet another crisis in Elisabethville developed, threatening an encounter between the UN on the one side and Katangese, together with the remaining foreign officers and mercenaries aided openly by their consuls, on the other. Rumpunch had taken the others by surprise and made a significant contribution towards the removal of foreign personnel in the Katanga service who were the major obstacle to Congolese reconciliation. The UN had apprehended a total of 315 non-Congolese in the Katanga gendarmerie, but 104 were missing. When the operation was stopped at noon on 28 August, the UN had it within its grasp to close the ring and remove all the unwanted individuals with perhaps a few remaining who could have hidden or vanished among the European civilians. The surprise element was gone, a second encounter would be costly, and it would not be surprising if some of the European civilians joined their countrymen on Katanga's side. Such a fight had to be avoided.

A cable received at this time from O'Brien called for an immediate response. In it he asked for instructions on how to deal with Munungo (who Tshombe believed was about to launch a coup), a possible civil war, and Munungo's designs on the UN and his threat to the life of Tombelaine. Hammarskjöld, in a carefully considered reply, told O'Brien that Munungo or anyone could be arrested when actually caught directing operations against the UN or the central government, but his present activities, as reported, did not justify this. For the time being, O'Brien should continue with his efforts to remove foreign officers and to press Tshombe to go to Leopoldville.

The situation in Katanga was again critical. Tensions were high, and the UN leadership in Elisabethville were under great pressure. The acrimonious European civilians; the three consuls who, by reneging on assurances to the UN, had been guilty of conduct generally thought to be the province of wily politicians, not of diplomats; a climate of hate against the UN, much publicised by an unfriendly and critical Western press; a whispering campaign of threats of violence; suspicion of a coup against Tshombe and the outbreak of civil war; the threat to murder a UN staff member—these had all added to the present ferment. At the Congo Club meeting that evening we discussed the situation in Katanga at length. Then, at a separate meeting that I had with Hammarskjöld and Bunche, it was obvious that Hammarskjöld was greatly concerned that our men in Katanga might resort to unauthorised actions that would have much wider and more serious implications than they could recognise. It was a concern shared by all of Hammarskjöld's advisers.

During the course of Rumpunch, I had noted and commented to Hammarskjöld and Bunche on actions by our troops that had not been previously approved by the Secretary-General, i.e. encircling Munungo's house and holding him there, and seizing Radio Katanga and the post and telegraph office. In the early euphoria of ONUC's success none of us wanted to rake this up. However, faced with the rising emergency in Elisabethville, I said at our consultations that unauthorised actions on our side were intolerable, and that ONUC command must seize effective control over military operations in Katanga. Another activity of the Katanga area command that incensed us was ONUC's provision of a guard of honour for the Belgian officers who were being expelled; this comic-opera exhibition did not conform to any military etiquette that I knew of. I was not alone in being unamused—Hammarskjöld informed Linner that this gesture had struck him as foolish and inappropriate.

In a cable to Linner late on 31 August, Hammarskjöld avoided, as was his style, saying explicitly that prior approval had to be sought for providing guards, a small matter of protocol, but he did imply that any serious matter had to be approved by him. Also, many reports originating from Elisabethville quoting O'Brien and Tombelaine were being distorted and misquoted giving a false impression which was not doing the UN any good. Hammarskjöld therefore told Linner that the UN representatives in the field should say less.

Munungo's open response to Rumpunch took two forms. He resumed a reign of terror against the Balubas which served two of his purposes: first, to resume Conakat's attempt to gain ascendancy in the north, and secondly to ensure that by harassing the Balubas more of them would turn to the UN for help, thus adding to its burden. Immediately after the end of Rumpunch Munungo's police and youth movement and Radio Katanga, supported by a whispering campaign, started a reign of terror against the Balubas. As the Balubas were harassed and beaten, more and more of them (reaching a total of 45,000 within a fortnight) sought UN protection. UN resources were already stretched in Katanga, and this made matters much worse.

On 31 August Munungo launched a new and more virulent propaganda offensive against the UN. Through Radio Katanga and pamphlets distributed by the Ministry of Information, his agents spoke of the 'atrocities and highhandedness of the UN', and complained that the

UN was driving Katanga to despair. On 1 September, a demonstration by 300 children in front of the UN offices shouted anti-UN slogans, stoned the building and burnt a UN vehicle. During the recent fighting, in a show of support for Katanga, Sir Roy Welensky, Prime Minister of the Federation of Rhodesia and Nyasaland, had denounced the UN action and moved his troops to the border of Katanga. Rumours were circulating that Rhodesia would send troops to aid Katanga and that its agents planned to bomb UN headquarters. Also there were rumours of an organised campaign, instigated by Munungo, to kill UN personnel, bomb ammunition stores and destroy small UN vehicle convoys. Unable to tolerate this any longer, O'Brien called on Tshombe to dismiss Munungo, but without avail. Tshombe blamed the Balubas for the disorder and made no reference to Munungo's mischievous role.

After a meeting with O'Brien, Linner and Khiari informed Hammarskjöld that the situation in Katanga was so delicate that urgent reconsideration of UN plans was necessary. They reported (as we already suspected) that the remaining mercenaries who were in hiding were actively organising guerrilla action against the UN. Tshombe was very much under the thumb of Munungo, whose inflammatory broadcasts were becoming a serious menace: in one public speech he had called for O'Brien's death. There were increasing tensions within the central government, and the ANC was planning an attack against Katanga from Stanleyville. Therefore urgent action by the UN was needed. Linner and Khiari suggested the following plan: the French, Belgian and British governments should prevent their consuls in Elisabethville from encouraging Tshombe to oppose the UN; a representative of the Secretary-General should go to Brussels to apprise the government there of the political realities in Leopoldville and Elisabethville to remove illusions created by Katanga; O'Brien should see Tshombe and urge him to end inflammatory broadcasts, arrests, terrorism and organised persecution by the Katanga Sûreté; and O'Brien should give Tshombe twenty-four hours to expel the remaining mercenaries, failing which the UN would round them up for expulsion.

In the event that this plan did not work, whereupon Linner and Khiari proposed that the UN should again take over the radio station, arrest troublemakers, and take steps to prevent the gendarmerie, the police and the Sûreté from interfering with UN operations. If required, the UN leaders would call on Tshombe, accompanied by a *commissaire d'état*, to obtain his approval for the arrest of Munungo and others guilty of common law crimes. If Tshombe agreed, the UN would execute the warrant of arrest and if he did not, then the *commissaire d'état* would order the Katanga provincial government to conform to the law, take temporary charge of the provincial administration, and then proceed with the proposed actions.

In New York we were well aware of the tensions, threats to life, the hate campaign and the large number of mercenaries who were at large looking for trouble. We were heading for another showdown in Katanga. O'Brien, a courageous man, had seen success elude him and was now even more determined to complete his task. Nonetheless, he had to avoid taking precipitous action, and Hammarskjöld told him and McKeown that while he understood the circumstances, he must without fail be fully informed in advance of any important moves and plans proposed so that he could communicate his views and directives as necessary. Meanwhile, he wanted them to remain strong and sit tight.[5]

With the mounting smear campaign against the UN, and harassment and even stoning of its personnel, the pressures on O'Brien and Raja were tremendous. The UN leadership in Katanga were at the centre of the tension, and it was not possible for them to break away, even briefly, for some calm thought, a vital necessity for military leaders and their civilian counterparts when facing momentous decisions. Thus it did not surprise us in New York that O'Brien and Raja wished to deal firmly with the situation. They had told Linner that they favoured tougher measures even if this meant bending the law. O'Brien had even suggested that Munungo should be neutralised and that a legitimate provincial government loyal to the central government be established in Katanga; in his view, Tshombe was likely to go along with these measures. Instead of informing Hammarskjöld immediately of O'Brien's and Raja's latest views, Linner arranged a meeting between O'Brien and Khiari at Kamina on 4 September.

Khiari, who had been named Chief of Civilian Operations after Linner became officer-in-chief, had in fact assumed, with Linner's encouragement and approval from New York, major responsibility for the diplomatic leadership of ONUC. His role at this time was thus no less crucial than that of Bunche at the beginning of the Congo operation, Cordier's at the time of the coup against Lumumba and Dayal's during the dramatic months that followed. Khiari was a shrewd politician and a skillful administrator and diplomat. He had been associated with Tunisia's independence movement and served as a minister in the Bourguiba government. He was a strongly nationalistic African and had little patience with the manoeuvring of the Belgians to retain dominance over a country which had already gained its independence from them by consent. He was intolerant of people like Tshombe and Kalonji who looked to the Belgians and the West to remain in power at the expense of the wider interests of their country. He believed in free enterprise but was against political manipulation by economic interests, which was what some of the Western states were doing in Katanga. He believed in negotiations and in the UN system. But his understanding of the UN peace and security operations was limited to his Congo experience, and when put to the test, he was willing to bend the rules to further his objectives. He was firm yet flexible in his dealings; in order to advance negotiations he could be very tough and did not hesitate to make a show of force and use it if necessary. His style was different from that of Hammarskjöld or Bunche, so assiduously followed by Dayal.

O'Brien's opinions had already made Hammarskjöld apprehensive; and Raja, having spent his career in command and staff appointments but with no UN peacekeeping experience, was ready to resort to what he was best trained to do, which was to fight. It was the combination of Khiari with O'Brien and Raja that determined the course of the eventful days that were about to unfold in Katanga.

Hammarskjöld and his advisers were caught up in issues raised by Linner, Khiari and O'Brien for the next few days and these consumed many hours. They met together, in small groups and separately with the Secretary-General. Hammarskjöld consulted the important member-states concerned, while his advisers talked to the UN experts and delegates to get a variety of views. My special task was to examine the military implications and discuss them with Bunche before we both saw Hammarskjöld. I had by now about a dozen members on my military staff from different countries. They had to update Force data, summarise and analyse situation reports, and get additional information from UN agencies with offices in New York. Meanwhile, I called or met all the military advisers in the missions to the UN, especially those with troops in Katanga, to obtain from their general staff headquarters information relevant to Katanga. At the same time I requested the military advisers at the missions of the United States and Britain, permanent members of the Security Council with consulates in Elisabethville, to exchange information with me. When they asked whether the UN had another military plan to arrest Europeans in the service of Katanga, I could honestly answer that we did not intend to do so and that our future actions would depend on the willingness of Katanga and the Western consulates concerned to co-operate with the UN in the implementation of the 21 February Security Council resolution which their governments had approved. In return, I wanted to know from them about the Katanga gendarmerie and the Europeans.

Rumpunch had shaken the morale of the Katangese. While Tshombe and other local leaders could find a role for themselves after reconciliation with the central government, men like Munungo could not, and were therefore determined to prevent a change. The missing European employ-ees of Katanga had indeed gone undercover, aided by the European civilians and Katangese in and around the capital. If the UN succeeded, they had everything to lose. Rumpunch had achieved complete surprise and caught them unprepared. They had also been surprised by the determined resistance put up by the UN troops (Ethiopian, Indian, Irish and Swedish) when attacked by the European-led Katangese. There had been a myth about the great fighting qualities of the mercenaries built on the fiction of fighting poorly-trained troops. The UN had destroyed this myth. While the mercenaries and their romantic admirers in the West were not ready to admit it yet, they now realised that they could only achieve success by denying the UN the element of surprise by their better intelligence network and by guerrilla warfare and acts of terrorism. ONUC was not adequately equipped to cope with any of these, although Egge was to gather some useful information.

I concluded that after Rumpunch surprise was no longer possible; besides, the UN would have to warn the public of any such future action. Only its timing, location and the size of troops could perhaps be kept secret. The possibility of using a ruse to mislead the opposition should be considered, but I hesitated to recommend such a course because I was not sure whether there was enough sophistication in the UN headquarters in Leopoldville and the UN Katanga area command to handle this.

While my staff and I were working on military questions at the Congo Club meetings, Hammarskjöld started to voice some of his thoughts. He wanted to ensure that all UN actions were supported by international law and UN resolutions, and therefore he would not condone any bending of the law. Thus, acting under the Security Council resolution of 21 February, the UN had to rely on its provisions and their interpretation as accepted by member-states, and the degree to which the Secretary-General could expect support. Hammarskjöld therefore concluded that another effort had to be made to persuade Tshombe to negotiate, and he instructed Linner accordingly. In case Tshombe should refuse, more drastic measures could only be considered if there were a threat of civil war or if the Adoula government collapsed.

Once Hammarskjöld had formulated a policy, I was able to complete my recommendations, one of which was that ONUC must be prepared for either an attempt by the ANC to invade Katanga, which was again likely to end in a disaster, or civil war breaking out if the province's future was not resolved. The latter provided a clear role for the UN. More troops would be required, and the move of the third Indian battalion, the Gorkhas, to Elisabethville was authorised. The UN secretariat ensured movement of ammunition and other essential supplies and stores, and improved air transport within the Congo.

O'Brien's efforts to persuade Tshombe to go to Leopoldville failed once again and he asked for authority to react immediately to acts of incitement and disorder. As the anti-UN propaganda gained in intensity, UN soldiers found alone were surrounded and stoned. UN vehicles were stoned and fired at. This forced the UN offices to move from Avenue Moero in the centre of the city to the castle on Avenue Fromot. When Hammarskjöld asked Linner for clarification of the proposed actions, he was told that O'Brien had envisaged seizing the radio station and arresting troublemakers, but that he had instructed O'Brien that no such action was to be taken until authorised. Linner hoped that by the time he returned from Brussels, O'Brien would have received Hammarskjöld's approval of his proposed actions. Hammarskjöld had told Linner to go to Brussels to inform the Belgian authorities of developments in Leopoldville and Katanga, and seek more support from them for the UN's policy in Katanga.

In his reply to Linner and O'Brien Hammarskjöld stated his guidelines. The UN could take preventive action to protect the lives of civilians when threatened by civil war; also to deal with incitement or preparation for civil war. Force could be used in self-defence, including the prevention of injury and abduction. The arrest of civilian leaders was only authorised when they were actually engaged in overt military action; an arrest warrant issued against a provincial leader by the central government or a *commissaire d'état* was a doubtful basis for the UN to carry out such arrests. Hammarskjöld realised that O'Brien would find little comfort in these guidelines, but the issues involved were complex. We were not an army of occupation or an army in support of its own government in the maintenance of law and order, but a UN peacekeeping force with a delicate mission and a weak mandate for its ability to use force.

The situation in Katanga worsened rapidly. Khiari was in charge while Linner was in Brussels, and Hammarskjöld had so far not received from him the detailed draft instructions that he had promised to send for approval. These were to be applied when all other measures suggested[6] had failed. The measures suggested by Khiari were to take over the radio station, arrest trouble-makers, and prevent the gendarmerie, the police and the Sûreté from interfering with the UN action. If it became necessary, O'Brien and Khiari should visit Tshombe, accompanied by the *commissaire d'état*, to get his approval for the arrest of Munungo. If Tshombe agreed, the UN would execute that order, but if he did not, the *commissaire d'état* would temporarily take over the provincial government.[7] In calling for details Hammarskjöld showed that he recognised the changes taking place and did not want the plan to be implemented without his approval. However, ONUC might take over the radio station as it had done on 28 August. He said he disliked the idea of the UN executing arrest warrants and that it should not risk being accused of acting prematurely and provocatively.

The arrival of the Gorkhas sharply increased tensions in Elisabethville. On the same day, the central government had issued arrest warrants for the Katangese government, appointed a *commissaire d'état* for

Katanga and told Khiari that the UN was expected to assist. In a cable asking for Hammarskjöld's approval, Khiari said that on Linner's return he would go to Elisabethville to brief O'Brien. Then Khiari told O'Brien that he was waiting for the Secretary-General's approval and that meanwhile preparations for the operation should begin. The next day, in another cable, Khiari informed Hammarskjöld that his instructions to O'Brien would coincide with the modifications suggested by the Secretary-General to the plan submitted a few days earlier by Linner and himself. He said that the plan was to take over the radio station and, if necessary, ensure that the gendarmerie, the police and the Sûreté did not hamper the UN in carrying out its operation. Hammarskjöld had never permitted action against the military and police and in fact had specifically advised ONUC to avoid antagonising them and rather to try and win them over. When Hammarskjöld pointed out this discrepancy between his instructions and Khiari's understanding, Khiari replied that his instructions to O'Brien were that action could only be taken after an understanding had been reached with the Secretary-General himself at Leopoldville. This referred to Hammarskjöld's acceptance of an invitation from Adoula to visit the Congo, which events in Katanga and their impact on the central government surely made vitally necessary this time.

On 10 September, Tombelaine was arrested by the Sûreté at the post and telegraph office. He was able to phone O'Brien who, by immediately gathering a platoon and some armoured personnel-carriers of the Swedish battalion under Colonel Jonas Waern and proceeding to the post office, procured Tombelaine's release. O'Brien now called on the Katangese to remove the Sûreté's Belgian personnel, who had been involved in the illegal seizure of a UN official.

As Hammarskjöld was preparing for his trip to the Congo, the situation in Katanga became rapidly worse. Linner's return to Leopoldville marked the completion of one of the first steps towards the start of the Khiari-O'Brien plan for Katanga. On 11 September O'Brien sent an ultimatum to Tshombe demanding that he go to Leopoldville for negotiations and that all non-Congolese personnel in the gendarmerie be removed within forty-eight hours, but the Katanga Council refused to let Tshombe go.

In a surprise move, the gendarmerie and mercenaries acted against the isolated Irish garrison at Jadotville and surrounded it. The Katanga government offered to withdraw its troops if the UN would accept a police guard at the nearby airport at Luano. The Irish company, commanded by Commandant Patrick Quinlan, had set up camp in a few villas a mile outside the town. The troops had gone there at the urging of the Belgian consul, in particular to safeguard the Europeans (mainly Belgians), and Quinlan had camped there for convenience and for quick access to the

European quarter; in doing so he had ignored tactical considerations. The invitation was obviously a ruse to entrap UN troops. When the company was surrounded by the gendarmes on 9 September, its electricity and water were cut off, leaving it with rations for only a week.

A relief column was sent to Jadotville from Elisabethville, but it was held up by a Katangese road-block at the Lufira bridge. Convinced of their success, the Katangese called on Quinlan to surrender, but he refused. Later that day the Irish camp was attacked by a Katanga aircraft, flown from Kolwezi and piloted by a mercenary.

When I left the UN secretariat after midnight that evening, no report on the incident at Jadotville had reached us in spite of the time difference of five hours. I had routinely glanced through the late evening wire services reports, and they made no mention of it.

I slept fitfully but had hardly lain down for an hour when I was awakened by a phone call from Dublin. It was Frank Aiken, the Irish Minister for Foreign Affairs. He was a man of great character, always calm and dignified. In an uncharacteristically tense and strained voice, he told me that the morning news in Dublin, based on wire service reports from Elisabethville, had reported that the Irish company at Jadotville had been captured and many soldiers killed in the fighting. The news had caused general shock in Ireland, church bells were tolling and the country was in mourning. I told him that according to my latest information the Irish were indeed hard-pressed, but they were holding their ground. It seemed to me that the Katanga Information Service had made another propaganda coup, one that could be extremely harmful to the UN. Any serious loss of Irish lives might well lead to the withdrawal of their troops and other personnel with serious consequences for the ONUC operation. The contributing countries had sent their troops for peacekeeping, not to wage war. I reminded Aiken of the workings of Katanga's public relations and how well they had wooed the Western press and media. They had always managed to reach the press hours ahead of the UN, whose reports had to be checked for accuracy before being released. I added that after our disastrous experience with the loss of UN lives at Port Francqui, ONUC had warned its troops to be cautious and not to fall for any ruse. I said that Irish troops were courageous and tough and surely they would put up a good defence.

I immediately called Bunche at his home, and he said that Boland had already spoken to him and that he would send a cable to ONUC asking for a report. We agreed to meet early at the office, and I immediately dressed and went there. My duty officer had not seen any new report on the Irish at Jadotville. Bunche came in soon after daybreak, and Hammarskjöld, alerted by Bunche, also arrived early. The morning wire services told the story we had heard from Aiken. However, it was reported that some Irish soldiers had survived and were in the gendarmerie's custody. Then, ONUC reports arrived informing us that the Irish troops were holding on in spite of threats and demands for them to surrender.

Soon after Linner returned from Brussels, Khiari and Fabry went to Elisabethville on 11 September and immediately had a meeting with O'Brien, Raja and their senior associates. Fabry showed them the arrest warrants the central government had issued for Tshombe, Munongo, Kibwe, Kimba and Mutaka. According to O'Brien, Fabry 'was smiling like a Machiavellian Santa Claus' as 'Khiari looked on benevolently'.[8] Khiari gave instructions for the arrest of the four ministers other than Tshombe. Waern expressed his reservations about arresting Munongo because such a move by the UN was expected and he was prepared for it. Therefore if the arrest of Munongo was central to Rumpunch, Waern did not think that it was for the UN to go ahead with it. O'Brien said that it should not be a condition *sine qua non*; the warrant was out for Munongo's arrest and Tshombe should know it. Khiari agreed.[9]

Khiari further instructed that Tshombe's residence be cut off but that he was to be arrested only as a last resort. O'Brien was to negotiate with Tshombe and make it clear that his only hope was in cooperating with the UN in the peaceful liquidation of Katanga's secession. Meanwhile, Radio Katanga and the post office were to be secured, and the offices of the Sûreté and the Ministry of Information were to be raided and have their files removed and their European and African officers apprehended if possible. The flag of the Congo was to be run up on public buildings alongside the UN flag. A *commissaire d'état*, yet to be named by Leopoldville, would arrive to take over authority, in cooperation with the UN and with Tshombe if possible. Further, the UN troops were to avoid a clash with the gendarmerie during the operation.

O'Brien said that fighting was likely to ensue. The Belgians had helped place a Colonel Muke as the head of the gendarmerie, and he would do anything that they and the European mercenaries told him to do. Radio Katanga had reported that the central government intended to disarm the gendarmerie with UN help—this was denied by ONUC. The radio had also reported that the UN planned arrests of ministers and that other actions were being discussed by them, which ONUC had not denied.

Khiari wanted the operation to be carried out before 3 p.m. on 13 September, just in advance of Hammarskjöld's expected arrival in Leopoldville or alternatively after his departure, which would probably be around 17 September. In deciding the timing, Raja said that if fighting broke out at the post office and the radio station, where he anticipated danger, it could be ended in two hours at the most. O'Brien insisted on urgency and after Raja's assurance on dealing with likely resistance, Khiari authorised the operation for the morning of 13 September.

The next day Khiari called on Tshombe, who said he favoured an African solution based on a confederation in the spirit of the Tananarive conference. He was willing to meet Adoula, but not in Leopoldville. Khiari explained that he had come to invite him to meet the Secretary-General in Leopoldville; Tshombe, instead, invited the Secretary-General to come to Elisabethville. Khiari's reply was that he was authorised to convey an invitation, not to discuss a venue. Tshombe said he would consider it.

Khiari, on returning to ONUC headquarters in Katanga, told O'Brien and Raja to start the operation at 4 a.m. the following day. He told them before his departure for Leopoldville, *'Surtout pas de demi-mesures'* ('Above all, no half-measures').[10]

Hammarskjöld left New York on the evening of 12 September. While he and his party were flying across the Atlantic, it was already another day in Katanga where fighting had resumed. The mercenary-led Katangese action in surrounding the Irish in Jadotville after having tricked them into going there rankled with the UN command, and provided a sufficient basis for the UN to take action in defence of its own troops. Raja and his staff were prepared for another showdown with the Katangese. However, Khiari had to convey the Secretary-General's invitation to Tshombe to meet in Leopoldville, but when that failed he authorised the UN Katanga area command to proceed with Operation Morthor (made up of Hindi words meaning 'breakthrough' and 'cut-off').

At the UN in New York we were taken completely by surprise. Khiari had assured Hammarskjöld before leaving New York that ONUC would not take any action without his specific approval; thus his instructions to O'Brien and Raja were at variance with his commitment to the Secretary-General. We had no inkling of the change in ONUC's plan of action, and in fact were not even aware of an operation called Morthor until we saw it in the news reports after it had been launched.

This operation, like Rumpunch before it, was intended to occupy certain strategic locations so as to neutralise the Katanga regime and disarm the gendarmerie; resistance was expected from the post office and Radio Katanga. At 4 a.m. on 13 September, the Indian Dogra battalion group, including a Gorkha company and a detachment of Irish armoured cars, set out to occupy the post office, radio station and airport, and take the Minister of Information, Samalenghe, into custody. The 35th Irish battalion group was to occupy the transistor at Collège St François, establish a road-block at the railway tunnel, secure the refugee camp near the Union Minière installation, and arrest the Finance Minister, Kibwe. The Swedish 12th battalion group, with a company of Gorkhas and a section of Irish armoured cars, went to occupy the radio transmitter at

Kilobilobe, secure the refugee camp and arrest Munongo. Tshombe's residence was to be surrounded and he was to be asked to co-operate with the UN in ending Katanga's secession peacefully.

When the Dogras reached the post office and asked the gendarmes to lay down their arms, a sniper from an adjoining building, which contained the Belgian consulate and housed some mercenaries, opened fire, killing an Indian soldier. The Indian troops thereupon charged and overpowered the gendarmes and captured the post office and radio station. At daybreak the gendarmes counter-attacked, but the fire of the Irish and Swedish armoured cars drove them back. The gendarmes now brought heavy automatic and mortar fire to bear on the Indian positions at the radio station, but the Indians held their ground. The Irish and Swedish battalion groups also captured their objectives in the face of heavy opposition. Kibwe was captured but Munongo and Samalenghe had vanished.

Within half an hour of the fighting breaking out, Tshombe phoned O'Brien to ask what the UN intended to do. After explaining his plans, O'Brien called on Tshombe to order his troops not to resist. Tshombe agreed, sent an officer to the gendarmerie headquarters and when the messenger returned half an hour later, called O'Brien to confirm that his orders had been passed to the Katanga forces to cease fighting. O'Brien then asked Tshombe to make a statement declaring the end of secession, to which Tshombe agreed, provided his personal safety was guaranteed. O'Brien gave him this assurance and said he would immediately send an escort to bring him to the UN residence where they could work out the details. When the UN escort reached Tshombe's residence, he had disappeared. Later it became known that he had gone to the house of the British consul, Dunnett, and then escaped to Northern Rhodesia. By the end of the day UN troops had seized all their objectives. At 8 p.m. Kibwe was persuaded to broadcast an appeal to the people to co-operate with the UN, but the appeal had little effect on the mercenaries leading the gendarmes and fighting continued.

While in Elisabethville the Katangese resistance under mercenary leadership appeared to be weakening, the Irish troops under siege in Jadotville were facing a serious threat. The Irish detachment at Collège St François was counter-attacked after dark by the gendarmerie and the Katangese paracommandos, and twelve of its soldiers were taken prisoner. An Irish platoon and a detachment of Irish and Swedish armoured cars under the command of Commandant Cahalane were sent to reinforce the Irish position at the college, but as they approached they were fired upon from a stationary ambulance, a bazooka wounding Cahalane and killing two Irish soldiers. The UN troops put up a determined resistance, resulting in six gendarmes and one mercenary officer being killed. Two UN armoured cars were hit in the engagement.

At daybreak a mercenary officer with a white flag warned the UN troops of their delicate situation and called upon them to surrender - which they refused to do. The mercenaries offered Cahalane safe-conduct to show him the gendarmerie positions to convince him of the hopelessness of the UN position in the area. Cahalane accepted the offer, examined the situation, and being convinced of the futility of fighting any longer, agreed to surrender to save unnecessary loss of life. Munongo sent an offer to the UN through a German TV correspondent for an exchange of the Irish prisoners with two Katangese Sûreté officials held by the UN, with the threat that otherwise he would have the Irish killed. This offer was declined, and as to his threat, Munongo was told that the Katangese held by the UN were in custody in accordance with the Geneva Convention and that it was expected that UN prisoners held by the Katangese would receive the same treatment.

While the UN troops were doing well in Elisabethville, with the exception of the ordeal of the Irish at Collège St François and Jadotville, the gendarmerie took the offensive at Kamina. Here the UN troops, consisting of the 1st Irish battalion less two companies, were confined to the base and were divided from the gendarmes only by the base boundary-wire. The gendarmerie had been restless for some days and had raided European houses in Kaminaville, forcing the white population to seek protection at the UN base. The gendarmes were under white officers and it was difficult to say whether the raids were encouraged by these officers or were merely the result of indiscipline among the troops. Certainly, at that time the behaviour of the gendarmes was not considered unusual and therefore the UN readily provided assistance to the victims.

Hammarskjöld's first notion of what was happening in Katanga came from a press despatch shown to him when his plane touched down at Accra. However, being acquainted with the nature of Katanga's propaganda and the support it enjoyed in the Western press, he did not give it any credence. After landing at N'Djili airport at 3 p.m. local time, he was occupied with the reception ceremonies and a visit to Adoula, and was therefore not able to learn about the fighting in Katanga until some hours later when he had reached Linner's villa where he was to stay. Linner, when asked by Hammarskjöld why the operation had been allowed to go ahead without his being consulted, explained that the situation in Elisabethville had developed in such a way as to require immediate action.

Not since Khrushchev challenged him in the General Assembly at the last session had Hammarskjold faced a crisis of such magnitude. It was clear to him that he had to stop the fighting in Katanga immediately. It was not a time to accuse his representatives in the Congo of exceeding their instructions and bending the law contrary to his wishes, and indeed it was not in his nature to engage in recrimination. His rebuke was only noticeable by those who knew him well—from the icy look in his eyes, deeper furrows than usual around his mouth and the subtlety (unlike a military dressing-down) with which he asked questions and stated his views. From Linner's villa they moved to the Royal where he questioned Linner, Khiari and McKeown for information so that he could learn what had gone wrong and consider how the situation could be sorted out. The prime objective of the operation was to round up the mercenaries, but with the outbreak of fighting this could no longer be done, as had been intended, in co-operation with the Katanga gendarmerie. Tshombe and Munongo had managed to escape, so Tshombe was no longer available to co-operate with the UN, and Munongo was free to conduct war against the UN. For the fighting to be brought to an end it was necessary to find Tshombe, and instructions were sent to O'Brien to do just that. On the basis of reports from Raja, McKeown insisted that fighting was expected to be over soon and therefore no initiative to end it was needed.

After dinner at Linner's villa with Adoula and his seven cabinet ministers and ONUC chiefs, Derek Riches, who had replaced Ian Scott as British ambassador, paid a call on Hammarskjöld to give the British reaction to the events in Katanga. We had seen a UPI report[11] stating that the British government had announced its regret at the Elisabethville fighting and said that its ambassador to the Congo was being instructed to contact Hammarskjöld as soon as possible and ask him to 'clarify' the situation. We learned of the meeting in a cable from Hammarskjöld later that day. Riches conveyed the shock and dismay of the British government and warned that its support for the Secretary-General would be withdrawn unless an explanation was given for the developments in Katanga, including various statements by O'Brien to the press, especially one that Katanga's secession had been ended. The Secretary-General was urged to do his utmost to end the fighting.

In explaining his vote on Security Council resolution S/4741 on 21 February, which was the basis of ONUC's action in Katanga, Sir Patrick Dean, the British Permanent Representative at the UN, had expressed his government's reservations over the use of force; according to the British view, ONUC had exceeded its mandate. Similar concern was expressed to O'Brien by the French and other Western consuls in Elisabethville about the UN force's ousting the secessionist government of Katanga. The US State Department expressed regret at the loss of life in the Katanga fighting, but said that the unity of the Congo was essential to economic progress and stability. Throughout Europe many newspapers voiced reservations over the UN troops' action to end the Katanga secession. In Brussels the conservative Catholic paper *La Libre Belgique* called the Katanga operation a premeditated crime and a mistake.[12]

While Hammarskjöld was in conference, Linner's staff were busy preparing a report for New York. We had already received a telex from Linner that morning stating that the objectives of the operation were to apprehend for evacuation the remaining foreign military personnel and officials of the Sûreté, after taking the security precautions necessary to perform that task. Linner's end-of-the-day report was approved by Hammarskjöld before being dispatched to New York in the early hours of 14 September.[13]

These and future reports on the situation in Katanga had not in any way changed the objectives set out by Hammarskjöld. There was no mention of the UN's attempting to end the secession of Katanga by the use of force. In explaining ONUC's actions in Leopoldville to Hammarskjöld, Linner, Khiari and Fabry contended that they had conformed to the Secretary-General's general instructions, and the outbreak of fighting was blamed on the opposition of European-led Katanga troops. Reports from Elisabethville made it clear that the European population, notably veterans and former police officials, were actively supporting the mercenaries and joining in the fight against the UN. However, O'Brien's statements to the press about the UN's ending the secession of Katanga did not seem to make sense and so he was advised to be careful when speaking to the press.

The first report on the fighting said that it had begun because, while the UN was resuming its task of apprehending and evacuating foreign military officers and personnel: 'An alert was set since arson was discovered in a UN garage. . . As the UN troops proceeded toward the garage premises, fire was opened on them . . . the UN troops returned the fire.' In an earlier telex Linner had reported the 'burning of UN vehicles', and this was stated to be one of the reasons for rounding up mercenaries. I had paid little attention to the earlier report on the events of 13 September, referring to UN vehicles and the garage, since vehicles were, after all, an appropriate target for attack. I only realised that there was something extraordinary about a UN vehicle garage when I read O'Brien's book *To Katanga and Back*,[14] in which there is a chapter describing Morthor, with the dramatic title 'Fire in the Garage'. Brian Urquhart, in his book, *Hammarskjöld*, said that Linner had reported the 'burning of UN vehicles in Elisabethville' early on the morning of 13 September, which I presumed was a retaliatory action by mercenaries once the operation to round them up had begun. Linner's report also stated that the UN garage premises were fired on from the building housing the Belgian consulate; it was not then known that a number of mercenaries were residing there. Later, when checking on the incident behind O'Brien's story, I learned that UN troops suspected arson in the UN garage and that troops proceeding to it were fired at. Somehow the word 'fire' had become ambiguous but it did not alter the basic fact that UN troops had been fired on while going about their peaceful business. Back in New York the press, radio and TV were full of reports of fighting in Elisabethville: they indicated that O'Brien had declared the end of secession in Katanga and that the UN had acted at the request of the central government. The arrest of Tshombe's ministers made big news, and the media reported the misuse by the UN troops of its Red Cross camp and vehicles by firing weapons from them, and that UN troops had fired at Red Cross vehicles. The UN action was condemned in Belgium and the United Kingdom; Spaak expressed concern over the developments and over O'Brien's statements. The French government did the same and reportedly said that the UN might have violated its Charter. The British ambassador to the Congo, as we have been seen, had already called on Hammarskjöld, and Lord Lansdowne, Under-Secretary of State at the British Foreign Office, was on the way to Leopoldville. Welensky, in a strong reaction, had sent troops to the border. Bunche reported these actions to Hammarskjöld and asked O'Brien for information - and for restraint. However, Hammarskjöld attributed these reports to Tshombe's propaganda, and did not want to press O'Brien for clarification at that time.

The Afro-Asian countries responded in various ways. The franco-phone African states, which were sympathetic to Tshombe, condemned the UN action, while the others praised it. There was praise for O'Brien from Nkrumah and Nehru. However, most diplomats in the UN's Delegates' Lounge in New York were left confused by the attacks on the world body in the West, notably by the local media in New York, and by the effectiveness of Katanga's public relations in the United States. Led by Bunche, each member of the Congo Club and the UN information service had to work hard to provide a correct picture of the events in Katanga.

The air attacks on our troops led ONUC to request Hammarskjöld for air cover, and he conveyed this to Bunche. I suggested that Ethiopia was the nearest country with troops in the Congo; it had a well-trained, though small air unit consisting of American F-80s. The Swedes had their own Saab fighters and could quickly reach the combat zone by staged flights. India had a sizeable air force, but their aircraft would probably have to be air-transported. Other possible suppliers were Iran, the Philippines and South Korea. Bunche decided on the first three of these and contacted their permanent representatives, while I spoke to their military advisers. I worked out possible flight routes and first asked the British for overflight clearance for Ethiopian aircraft over Kenya and Uganda. All three governments readily agreed. However, India decided to send a Canberra light-bomber unit because of the distance; it asked for 1,000 lb. bombs from Britain and flight clearance over Tanganyika, and, not unexpectedly, the British balked at both requests. More troops were needed in Elisabethville, and therefore Hammarskjöld made a request through the US embassy in Leopoldville for US air transport to move troops from Stanleyville to Elisabethville, but this too was declined.

By now Hammarskjöld was busily engaged on the situation in Katanga and had postponed his return to New York. He sent McKeown to Elisabethville to learn what was happening at first hand. Meanwhile, O'Brien had been arranging to meet Tshombe at the British consulate. Hammarskjöld, in answering O'Brien's request for instructions on how to deal with Katangese ministers, told him that his major task was to remove non-Congolese military personnel and political advisers. Any of the ministers who had interfered with the UN operation, incited civil war or participated in disturbances were to be taken into custody, unrelated to the warrants issued by the central government. Tshombe should be contacted immediately— he should meet the *commissaire d'état* and be persuaded to come to Leopoldville—but he did not appear. O'Brien was not informed by Dunnett that Tshombe had gone to Rhodesia on 13 September.

Meanwhile, on the afternoon of 14 September a company of the gendarmerie with some armoured cars established a road-block between Kamina base and the town and attacked the base. The Irish knocked out two armoured cars and wounded twenty gendarmes without suffering any casualties themselves. The Katangese mortar fire had damaged the control-tower and the UN's radio, but the aircraft control radio was still operating, making it possible to communicate with Elisabethville and Leopoldville through the control-tower at Luluabourg. Later that day, the gendarmes pressed another attack, this time supported by about 5,000 civilians from the town and villages nearby. A Katangese aircraft strafed the UN positions. The Irish found they were too thin on the ground, and therefore the base commander, Lt. Col. John O'Donovan, withdrew his isolated garrison which had been guarding the Kilobilobe power-station (providing electricity to Kamina) and reduced his defences on the base to a manageable size. Aware of the importance of the base, ONUC ordered two Indian Jat infantry companies to be flown from Leopoldville. They arrived just as the gendarmes were making another attack, and the sight of UN reinforcements was enough to put them to flight—they left their weapons and equipment and took to the bush. The area tribal chief claimed that his people had been engaged in fighting the UN without his authority; he protested vigorously to Tshombe and made peace with the UN base troops, reopening the provision of supplies and movement of labour to the camp.

In his determination to regain control of North Katanga, and faced with the loss of his Belgian military advisers, Tshombe had, the previous few weeks, placed several European mercenaries with his units in the area. Subsequently, the gendarmerie had steadily sought to increase its control over the local population, often by brute force, but the arrival of the Indian troops had given the UN enough manpower to prevent atrocities by the Katangese and provide some security for the local population. Only three days before Morthor the gendarmes had tried to remove a UN road-block manned by the Ghanaians near Albertville airfield, but this was foiled, and they were unable to enter the airfield. After fighting had broken out in Elisabethville, the gendarmes set up a checkpoint on a bridge on the road from Lake Tanganyika to the town and instituted a check on passes of North Katangese.

At 6.30 p.m. on 14 September in Jadotville, the Irish garrison was again given an ultimatum to surrender, and again refused. The next day it was subjected to successive air attacks in which three of its soldiers were wounded. At 2 p.m. on 16 September, Quinlan sent an SOS to his battalion commander and then went off the air. A second relief column, consisting of Irish and Gorkha troops, supported by a section of the Irish armoured-cars and the Swedish armoured personnel-carriers, was sent from Elisabethville to relieve the Irish garrison, but it ran into heavy fire from strongly fortified gendarmerie positions around the Lufira bridge and so could do nothing to assist the besieged garrison. The next day, a UN helicopter managed to land in the garrison camp with food, medical supplies and ammunition. The relief column at the Lufira bridge made a fresh attack the next day and attempted to push its way through, but it was repulsed by strongly entrenched gendarmes; it was also repeatedly strafed and machine-gunned by the Katangese Fouga jet, resulting in four Indians and one Irish soldier being killed and twelve Indian and four Irish soldiers wounded.

On 15 September, Hammarskjöld continued to receive reports from Leopoldville and a string of visitors. The Congolese parliament voted to invade Katanga. Welensky called for a ceasefire and the restoration of Tshombe's government in Katanga. Moreover, there were reports from UN headquarters in Elisabethville that Rhodesian military were actively supporting Katanga and had been seen inside the territory. Welensky's support for Tshombe was well known, and it appeared that with British backing he had dared to violate the international border and provide Tshombe with surreptitious military assistance to oppose the UN. He said that 'the people were rallying around President Tshombe and his troops were mounting an increasingly stubborn resistance.'[15]

The Soviet Union had supported the unity of the Congo, and according to a commentator on Moscow Radio, 'initial UN victories over Katangese troops had come as a surprise to the UN command.'[16] However, 'under pressure from the United States, Britain, Belgium and other Western powers, the United Nations forces had been instructed not to pursue their advantage.'[17] Hammarskjöld had initiated military operations against the Tshombe forces, he went on, 'to give the impression of implementing UN resolutions on Congolese unity before the 19 September opening of the General Assembly.'

In the evening Hammarskjöld was informed of Radio Katanga's report of the disaster at Jadotville. He had been thinking all day of how to arrange a ceasefire, but Tshombe had disappeared. Although the Katangese report on the fate of the Irish could have been exaggerated, it further strengthened his determination to find a way to end the fighting. He informed Bunche by telex that when he had seen Lord Lansdowne in the morning, he had sought his help in reaching Tshombe to arrange a ceasefire. Lansdowne's visit had become controversial since it appeared to be a further instance of British pressure on the Secretary-General in support of Tshombe. The Congolese government were also upset, as it seemed to them that the British were interfering with the UN on Tshombe's behalf. Although the UN officials and others who were around when Hammarskjöld and Lansdowne met viewed it as the final impetus to Hammarskjöld to seek negotiations with Tshombe, the Secretary-General's own reports to Bunche, seen by me and others of the Congo Club, made it clear that the request to Lansdowne for ceasefire negotiations was his own idea.[18]

On 16 September, Welensky, after meeting two of Tshombe's ministers, released a message from Tshombe in which he made a ceasefire conditional on the UN's withdrawal from Katanga; otherwise he threatened to wage total war. It was a difficult day for Hammarskjöld. His senior UN aides, especially Khiari and O'Brien, depressingly viewed his moves from the opposite point of view to his own. The voices of approval for the UN's action in Katanga could hardly be heard above the loud and persistent cacophony of criticism, pressures and even veiled threats. When I went to Leopoldville soon after those days, their memory was still fresh and painful to the senior ONUC civilian and military staff.

Hammarskjöld had faced a most difficult challenge from the Soviet Union during the last Assembly session. Under his vigorous leadership the UN operation had moved toward achieving its goals. A national government had emerged in Leopoldville, with first Gizenga and then Kalonji being reconciled. Law and order had improved throughout the land. Only the secession of Katanga remained to be resolved, but at this crucial juncture, when the Soviet Union already opposed the Secretary-General, Britain and France had openly sided with Tshombe and dealt harshly with Hammarskjöld. Later that day when Edmund Guillion, the new United States ambassador, came to see Hammarskjöld with a message from President Kennedy, Secretary of State Dean Rusk and Lord Home, the

British Foreign Secretary, asking Hammarskjöld to remain in the Congo as long as hostilities continued 'to show the seriousness with which the responsibilities of the Secretary-General under UN resolutions are being carried out',[19] it was seen as implying that the Kennedy administration, which had stood solidly by Hammarskjöld, had also abandoned him and joined its Western allies in their concern to protect their common economic interests in Katanga.

In Jadotville, meanwhile, the situation took a slightly different turn before it got worse. On 16 September, the Katangese gendarmes had refused to obey their foreign officers and had stopped attacking the Irish troops. A ceasefire was agreed, including a provision that the Katanga jet fighter would be grounded and the gendarmerie's road-block on the Elisabethville-Jadotville road removed. The Katangese gendarmes provided the Irish troops with fresh food and other commodities, and it was agreed that a joint tour of Jadotville by UN officers, the gendarmerie and local authorities would be carried out the following morning. But early the next day the situation suddenly changed. The Irish garrison was again surrounded by the gendarmes and came under heavy fire from their mortars and machine-guns. By evening the garrison faced being overwhelmed, and with its food running out was forced to surrender. The Katangese claimed that fifty Irish soldiers had been killed and about 100 taken prisoner. This news brought an angry reaction in Ireland. Prime Minister Sean Lemass indicated that the Irish troops might be pulled out, and immediately despatched his Foreign Minister Frank Aiken to the Congo on a fact-finding tour.

On 17 September, another attempt was made to occupy the Albertville airfield. When the UN troops stopped the gendarmes, the latter opened fire. An Indian armoured car in support of the Ghanaians returned fire and destroyed three Katangese jeeps. That night the gendarmes attacked the main Indian camp in the town and surrounded the Indian hospital. Colonel Hazari rallied his troops, including the engineers, men of the heavy mortar battery and the remaining armoured cars, and routed the gendarmes. The latter requested a ceasefire, to which Hazari agreed on condition that they and other armed Katangese deposited their arms with the UN. This demand was accepted, and resistance to the UN in the Albertville area ended. During the following week, UN troops took the surrender of Katangese troops and police at Nyunzu and Manono, and disarmed the *Groupe Mobile* at Nyemba. By 25 September all resistance by the Katangese to the UN was ended and life in North Katanga returned to normal.

Early that morning, O'Brien had conveyed to Tshombe through Dunnett, the British consul, an offer to meet him unescorted anywhere in Katanga. When informed of this approach, Hammarskjöld instructed

O'Brien that if this meeting took place, he was to use a brief that he, the Secretary-General, had prepared for negotiations with Tshombe,[20] explaining the UN position and suggesting an unconditional ceasefire, provided that Tshombe accepted the basic attitudes that were binding on the UN. It emphasised that the solution to the situation in the Congo, was through reconciliation. Once a ceasefire was in effect, then the UN would resume its discussions and try to bring about a meeting between him and Adoula. Hammarskjöld also wanted Tshombe to reaffirm his stand on the 28 August agreement he had made with O'Brien, when the objective of the UN was to remove mercenaries. Therefore, the 104 mercenaries still remaining were to be removed in the same way as 400 had been removed in August. A serious civil war risk remained in the Congo and therefore a halt in military movements should follow a ceasefire: this was essential in the context of the implementation of the Security Council resolution of 21 February. If the British consul could not arrange such a meeting, then O'Brien was to send Tshombe Hammarskjöld's note in the form of an official letter from the Secretary-General through the consul, with an additional paragraph proposing a personal meeting with Hammarskjöld.

O'Brien did not like the contents or the tone of Hammarskjöld's note, or his intention to go to Northern Rhodesia to meet Tshombe. His cables to Hammarskjöld were explicit that at that stage only he should meet Tshombe and that a visit by Hammarskjöld would be tantamount to surrender by the UN. O'Brien wrote in his book about a year after these events:

> From the outset, of course, we had been looking for a ceasefire, but the word ceasefire took a different meaning with the passage of time. At 4.45 a.m. on 13 September, if his house had been sealed off, it would have meant unconditional surrender by Tshombe. A little later that morning, if Mr Dunnett had been good enough to contact me, it could have meant a satisfactory settlement. But now with Tshombe in Northern Rhodesia, and after S/4940 and all it implied (and later the capture of the Irish company), the word ceasefire was more likely to mean, at best, stalemate and return to *status quo*.[21]

As the man in charge of the Katanga operation O'Brien was directly responsible for the orders given to the troops and for assuring their implementation. Tshombe's house was not surrounded by UN troops in time and he escaped. Dunnett, for obvious reasons, did not inform O'Brien that Tshombe was at the British consulate seeking sanctuary from O'Brien and the UN troops. Under the circumstances, O'Brien was the last person in the world with whom Tshombe would have shared his plan for escaping to Northern Rhodesia. As to the fate of the Irish at Jadotville, O'Brien had ignored the correct advice he had been given by Raja not to send a company of infantry off on its own, given the circumstances of hostility with the Katangese and their European mercenaries. I propose to comment on O'Brien's last point later.

Before dawn on 17 September, Dunnett brought Tshombe's reply to Hammarskjöld's letter. Tshombe agreed to a meeting in Ndola and to a ceasefire and requested that the UN troops be confined to their camps and that troop movements be stopped. In forwarding this message, O'Brien added that he believed the Secretary-General did not thoroughly understand the situation in Katanga and should therefore travel via Kamina where O'Brien could join him on the flight to Ndola and brief him. On the other hand, on the basis of available evidence, we in New York were more convinced even than Hammarskjöld in Leopoldville that it was O'Brien and his associates in Katanga who misunderstood the UN's position or, if they did understand it, were ignoring it. The media reports of the statements by a UN spokesman in Elisabethville continued to refer to the implementation of the Security Council resolution of February 21 and ending the secession of Katanga. Hammarskjöld had to send O'Brien a curt message to adhere to accurate and impartial reporting and to take the letter along for his meeting with Tshombe.

The Secretary-General replied to Tshombe that he could not accept the conditions that were being put forward for a ceasefire and for the meeting. He insisted on an unconditional ceasefire and that both parties should meet to discuss all modalities. He concluded by stating that he could not agree to meet Tshombe until there was a preliminary accord. This was normal practice.

In a cable to Bunche early that day, Hammarskjöld expressed optimism. The first reports of the action of the K atanga gendarmes in lifting the siege of the Irish troops at Jadotville, in defiance of the orders of their European officers, was encouraging (the situation reversed itself later in the day). Besides, Tshombe had at first agreed to meet O'Brien at Bancroft in Rhodesia, which opened the way for Hammarskjöld to ask for a meeting himself.

After spending the day seeing Adoula, Lansdowne and his own staff, Hammarskjöld was ready to leave for Ndola and waited for Tshombe's reply. A chartered DC-4 was on standby for the journey, but the ONUC commander's DC-6, *Albertina*, a faster plane than that which had taken McKeown to Elisabethville, was also available to fly the Secretary-General. It had been subjected to rifle fire at the Elisabethville airport, but on its return it was checked and an exhaust pipe damaged by a bullet was replaced. The DC-4, which was now spare, was given to Lansdowne so he could fly ahead to facilitate the meeting in Bancroft.

Hammarskjöld received Tshombe's agreement to the points he had raised, and left for Ndola at 5 p.m. He was accompanied by Wieschoff,

Fabry, Alice Lalande (Linner's secretary, who had been assigned to work for the Secretary-General[22]) and William Ranallo, his personal aide. Captain Per Hallonquist and an experienced crew were in charge of the plane. Because of the activities of the Katanga Fouga fighter, the departure time and its flight plan were kept secret. Hallonquist had told another Swede at ONUC air operations that the destination was Luluabourg. Four hours later, *Albertina* contacted Ndola and asked for the estimated arrival time of Lansdowne's plane. It gave its own estimated arrival at 12.35 local time (10.35 GMT). Half an hour later, *Albertina* reported to Ndola that it was at the southern tip of Lake Tanganyika and expected to reach its destination at 12.20. It was told in turn that Lansdowne had landed at . 10.35. Ten minutes before its expected arrival it reported to the tower that the airport lights were in sight and was told to report again when it reached 6,000 feet altitude. This was the last communication from the aircraft.

Lansdowne's place was on the runway when *Albertina* flew over it at 2,000 feet. People anxiously waited for Hammarskjöld's plane; when nothing was heard for some time, Lansdowne took off for Salisbury and the airport closed down for the night. At some distance from Ndola, there were reports that an explosion had been heard, but it was many hours before it became known that *Albertina* had crashed on its approach run at about 12.11. When officials reached the site, the plane was burnt out, but it was evident that its wheels and flaps were down and after cutting through trees and ground it had somersaulted, broken up and burst into flames. There was one survivor, Harold Julien, a field security officer, but he was badly burnt and unconscious and never recovered. Others in the aircraft were burnt, except for Hammarskjöld, who had been thrown clear and escaped the fire. He was found lying on the ground near a bush with a tuft of grass in one hand, his face serene. He had multiple severe injuries and could only have lived a short time.

Unaware of what had happened and anxious to know of Hammarskjöld's arrival, I began to monitor the early morning broadcasts on 18 September. WQXR, the radio station owned by the *New York Times*, reported at 5 a.m. that the Secretary-General and Tshombe had met at Ndola. At about 7 o'clock I heard the newspaper delivery man drop my papers at my apartment door and I hurriedly picked them up. The three major papers that I read in the morning—the *New York Times*, the *Herald Tribune* and the *Christian Science Monitor*—carried an Associated Press report of Hammarskjöld having had a meeting with Tshombe, saying that the two had driven to Kitwe, 30 miles away, for what was described as a crucial discussion. When I reached the office, Bunche told me that the British had informed ONUC that *Albertina* had not reached Ndola, and there had been no contact with the aircraft after it last reported to the Ndola control tower and was seen flying over the airport.

Cordier, Bunche, Narasimhan and I were shuttling in the corridor between each other's offices and becoming more and more anxious as the time passed. A few hours later we learned of the crash, but hoped that Hammarskjöld and the others might have survived. By the afternoon it had been confirmed that Hammarskjöld was dead.[23]

The members of the Congo Club had by instinct come to Cordier's office and we silently shared our shock and grief. We all had many questions in our minds and I could sense that my companions shared my bewilderment and my anger at the Katangese, the white mercenaries and their backers for preventing the success of Rumpunch, thereby creating conditions leading to Morthor which had turned into a bloody war. There was anger at O'Brien, Linner and Khiari for ignoring Hammarskjold's instructions and leading the UN into a disastrous mess which had cost the life of its Secretary-General. Just sitting together seemed to help and we were soon galvanised into action. All matters related to the accident and above all the ceasefire negotiations with Tshombe had to be taken care of.

Khiari was selected to represent the UN and was told by Bunche to follow the directions Hammarskjöld had stated in his letter to Tshombe. Khiari flew to Ndola on 19 September and the next day a provisional ceasefire agreement was signed. They agreed to the following: there was to be an immediate ceasefire, effective at one minute past midnight on 20/21 September; a mixed commission of four members with full powers would be put into the field immediately to implement the clauses of the agreement and seek means of settling relations between the UN and Katanga forces, including the positioning of the troops; no troop movements to reinforce garrisons or any other position would be forbidden (this would apply to all men of both sides, arms, ammunition and other weapons); the two parties would keep their freedom of movement for food supplies; and the exchange of prisoners should be carried out at the direction of the joint commission.

Shortly after the ceasefire, Bunche sent me to the Congo to examine various facets of the operations and, although Hammarskjöld's death was the subject of official inquiries, to find out what I could about the circumstances of the air crash. A final reckoning of Morthor revealed that the Western press had shown the fighting as being bloodier that it actually was. Eleven UN personnel and fifty Katangese had been killed. The UN wounded were about six times the number of killed, whereas the exact number of the Katangese wounded was not known. At the military level, the Katanga troops were in some respects better equipped than the UN forces. They had the new FN rifle, the same as the NATO issue, whereas the Indian troops had Second World War rifles; also, the Indian armoured cars were Second World War vintage while the Katangese had newer models. Katanga's one Fouga jet trainer, modified as a fighter, gave it complete air superiority because the UN, which was well off with transport aircraft, had no fighters and no anti-aircraft guns. But the primary cause of the failure of this operation was at the level of the UN leadership, both political and military.

At the military level I was amazed to learn that Raja had received no orders from McKeown to implement Morthor. When I asked him why he had launched the operation without specific orders from his Force Commander, he said that at the meetings with Khiari and O'Brien he had been told that the orders to go ahead were from the Secretary-General. When I reminded him that he was under the command of the Force Commander and not the political representatives of the Secretary-General, he rested his explanation on what he had already said. When I asked McKeown if he was aware of the instructions carried by Khiari to Katanga and if Khiari had his authorisation to convey the go-ahead signal on his behalf to Raja, he said that he had learned of the operation only after it was launched. Thus there was a complete breakdown in the military command. Unacceptable as it might be, the only explanation of the breakdown was that Katanga was too far away and that the UN representative there had developed a degree of independence. But if this was permitted at a political level because of the history of difficulties the UN had had in dealing with Leopoldville and Elisabethville there was no reason for it to be allowed at the military level.

The second military problem was the relationship between the Katanga area headed by Raja and the South Katanga sector under the command of Jonas Waern. This sector had been first an Irish and then a Swedish command, but once the reorganised Katanga area was established under Raja, his Indian headquarters was imposed on top of Waern's. Thus the South Katanga sector, which had been a Swedish preserve, was taken over by the Indians. This had never been intended by us in New York when we selected Raja as commander of Katanga area; my intention had been that in establishing his area headquarters in Elisabethville, he would command his sectors through the sector commanders. The sectors were North and South Katanga and Kamina. Intended or not, it was not long after Raja's arrival that Rumpunch occurred, to be immediately followed by Morthor, and he took over command of the operations in Elisabethville. This was resented by Waern.

In appointing Raja as the area commander, the Secretary-General had left the details of the staff work involved to the Force Commander. An area headquarters to command a mix of nationalities should not have been based on the Indians alone. The Indians had arrived with a fully-staffed brigade headquarters, which provided an easy framework around which an area headquarters could be organised by adding staff from other contingents to it; Raja should have been provided with a deputy or a chief

of staff from one of the other contingents and a few non-Indian staff officers
to make his staff more representative. Another easy way would have been
to appoint liaison officers from other contingents who would deal directly
with the area commander himself. None of this was done. On first setting
up the Katanga area command I had done just this, but then I was the
commander in all but name. Since I had been kept out of the Congo, I had
no way of knowing that basic management matters had been ignored.

In any multinational force, intercommunications, especially at a
personal level, are a constant problem. The common language of
command for the UN in Katanga was English; however, the knowledge of
English varied between officers and their accents had the pronounced
flavour of their own language. While this did create difficulties, the
differences in their personal characteristics and in the policies of their
countries had a profound effect on their behaviour. O'Brien was an Irish
diplomat, anti-colonial, audacious and brilliant, and he bristled at the least
sign of power pressures, particularly from the British. He had come to the
conclusion that the threat of the use of force, combined when necessary
with its application, was essential to persuade the Katangese towards
conciliation with the central government. Khiari shared his attitude. The
Irish troops would go along with him and certainly McKeown was not
likely to interfere.

The Indian government had stated its support for the central
Congolese government and favoured the implementation of the Security
Council resolution of February 21 in its totality with the least possible
delay. Raja, a taciturn man, was well prepared for command of a brigade,
but was new to international leadership; he looked for guidance to
O'Brien, to whom he was grateful for his appointment, and was anxious
to do what he was asked. His troops were professional soldiers, highly
trained for combat. He and other senior Indians were Second World War
veterans and had had additional battle experience after Indian independence in Kashmir and in dealing with insurrections on India's eastern
border. Waern, towering in height and an ADC to his King, was the
epitome of a Swedish aristocrat. With the exception of some volunteers
who had fought in various European wars, Sweden had been continuously
at peace for a century and a half. Swedes were proud of their country's
history and their prowess at arms, and therefore did not like to have their
lack of combat experience rubbed in. Waern, like other good Swedish
commanders whom I have known, was aware of the shortcomings of his
troops and therefore wished to use them cautiously. However, the Swedish
government followed the guidelines for the UN operation in the Congo,
and certainly would not have approved of Waern readily agreeing to
become involved in Morthor as O'Brien had intended. In fact, Waern's
instructions from his government were the same as those Hammarskjöld

had issued to the UN in the Congo.

During the final planning of Morthor, Waern was the only commander present who questioned the advisability of attempting to arrest Munongo. He said 'that it was easier to speak of arresting Munongo than actually to do it. On the last occasion, i.e. Rumpunch, the Katangese had been taken by surprise. There was no question of surprise now.'[24] He went on: 'The UN force was not a police force. . . . If Munongo's arrest was a *sine qua non* condition for the success of the operation then it would be better not to go ahead.' Khiari and O'Brien quickly assured him that Munongo's arrest was not to be a *sine qua non* condition; the essential thing was that a warrant for his arrest was out and that Tshombe should know about it. However, the operational plan required the Swedes to surround Tshombe's and Munongo's houses, which they did not do. O'Brien attributed this to a failure to understand orders given by Raja. I concluded that Waern had raised two critical issues at the planning meeting: first, that surprise had been lost and, secondly, that his troops were being called on to implement an order which was beyond the limits of his government's directive regarding the role of Swedish troops in the Congo. Waern was right since at the UN the Secretary-General had entered into agreements with troop-contributing countries that included their role within the limits of the UN resolutions. Operation Morthor had not been envisaged by the Secretary-General, nor could it have been approved under the authority vested in him by the Security Council.

Waern's non-compliance with Raja's orders did little to improve their relations, and thereby became yet another factor leading to the failure of this operation. The two also had a different style of command. Raja, having issued his orders, was cautious and ran the operation from his headquarters, while Waern, careful not to exceed his national directive and using his troops to avoid unnecessary casualties by operating within the framework of a self-defence role, controlled his operations from a radio-fitted APC. He moved from one trouble-spot to another, watching over his men and personally directing his subordinate commanders. Because of his height, the APC gave him little cover above his knees, but being a high vehicle, it put him in a commanding position. He was remarkably brave and an inspiring leader, and I still wonder how, being such an easy and important target, he escaped being hit. This difference in style of the two senior military officers further increased friction between the two, with Waern saying that Raja had taken cover in his bunker and stayed at headquarters, and Raja saying that Waern had charged around playing the hero. Overseeing them required an effective military command, not a loose form of political direction, and the lack of it made the failure of that ill-conceived, badly-directed and unauthorised operation all the more uncertain.

My inquiry into the circumstances surrounding the air crash that caused the deaths of Hammarskjöld and our other UN colleagues was carried out in Leopoldville and Elisabethville. Katanga's armed Fouga trainer jet had attacked a UN DC-4 in the air, damaging it, and had hit several UN aircraft and troops on the ground. Concerned for Hammarskjöld's safety, Linner and his civilian staff had dealt directly with Captain Hallonquist and when McKeown took the DC-6, *Albertina* to Elisabethville, he was asked to send it back in case the Secretary-General needed it to go to Northern Rhodesia. Thereafter, the commander of the ONUC air force, the Canadian Wing-Commander Jacques Forest, and his staff had not been informed of Hammarskjöld's plans. This and the fact that Linner and his confidants had dealt with the Swedish crew of the aircraft was a major omission, however important the need to maintain the secrecy of the flight might have been. The failure to give the air commander the information he needed led to two situations which would prejudice the flight. First, the aircraft was hit at Elisabethville, and the damaged part was replaced at Leopoldville. It was civilian-chartered, and its maintenance was carried out by a Belgian company on contract. To ensure flight safety, I had encouraged the UN air force to introduce all safety checks, which included a flight check on all UN aircraft. The civilian charter was not part of this system, but whenever we had a chartered plane for a VIP flight, it was flight-tested with a UN air force officer on board. *Albertina* did not receive flight clearance from the UN air force before it carried the UN's pre-eminent VIP.

The other problem was that the flight route had not been cleared by the UN air force, and so, instead of obtaining all the relevant information about the route (the UN had its aircraft flying all over the area), the captain of *Albertina* was left to choose his own route, and did not inform the UN air force of the flight plan. When it was late arriving at its destination, there was nothing anyone could do to locate it. The UN was netted in the global air rescue network, which it could have altered, bringing its own aircraft from Elisabethville or Kamina to look for *Albertina*. After *Albertina* was flown back to Leopoldville and found to need repairs, Hallonquist and perhaps other crew members flew another aircraft of the same Swedish charter company to Kasai to fill in flying time. On their return that afternoon they were told of Hammarskjöld's plan—not the normal practice for a VIP flight.

Another possible cause of the accident could have been an error in selecting the altitude for N'dola airport due to confusion with a small airfield called N'dola near Leopoldville, which is almost at sea level, as opposed to Ndola airport in Zambia (then Northern Rhodesia) which is much higher. All the evidence suggested that for some reason *Albertina* made its approach run too low and ploughed into the trees and the ground.

Had there been a navigational error or a failure of the controls? We would never know. I have been told quite recently that after similar types of accidents with DC-6 aircraft, ICAO found that there was a design fault with its altimeter and ordered a modification. This would certainly explain the accident. I was completely satisfied that there was no sabotage and that the plane had not been hit by fire from weapons.

In the last week of September, life gradually returned to normal in Elisabethville. UN and Katangese officials agreed to establish joint commissions to supervise the ceasefire. On 30 September, UN troops were withdrawn from the Lido Hotel and the BCK hospital, although the post office, the transmitter station, the airfield and the US consulate continued to be guarded by UN troops. Tshombe promised to lift the economic sanctions against ONUC personnel in Katanga and offered safe conduct to Balubas who wished to return to Kasai. Simultaneously, Prime Minister Adoula announced from Leopoldville that officers and men of the Katangese gendarmerie would be permitted to serve with the army of the central government if they so desired.

While the UN in New York was looking for a new Secretary-General, the Congo Club, under Bunche's able direction, continued to conduct the Congo operation in keeping with Hammarskjöld's policies. This was our tribute to a great Secretary-General, a masterly diplomat and a superb leader.

NOTES

1. On my recommendation and with General McKeown's agreement, the Secretary-General appointed Michel to replace Iyassou as Chief of Staff, who was due for rotation having completed a year in the Congo. Queen Elizabeth II was paying a state visit to Ghana and Michel was appointed equerry for her visit, but during the preparation for her journey to Ghana, the aircraft carrying Michel and other senior Ghanaian officers crashed, killing all aboard. Michel's tragic death ended a brilliant career and was a great loss to the UN and to his country.

2. *The Congo Operation, 1960-63,* New Delhi: Historical Section, Ministry of Defence, Government of India, 1976, p. 62, footnote 2.

3. Republic of Congo. Ordinance 70/1961.

4. Appointment of state commissioner was authorised by the *Loi fondamentale* for each province, and had to follow an elaborate procedure. None had been appointed hitherto.

5. See Brian Urquhart, *Hammarskjöld* (New York: Harper and Row, 1984), pp. 556-65, a comprehensive account of Hammarskjöld's actions before the breakout of renewed fighting in Katanga.

6. See pp. 254-5.

7. See Urquhart, op. cit., p. 563, for more details.

8. Conor Cruise O'Brien, *To Katanga and Back: A UN Case History* (New York: Simon and Schuster, 1962), p. 247.

9. O'Brien, op. cit., pp. 247-52.

10. O'Brien, op. cit., pp. 246.

11. *New York Herald Tribune,* 14 Sept. 1962.
12. *New York Herald Tribune,* 15 Sept. 1961.
13. UN Security Council document S/4940, 14 September 1961.
14. Urquhart, op. cit., p. 574.
15. *New York Times,* 15 Sept. 1961.
16. Ibid.
17. For more details, see Urquhart, op. cit., pp. 279-580.
18. UN Archives, unpublished correspondence.
19. United Nations. Security Council document S/4940, 14 Sept. 1961.
20. O'Brien, op. cit., p. 284.
21. Alice Lalande had been my secretary, an excellent one, when I was Chief of Staff, UNEF. She had returned to New York and on my recommendation was posted as secretary to Dayal.
22. Later that day Associated Press admitted that a mixture of misinformation, mistaken identity (the arrival of Lansdowne was taken to be that of Hammarskjöld), and tight security at Ndola airport had led to the erroneous report that Hammarskjöld had arrived at Ndola.
23. O'Brien, op. cit., p. 249.
24. Conversation with Brian Urquhart.

12

THE END OF KATANGA'S SECESSION

The end of the first round of fighting between the UN troops and the Katanga gendarmerie, including Operations Rumpunch and Morthor, left Tshombe feeling like a winner. He had regained all that he had lost. His troops had defeated the UN troops at Collège St François and Jadotville, and humiliated them by taking nearly 190 prisoners; furthermore, they were holding the UN troops in check in Elisabethville and Kamina. The British, French and Belgians had supported him against the UN, and in the end even the Americans had opposed the UN action against Katanga. His southern neighbours, the white Rhodesians, were jubilant and, together with South Africa, launched an anti-UN campaign in support of him. Angola and Congo-Brazzaville also joined in this effort.

When Tshombe returned to Elisabethville, he was more confident and aggressive than before. He refused to deal with O'Brien, who was recalled to New York for consultations and for a decision to be made on his future role in the Congo operation, and with Georges Dumontet, an able French UN secretariat official who had only recently been posted to Elisabethville, was appointed to replace him. Adoula and Khiari were not pleased at the appointment of a French national at this critical juncture in the UN's relations with Tshombe; besides, during his previous tenure in the same job, Dumontet had got along very well with Tshombe and Munongo, which in the changed circumstances was not considered by the central government and the senior UN officials in the Congo to be an appropriate qualification. George Ivan Smith, a friendly and effusive Australian who was completely trusted by Hammarskjöld and his other colleagues, had already been sent to Elisabethville to help O'Brien with public relations. He was now asked to remain and Urquhart was sent to take charge as soon as O'Brien's future was resolved.

Adoula was opposed to the ceasefire agreement in Katanga, and announced that the central government would resort to its own means of ending Katanga's secession. By the third week of October, in a co-ordinated effort with Lundula, Mobutu—who had already airlifted the ANC to Luluabourg—launched an attack against the Katanga gendarmerie from Kasai while the Stanleyville ANC attacked from Kivu. On the pretence of going to Stanleyville on leave, Gizenga left the capital and then refused to return to carry out his functions as Deputy Prime Minister. Tshombe's response to the ANC attacks was to launch counter-attacks. He also obtained twenty additional aircraft for use as fighters, and recruited more white mercenaries.

The mood of the Afro-Asians at the UN was bitter, and Hammarskjöld's death had shocked them into renewed efforts to end the Katanga secession. Sensing this, the American ambassador, Edmund Guillion, under instructions from Washington, renewed his country's efforts to arrange for Tshombe to meet Adoula. The British policy had all along been to seek a negotiated solution, and even the Belgian Foreign Minister Spaak joined in this effort for a dialogue between the two Congolese leaders. In a meeting with Khiari, Tshombe had conveyed his willingness to see Adoula but asked for a neutral site rather than Leopoldville. Like so many others, Adoula had little faith in Tshombe's verbal acceptance of a dialogue; there had been meetings and agreements, but nothing had changed. Thus, understanding the limitations of the ANC, he pressed ahead with military action and agreed at the same time to have another meeting with Tshombe.

The Katanga forces put up a stiff resistance and their aircraft began bombing military and civilian targets, causing much suffering. The ANC, poorly equipped and badly directed, were checked at Kaniama. The Stanleyville troops were even worse off and they killed, raped and pillaged at will in their attempt to live off the land. The Katangese stopped them at Kongolo. Bomboko dropped hints that his government might seek Soviet assistance to crush Katanga's resistance unless the UN acted decisively. It was clear to us at the UN that Katanga's increased air power had to be faced and that our troops should be readied to face its reorganised force led by mercenaries. Two things had to be done immediately: first, new and stronger pressures had to be used to persuade Tshombe to remove the mercenaries; and secondly, the Indian Canberras had to be provided with bombs to immobilise Katanga's air force on the ground. So that ONUC could act, Bunche renewed his efforts to gain support from the states concerned.

The ink was hardly dry on the ceasefire accord when Katanga resumed its propaganda campaign against the UN. As new pressures were applied by the West to persuade Tshombe to negotiate, he left for Geneva; it later became known that he had hoped while there to see a senior American official to solicit support, but he was not successful in this move. Aware of the views of the Afro-Asians, President Kennedy had already decided to strengthen the UN troops' capability and at the same time to press Tshombe to negotiate with Adoula. The Americans had considered stationing some Globemasters at Leopoldville for troop and logistical airlifts, and sounded us out on the feasibility of placing a fighter aircraft unit at our disposal, or merely one fighter aircraft for which we would have to find a suitable crew from among the member states.

Meanwhile, on the recommendation of the Security Council, the General Assembly elected U Thant Secretary-General of the UN on 3 November. He was then serving as Burma's Permanent Representative in New York and Acting Secretary-General. The Congo Club members were delighted with the election of U Thant, whom we already knew well as the Chairman of the second Congo Conciliation Commission. Hammarskjöld had thought so highly of him that he would have liked to appoint him in Dayal's place, but it was no longer possible when he was elected chairman of a related committee. Another diplomat whom Hammarskjöld greatly admired and thought a possible successor to himself was Mongi Slim, the President of the General Assembly, but as an Arab he would have been unacceptable to Israel and its friends, including the United States. Besides, the French would have opposed his election after the Bizerta incident.[1] The Arabs might have objected to U Thant since Burma had diplomatic relations with Israel, but this problem vanished when both the Egyptian and Israeli Permanent Representatives urged him to be a candidate.

The major obstacle to the final selection of U Thant was the Soviet stand on its *Troika* idea.[2] After Hammarskjöld's death, the Soviets had made it clear that they would not settle for anything less, but a member of the Soviet delegation met U Thant and said that while they would continue to insist on a Troika in principle, they would accept as an interim measure an acting Secretary-General and three Under-Secretaries-General, acting collectively. U Thant replied that his government was opposed to a Troika in place of the Secretary-General, and besides he was not interested in the job. The truth, however, was that he would not accept the job under such conditions. It took a few weeks for the United States and the Soviet Union finally to agree on U Thant and for him to accept. The Troika idea was buried, but in his discussions with both the great powers, U Thant spoke of his concept of the Secretary-General's role as requiring consultations and greater reliance on under-secretaries. One of his important qualifications was that at this time he carried no political baggage, and was thus not limited in his ability to deal or work with any people because of their nationality, race, ideology or geographical situation.

As for the Congo operation, the immediate change came when U Thant delegated the responsibility of managing it to Bunche. The Congo remained one of the big issues before the UN, but it was no longer the all-consuming concern it had become towards the end of Hammarskjöld's life. This change had a major impact on my role. Hammarskjöld had personally directed the Congo operation and concerned himself with every detail. His aides were responsible for various aspects of the operation and reported to him. Now U Thant concerned himself with the higher political conduct of the operations, leaving the implementation of his political decisions to Bunche.

This gave Bunche responsibility for interpreting political decisions into the military direction of ONUC. Unlike Hammarskjöld, U Thant was not interested in military details, and I now had to take these up with Bunche. In the past, when I had expressed a different viewpoint from that of Bunche or any of the other aides, Hammarskjöld had made the final decision; now it rested with Bunche. I did not find this arrangement satisfactory, and told U Thant so. I had tremendous regard for Bunche's ability, but felt that he might overrule me due to political considerations and that, although I would defer to his judgement, my advice on military matters should not be ignored. U Thant said that I should try to persuade Bunche to accept my views and that he would prefer me to settle any differences that emerged with Bunche directly. Nevertheless, I was *his* military adviser, with free access to him, and continued to give him advice.

During the attempts by the ANC to attack Tshombe's forces in Katanga, the Stanleyville ANC had established a garrison at Kindu. Here 200 Malayan UN troops guarded the airport and the river-rail terminal. On 11 November, a UN C-119 transport aircraft, crewed by Italians, flew two armoured cars into Kindu for the Malayans. The crew was taken to the Malayan officers' mess and then, shortly after their arrival, the mess was surrounded by 260 ANC troops, some sixty of whom were from Stanleyville. The Italians were arrested on the charge of being spies for Katanga and removed to the local prison. There they were shot, and their bodies were dismembered and the pieces distributed to the crowd.

Unaware of the fate of the Italians, the Malayan commander entered into negotiation with the ANC commander Colonel Pakassa, a cousin of Gizenga, who pretended not to know where they were; later he said they had escaped. In spite of personal intervention by General Lundula, who was flown in by the UN from Stanleyville when the killing of the Italians became known, no punitive action was taken.

The death toll was thirteen, and about a year later, when the Italian Air Force dedicated a memorial in honour of these men at its base near Pisa, I represented the Secretary-General at the ceremony. Although the

Italian government never said anything publicly, it withdrew its air contingent from ONUC and expressed the view privately that the UN had failed to provide security. Probably the killing of the Italians could have been avoided, and unquestionably there were errors on the part of the UN troops in Kindu. A UN call for an inquiry and disciplinary action was rejected by Adoula, who asserted that the UN had no jurisdiction and ordered his own inquiry. Indeed, since there was now a duly-elected government in power at the centre, which the UN had done a great deal to help establish, it was imperative that we should now support its authority.

The tragedy at Kindu was followed by the ANC's misconduct at Luluabourg: they surrounded the airport to prevent its use by the UN, and Adoula had to fly down with Khiari to persuade the ANC to evacuate it. Adoula's government was also persuaded by the UN officials in Leopoldville to agree that Bomboko, the Foreign Minister, should sign the Status of the Force Agreement, which he had initialled the year before. This gave the UN freedom of movement throughout the whole country, as well as certain immunities and privileges.

Since Hammarskjöld's death, the members of the Security Council had been engaged in the search for a stronger mandate for the UN troops to deal with Katanga. Tshombe's renewed propaganda campaign and assertion of his authority, with the help of foreign mercenaries and in the face of international opposition, had added to the determination of the member-states to act. On 24 November, the Security Council[3] authorised the Secretary-General to take vigorous action, including a requisite measure of force if necessary, to end the secessionist activities in Katanga and deport foreign military and political personnel not under the UN command. This resolution was received enthusiastically in Leopoldville, by the UN command, by troop-contributing countries, and in most African and Asian countries. It was not received well by Katanga or by its outside supporters: the British, as before, objected to the authorisation of the use of force, and France opposed UN peacekeeping by all means short of vetoing it in the Council

The following day, Tshombe made a highly inflammatory speech calling on all his forces to fight the UN force if it attacked Katanga. Inevitably, it was now only a question of time before this reckless incitement would lead to some ugly incident or violence.

On 28 November George Ivan Smith, the Acting Representative of the UN in Katanga, and Brian Urquhart, who had just arrived in Elisabethville, were invited to a reception by Lou Hoffaker, the US consul, in honour of a visiting US senator, Thomas Dodd of Connecticut, and his wife. Afterwards there was a dinner for the senator at the house of Sheridan Smith, the representative of the Mobil Oil Company, to which George

Ivan Smith and Urquhart were also invited. Accordingly, after the reception, the two UN officials went to the Mobil Oil house, which was opposite that of General Muke, commander of the Katanga gendarmerie. The General's para-commando guard, seeing the UN car, surrounded it, but after some discussion allowed it to go on its way. Shortly after the guests arrived, the para-commandos broke into the house, pointing their guns, apparently looking for the two UN guests. Two other guests, a Belgian businessman and Denzil Dunnet, the British consul, tried to calm the soldiers but to no avail, and George Ivan Smith and Urquhart were dragged out of the house and thrown into the back of a truck, all the while being hit by rifle butts. Urquhart was badly hurt and bleeding profusely. The Belgian businessman, disregarding his own safety, plunged in to help the victims, and was also beaten.

At this stage, Senator Dodd's party arrived, accompanied by a motor-cycle escort. Hoffacker, the US consul, jumped out of his car and grabbed Smith. Others coming to the rescue managed to extricate Smith and the Belgian; however, the soldiers managed to get away with Urquhart in their truck. Senator Dodd and Hoffaker took Smith to Tshombe's house where they also found Kimba and Munongo, who promised to help. Munongo, accompanied by Tshombe himself, went off to find Urquhart. After some time, he phoned demanding the release of Katanga personnel arrested by the UN, but since there were none, he was persuaded to facilitate Urquhart's release. In the morning he was released and taken to the hospital.

Urquhart had suffered various head injuries, a broken nose and two cracked ribs, and been through a night of terror. He had been taken to a para-commando camp and held there as prisoner. He was most afraid that the Indian troops would try to rescue him, for the soldiers holding him were terrified of the traditionally fierce Gorkha warriors and panicked in fear of them every time a car approached the camp; he was told that if one Indian soldier entered the camp, he would be shot. 'I believed them,' Urquhart later said, 'I was more sure that I was going to die there.' The arrival of Tshombe and Munongo saved him.

Raja had sent out a number of patrols to look for Urquhart, and Major Ajit Singh of the 3/1 Gorkhas, with his driver Rifleman Narayan Bahadur Gurung, was reported missing. The next day our troops found the body of the driver, who had been shot in the back at close range. Ajit was never found. According to unconfirmed reports he had been taken to Jadotville and then Kolwezi where he was murdered by the Katangese. This entire episode was unique in that there could have been no mistaking the identity of the UN representatives. Essentially it had to have been premeditated, and to be the result of the vilification begun by none other than Tshombe himself.

After this affair the authorities realised that they had perhaps gone too far. Munongo declared in a press statement that 'the guilty parties will be sought out and punished according to the law. So long as the United Nations does not attack, we remain calm.' But the propaganda had had its effect.

Soon afterwards, Tshombe went on a visit in Europe, leaving Munongo in charge in Elisabethville. On 2 December, some drunken gendarmes molested a local woman and some workers at the airport, and an Indian guard there immediately disarmed them and told them to maintain order. The gendarmes retaliated when they returned to their trenches by opening fire on the UN troops. The Indians returned the fire and the gendarmes surrendered. A series of incidents followed where the gendarmes who were manning posts in the city made arbitrary arrests of UN and Red Cross personnel; they abducted a group of Norwegians and an Argentinian officer and fired shots at random. George Ivan Smith tried to persuade Kimba to withdraw his troops from the city. He was joined in this by the American and British consuls, but it made little difference.

The situation took a more serious turn when the gendarmes opened fire on a party of Swedes, killing one of them. Smith telephoned Kimba to protest and to insist that the gendarmes be immediately withdrawn to their camp. Kimba interpreted this as an ultimatum and issued a press statement that 'the Government of Katanga most vehemently rejects this ultimatum. It is ready to negotiate, but will meet force with force.' By now the gendarmes held eleven Swedes, two Norwegians and Major Ajit Singh.[4] Both Smith and Urquhart tried hard to persuade Kimba to order the release of our people, but to no effect. On 4 December, Smith and Raja toured the city and its outskirts to learn the situation at first hand. Returning from the airport, they found that the gendarmes had set up a road-block which cut the city surface links between the airport and ONUC headquarters. They were forced to return to the airport, where they remained in the critical days that followed.

With the help of the American and British consuls Urquhart again pressed Kimba to remove the road-blocks and order his troops to return to their camp for by this time it was obvious that the gendarmes were acting under the orders of their foreign officers and that Kimba had no control over them. It was also evident that they were following a concerted plan to isolate the UN troops and their headquarters. A Katanga Dornier plane had flown over the airport, presumably on a reconnaissance, while the gendarmes had encircled the airport to cut it off from UN locations. It had also been reported that Kimba and Munongo were trying to leave the city to go to Jadotville. The UN command had no choice but to remove the road-blocks to regain freedom of movement. This operation was named Unokat.

Realising that more troops and ammunition were needed to deal with the deployment of the gendarmerie, who outnumbered them, the UN plan called for a defensive operation with limited efforts to reopen surface communications. This lasted till about December 13. Once the reinforcements were in position, the UN command could press forward to remove all road-blocks. Above all, it was essential to reopen the airport road and to enable Smith and Raja, who were marooned at the airport, to return to ONUC headquarters. Luckily Urquhart was present and had taken charge. A platoon of Gorkhas with three Irish armoured cars charged the road-block, meeting stiff resistance. Captain G.S. Salaria, the commander, personally led the charge on the gendarmes and cleared the road-block, but was killed in the action.[5]

In the first week of November, I helped organise a Fighter Group under the ONUC Air Command, which was placed under Colonel Sven Lampell of Sweden. The group consisted of an Indian fighter squadron of six British-made Canberra interdictors under Wing-Commander Anthony Soares, a Swedish fighter squadron of five Saab J29 single-seater jet fighters under Lt. Col. Sven Everstal, and an Ethiopian fighter squadron of four US-made single-seater Sabre F86F supersonic fighters led by Major Assefa Gebregzil. The Swedish fighters were sent to Kamina, while the other two units were kept at N'Djili airport in Leopoldville to avoid causing undue alarm to the Katangese. The Canberras had the range to reach Katanga and back, while the Ethiopians could be moved forward when needed. At last the UN could meet the menace of the Katangese air force, and when the latter bombed Elisabethville airport on 6 December, the UN aircraft were ordered into action. The Swedish fighters attacked a train east of Kolwezi and later that day, as the weather improved, the Indian Canberras hit the airports at Jadotville and Kolwezi, destroying the one Fouga fighter which had caused such damage to ONUC during the first two rounds of fighting in Katanga, as well as three transport aircraft.

The same day, the Swedish troops attacked the road-block and forced the gendarmes to withdraw. Smith and Raja were able to return to headquarters. Unokat covered the entire province of Katanga, and the operation required redeployment. In New York the Americans assured us that we would receive air transport support within the Congo—a notable change in their policy from the past, when they had insisted on providing airlift from the outside to a destination chosen by us. Our priority for airlift was to concentrate a sufficient number of our troops, weapons and ammunition to deal with some 4,000 Katanga gendarmes. The situation of our troops at the beginning of December can be summarised as follows.

In Elisabethville the Indian troops included two infantry battalions, 1 Dogra and 3/1 Gorkhas less a company, plus ancilliary troops; both the Irish and the Swedes had one battalion, and Malaya had two groups of reconnaissance scout cars. Besides Katanga headquarters, there was a Canadian signals detachment. At Kamina base there was an Indian battalion, 2 Jats, and ancilliary troops, and a Canadian signals detachment; at Kabalo the 25th Ethiopian battalion less one company; at Nynzu-Niemba one Irish battalion group; at Manono one Gorkha company, one Indian armoured-car troop and heavy mortar troop, and an Ethiopian company; and at Albertville troops of the Indian brigade headquarters, an Indian armoured car squadron less one troop, and mortar battery headquarters, and a detachment of Canadian signals and some other ancillary troops.

During the second week in December, reinforcements were flown into Elisabethville. These consisted of a Gorkha company and a troop of Indian heavy mortars from Manano, the Indian armoured-car squadron less one troop from Albertville, an Ethiopian battalion from Oriental, and the remaining Malayan scout cars from Kindu. In a rotation of the Irish and Swedish battalions, some of the men due to return home were kept temporarily to provide some extra manpower for the units.

On 8 December, the UN troops in Katanga were reorganised into two brigades. One, under the command of Colonel Waern, consisted of 14 Swedish battalion and elements of 12 Swedish battalion which had been left behind, 36 Irish battalion plus the remaining men of the outgoing battalion, the Irish armoured cars, and six Swedish APCs. This brigade was responsible for the airport, the railway line and the area to the east of it. The second brigade was under the command of Lt. Col. M.G. Hazari and consisted of 1 Dogra, 3/1 Gorkhas, 31 Ethiopian battalion, a Malayan squadron and four Swedish APCs. Its area of responsibility lay west of the railway line.

The instructions from U Thant were clear and precise: to take the necessary action to ensure the freedom of movement of the UN troops and to restore law and order in Katanga so that the UN resolutions could be implemented. There is no need to go further into the details of the military operations other than to emphasise that it was the first of a series of operations in Katanga authorised by the Secretary-General and therefore properly co-ordinated at all levels.

There was intense fighting in Elisabethville at the railway tunnel, the airfield, Camp Massart, the headquarters of the Union Minière and the golf course. Elsewhere the heaviest fighting was in Manono: the gendarmes there attacked the Ethiopian garrison, were repulsed, and then returned, which caused ONUC command to fly in reinforcements from Kabalo. With air support, the ONUC attack was initiated and heavy casualties were inflicted on the gendarmes. By 12 December the UN troops had occupied Manono and taken many prisoners, and a week later most of the UN's objectives had been achieved. There was, however, a price to pay for this fighting; the UN lost twenty-one men killed, and 100 were wounded. The Katangese were thought to have lost twenty dead and suffered many additional casualties—the details were not known to the UN. Fifty-eight of their men were captured.

In New York, what most concerned U Thant and his Congo team was the abuse of the Red Cross by the Katangese for their advantage; during Rumpunch and Morthor this had already been reported. The British press had carried extensive accounts of UN troops firing on the Red Cross. On investigation, we learned that there were estimated to be *ten* Red Cross vehicles in Elisabethville, yet Olivet, the representative of the Red Cross International Committee, reported that although the number of his vehicles had not increased, almost double the official number of vehicles, with red crosses painted on them or carrying the flag, had been seen. These fake Red Cross vehicles carried gendarmes, munitions, mercenaries and armed European civilians who were opposed to the UN. It was inevitable that UN units had to return fire on these vehicles when they themselves were fired upon. Olivet was disturbed on first learning of these incidents, but he then realised that the culprits were from the other side, and he complained to the Katangese authorities. They retaliated by abducting him and some ten days later his body was found buried in a shallow trench.

Once Tshombe became aware of the extent of the UN operation, he sent a message to President Kennedy on 15 December to the effect that he was ready to negotiate with Adoula on the various aspects of the Congo problem. Kennedy immediately passed on this information to U Thant and Adoula. U Thant instructed his representative in Leopoldville to arrange a meeting between the two Congolese leaders and made Bunche (who was already in the Congo) and Robert Gardiner available. Kennedy also nominated his ambassador in the Congo, Edmund Guillion, as his personal representative to facilitate the talks. Kitona, a former Belgian base near the mouth of the Congo river, was suggested as the place for the meeting. However, on the basis of two past experiences with Tshombe, no one, least of all the UN, was going to trust him with a ceasefire. The fighting would continue until UN troops had control of the military situation. On 18 December, Tshombe agreed to travel by road to N'Djili airport in Leopoldville and from there in a United States aircraft to Kitona. The following day Raja ordered an end to the fighting. The troops nonetheless remained on alert.

U Thant had approved Unokat on the basis of the Security Council resolution of 24 November, which had authorised him to take vigorous action, including the use of a requisite measure of force if necessary, to apprehend and remove all foreign personnel not serving with the UN. This was the third round of fighting with Katanga caused by the UN's attempt to deal with the question of mercenaries and other unauthorised foreigners, but the first in which the UN acted under a strengthened mandate. Some critics compared it to an *enforcement* action and therefore not *peacekeeping* as developed by the UN. However, the troop-contributing countries accepted the new mandate as clarifying the exercise of the right of self-defence. The UN lawyers and experts in international law had followed the evolution of UN peacekeeping and the challenge of the operations in the Congo. Most of them agreed with the UN's interpretation that the new mandate had not altered ONUC's peacekeeping role, although it bordered on enforcement action.

The situation in Katanga had altered radically. ONUC controlled the whole province, with the exception of pockets around Jadotville, Kolwezi and Kipushi. Kolwezi had the major mining installations and any thought of UN troops moving in that direction sent shock-waves to their owners and managers. At least it had done so hitherto. The UN had accepted an offer of 100 Congolese troops, and had issued them with UN blue helmets and insignia. At the conclusion of Unokat, the UN handed over North Katanga to the central government. Chief Kasongo of Kamina had also been kept in his place. While he had complied with the arrangements arrived at after Morthor, the morale of his fighters was low, akin to that of the Katanga troops in the area, and the UN did not expect any problems. It was not surprising that Tshombe and his supporters were ready to negotiate.

Adoula and Tshombe signed the eight-point Kitona Declaration on 21 December. The main points of the Declaration were that Katanga would end its secession and recognise the authority of the central government and the Republic of the Congo; it would accept the *Loi fondamentale* and its representatives would participate in the commission appointed by the central government to consider the draft resolution; the Katanga gendarmerie would be placed under the command of President Kasavubu; and Tshombe would accept all UN General Assembly and Security Council Resolutions in respect to the Congo and facilitate their implementation. Furthermore, Tshombe agreed that the Katanga members of the central parliament would participate in its sessions; the UN agreed to transport and look after them. Kitona proved to be a historic step towards the reunification of the Congo.

ONUC kept up a steady pressure on Tshombe as well as on Union Minière, which had suffered during the economic blockade Tshombe had ordered, to increase Katanga's ties with the central government. Having now reached an accord with Tshombe, who had enjoyed Western support, Adoula could now begin to deal with Gizenga, who was supported by the Eastern bloc. Gizenga had left Léopoldville to return to Stanleyville in October 1961, whereupon Adoula asked him to return to defend himself against secessionist charges. A week later, fighting broke out between pro-Gizenga troops and the government-controlled ANC. Adoula asked for assistance from the UN, and its troops intervened to restore law and order. The central government dismissed Gizenga from his post and the ANC arrested him and brought him to the capital. He was subsequently imprisoned on the island of Bulabema in the Congo river, and thus the second major secession in the Congo came to an end.

Meanwhile, Tshombe, chafing under the restrictions of the Kitona Accord, delayed its full implementation; he had returned to his old habits of attempting to sustain secession by smuggling mercenaries, arms and aircraft into Katanga. He came to Leopoldville twice, staying for several weeks each time, to negotiate with the central government, in the presence of UN representatives, on the exact steps to be taken to end secession. By the end of June, the talks were abandoned.

While the greatest problem for the UN continued to be Katanga, it also faced a financial crisis, which even the sale of bonds to meet the expenses of the Congo operation had not resolved. The beginning of 1962 also brought many changes in ONUC. Robert Gardiner, the able and brilliant Ghanaian, had replaced Linner as officer-in-charge, and General McKeown had returned to his post in Ireland as army chief of staff, to be replaced by General Kebede Gebre of Ethiopia. On completion of a year's duty, Brigadier Raja and his brigade group of 4,907 officers and men returned home and were replaced by new troops. In order to overcome some of the difficulties encountered in the command and control of the UN troops in Katanga, I recommended a number of improvements in consultation with ONUC, which were implemented. When the command of troops in Katanga had last been reorganised before Rumpunch, I had intended, by placing Raja in overall command, that he and his Indian brigade headquarters should provide the command and control element. But I did not know until I visited the Congo after Hammarskjöld's death that ONUC command had let Raja leave his Indian brigade headquarters at Albertville and helped him to set up an *ad hoc* Katanga area headquarters. In the past we had appointed unit commanders to command the Katanga area, and because their headquarters were not organised for the command of additional units, *ad hoc* arrangements had been made to assist them. But since we now had a well-organised Indian brigade headquarters, I felt that it would provide a more cohesive arrangement for command. However this was not to be. For the future, I wished to avoid this weakness in command, and form a suitable organisation to manage ONUC military operations in Katanga.

Our new arrangements included an Indian brigade group under the command of an experienced and battle-decorated officer, Brigadier Reginald S. Noronha, which would operate as a cohesive force, as initially intended by the Indian government; this was a militarily sound policy which I supported. A separate Katanga area headquarters was established and provided with an international military and civilian staff; at the UN's request a qualified Indian, Major-General Dewan Prem Chand, was appointed to command it. The UN representative in Katanga had also changed. Brian Urquhart had replaced George Ivan Smith, and early in the year José Rolz-Bennett, a Guatemalan from the UN secretariat, had taken over.

The UN troop strength in the Congo in March 1962 was 16,710,[6] some 1,300 below my estimate of the minimum requirement. The military situation in Katanga was again becoming confused. The UN controlled the areas where its troops were deployed, but because the joint commissions required Katanga's cooperation, which was not forthcoming, they were ineffective. The mercenary-led gendarmerie was increasingly active: they attacked the ANC at Kongolo and Kabalo, and seized those towns, and at Kamina it even engaged the UN. However, the UN was able to solve the Baluba refugee problem. Fellow tribal chiefs in Kasai offered them land, and the UN was able to transport the refugees and assist in their relocation to safer areas over which it exercised control.

The so-called 'Katanga Independence Day' brought many gendarmes to Elisabethville. This caused concern to our troops, and a roadblock was set up on the road leading to the African *communes*. The Katangese reacted violently to this and organised an anti-UN demonstration. A mob of 2,000 women and children came to the UN post, which was manned by Indian troops of 4 Rajputana Rifles; they threw stones, damaged UN vehicles and manhandled UN soldiers, snatching their helmets and badges and spitting at them. When the mob went out of control, the UN troops drove them back with batons. Later, when Brigadier Noronha arrived, he too decided to use batons, and fired nine warning shots into the air. The crowd immediately withdrew and the demonstration broke up. The Katangese later complained that the UN troops had caused the death of a woman and a girl, and wounded fifteen others. Realising that his Western supporters were likely to be responsive, Tshombe accused the Indians of assaulting, molesting, killing and wounding African women. ONUC ordered a high-level inquiry, which concluded that the charges were false. The incident proved the fragility of any arrangements with Katanga and the determination of Tshombe and other Katangese leaders to maintain their independence of the central government. The UN troops had to be alert since such an incident could easily spark off renewed fighting.

U Thant was under considerable pressure from the Congolese government, backed by the Afro-Asian lobby, to strengthen his efforts for reconciliation between Adoula and Tshombe. On 20 August, he presented his 'plan for National Reconcilation' to Adoula and, when Adoula had accepted it, delivered it to Tshombe four days later.Thereafter, negotiations between the central government and Katanga, with the assistance of the UN, included the implementation of the Kitona Accord and U Thant's plan.[7] The plan included such proposals as a federal constitution, the division of foreign exchange proceeds on an equal-sharing basis, the reintegration of the gendarmerie into the ANC, and a general amnesty. If it were not respected, four successive phases of increasing economic pressures on Katanga would follow, leading ulti-mately to a boycott of its products and the interruption of all economic relations and communications with it.

On 3 September Tshombe accepted the proposal, but objected to the time-limit, which he complained was an ultimatum. U Thant, a man of peace, had little patience left for Tshombe: on a visit to Helsinki, when asked about him and his secessionist movement at a press conference, he characterised Tshombe and his colleagues as 'a bunch of clowns' who were not to be taken seriously in their negotiations with either the central government or the UN.

On 10 September, pushing ahead with his plan, U Thant wrote identical letters to Adoula and Tshombe, enclosing a detailed programme for the plan's implementation. It dealt with the drafting of a new constitution and the creation of three joint commissions, with the partici-pation of UN experts, to establish the administrative details of the military, monetary and revenue provisions of the plan. Also included were several transitional steps to be taken by the parties for the reintegration of Katanga into the Congo: the taking of an oath of allegiance to the President of the Republic by all gendarmerie officers, the dissolution of Katanga's 'foreign ministry' and withdrawal of its representatives abroad, the proclamation of an amnesty by the central government, and the offer to assign a number of ministries to Katanga's Conakat party.

Tshombe, true to himself, offered little co-operation. The draft of the federal constitution was prepared with the assistance of international experts, and submitted to the two chambers of parliament and to the conference of provincial presidents in October, but Tshombe refused to attend. After the joint commissions were established, the central govern-ment insisted that their role was to implement the plan, whereas the Katangese maintained that their work could only serve as a basis for discussion. Consequently, little progress could be made. By the middle of November, it was clear that Tshombe was playing for time, hoping that the UN's financial crisis would lead to reductions in the UN Force, and thus impair its ability to act vigorously.

Since August, the attitude of the Katanga gendarmerie towards UN troops had become hostile. Their attempt to establish a road-block in the city had to be stopped, and the block and the troops guarding it physically removed. A UN patrol near Elisabethville airport was fired upon and our troops returned the fire, killing two gendarmes. Tshombe declared, 'I do not believe in U Thant's good faith any longer, nor in the Western nations which guaranteed U Thant's plan.'[8]

In September, an unarmed UN transport aircraft was shot down by the gendarmes near Kamunza, killing the two men aboard. U Thant agreed to a request by ONUC to bring in anti-aircraft artillery and I was able to obtain a battery each from Indonesia and Norway.[9] A few days later, a mine was placed by the gendarmes in the path of the Gorkhas which resulted in two of the latter being killed and three wounded.

By the middle of October, a ceasefire signed between the ANC and the gendarmerie was repudiated by Adoula's representatives on the basis that ceasefires are agreed to by sovereign states at war whereas Katanga was only a province of the Congo; the next day fighting erupted between the rival forces. Adoula called for the application of sanctions against Katanga since the deadline for the implementation of U Thant's plan had already passed. Tshombe retorted that such a move would lead to a renewal of fighting between the UN and Katanga's troops. It was a most difficult situation for Adoula's government, threatening its survival. Realising that Britain and Rhodesia were not going to co-operate in applying sanctions, U Thant told the Advisory Committee that the implementation of his plan could not be deferred any longer.

We had received reports that mercenaries, arms and equipment were reaching Katanga by many routes in addition to the traditional ones that we knew, e.g. by air to Elisabethville, by surface routes from Angola and Northern Rhodesia, and by air to Kolwezi. On 8 October, the Secretary-General stated in a comprehensive report to the Security Council[10] that the Katanga mercenaries had rebuilt their strength to their 1961 level of between 300 and 500 and that Katanga seemed to be preparing for an offensive. ONUC had verified the arrival of twelve US-made aircraft and there were three others from South Africa equipped with French rockets. There was also evidence of new runways and under-ground shelters being constructed in Katanga. The renewed military activity and hard evidence of the return of mercenaries in large numbers, as well as the arrival of new aircraft, provided sufficient information to enable us to anticipate the gendarmerie's likely future actions. Major Georges Foulque, formerly of the French army and a colonel in the Katanga gendarmerie, had led these forces during Unokat and was still in command with another former French officer. They were spoiling for a fight.

My concerns during the preparation of our military plans in the event of renewed fighting were twofold. I wanted to ensure that ONUC would conduct the operation approved by the Secretary-General as an integrated military force, all the way down from the Force Commander to the area command, the air force and brigade units. My second concern related to ensuring that personnel, equipment, ammunition and stores were pre-positioned near expected areas of action. The possibility that our troops might be required to go to Jadotville and Kolwezi, which meant crossing several rivers, necessitated bridging and river-crossing equipment. We required massive airlift capability, and although by now we had some sixty-five UN transport aircraft, the largest were DC-4s. We needed the US Military Air Transport Service (MATS): in spite of opposition on political grounds to placing so much reliance on US aircraft, I persisted. When our request reached the US Department of Defense, they were surprised and alarmed at the size of our requirements.

In meetings with the military staff of the US Permanent Mission to the UN, I gave the details of our requirements which had been passed to the Defense Department. The latter now called me to the Pentagon to explain our needs to their Chiefs of Staff. The Military Assistant to the Chief of Defense Staff (CDS), General Maxwell Taylor, explained the protocol for my appearance there: I would have two minutes in which to present my request. I was conducted to the conference room at the exact time for my appearance and Taylor came out, greeted me and invited me in. Around a large oval table sat the Secretary of Defense, Robert McNamara, and his other chiefs of staff. I recognised only General LeMay with a fat little cigar in his mouth. While I made my case, he listened with an amused look. He was the only one to ask a question since it was his aircraft I was bidding for. He asked, 'Are you confident of success and will you look after my boys?' I replied, 'I am certain of success if we get the aircraft. We will take good care of your men. Sir, we need them for our success.' Taylor rose from his chair and walked me out of the room, shook hands and said, 'You will soon hear from my staff.'

In a couple of days, I received a call from the US Mission to say that we could count on *their* support, but they had to attend to anticipated problems from the Congress. Later that day, a member of their mission came over to see Bunche and said that the United States was most sympathetic to our request for an airlift, but because of its extraordinary size and in order avoid any political objections, the Department of Defense had decided to send a Pentagon lieutenant-general, Louis W. Truman, to the Congo to examine our request. I welcomed this approach. In fact, General Truman reinforced my estimate and was full of praise for the UN command in Katanga. We received the aircraft, which proved to be an essential ingredient of our success.

Tshombe's anti-UN campaign was gathering momentum and early in December was extended to the representatives of the diplomatic community, whose countries had endorsed U Thant's plan, such as the

United States, Italy and even Belgium. In July, the Katangese had seized several rail wagons carrying UN stores near the Northern Rhodesia border, and their officials refused to release them, contrary to the agreement made at the end of the last battle. It was time to change UN tactics since our efforts to negotiate with Tshombe had proved fruitless. After consultations with the Congo Advisory Committee, U Thant switched from his policy of persuasion in dealing with Tshombe to pressure, just short of resorting to force. Two methods were decided. First, measures to implement decisions relating to integration were introduced, whether or not Tshombe agreed. These included providing protection for Union Minière installations, once it decided to stop payments to Katanga, as well as for Congolese immigration and customs officials operating at Elisabethville. The second series of actions were to be taken by the UN troops for their own security. They had withstood harassment and provocative road-blocks, and now they would assume a vigorous posture to remove them to regain their freedom of movement. Our men were not to use force except in self-defence, if fired upon first.

The mercenary-led Katangese troops played into the hands of the UN troops and facilitated the task of ending the secession. On 24 December, the opening shot of the last round of fighting in Katanga occurred when the UN's Ethiopian troops manning the Lumumbashi road-block were fired upon by gendarmes from their Union Minière base. Intense firing continued for several hours; then the Ethiopian commander withheld fire while calling on the gendarmes through his loud-hailer also to stop firing.

The same day, a UN helicopter with a Norwegian crew and six Indian officers and NCOs was shot down over the Union Minière area and forced to land near the golf course, which was being held by the gendarmes; Second-Lieutenant Surendar Singh Kang of the mortar battery had been wounded by the same bullets that had brought down the helicopter. The captors were so busy beating and brutalising the UN personnel that they overlooked Kang's serious wounds and the fact that he was bleeding to death. He was finally taken to a hospital where he died on the operating table.

The UN troops were placed on alert and all exits from the city were blocked to prevent the departure of Katangese leaders to ensure their availability in case they were needed by the UN. Elihu Mathu, the new (Kenyan) UN representative in Katanga, contacted Tshombe for the release of the aircraft, and Noronha called the gendarmerie commander, Muke, on the telephone: neither he nor any of his staff was available. In a bold move, Noronha, equipped only with his swagger-stick and a loud-hailer for his French interpreter, went to the crash site to persuade the gendarmes to release the aircraft. At this point, Major Moboye, Tshombe's staff officer, arrived and obtained the release of the personnel and arranged for the UN mechanics to repair the damaged aircraft and have it flown back to the UN air base.

The day after Christmas, the gendarmerie again opened fire on the UN troops on the road to Jadotville. We did not return the fire. The following day they fired on several UN positions in Elisabethville and Jadotville, and again our troops did not retaliate. They were provoking the UN to act; however, even though the quality of our troops was as good as before, we now had effective command and control. Next, the Katangese cut off water, electricity and telephone lines linking the UN in Elisabethville with its other bases.

Katangese firing had not ceased, while our guns remained silent. Tshombe was persuaded to visit the area of the golf course where his troops were keeping up intense firing, but there was little he could do, and perhaps little that he wanted to do. On 28 December, U Thant instructed Robert Gardiner to go to Elisabethville to meet Tshombe, and to warn him that if firing on the UN personnel did not cease and if road-blocks were not removed, the UN troops would act to regain their freedom of movement, but Tshombe left Elisabethville surreptitiously before Gardiner could get to see him, and was reported to have gone to Salisbury with Munongo and some of his other cabinet colleagues. Meanwhile, his troops increased the intensity of their fire. On 29 December the Indian brigade intercepted a message from the commander of the gendarmerie to his air force commander at Kolwezi ordering the bombing of the Elisabethville airfield during the fight. Now the die was cast. With the approval of the Secretary-General and under the direction of ONUC command, the Katanga area commander, Major-General Prem Chand, ordered operation Grand Slam to begin at 1600 that day.

The operation was carried out in two phases. The first phase included the elimination of road-blocks in Elisabethville and of the gendarmerie positions that were being used for firing at the UN, to enlarge the UN control and gain greater freedom of movement. The second phase was to advance towards Kipushi and Jadotville if the political and military leaders considered it necessary in the light of how the first phase had fared. An advance to Kolwezi was considered but this part of the plan was not finalised, since it would depend on the same factors as the second phase, as well as the availability of bridging and water assault equipment.

The Gorkhas quickly captured the gymnasium, and 4 Madras secured the radio colony. The Madrassis found Karavia, a camp vacated by the gendarmes, with a large quantity of stores and equipment they had left behind in their hasty withdrawal. Meanwhile, the Ethiopians, Irish and Swedes moved into Elisabethville, overcoming stiff opposition, and captured all their objectives. During the night, the Katangese put up strong resistance at Kasapa, 5 miles east of Karavia. In the morning, the Ethiopians made a frontal attack and in a wide encircling move two Gorkha companies and some armoured cars captured Kasapa. Two companies of Rajputana Rifles, supported by heavy Indian mortars and machine-guns, secured the "Martini Board Area" (so-called because of the presence of a hoarding advertising that brand of liquor) after a fierce battle, including an assault on gendarme trenches. In the charge, the Indians lost an officer and a soldier; the gendarmes had nine killed and three captured.

An Ethiopian battalion with an Indian armoured-car squadron and heavy mortar battery moved rapidly and by noon on the 29th had seized Simba hill, which was about half-way to Kipushi and only 300 yards from the Northern Rhodesia border. Here the 35th Irish battalion, accompanied by two Indian support sub-units, took over the advance to Kipushi from the Ethiopians. The retreating Katangese demolished the bridge over the Kafubu river 3 miles east of Kipushi, but the Indian engineers dismantled a Bailey bridge in Elisabethville overnight, transported it to the Kafubu river and had reconstructed it before noon. The next morning, the UN troops continued their advance and captured Kipushi. The following day, 4 Rajputana Rifles secured an important road and track junction east of the airport and radio installation at Kilobilobe, and the Ethiopians captured Keyberg, 8 miles south-west of Elisabethville, blocking that approach.

By the end of 30 December, the UN troops had secured all the objectives of Phase 1. The next day the Swedes occupied Kaminaville and ONUC demanded that all Katanga civil and military aircraft be grounded, otherwise the UN would destroy them from the air.

In New York we were delighted at the successes of our troops and U Thant, in a cable to Kebede Gebre, asked him to exploit these to the full. The UN troops should eliminate the gendarmerie from the entire area of Elisabethville and as far beyond as our strength would allow and thereafter we should not hesitate to proceed as far as possible along the road to Jadotville.

This message was in response to my urging both U Thant and Bunche that we had to exploit our success and take full advantage of the disarray and demoralisation of the gendarmerie. U Thant was willing, but he had been obliged to agree, on British and Belgian insistence, not to allow the UN troops to go beyond the Lufira river. These two governments were acting under strong pressures from the Union Minière (Belgian) and Tanganyika Mining (British), which feared that the white mercenaries might try to blow up the mining installations on their own initiative or in response to threats already made by Tshombe to do so. In fact, Tshombe had escaped to Kolwezi and his presence there caused us considerable anxiety.

Having carefully followed the behaviour pattern of the white mercenaries, I had come to the conclusion, with which my military colleagues agreed, that they would fight to the last Katangese, but would cut and run when faced with the option of having to fight to the last of their own ranks.

Considering what was involved, none of us could take the risks that were possible in normal combat. Thus the commanders in the field and we at headquarters were cautious in giving free rein to the leading troops who were then heading towards Lufira. Since there was not enough motor transport, Noronha decided to move only 4 Madras, the ancillary troops and his headquarters by road. The remainder of the Indian brigade were to travel by road up to the Lufira and wait for the outcome of the advance. Noronha arranged two side operations in order to secure the Jadotville-Elisabethville road junction and the power-station that supplied energy to Jadotville.

Apart from one short, sharp engagement that left each side with casualties, the UN troops rapidly reached the Lufira. The Indian troops made a bypass around a bridge formerly spanning the Lukutwe river, which had been destroyed by the withdrawing troops. Surprised at the rapid move of the UN troops, the mercenaries were not able to blow up the bridge on the Lufira, 7 miles up river. When the Katangese finally withdrew to the east bank along the main road, they blew up the railway bridge. After 4 Madras had secured the near bank of the river, the Rajputana Rifles moved forward to find crossing places, and succeeded in crossing on the submerged girders of the demolished bridge, which had not fallen deep enough to prevent the infantry from walking over it. By the afternoon, the UN troops had secured a bridgehead across the river.

We did not yet have any bridge equipment in Katanga; the Americans had agreed to provide it, but had explained that there were procurement delays. I suspected that the Americans were hesitating to airlift because they too were under pressure from the British and Belgians to make sure that UN offensive capability did not cross over the Lufira. The highly skilled Indian troops, especially adept at river and canal crossing and trained to look for every possible opportunity to get over a water obstacle, saved the situation for the UN. The Madrassis found a small raft which they towed to the bridge site, and with the help of a ferry started hauling weapons, ammunition and troops across.

The mercenaries retaliated by pushing a rail wagon, loaded with explosives, towards the bridge, which exploded on impact. Two of our men were wounded, but the submerged bridge girder remained usable. In a daring assault, our troops captured the two mercenaries responsible for the attempt to destroy the bridge and later a mortar site, which was making ferrying hazardous. Meanwhile, a UN Sikorsky helicopter had arrived to ferry equipment across, and five jeeps were carried over as well. Now Noronha decided to resume the advance. About 4 miles short of Jadotville, the leading UN troops encountered a minefield, but by the evening the main body of the brigade had joined the leading elements, and while the mines were being cleared supplies were brought up.

The news that the Indians had reached the Lufira and succeeded in crossing the river and establishing a bridgehead was joyfully received by the Congo Club, the troop-contributing countries and most of the world. However, it caused panic in Belgium and the United Kingdom. They stirred up their friendly newspeople, lobbyists in Washington and their allies at the UN to urge a halt to the advance of the UN troops. The economic interests of both countries and Britain's political interest in Southern Africa had created the situation in which they now found themselves. But now the tail was wagging the dog: Tshombe, crazed by his losses, or his associate Munongo could order the mining installations to be blown up, or the white mercenaries could do it or even hold the economic interests hostage.

The success of the UN troops, made up as they were of Ethiopians and Indians as the largest contingents—and, perhaps even more galling, led by Indian officers in their first major military action abroad since the departure of their British masters—was ignominious enough in the context of the Congo and the rest of Africa, where the former colonial powers were determined to maintain a hold. Eventually, President Kennedy was prevailed upon to insist that U Thant order his troops to halt at the Lufira.

Kennedy's request reached U Thant by the time our troops were ready to cross the river. Therefore, all he could do was tell ONUC not to advance to Jadotville. By now I had come to believe that the white mercenaries would all run with their money to save their lives; neither their political rhetoric nor their martial ability had ever impressed me. I explained to U Thant and Bunche that once troops were in hot pursuit, it was virtually impossible to stop them until they were exhausted or were running out of essential supplies.

Urged by the British, the Belgians and particularly the United States, U Thant made the political decision to order a halt to our advance; I kept quiet while the cable giving these instructions was being drafted by Bunche to send to ONUC. Later, during another conversation, U Thant took me aside and asked what was going to happen in Katanga. I realised that he wanted me to be frank rather than diplomatic. I therefore said that I expected that by the time his order reached Noronha in the field (I knew from reports that he was with his troops at the head of the column), he would already have gone for Jadotville and probably secured it.

Then he asked what was likely to happen after that; I replied that Noronha would probe forward, looking for new ways to reach Kolwezi without harming it, but that he would not attempt to secure it without Prem Chand's approval. U Thant relaxed and his eyes had that same look as when he told us one of his many funny stories. No one else questioned me and I did not intend to volunteer this information myself; after all, it was conjecture, but based on my personal knowledge of senior military officers like Prem Chand and Noronha. Furthermore, they were both infantrymen and therefore likely to be more cautious than I, who, because of instinct and training, would have ridden forward harder.

Prem Chand received U Thant's order in the evening of 3 January, while visiting the forward troops. He had been apprised of the military situation and information from Jadotville indicated dissension between the gendarmes and the mercenaries. Besides, a decision to halt the operation at this critical stage was .nilitarily unsound. He informed Kebede Gebre accordingly and ordered his troops to resume their advance. Leaving most of the Rajputana Rifles to defend the bridgehead on the Lufira, Noronha had pushed forward with a few jeeps and moved his mortars and machine-guns by helicopter. It was raining heavily, which slowed the movement down, but the troops pushed forward relentlessly. On reaching the Likasi river just before Jadotville, they found that the bridge had been blown; quickly they discovered a cart-track off the main road and continued their advance along it on foot.

On the outskirts of the town, Noronha was met by some officials and together with them drove into the town where he was received by the mayor. There was no resistance and the attitude of the Africans and the Europeans, including the Union Minière officials, was friendly. While these dramatic events were unfolding in Jadotville, a tragic incident occurred just outside it. As the Madrassis were advancing along the road toward the town, two cars carrying civilians drove through the troops at high speed. The cars ignored signals to stop and were fired at, resulting in the deaths of two European women in the back seat of one of them. The Indian soldier who had fired had not been able to see any passengers in the car. Western television and the British press played up this incident as an act of brutality by Indian troops, but an inquiry by Humphry Berkeley, a British Conservative M.P., exonerated the Indians, attributing what had happened to the faulty judgement of the European driver of the car. Thus it was listed as an accident of war.

Meanwhile, Belgium demanded an explanation of why ONUC troops had crossed the Lufira river and entered Jadotville, thereby violating the assurances U Thant had given that the UN troops would halt at the river. U Thant had pledged that the UN troops would not advance to Jadotville; thus he had to concede that his instructions to ONUC had been violated and he found this hard to explain. He therefore ordered Bunche to make an immediate on-the-spot investigation and prepare a report for the member-states who were demanding an explanation. Bunche left New York on 3 January 1963 and on arrival in Leopoldville the next day, discussed the Jadotville events with Robert Gardiner and Kebede Gebre. He then went to Elisabethville to meet Elihu Mathu and Prem Chand. Mathu had been in hospital for some weeks and therefore George L. Sherry from Bunche's office had been sent to Elisabethville to attend to his duties. Accordingly, Sherry and Prem Chand accompanied Bunche after his arrival in Elisabethville.

In the mean time, the media were reporting Bunche's mission as an attempt to inquire into the 'serious breakdown in effective communications and co-ordination between UN headquarters and the Leopoldville office'. Unfortunately, there were distorted reports and allegations that 'authority had been exceeded' and that 'heads would roll.'

In a special report on the events,[11] Bunche concluded that the breakdown in communications was not deliberate and that the crossing of the Lufira river into Jadotville had not been a blatant act of disobedience to the Secretary-General's orders. Communications from New York were subject to delay because of the time difference of six or seven hours and an overload of staff and coding facilities, which sometimes placed 'priority' messages as much as forty-eight hours behind, especially when they had to be coded for security reasons. Thus, by the time the troops had received the order not to cross the Lufira they had crossed it. Likewise, it was difficult for troops to report their every move back to New York for approval, especially when such a delay might mean the loss of winnable objectives and even of lives while they waited for the next action to be approved.

Also, the commanding officer of the Katanga area considered that since there had been agreement on ONUC's initial plan to regain freedom of movement for the UN troops, there was no necessity once the operation was under way to receive clearing orders for each step, especially since it would have to be cleared first in Leopoldville and then in New York. With these factors complicating the situation, when the troops were under fire at the Lufira river, they pushed on across it. Finding little opposition on the other side, and much more local encouragement than they had anticipated, they continued on to Jadotville, a phase of the plan that was to be deferred till the arrival of reinforcements of troops, air support and river crossing equipment.

So, under these circumstances, the accusations of a breakdown in communications and co-ordination between the Secretary-General and the ONUC force were unfounded. Bunche concluded the report: 'Experienced military men . . . are not accustomed to the need for clearing each military move before it is made, once a plan is approved. It has to be soberly reckoned with at the United Nations Headquarters that once a fighting situation develops - and particularly when a plan is being executed in an area of combat activity - efforts to regulate details of military moves and tactics by political levers at Headquarters may put a lot of men's lives in jeopardy. Once a military action is on foot there can be no push-button action at Headquarters to control that action in response to political or other considerations, without doing violence to sound military judgement and tactics at serious cost to the security of the troops involved and of the local population.'[12]

In almost all its communications, ONUC had urged the Secretary-General to hurry the transport of bridging and other water-crossing equipment. Finally, the United States agreed to our request and on 6 December the equipment began to arrive at Elisabethville by way of US Air Force Globemasters. Meanwhile, with UN technical assistance, the railway from Elisabethville to Northern Rhodesia and Jadotville was reopened. The advance toward Kolwezi was also resumed. The advancing Indian troops found the rail and road bridge at Mulungwishi demolished, but our troops crossed the river and established a base. A platoon found that the rail and road bridges over the Dikulwe river, 45 miles from Jadotville, had also been destroyed. A sharp fight with the gendarmes ensued, but our troops forced them to withdraw. A detour via Kakanda allowed our troops to reach Guba, on the other side of the Dikulwe. Then, using an existing track, the troops were able to use their jeeps to reach the Dipeta river. The Katangese there withdrew, after blowing up the bridge. Meanwhile, other Indian troops captured Shinkolobwe and the Ethiopians secured Sakania.

On 15 January, the gendarmes were reported to have returned to Sakania. The Rajputana Rifles were ordered to remove them, but met stiff opposition. Air support was called for and UN Swedish aircraft attacked targets 2,000 yards ahead of our troops dislodging the resistance and enabling our troops to seize the high ground in the area. This was the first time that anything like this had happened in the Congo. Later that day, our troops secured the airfield at Kamatanda. That night the Indian engineers built a foot-bridge across the Dipeta and weapons and stores were carried manually to the far bank. A detour over Dikulwe was found; also an intact bridge over the Kolwezi river was secured. The main bridge astride the main road had been destroyed.

The administrative situation of our troops in Katanga was weak. They had no heavy transport to support so rapid an advance over such a long distance. We had a few helicopters and enough aircraft, but because of rain these could not be put to full use. There were only a few water trucks and just one drinking point for the advancing troops. The railway carried supplies and fuel up to the Lufira, from where it had to be hauled manually across to the few available vehicles on the other side. Logistically, our troops were already beyond their supply lines and at considerable risk. Besides, as they moved closer to Kolwezi, they caused increasing alarm to the Western economic interests. U Thant now ordered that no advance towards Kolwezi should take place unless he authorised it. Noronha kept his troops on the move by changing their direction, so that while they did not cross the given line, they extended their area of control.

In the meantime, ONUC was preparing, at the request of the local railway authority to open a line to Sakania on the Rhodesian border. Tshombe, after a brief return to Elisabethville, set out for Makambo on 10 January ahead of the ONUC troops, who had the declared purpose of ensuring their own freedom of movement. In fact, UN troops had already established their freedom of movement, so Tshombe must have had some other intention. On 12 December, he briefly returned to Elisabethville and then left for Kolwezi.

ONUC had received information that the mining installations at Kolwezi were planted with explosives and that the bridge over the Lulaba river near the Lufira power plant was also in danger of destruction. Western states which had consuls in Elisabethville made vigorous representations to Tshombe to call a halt to the destruction of the wealth of the Congolese people.

On 14 January,[13] the Belgian government transmitted a message from Tshombe to U Thant. It conveyed the results of his meeting with his Ministers in Council at Kolwezi, announcing their readiness to allow UN movement throughout Katanga and to return to Elisabethville for the complete implementation of U Thant's plan. In return, the Council asked for freedom of movement in the province and security for the Council members. The Katanganese declared that they would immediately remove all mines and other explosives placed at vulnerable points.

On 17 January Sherry and Prem Chand, representing ONUC, received Tshombe at their headquarters in Elisabethville to discuss the modalities for the entry of ONUC troops into Kolwezi.[14] Assured of personal protection, Tshombe signed an agreement ordering his troops not to offer any resistance and to surrender their arms to the UN troops. He agreed to allow ONUC freedom of movement throughout Katanga and a date was fixed for UN entry into Kolwezi.

Our troops immediately moved forward and found the bridges over Lulaba, which provided the water for the dam that generated power for the mining installations in Kolwezi, ready to be blown. The approaches were heavily mined and dynamite charges had been laid everywhere. Indian engineers were now ordered to remove all the charges and clear the mines.

As had been arranged, Noronha met the representatives of Katanga and Union Minière at Pumpi railway station. The whole party proceeded to Kolwezi, followed by the Rajputana Rifles group. From Lulaba Noronha went forward with a small group and entered the town, while his brigade rapidly occupied other important centres. On 21 January the UN announced the end of military operations, declaring that the Katanga gendarmerie had ceased to exist and that all important centres in Katanga were under UN control.

On 23 January, Joseph Ileo was appointed State-Resident at Elisabethville by the Prime Minister of the central government, and his arrival in the capital of Katanga marked the end of the secession. Six days later, U Thant, at a press conference in New York, stated that the military phase of the ONUC operation had been completed and that, beginning in March, UN troops would gradually be withdrawn from the Congo.

The Indian government, after the debacle it had suffered in its war with China in the fall of 1962, was under pressure from parliament to withdraw its contingent from the Congo, and had informed parliament that the troops would return home in January 1963. At U Thant's request, India agreed to allow its troops to complete their task in Katanga, and the date was moved forward to March. These fine troops were still among the first to leave the Congo.

Meanwhile, the reintegration of Katanga was being pursued smoothly and peacefully. Twenty-five Katanga gendarmerie officers were transported by UN aircraft to Leopoldville, where they took an oath of allegiance to the Congolese President, an action which signalled the integration of their force into the ANC.

While the UN troops were busy in South Katanga, some pockets of resistance remained in North Katanga, where the gendarmerie, led by mercenaries, still held out. Although I was reluctant because of past experience to assign the Nigerian brigade to this task with their seconded British officers who had misgivings about expelling white mercenary officers, they were the only sizeable formation available and were good. They established a command post in Kongolo and deployed their 3rd Battalion from Luluabourg and the Royal Malayan Rifles from Bukavu. Each of the battalions was accompanied by its armoured cars as they converged on Nyunzu and cleared the areas north and south of the Kongola-Nyunzu road. On completing the operation, these troops returned to their previous locations. This was accomplished by 12 March.

Just before the last round of fighting in Katanga, Adoula had requested U Thant to help obtain aid for the training of the ANC from countries friendly to the Congo; he had in mind Belgium, Canada, Italy, Israel, Norway and the United States. Although the UN had the responsibility for providing assistance in the reorganisation of the ANC, it was up to the Congolese to determine the countries of their choice, and we were to do everything possible to help. After consultations with the Congo

Advisory Committee, Adoula was advised that the initial technical assistance mission should include Ethiopia, Nigeria and Tunisia.

Presumably under pressure from his Western supporters, Adoula conveyed to U Thant that he could not understand the delay from the UN side in providing training assistance for the ANC. In April 1963, he decided that his government would make its own choice of countries to provide training assistance, and informed U Thant accordingly. At the UN, we particularly appreciated the importance of reorganising the ANC, since it would facilitate the earlier withdrawal of our troops; however, it was not politically feasible for us to co-operate with the Congolese in this respect, for we could not endorse bilateral military aid. But in early May, asserting its right to seek bilateral aid, the Congolese government went ahead and requested the three countries mentioned above for aid. On 28 June, it signed an agreement to this effect with Belgium. This marked the beginning of the end of any UN effort to help in the reorganisation of the ANC.

Immediately after the ending of the Katanga secession, as we have seen, U Thant declared that the UN military operation would now be gradually phased out, and civilian technical assistance increased. Adoula then asked U Thant that ONUC remain for an extended period because the ANC was not yet in a position to maintain order. However, the Secretary-General was acting in response to ONUC's financial straits, and on 26 April a UN spokesman declared that this problem would oblige the UN to withdraw its troops from the Congo before the end of 1963. The Soviet Union had called for the early withdrawal of the force, and many states had failed to meet their financial obligations, placing the Congo account into additional debt. A UN bond, issued to pay for ONUC, was undersold and so U Thant had no choice but to scale down the force to reduce costs.

Adoula had written to U Thant asking that a UN force of 3,000 men remain till July 1964. The general situation in the Congo had improved, although some clashes were still occurring, mostly in Katanga, calling for a response from UN troops. Therefore, U Thant presented Adoula's request, which was endorsed by Belgium, to the Congo Advisory Committee. However, when Mobutu returned from Israel, where he had completed a parachute course together with 200 of his paracommandos, he declared that ONUC had already stayed too long in the Congo and that the ANC was capable of maintaining order. Adoula arrived in New York in early October, still seeking support for his request that UN troops remain till June 1964. His efforts were successful.

There were reports from Katanga that Tshombe was only waiting for the departure of ONUC to make moves to regain power. He accused Ileo of scheming to arrest him, but eventually he left for a visit to Europe.

In September, there was an outbreak of lawlessness in Maniema province, which forced Kasavubu to declare an emergency, and incidents in Goma and other areas in Kivu province, and in Bumba in Moyen Congo province, also led to emergencies being declared. Then in January 1964 fighting in Kwilu placed yet another province under emergency. In all these situations, the UN provided assistance in one form or another with troops, planes, helicopters and transport. Besides, the UN Force had to provide security to technicians stationed in disturbed areas or evacuate them, as happened in Kwilu.

At ONUC headquarters there were a number of changes. On General Gebre's return to Ethiopia in July 1963, the UN's Norwegian air commander, General Christian R. Kaldagar, was appointed Acting Force Commander as an interim arrangement. In January 1964, Major General J.T.U. Aguiyi-Ironsi of Nigeria was appointed Force Commander. Robert Gardiner left in May 1964 and was replaced as Officer-in-Charge at ONUC by a Haitian diplomat, Max Dorsinville.

By January 1964, we had been able to reduce the strength of the UN force from its 1963 level of 19,800 men to 5,470 largely by not replacing troops due for rotation. The major troop-contributors remaining were Ethiopia (1,718), Ireland (355), Nigeria (1,025) and Sweden (396). In addition, an ANC battalion (782) remained in ONUC service. With Katanga reasonably secure the primary mission of the UN troops was to maintain their presence and help in keeping law and order.

The Congolese government was busy negotiating bilateral agreements for aid, notably with Belgium and the United States. These measures heralded the gradual reduction of UN operations, i.e. reducing the number of UN troops and changing the UN's role from that of a major player to its normal role of technical assistance. The UN expected the ANC to play its part in maintaining law and order, except when this proved problematical; thus, ONUC had to take action in January when two ANC companies in Stanleyville mutinied and there was a demonstration by about 300 Lumumbists. However, in May, when rebel activities in Kivu, led by Gaston Soumialot, caused Adoula to request assistance from the UN force, ONUC headquarters demurred. We were reluctant to become involved in an operation at so great a distance just as we were arranging the final phase of withdrawing our troops from the Congo. Eventually, Adoula despatched Lundula to deal with the rebels, and on 6 June, realising the UN's situation, he retracted his request for help.

During June, rebels had gained control over most of Kivu and were advancing towards Albertville. The UN troops in Katanga, as they reduced their numbers, were no longer able to protect roads to Northern Rhodesia. On 16 June, the US Department of State confirmed[15] what was already being reported by the media, namely that some American civilian pilots were participating in the operations against rebel troops in the eastern part of the Congo. It was common knowledge that the United States, as part of its military assistance, had provided aircraft with civilian crews—who, incidentally, were rumoured to be Cuban expatriates. The next day, an official in Washington announced that US citizens would not fly any more combat missions: 'Our understanding is that these US citizens will not in the future be called upon by the Congolese government to engage in operational missions in the police action within the Congo.'[16]

Late in June, a Belgian journalist, Pierre Davister, came to Leopoldville where he discussed with Adoula and Mobutu their requests that Tshombe should return to the Congo. On 25 June 1964, Adoula decided that he was prepared to resign his position and participate, if necessary, in a government led by Tshombe. The same day, Tshombe met Davister in Brussels, and later had meetings with Spaak and the US ambassador in Belgium, before leaving for Leopoldville with Davister. On arriving there the next day, he met Kasavubu, Adoula and Mobutu. He then declared that a reconciliation among all the Congolese factions was necessary to save the country and that all political prisoners, including Gizenga, should be released.

While these critical negotiations between the Congolese leaders were going on, the remaining ONUC troops were preparing to leave. U Thant asked me to fly to Leopoldville to facilitate their departure as well as to say my farewells to the Congolese leaders.

On 30 June, Kasavubu announced the dissolution of the parliament and the resignation of Adoula and his government. Apparently, Western economic interests had prevailed and succeeded in persuading the Congolese leaders to turn to Tshombe to lead them at the time when the UN troops were leaving. I saw the last Nigerians and Canadians fly out of the Congo. On the flight to Nigeria was General Ironsi, who always carried a symbolic stuffed lizard instead of a cane. As the gangway ladder of his aircraft was removed, he waved it, seeming to say farewell on behalf of thousands of UN troops who had served, at great sacrifice, to bring peace to the Congo.[17]

I could hardly wait for my commercial aircraft to ready itself to depart for Brussels from where I would return to New York. When we were finally in the plane, and as it rolled down the runway, I sank back in my seat and said to my military aide, 'Thank God it's over'—also remarking that we had done what we could and it was now up to the Congolese.

NOTES

1. In 1958, all French troops in Tunisia were withdrawn, except for some near the frontier and the naval base at Bizerta. President de Gaulle insisted that their presence in Tunisia was necessary for French security and for more than two years fruitless negotiations concerning their removal continued. On 16 July 1961, Tunisian troops surrounded the naval base at Bizerta while volunteers moved south to harass the French garrisons there. Fighting broke out, leading to UN intervention.

2. Because of the Soviet Union's dissatisfaction with Hammarskjöld, Khrushchev, in an address to the General Assembly on 26 September 1960 (UN Document, SG/964), suggested abolishing the executive office of Secretary-General and replacing it with three persons, representing respectively the Western powers, the socialist states and the neutral countries. This concept became known as the Troika.

3. Security Council Resolution S/4989/Rev. 2 of 24 November 1961. The votes were nine in favour, none against, and abstentions by Britain and France.

4. His probable death was not known at the time and in fact he still remains listed as 'missing in action' on the books of the Indian Army.

5. He was posthumously awarded India's highest decoration for valour, the *Param Vir Chakra*.

6. Austria, 45; Canada, 285; Ireland, 700; Italy, 62; Liberia, 238; Malaya, 1,461; Nigeria, 1,683; Norway, 24; Pakistan, 672; Sierra Leone, 110; Sweden, 767; Tunisia, 548; other countries, 707.

7. UN Document S/5053/Add. 11, 20 August 1961.

8. *New York Times,* 13 September 1961.

9. The Indonesians asked the UN to arrange delivery of ammunition for their Soviet-made guns. Since the Soviets did not contribute to ONUC, the UN field service was hampered in ordering them. I asked the Indonesians to bring their own ammunition with them and we would try to purchase it somehow—which we did.

10. UN Document, S/5053/Add. 12.

11. UN Document, S/5053/Add. 14, 10 January 1963, pp. 53-9

12. Ibid., pp. 58, 59.

13. UN Document, S/5053/Add. 15 (Annex V).

14. UN Document, S/5053/Add. 15 (Annex IX).

15. *United Nations Peacekeeping in the Congo, 1960-1964* (Washington, DC: Brookings Institute), 30 June 1960, vol. IV, p. 97.

16. Ibid.

EPILOGUE

When the secession of Katanga came to an end, U Thant announced the early withdrawal of the UN force. ONUC had been in the country for three years, and clearly it could not stay for ever. The Secretary-General felt that the unification of the country under a government of national reconciliation provided a suitable point for the UN to withdraw and for the Congolese to assume their full responsibilities. Besides, he could never forget that the Congo operation had led to the death of a Secretary-General and shaken the UN's very foundations. Then there was the inescapable fact that the UN's financial burden was mounting, with the potential for endangering the very existence of the organisation. This came to the crunch in 1964, when the United States attempted to apply Article 19[1] to the Soviet Union for non-payment of its peacekeeping dues for more than two years.

The months following the coerced return of Katanga to the nation saw a measure of optimism in the Congo. News from there disappeared from the headlines of the world's press. The Belgians had developed a rich colony through the close interlocking of state, church and capital. The Congolese élite was built around clerks and other subordinate government and commercial employees at different urban centres. Some ethnic groups were favoured over others and all grew up in isolation from African nationalism elsewhere and the rapid changes taking place internationally. It was not till the Brussels 'Expo' of 1958 and subsequent contacts that Congolese eyes were opened to other influences. Thus the Congolese national movement was a product of Congolese and Belgian colonial interaction. Essentially, the decolonisation formula prescribed a set of African institutions to be run parallel to a bureaucracy managed and an army led by Europeans. This arrangement proved too fragile to withstand the other forces released within the newly-independent state.

The mutiny of the Force Publique and the removal of its white officers led to a European exodus from the Congo and Belgian military intervention. At this stage the UN was invited to supervise the withdrawal of Belgian troops and to assist in restoring law and order. Although the UN did not entirely succeed, it was able to maintain peace through most of the country and to restore normal life. Of the three basic institutions created by the Belgians, two survived—the church and the capital Leopoldville, now Kinshasa. As to the third, the bureaucracy, while the Congolese accepted massive UN technical assistance, they could not wait to reinstate Belgian bureaucrats to run their system. The void—filled by the UN to restore a semblance of order—led to the return of past practices familiar to the Congolese. Thus the UN temporarily replaced the vanished colonial system of officialdom without having its authority.

When the parliament reconvened in 1962, the leadership was too much occupied with administration at national and provincial levels. Leopoldville was the main centre for politics, and among the élite there was competition for influence and power as well as interaction with external interests. The legislators and parliamentarians quadrupled their salaries and refused to apply budgetary restraints on the country's spending. The political parties had ceased to play their roles; a few leaders dominated the scene, working to maintain their personal influence and power in order to achieve benefits for themselves, rather than their parties. This political process went no further during the remaining UN operations, and when eventually the parliament was adjourned, there was little protest.

Lumumba's fall was brought about by individual politicians working together and not by any action of the political parties working in concert. He made more enemies than friends and thus encouraged his rivals. Those presenting the most serious threat to him were President Kasavubu; Bomboko, the Foreign Minister; Nandeka, the security chief; and subsequently Mobutu, the army chief of staff. These four had gained prominence by virtue of their positions rather than the votes they could muster in the legislatures. It was Lumumba who could carry the majority in the parliament though not in the Senate; despite the opposition to him, it was only he who had the ability to rally political parties at the national level, which was not what had been intended by the three basic institutions designed to share power. He was too radical in the ambition he felt to move towards independent nationhood; this was contrary to the intentions of the Belgians and other interested parties, who wanted to retain power and influence in the Congo. Thus there was no place for Lumumba in this setting, and he had to be removed.

Lumumba's African, Asian, and Soviet-bloc friends did help, but their political assistance had to be within the framework of the UN General Assembly with all its limitations. Any military support had to conform to the resolutions of the Security Council, where three out of the five permanent members were allies of Belgium. In the economic field, only a government enjoying the approval of the Belgians could expect aid; so high was their stake in the Congo. This was equally true of the United States which, leaving aside the Belgian factor, was determined to oppose and even attempt to bring down any Congolese regime which leaned towards the Communist world. Although Lumumba had many influential friends among world leaders, they were unable to match the resources of his opponents.

Lumumba lost the support of the West from the beginning of the country's independence. His verbal assault on the Belgians and on King Baudouin himself during the independence ceremony soured relations and sparked the mutiny of the Force Publique. His courting of Nkrumah, Sekou Touré and their Soviet friends antagonised the United States and their Western allies. The intervention by the UN was intended to keep East-West rivalry out of the Congo, but it was always omnipresent. Yet, because Lumumba lacked experience of international gamesmanship, he was unable to play the East off against the West to his advantage. The West, with its enormous interests in the Congo, was determined to win, but Lumumba, who might have worked in harmony with the goodwill of the country's former colonial masters, deliberately threw it away. There is hardly any state which, on gaining its independence, could have afforded to lose the co-operation and support of the departing colonial power. The entire infrastructure of a colonial state was created by the rulers for economic exploitation. Bereft of its past rulers, lacking their support and even having earned their open hostility, Lumumba faced unavoidable downfall. Not only did he lack experience, in spite of his appeal across the political spectrum; he was also not of a calibre equal to such contemporaries as Kenneth Kaunda of Zambia, Julius Nyerere of Tanganyika, Kwame Nkrumah of Ghana and Sekou Touré of Guinea. At this critical time instead of strengthening the foundations of the young state, he weakened them.

The UN might have been more helpful to Lumumba, although it would be foolish to claim that it could have guaranteed him success. It was Lumumba who finally blew this possibility. Both Ralph Bunche, who was known as the most patient of men, and Dag Hammarskjöld, who made every sacrifice to work for the Congolese, were treated badly by him. They had pre-eminently fulfilled their obligation to the UN's mission in the Congo, but Lumumba insulted and humiliated them. And when his troubles got worse, neither these two nor many of the less senior UN staff who had witnessed his behaviour could do much since he had made it impossible for us to deal with him on any normal terms. In contrast to other African leaders who had led their nations to independence, Lumumba was unprepared to become the chief minister of a democratic state when it became decolonised, especially one as large and diverse as the Congo. It cannot be denied that he had acquired some political experience, but his nature was that of a fiery demagogue. His temperamental weaknesses made him his own worst enemy. He was arrested, not because he decided to disappear from his house in Leopoldville but because of his rashness in emerging into the open in hostile territory. Once arrested, his death was foredoomed. Beyond pleading for humane treatment, there was nothing the UN could do to save him.

From the outset, a major problem in the Congo was that the ANC was a disorderly rabble and its officers lacked any semblance of control. At the same time, every politician sought the support of troops from his own ethnic group. Mobutu by contrast was attempting to establish his control over them all with the help of the UN under the guidance of General Kettani, ONUC Deputy Force Commander and military adviser to the Congolese. This help enabled Mobutu to gain control of the military police and the loyalty of the Thysville garrison commander, whose command included the ANC's only armoured unit. Moroccan training teams also helped to raise a commando unit and a parachute unit. It was only the loyalty of these troops that made the September 1960 coup possible.

Mobutu was under the protection of the UN when he announced his coup, and his power-base was built around the troops it had trained. A couple of days earlier, fearing that a fresh mutiny might break out because the soldiers had not been paid, the UN authorised Kettani to offer Mobutu a sizeable sum of money to pay part of the soldiers' dues. Mobutu declined the offer since he had already been generously helped by another benefactor, who did not wish the UN to gain special influence. These developments led to allegations that the UN was involved with Mobutu in his coup. On the other side of the picture, Lumumba, like other Congolese leaders, was also under the protection of the UN whose troops had twice saved him from serious bodily harm, if not from being killed.

ONUC troops had guards at all vulnerable points and were able to prevent the ANC from entering such areas, but Mobutu was able to seize control of other installations. His troops made several attempts to seize Lumumba, but these were foiled by the UN; prevented from gaining entry to his house, the ANC surrounded it. The UN had no mandate, by any stretch of the imagination, to fight the ANC around Lumumba's house, apart from controlling the entrance, which they did. It was the closing of the radio station and the airports by the UN at this time which became controversial both in the Congo and at the UN, especially in view of the fact that, while Lumumba was denied access to the radio, his rivals were free to broadcast from across the Congo river on Brazzaville radio. Closing the airports was less controversial.

The UN, with the direct participation of United States diplomats, succeeded in establishing a democratic regime under Adoula. A Western parliamentarian from of government is based on a division between government and opposition; in the course of a debate, one prevails over the other and the majority wins the point. However, in the African style, dialogue or palaver must go on and on until negotiations have proceeded to the point where the parties are ready for compromise. In the Congo, they called it a *buntu*, or an African arrangement. The West had no patience with this; they wanted results quickly, and were already looking for other solutions to the Congo dilemma. Mobutu had the loyalty of the troops, but his dominance was primarily in the capital; at this time, too, he clearly lacked political *savoir-faire*. Adoula had not succeeded, so Tshombe became the choice.

The dramatic turn of events which led to the rise in Tshombe's political fortunes was caused by his stubborn refusal to move forward in the process of reconciliation with the central government unless forced to do so. He still enjoyed the confidence of Belgian and Western economic interests, while Adoula was unable to govern due to political dissension, failure of the economy and a breakdown of central authority over the provinces, particularly those in the north and the north-east. Just as Kasavubu dissolved the parliament later in 1963 and granted Adoula full legislative powers to draft a new constitution within 100 days, Adoula was fighting for his political survival. The economic rundown and accelerating inflation had increased hardship and generated strong opposition. The trade unions demanded quick reforms and early relief, and civil servants were calling for a strike. The pro-Lumumba group called for the release of Gizenga, held on an island near the mouth of the Congo river. The three deputies responsible for this agitation, who had been arrested under the emergency backed by the military courts, were released by the troops and escaped to Brazzaville—an ominous sign of the army's unreliability in relation to the government. A few days earlier, some troops at Luluabourg mutinied, demanding arrears in pay; although the mutiny was put down, the attitude of Mobutu's élite troops was questionable.

Adoula had excluded Mobutu and Nandeka, the security chief, from the emergency committee to deal with the situation in Leopoldville. While Adoula was sustained by the support of the United States, he was unsure of it at this stage. Kasavubu had done away with the *Loi fondamentale* negotiated between the Congolese and the Belgians before independence. By dissolving parliament and giving new powers to Adoula in 1962, Kasavubu had put an end to a government of national conciliation. This left Adoula alone to administer the country, and to draft a new constitution, a task which he could have performed only with the co-operation of all the prominent political leaders, something that proved difficult to achieve. Besides, Adoula needed external support, particularly from the United States and Belgium.

By mid-April 1964, as the deadline for ONUC's withdrawal came closer, the ability of Adoula's government to administer and maintain order in the Congo was still questionable. He had a relatively strong government and had established and improved relations with Belgium. Paul Henri Spaak, Belgium's Foreign Minister, had come to the Congo indicating support for him, whereas Belgium had previously favoured Bomboko and Tshombe to head the government. During his visit, Spaak resolved many outstanding issues, including financial problems which had remained dominant ever since independence. A visit by W. Averell Harriman, United States Under Secretary of State for political affairs, signalled President Johnson's support for Adoula. On the other hand, relations between Adoula and the UN had deteriorated. He had refused to receive Max Dorsinville, a UN-appointed Officer-in-Charge of Haitian nationality, and to accept the credentials of Babiano Osorio-Tafall, an experienced Mexican diplomat heading the UN civilian operations, as the representative of its Technical Assistance Board—although he did eventually agree to the latter appointment.

The UN faced enormous difficulties in meeting the ONUC budget. ONUC had been given an extension, and it was unlikely to receive another one. Besides, no one in the Congo seemed to want the ONUC presence any more. Mobutu, smarting under the UN's continuous criticism of his ill-trained troops, insisted that he needed no further help from it. The publicised logistical support the UN had given to the Congolese troops in their operations in the northern and north-eastern regions did little to improve its relations with the ANC. Adoula's government was faced with the prospect of the Congolese army of 35,000 men having to take over the country's internal security from the UN force of 4,200. The informed view at the UN, which I shared, was that although there was no way that ONUC could possibly remain in the Congo, its departure would lead to chaos; and this is precisely what happened.

Mobutu ruled over the Congo (renamed Zaïre) from then up till the time of writing—a quarter of a century. He provided a measure of normality to the vast and diverse land, and succeeded in keeping it unified in spite of breakaway attempts. He dealt with revolt firmly and when his own troops failed, as they did twice in Shaba (as Katanga is now named), he obtained help from Belgium, France, the United States and Morocco.

Before the end of 1963, Adoula's government faced serious opposition across the Congo. After the parliament was dissolved, a number of

Lumumbist parliamentarians, having thereby lost their immunity from arrest, moved across to Brazzaville and formed the Comité National de Libération (CNL) to bring down the Binza group in power in Leopoldville. Pierre Muele, another Lumumbist, established guerrilla camps in Kwilu, and his followers gained control of the province, forcing the ANC to withdraw. There was insurgency in Kivu, and the Lumumbist Gaston Soumialat established a so-called Eastern Front. His forces defeated Mobutu's troops in Baille, near Burundi's border and humiliated the ANC in Kivu. From there they moved south and joined forces with anti-Sendwe *simbas,* which gave them control over most of North Katanga.

The apparent collapse of the ANC led sympathetic African states to consider the formulation of an African command to assist with internal security, but the African states were badly divided after the murder of Lumumba and unable to offer any viable alternative. What sympathy there was for the Congo among African states mostly vanished with the appointment of Tshombe as Prime Minister.

Relying on the support of Belgium, the West and some African states, Tshombe was left to do what he knew best. He called his old Katanga gendarmes into service, recruited 400 white mercenaries, and obtained logistical and transport support from the United States. The eventual capture of Stanleyville followed a dramatic US airlift of Belgian paratroopers to prevent a complete massacre of European hostages, of whom some had already been killed and others died during the rescue operation. However, Tshombe also proved incapable of dealing with internecine squabbles and fighting, and this brought Mobutu to power, with his rag-tag ANC. Belgium and the West concluded that there was no other choice if their interests were to be safeguarded and the country kept free from Communism.

Mobutu's style of governing was not much different from that of most other African leaders, as an authoritarian presiding over a single-party polity. He amassed a fortune and distributed largesse among his courtiers and supporters. This was not what the UN expected to leave behind, but such expectations were misplaced, for why should Zaïre have been expected to be different from the rest of Africa south of the Sahara? There are exceptions, but they are in a small minority.

I often told Mobutu during the UN operation that he had the making of a great leader, but that he must gain experience and build up the ANC and a political base before venturing into national leadership. His September 1960 coup was premature and went nowhere; only in 1965 was he able to gain political power (with the help of the United States who perceived in him an ally in their worldwide anti-Communist crusade), but then it took him many years to consolidate it. He finally emerged as a strong African leader, and used his experience and prestige in brokering dialogue between the frontline states and South Africa. This was a useful contribution.

Mobutu has been forthright in expressing his appreciation of what the UN peacekeeping force did in maintaining law and order, dealing with revolt in the north-eastern and Kasai provinces, and ending the secession of Katanga. He had fond memories of Kettani and the Moroccan officers who helped to train his troops, while remaining firm in his view that the Belgians were the best people to reorganise and retrain the ANC, since they were familiar with his troops and with conditions in his country. Furthermore, it was and is the sovereign right of his country to accept offers of assistance made to the ANC.

Mobutu had no rancour against any of the main UN actors during the ONUC operations; he understood the constraints under which they operated and, like all Zaireans old enough to remember, was aware of the useful and historic role of the UN immediately after their country's independence. He was appreciative too of the many subsequent technical assistance programmes. At the time when this book is going to press, his long hold on power is slipping, amid scenes that recall the appalling chaos of 1960. How this will end only the future can tell.

When one evaluates ONUC's operations after nearly three decades, it is clear that it achieved most of its goals. It kept the country unified, and prevented the global East-West rivalry from igniting dissidence, and the revolt from within the state from becoming a major conflagration. ONUC also helped to bring about a political reconciliation, although this did not last beyond its departure. ONUC was also able to render massive technical assistance and development aid. On the other hand the UN was not able to advance the country to stability and democracy. It was not permitted to train the ANC and, had such an opportunity been available, it probably could not have achieved much more than bilateral assistance.

In terms of manpower, ONUC was an enormous civil and military operation, which remains unmatched in the UN's annals so far. Thousands of UN civilians and many thousands of military served in ONUC. At the helm of the operation was the UN Secretary-General—first Hammarskjöld and then, after his death, U Thant. Hammarskjöld's staff for ONUC, which became known as the Congo Club, changed frequently, except for Bunche and myself, who remained throughout the operation.

There are many men and women who contributed to the achievements of ONUC. As I look back to those years of the UN's toil and suffering, some emerge more prominently than others for their service to ONUC (omissions are not intentional, as I have had to rely on memory alone). Hammarskjöld is at the head of this list, followed by Bunche and then U Thant. Cordier played a key role for most of the time until he left the Secretary-General's cabinet. Frederick Boland of Ireland and Mongi Slim of Tunisia were prominent at the political level in the General Assembly and Security Council. Brian Urquhart and F.T. Liu served courageously in the field and rendered great service with their work behind the scenes in Bunche's office. George Sherry played an important role in the final chapter of Katanga.

In the Congo, first Bunche and then Dayal head the list. Robert Gardiner, an exemplary civil servant, played a quiet, yet important role in the Congo conciliation negotiations, Mahmoud Khiary and Conor Cruise O'Brien showed brilliance in their efforts to end the secession in Katanga, but none the less they led ONUC to its major disaster. Some additional comment is necessary here.

O'Brien, an able and impressive diplomat-scholar, with a sympathetic understanding of the problems of decolonisation, set out, I am sure, intending to serve the UN faithfully and its Secretary-General loyally. He could speak and write with eloquence. When he agreed to turn over the mercenaries to their consuls in Elisabethville to be returned to their countries, he accepted the assurances given. But the consuls proved untrustworthy and allowed the mercenaries to disappear, only to return to Katanga surreptitiously and resume fighting. Furthermore, O'Brien took his instructions from Khiary, who, it was understood, acted with the approval of the Secretary-General. This, in fact, was not the case. O'Brien, believing that his instructions from Khiary had Hammarskjöld's approval, was shocked at what he believed to be a turn-around by Hammarskjöld, presumably under Western pressure. On the other hand, Hammarskjöld had at no time given his approval to the new operations in Katanga and viewed the recent action as a violation of his instructions. Ignorant of what had actually occurred at that time, O'Brien and Hammarskjöld, each felt let down by the other, which led to much acrimony. Hammarskjöld made an inspired choice in appointing O'Brien as ONUC representative in Elisabethville. The tragedy was that the two 'aces' were 'trumped'. As for Khiary, it is clear that he issued instructions on the basis of what he had recommended to Hammarskjöld and not what had been approved. Khiary and Linner remained silent on their roles at this critical point; therefore, the chronicler has to fall back on what is known to the UN and on personal inquiries. Undoubtedly they had a style which did not conform to what Hammarskjöld expected of international civil servants. In addition to these, John Olver and Habib Ahmed were painstaking and sympathetic administrators. In the civilian operations team, Bibiano Osorio-Tafall facilitated the departure of ONUC and the resumption of the UN's development and assistance programme.

Among the military in the Congo there were many changes. At the head of the force, Alexander, as the Acting Commander, provided professional leadership. Kettani served with distinction, and of the Chiefs of Staff Iyassou and the Canadian Brigadier Jimmy Dextras were outstanding. At the operational staff level, Mitra and Azim were a hard act to follow. 'Nanna' Madan was prominent in logistics and remained beyond his intended tenure of one year. As for air transport, Carpenter and Carr deserve credit for organising it as a safe and reliable service. The nursing officers of the Indian and Ghanaian contingents gave comfort, and the medical staff of the Indian General Staff healed the wounded and cared for the sick (including the Congolese), thus contributing greatly to ONUC's morale.

There were many fine contingent commanders, and it is invidious to name only a few. Since the operations in Katanga presented the hardest military challenge, it was contingent commanders like the Swedish Colonel Jonas Waern, the Indian brigade group commander 'Reggie' Noronha, and the overall Katanga area commander General Prem Chand whose achievement perhaps deserves pride of place.

Among the foreign diplomats in the Congo, the Americans emerged as major supporters of ONUC, and here Edmund Guillion and his deputy (later his successor) McGodley stand out. It has to be noted too that they were sometimes opposed to ONUC's responses to particular situations.

The UN made heavy sacrifices to pull the Congo out of the morass of utter chaos into which it had sunk. In the process, it lost its Secretary-General[2] and many others, who suffered at the hands of the very people they had come to help. The situation of Zaïre today is again perilous and its future uncertain. The UN, on the other hand, is strong and united as it has scarcely been since its foundation. Its duty thirty years ago was clear. The sacrifice, suffering and humiliation of those days were not in vain, and can be recalled with pride.

NOTES

1. *Article 19*: A member of the United Nations which is in arrears in the payment of its financial contributions to the Organization shall have no vote in the General Assembly if the amount of its arrears equals or exceeds the amount of contributions due from it for the preceding two full years. The General Assembly may, nevertheless, permit such a Member to vote if it is satisfied that the failure to pay is due to conditions beyond the control of the Member.

2. Former members of the Congo Club and many members of the Secretariat meet in the Meditation Room near the public entrance to the UN to commemorate by silent prayer the deaths of Hammarskjöld, and of Wieschoff, Fabry, Lalande, Ranallo, Justin and others who were killed with the Secretary-General. The occasion also serves to commemorate all who have given their lives in UN peacekeeping.

APPENDIXES

A

COMMAND STRUCTURE OF THE U.N. CONGO OPERATION

NEW YORK

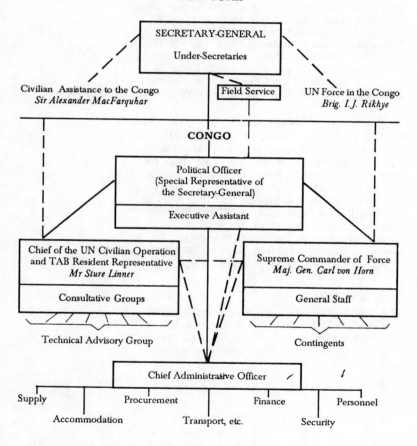

Note. This organisation chart was included with the Secretary-General's second report on the Congo operation and was circulated as U.N. Document S/4417, Add. 5, SCOR, Fifteenth Year, Supplement for July, August, September 1960 (11 August 1960), p. 66.

B

HIGHER CIVILIAN AND MILITARY COMMAND IN THE CONGO, 1960-1964

Special Representatives of the Secretary-General

Ralph J. Bunche (US), 13 July 1960 - 27 Aug. 1960
Andrew W. Cordier (US), 27 Aug. 1960 - 6 Sept. 1960
Rajeshwar Dayal (India), 8 Sept. 1960 - 25 May 1961
Indar Jit Rikhye (acting) (India), 3-23 Nov. 1960
Mekki Abbas (acting) (Sudan), 10 Mar. 1961 - 20 May 1961
Sture Linner (Sweden), 20 May 1961 - 10 Feb. 1962
Robert Gardiner (Ghana), 10 Feb. 1962 - 1 May 1963
Max H. Dorsinville (Haiti), 1 May 1963 - 30 Apr. 1964
Bibiano F. Osorio-Tafall (acting) (Mexico), 30 Apr. 1964 - 30 June 1964

Representatives in Elisabethville

Ian E. Berendsen (New Zealand), Aug. 1960 - Mar. 1961
Georges Dumontet (France), Mar. 1961 - May 1961
Conor Cruise O'Brien (Ireland), June 1961 - Nov. 1961
Brian E. Urquhart (UK), Nov. 1961 - Jan. 1962
George Ivan Smith (acting) (Australia), Dec. 1961
George Dumontet (acting) (France), 27 Dec. 1961 - Jan. 1962
José Rolz-Bennett (Guatemala), Jan. 1962 - June 1962
Jean Back (France), June 1962
Eliud Mathu (Kenya), June 1962 - May 1963
George L. Sherry (acting) (US), Jan. 1963 - Feb. 1963
A. Nashashibi (Jordan), May 1963 - June 1964

Force commanders

Maj.-Gen. Carl von Horn (Sweden), Aug.-Dec. 1960
Lt.-Gen. Sean McKeown (Ireland), Jan. 1961- Mar. 1962
Lt.-Gen. Kebede Gebre (Ethiopia), Apr. 1962 - July 1963
Maj.-Gen. Christian R. Kaldager (Norway), Aug. - Dec. 1963
Maj.-Gen. J. T. U. Aguiyi Ironsi (Nigeria), Jan. - June 1964

UN commanders in Katanga

Col. H.W. Byrne (Ireland), Aug. - Dec. 1960
Brig. K.A.S. Raja (India), Mar. 1961 - Apr. 1962
Maj.-Gen. D. Prem Chand (India), May 1962 - Apr. 1963
Col. Worku Metaferia (acting)(Ethiopia), Apr. 1963
Brig.-Gen. Abebe Teferra (Ethiopia), June 1963 - June 1964

C.1. MANPOWER CONTRIBUTION TO UN MILITARY EFFORT IN THE CONGO

AUG. 2, 1960 - JUNE 30, 1964

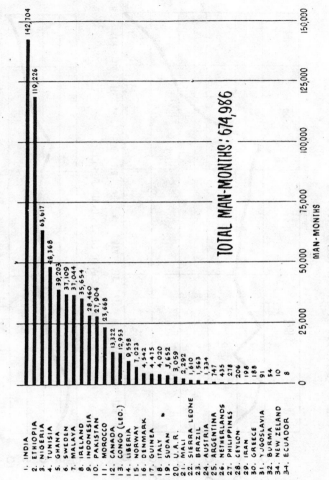

TOTAL MAN-MONTHS: 674,986

	MAN-MONTHS
1. INDIA	142,704
2. ETHIOPIA	119,226
3. NIGERIA	63,617
4. TUNISIA	48,368
5. GHANA	39,203
6. SWEDEN	37,109
7. MALAYA	37,044
8. IRELAND	35,654
9. INDONESIA	28,460
10. PAKISTAN	27,904
11. MOROCCO	23,668
12. CANADA	13,322
13. CONGO (LEO.)	12,953
14. LIBERIA	9,558
15. NORWAY	7,023
16. DENMARK	4,542
17. GUINEA	4,415
18. ITALY	4,020
19. SUDAN	3,652
20. U.A.R.	3,059
21. MALI	2,292
22. SIERRA LEONE	1,610
23. BRAZIL	1,563
24. AUSTRIA	1,334
25. ARGENTINA	747
26. NETHERLANDS	435
27. PHILIPPINES	278
28. CEYLON	206
29. IRAN	198
30. GREECE	188
31. YUGOSLAVIA	91
32. BURMA	54
33. NEW ZELAND	10
34. ECUADOR	8

Source: Brookings Institution, prepared from official UN records.

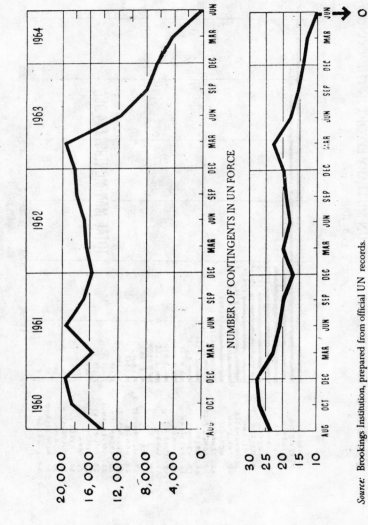

C.2. STRENGTH OF UN FORCE IN THE CONGO, 1960-1964

NUMBER OF CONTINGENTS IN UN FORCE

Source: Brookings Institution, prepared from official UN records.

C.3. CHANGES IN UN FORCE COMPOSITION (MAJOR COMBAT UNITS)

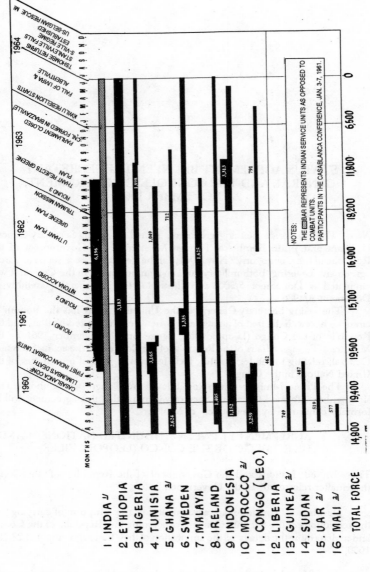

Source: Brookings Institution, prepared from official UN records.

D

STATUS AGREEMENT BETWEEN THE SECRETARY-GENERAL AND THE CONGOLESE GOVERNMENT, 27 NOVEMBER 1961

Note. This elaborate Status Agreement, signed by Acting Secretary-General U Thant and Justin Bomboko, Foreign Minister of the Government of the Republic of the Congo, on 27 Nov. 1961, can be regarded as a status of forces agreement covering both military and civilian personnel in the Congo. It was circulated as Document S/5004 and distributed to the General Assembly as Document A/4986.

The acting Secretary-General of the United Nations has the honour to circulate herewith the text of an agreement between the United Nations and the Republic of the Congo (Leopoldville), signed on 27 November 1961 by the Minister of Foreign Affairs of the Republic of the Congo and the acting Secretary-General, relating to the legal status, facilities, privileges and immunities of the United Nations in the Congo.

The Prime Minister of the Republic of the Congo, who authorized the signing, has informed the acting Secretary-General that this agreement will be formally confirmed by the Council of Ministers.

AGREEMENT BETWEEN THE UNITED NATIONS AND THE REPUBLIC OF THE CONGO (LEOPOLDVILLE)

The United Nations and the Government of the Republic of the Congo (hereinafter referred to as 'the Government'):

Desiring to conclude an agreement for the purpose of carrying out the resolutions of the Security Council concerning the Republic of the Congo, and to determine the details of the application of their basic agreement of 27 July 1960;[*]

[*]*Ibid,* Fifteenth Year, Supplement for July, August and September 1960, document S/4389/Add.5.

Recalling the request of the Government to the United Nations for military assistance and its acceptance of the resolutions of the Security Council; and

Having regard to the provisions of the United Nations Charter for mutual assistance in carrying out the measures decided upon by the Security Council, and for the privileges and immunities necessary for the fulfilment of the purposes of the United Nations,

Have agreed as follows:

Respect for local law and international status

1. Members of the United Nations Force in the Congo and all officials serving under the United Nations in the Congo shall respect the laws and regulations of the Republic of the Congo. They shall refrain from any activity of a political character in the Congo and from any action incompatible with their international responsibilities. The Special Representative of the Secretary-General shall ensure the observance of these obligations.
2. The United Nations shall possess sole competence with respect to decisions concerning the composition of the military units sent to the Congo, it being understood at the same time that the United Nations shall, in determining their composition, give every consideration to the opinion of the Government as one of the most important factors to be borne in mind in connexion with recruitment.
3. In so far as consistent with the relative provisions of the United Nations Charter and the independent exercise of its functions, the Secretary-General shall pay all due attention to any pertinent information transmitted to him by the Government concerning United Nations officials who have been assigned to duty with the United Nations in the Congo, as well as concerning local personnel employed by the United Nations.

Entry, exit and identification

4. Members of the Force shall be exempt from passport and visa regulations and immigration inspection or restrictions. Officials serving under the United Nations in the Congo and members of their families living at their expense shall be exempt from immigration restrictions and alien registration.
5. The first entry of members of the Force into the territory of the Republic may be by military movement order, a national military identity card and the certificates of vaccination as provided in international conventions. Thereafter the personal identity card issued to them under the authority of the Special Representative of the Secretary-General shall be recognized by all authorities as valid and sufficient identification. Members of the Force shall be bound to present their identity cards, if requested, but not to surrender them.
6. The United Nations *laissez-passer* shall be recognized as a valid travel document. This *laissez-passer*, as well as the personal identity cards issued to United Nations officials in the Congo by the Special Representative of

the Secretary-General, shall be recognized by all authorities as valid and sufficient identification.

7.   (a)   Requests for visas made by holders of a *laissez-passer* and accompanied by a certificate stating that these officials are travelling on United Nations business shall be given the speediest possible consideration.

(b)   The same privileges shall be granted to experts and other persons who do not hold a United Nations *laissez-passer* but who carry a certificate stating that they are travelling on United Nations business.

(c)   Persons granted the privileges referred to in this article shall obtain the certificates of vaccination as provided in international conventions.

(d)   Persons holding a *laissez-passer* and also experts or other persons travelling on United Nations business who come from a country where the Republic of the Congo is not represented, or who are unable for any other reason to obtain a visa before their arrival in the Congo, shall be permitted to enter without a visa which shall be delivered to them after their arrival by the Ministry of Foreign Affairs.

8.   The Government shall be kept informed of the following:

(a)   the arrival and departure of military units serving in the Force, as well as their numbers and nationality;

(b)   the arrival and final departure of members of the Force who are not transferred at the same time as the rest of their national contingent;

(c)   the arrival and final departure of officials serving under the United Nations, or the termination of their services;

(d)   the arrival or final departure of a member of the family of an official serving under the United Nations, or of a member of the Force;

(e)   the appointment or discharge of persons residing in the Congo as officials employed in the service of the United Nations.

9.   Members of the Force shall be subject to the exclusive jurisdiction of their respective national State in respect of any criminal offences which may be committed by them in the Congo. Officials serving under the United Nations in the Congo shall be immune from legal process in respect of all acts performed by them in their official capacity. They shall be immune from any form of arrest or detention.

10.   In respect of matters not falling within article 9, the Government in the exercise of its sovereignty undertakes to refrain from any act of arrest, detention, seizure of personal property, or other form of legal process against members of the Force or officials serving under the United Nations in the Congo or their dependants until after completion of the following procedures:

(a)   If the authorities of the Government possess evidence that an official or a dependant of such official has committed an offence against the penal laws of the Republic of the Congo all such evidence shall be communicated to the Special Representative of the Secretary-General, who shall conduct any supplementary inquiry necessary to obtain evidence. The Government and the United Nations will then arrive at an agreement as to whether the international Organization should institute disciplinary procedures within the terms of its appropriate regulations or whether the Government shall institute legal action. Failing an agreement, the matter shall be submitted to arbitration at the request of either Party;

(b)   If as a result of any act performed by a member of the Force or an official in the course of his official duties, it is alleged that loss or damages that may give rise to civil proceedings has been caused to a citizen or resident of the Congo, the United Nations shall settle the dispute by negotiation or any other method agreed between the parties; if it is not found possible to arrive at an agreement in this manner, the matter shall be submitted to arbitration at the request of either party;

(c)   If evidence is submitted of the existence of an obligation at civil law binding upon or in favour of a member of the Force or an official serving under the United Nations in the Congo or a dependant of such member of the Force or official, and arising out of his presence in the Congo but not related to his official duties, the United Nations shall use its good offices to assist the parties in arriving at a settlement. If the dispute cannot be settled in this manner, or by any other agreed mode of settlement, it shall be submitted to arbitration at the request of either party.

11.   The foregoing arrangements concerning jurisdiction are made having regard to the special functions of the United Nations in the Congo, and are not for the personal benefit of members of the Force or officials in the service of the United Nations. The Special Representative of the Secretary-General shall arrange for any arbitral procedure necessary to hear and decide such disputes as have to be submitted to arbitration under the provisions of article 10. They may, should they find it warranted, establish a claims commission and instruct it to consider all or any types of claim listed in article 10.

12.   The Supreme Commander of the United Nations Force in the Congo shall take all appropriate measures to ensure the discipline and good order of members of the Force. For this purpose United Nations military police may undertake the surveillance of the premises occupied by the United Nations, the areas in which the Force is deployed, and, in liaison with local authorities, wherever necessary to maintain such discipline and order. The military police shall have the power of arrest over members of the Force.

13.   A member of the military personnel or an official serving under one of the parties to the present agreement may not be arrested by the authorities of the other party, unless the competent authorities to whom he is responsible are unable to act with the necessary speed to apprehend him at the time when he commits, or attempts to commit, an offence which may result in serious harm to persons or property; however, a person apprehended in this way, as well as any object seized in connection with the offence, must be delivered immediately to the nearest authority to whom the person in queston is responsible. These provisions shall be without prejudice to the right possessed by the ONUC, under its authority to assist in preserving order, to take into custody other persons in order to deliver them to the authorities, whether Congolese or not, to whom they are responsible.

14. The United Nations and the Congolese authorities shall assist each other in the carrying out of all necessary investigations into offences which are of concern to either or both parties, in the hearing of witnesses, and in the collection and production of evidence.

Privileges and immunities

15. The United Nations, its property and assets, and the property and assets in the Congo of the States participating in the United Nations Force shall be immune from every form of legal process, from search and requisition and from any other form of governmental interference. The documents of the United Nations and of the participating States shall be inviolable, wherever they may be.

16. The United Nations, its property and assets, and the property and assets of the States participating in the Force situated in the Congo for the purposes of the Force shall be exempt from:

(a) Taxes of every kind. It is understood, however, that the United Nations shall not request exemption from taxes that do not exceed the mere remuneration of services performed by public utilities;

(b) Customs duties and from prohibitions or restrictions on imports and exports relating to articles imported by or on behalf of the United Nations or by the participating States in application of any part of the United Nations programme in the Congo. The right of the United Nations to import goods free of duty includes the right to import certain articles for sale exclusively to members of the Force and to officials of the United Nations, in service institutes and canteens. It is understood, however, that articles thus imported free of duty shall not be resold on Congolese territory to third parties, save at conditions approved by the Government;

(c) Customs duties and from prohibitions and restrictions on imports and exports in respect of their publications.

17. Arrangements shall be made for the remission or return to the United Nations of the amount of any duties and taxes which are included in the price paid by the United Nations in any important purchases which it may make in the Congo.

18. (a) Members of the Force and officials serving under the United Nations in the Congo shall be exempt from direct taxes. They shall be exempt from personal contributions. Their papers and documents shall be inviolable;

(b) Members of the Force and officials serving under the United Nations in the Congo shall have the right to import free of duty their personal effects when taking up their posts in the Congo, and subsequently, such articles as the United Nations administrative services may certify as being required by these persons by reason of their presence in the Congo under the United Nations, it being understood that articles imported in this manner shall not be sold on Congolese territory to third parties, save at conditions approved by the Government;

(c) Members of the Force and officials serving under the United Nations are exempt from inspection of their personal baggage, unless there are good reasons for supposing that it contains undeclared articles not covered by the exemptions referred to in paragraph (b) of this article, or articles, the import or export of which is prohibited by law or falls under the quarantine regulations of the Republic of the Congo. In such cases, the inspection shall be carried out only in the presence of the member of the Force or official concerned, or of his representative.

19. As regards the rules of precedence observed in the Republic of the Congo, the Special Representative shall immediately follow the President of the Republic; in particular, he shall take precedence over all the heads of diplomatic missions.

20. The funds, currencies and accounts of the United Nations are free from financial controls.

21. The Government shall, if requested by the United Nations, make available to the United Nations against reimbursement in United States dollars or other currency mutually acceptable, Congolese currency required for the use of the United Nations activities and programme in the Congo, including the pay of the members of national contingents, at the most favourable official rate of exchange.

22. Officials serving under the United Nations in the Congo shall be accorded the same facilities in respect of currency or exchange restrictions as are accorded to officials of comparable rank forming part of diplomatic mission to the Government.

23. On their departure from the Congo members of the Force shall be entitled, notwithstanding any foreign exchange regulations, to take with them such sums as are certified by the competent United Nations finance officer or the paymaster of the contingents as having been received in pay and emoluments from the United Nations or the national Government in question for service in the Congo and are a reasonable residue thereof.

Premises

24. The Government shall provide, in agreement with the United Nations accommodation service, such buildings or areas for headquarters, camps or other premises as may be necessary for the accommodation of the personnel and services of the United Nations and enable them to carry out their functions. Without prejudice to the fact that all such premises remain Congolese territory, they shall be inviolable and subject to the exclusive control and authority of the United Nations. This authority and control extend to the adjacent public ways to the extent necessary to regulate access to the premises. The United Nations alone may consent to the entry of any government officials to perform duties on such premises or of any other person. Every person who so desires for a lawful purpose shall be allowed free access to the premises placed under the authority of the United Nations.

25. If the United Nations should take over premises previously occupied by private persons and thus represented a source of income, the Government shall assist the United Nations to lease them at a reasonable rental.

Flag
26. The Government recognizes the right of ONUC to display the United
Nations flag on its headquarters, camps, posts or other premises, vehicles
and vessels and otherwise as determined by rules of the Special
Representative of the Secretary-General. Other flags or pennants may be
displayed only in exceptional cases, such as the national holiday of the
contingent concerned, and in accordance with conditions prescribed by
the Special Representative.

Local personnel
27. (a)   The United Nations may recruit locally such personnel as it requires.
(b)   The terms and conditions of employment for locally recruited personnel shall be prescribed by the Special Representative of the Secretary-
General and shall generally, to the extent practicable, follow the practice
prevailing in the locality.
(c)   No Congolese authority shall seek to influence local personnel
directly or indirectly in the performance of their duties. All decisions
as to their recruitment and the continuation or cessation of their
employment shall lie within the sole authority of the Special
Representative of the Secretary-General; the latter, however, shall decided
only after due consideration of the evidence submitted to him.
(d)   Any dispute concerning the terms and conditions of employment
of locally recruited personnel shall be settled ` in accordance with
administrative procedures to be established by the Special Representative.
28. The privileges and immunities granted in accordance with the provisions of
the preceding articles shall not be extended to Congolese nationals or other
local staff who were subject to Congolese jurisdiction at the time of their
recruitment by the United Nations in the Congo. Locally recruited
members of the staff of ONUC shall enjoy immunity only from legal
process in respect of acts performed by them in the course of their official
duties. The Government shall exercise its jurisdiction over them in such a
manner as will not hamper the conduct of the affairs of the Organisation.
29. (a)   Subject to the provisions of paragraph (c) of this article, officials and
employees of the United Nations in the Congo other than Congolese
nationals shall be exempt from the social security provisions in force in the
Congo in respect of services rendered to the Organisation.
(b)   The exemption provided in paragraph (a) of this article shall also
apply to private domestic servants employed exclusively by officials of
the Organisation, provided that they are not Congolese nationals or do not
reside permanently in the Congo.
(c)   Any official of the Organisation who employs in his service persons not
covered by the exemption provided in paragraph (b) of this article shall be
required to fulfil the obligations imposed on employers by Congolese
legislation concerning social security in the Congo.
30. The Government shall afford the members of the Force and the officials
serving under the United Nations in the Congo full freedom of movement
throughout Congolese territory and to and from points of access to

Congolese territory. This freedom shall extend to the operation of vehicles, aircraft, vessels and equipment in the service of the United Nations.

31. The United Nations shall have the right to the use of roads, bridges, waterways, port facilities and airfields without payment of dues, tolls or charges by way of registration or otherwise, except for charges collected directly or remuneration for specified services.

32. United Nations vehicles, aircraft and vessels shall carry a distinctive United Nations identification mark. They shall not be subject to the registration or licences prescribed by Congolese laws or regulations.

Communications

33. In all matters of official communications the United Nations shall enjoy conditions not less favourable than those accorded by the Government to any other Government or diplomatic mission. No censorship shall be applied to the official correspondence or other official communications of the United Nations or of the contingents of the Force in communicating with their Governments.

34. The United Nations and the contingents shall have the right to use messages in code or cipher and to despatch and receive their correspondence by courier or valise, which shall have the same privileges and immunities as diplomatic couriers.

35. The Government recognizes the right of the United Nations to make arrangements through its own facilities for the sorting and transport of private mail addressed to or despatched by members of the Force or officials serving under the United Nations in the Congo. The Government shall be informed of such arrangements. The Government shall not interfere with or censor such mail in any way.

36. The United Nations shall be authorized to install and operate in the Congo radio sending and receiving stations which shall be connected at appropriate points with the United Nations radio network and be able to communicate therewith. The United Nations shall duly communicate to the Government and to the International Frequency Registration Board the frequencies used for the operation of these stations.

37. The United Nations shall enjoy throughout the Congo the right of unrestricted communication by radio, telephone, telegraph or any other means, and of establishing the necessary facilities for maintaining such communications within and between premises of the United Nations, including the laying of cables and landlines and the use of fixed and mobile radio sending and receiving stations.

Public services

38. The United Nations shall have the right to the use of water, electricity and other public services at rates not exceeding those enjoyed by other comparable consumers. The United Nations shall have the same priority as essential Government services in the event of the interruption or threatened interruption of the said service.

Uniform

39. Members of the Force shall normally wear the uniform prescribed by the Supreme Commander but may wear civilian dress under conditions determined by him. Members of the Force while on duty shall be entitled to possess and carry arms in accordance with the regulations applicable to them.

Death of members of the Force

40. The Supreme Commander shall have the right to take charge of and dispose of the body of a member of the Force who dies in Congolese territory and may take steps for the disposal of the personal property of such member.

Liaiaon

41. The Special Representative and the Government, as well as the Supreme Commander of the United Nations Force and the Supreme Commander of the Armée nationale congolaise shall take the measures necessary to ensure close liaison between ONUC and the Congolese authorities at both national and local levels. Notwithstanding this principle and subject to any agreement providing otherwise, official matters for which the United Nations is responsible in the Congo shall be taken up with the Minister of Foreign Affairs or his intermediary. Liaison officers shall be appointed to the staff headquarters on a reciprocal basis and, to the extent that their presence may be useful, to the regional commands of the Armée nationale congolaise and the United Nations Force.

42. At airports necessary for the effective functioning of the Force, the United Nations alone shall control arrivals and departures of aircraft operating on its behalf, whether these are transporting civilian or military personnel or supplies. Except in cases covered by resolutions of the Security Council or the General Assembly, civilian officials of the Government shall control all other arrivals and departures. Liaison shall be maintained between ONUC and the Congolese authorities at each airport in order to prevent any conflict of functions in the application of this provision.

43. In fulfilling their liaison duties, both parties shall take fully into account the essential differences in their mandates:

(a) Full responsibility for the implementation of domestic legislation and regulations shall remain with the Congolese authorities. The United Nations shall be as an international Force and as such its responsibilities shall be exercised for the purposes of maintaining public order, peace and security; in so doing it shall not apply domestic regulations and procedures, but shall act in accordance with its interpretation of the mission assigned to it by the Security Council.

(b) In the performance of their duties, the Congolese authorities responsible for enforcing the law shall have the right to resort to force in conformity with the law. The United Nations shall not have recourse to the use of force except as a last resort and subject to the restrictions imposed by its mandate and by the resolutions of the Security Council and the General Assembly.

44. In view of the impossibility of having two security systems acting in competition, both parties undertake to co-ordinate their actions in the maintenance of public order and shall adopt the principle of mutual consultation. Whenever the actions of any units of the army, *gendarmerie* or police might create a conflict of competence in the maintenance of public order, the authorities concerned shall proceed to immediate consultations with the nearest unit of the United Nations Force. Such conflicts shall be adjusted by agreement, in a spirit of understanding and co-operation. In particular, if a situation arises in which it appears that the use of force is necessary, the authorities concerned shall first immediately enter into consultation with the nearest unit of the United Nations Force.

Supplementary provisions
45. Any supplementary provisions necessary for the carrying out of this agreement shall be made by agreement between the Special Representative of the Secretary-General or as the case may be by the Supreme Commander of the United Nations Force, and the appropriate Congolese authorities designated by the Government.

46. The United Nations and the Government shall from time to time, at the request of either Party, review the provisions of this agreement in the light of the progressive development of the Congolese civil service and shall agree on any necessary amendments thereto. Any dispute between the United Nations and the Government concerning the interpretation and application of this agreement which is not settled by other means agreed between the parties shall be referred for arbitration to a tribunal consisting of three arbitrators whose decision shall be final. The Secretary-General of the United Nations and the Congolese Government shall each appoint one of the three arbitrators. The third arbitrator shall be a chairman appointed by agreement between the Secretary-General and the Congolese Government. If, within one month from the date on which either party has requested arbitration, the two parties have failed to agree on the appointment of a chairman, the President of the International Court of Justice shall be requested by either party to appoint a chairman. Should a vacancy occur in the tribunal for any reason, it shall be filled within thirty days in accordance with the method provided in this article for initial appointments. The tribunal shall commence to function as soon as its chairman and one of its other members have been appointed. Two members shall constitute a quorum of the tribunal and with respect to all of its deliberations and decisions a favourable vote of two members shall suffice.

47. The Central Government of the Republic of the Congo shall have the ultimate responsibility for the fulfilment of such obligations by the competent Congolese authorities, whether central, provincial or local.

Duration
48. Upon the signature of this agreement by the duly authorized representatives of both parties, it shall be deemed to have taken effect as from the date of

arrival of the first elements of the United Nations Force in the Congo. The provisions of the agreement which relate specifically to the Force or its members shall remain in effect until the departure from the territory of the Congo of the last elements of the Force and its equipment. Those provisions which relate generally to the United Nations or officials serving under the United Nations in the Congo shall remain in effect until this agreement has been superseded or until such other date as shall be agreed between the parties.

In witness whereof the undersigned, on behalf of the parties, have signed this agreement at New York, on 27 November 1961, in duplicate in French.

For the United Nations
(Signed) U THANT
Acting Secretary-General

For the Government of the
Republic of the Congo
(Signed) Justin BOMBOKO
Minister for Foreign Affairs

INDEX

343

352   *Index*